Making Sense of Music

Making Sense of Music

SUSAN McCLARY

OXFORD
UNIVERSITY PRESS

Oxford University Press is a department of the University of Oxford.
It furthers the University's objective of excellence in research, scholarship,
and education by publishing worldwide. Oxford is a registered trade mark of
Oxford University Press in the UK and in certain other countries.

Published in the United States of America by Oxford University Press
198 Madison Avenue, New York, NY 10016, United States of America.

© Oxford University Press 2025

All rights reserved. No part of this publication may be reproduced, stored in a retrieval system,
transmitted, used for text and data mining, or used for training artificial intelligence, in any form or
by any means, without the prior permission in writing of Oxford University Press, or as expressly
permitted by law, by license or under terms agreed with the appropriate reprographics rights
organization. Inquiries concerning reproduction outside the scope of the above should be sent
to the Rights Department, Oxford University Press, at the address above.

You must not circulate this work in any other form
and you must impose this same condition on any acquirer.

CIP data is on file at the Library of Congress

ISBN 9780197779767 (pbk.)
ISBN 9780197779750 (hbk.)

DOI: 10.1093/9780197779798.001.0001

Paperback printed by Marquis Book Printing, Canada
Hardback printed by Bridgeport National Bindery, Inc., United States of America

The manufacturer's authorized representative in the EU for product safety is
Oxford University Press España S.A., Parque Empresarial San Fernando de Henares,
Avenida de Castilla, 2 – 28830 Madrid (www.oup.es/en).

Contents

Foreword by Peter Sellars   vii
About the Companion Website   xi

Fundamentals: An Introduction   1

I. WHY I DO WHAT I DO

1. A Life in Musicology: Stradella and Me   27
2. In Praise of Contingency: The Powers and Limits of Theory   45
3. Evidence of Things Not Seen: History, Subjectivities, Music   63
4. Writing about Music—and the Music of Writing   82
5. The Bodies of Angels   93
6. The Lure of the Sublime: Revisiting the Modernist Project   104
7. Playing the Identity Card: Of Grieg, Indians, and Women   120
8. The Object/the Objective of Analysis: The Case of Florence Price   135

II. MESSING WITH EARLY MUSIC

9. Unwashed Masses: Music for the Morning After   153
10. Tumescence and Detumescence in a Monteverdi Madrigal   166
11. Doing the Time Warp in Seventeenth-Century Music   179
12. In the Realm of *All* the Senses: Two Sarabandes by Élisabeth-Claude Jacquet de la Guerre   196
13. Salome in the Court of Queen Christina   216
14. Adorno Plays the *WTC*: On Political Theory and Performance   232

III. SEX AND GENDER REDUX

15. The Classical Closet 249
16. Soprano Masculinities 260
17. Sister Campers 279
18. Kaija Saariaho, Mater 291
19. Mahler Making Love: Mengelberg's Adagietto 302

Index 329

Foreword

As I write these words, all of the January 6th Insurrectionists have been unconditionally pardoned; the U.S. Army is on its way to the border with Mexico; Guantánamo is being refurbished by profiteering corporations as a massive concentration camp; immigration raids are ramping up in large and small cities across the country; transgender care is being outlawed; diversity, equity, and inclusion are being formally terminated in public and private institutions; restrictions are being placed on the teaching of Black history; libraries are being censored; USAID is being foreclosed; even the National Weather Service is facing mass firings; the United States has sided with Russia against Ukraine; and an order from the State Department has halted all aid to South Africa until white land owners are resettled as "refugees." Decades of climate legislation are being rescinded: billionaires are getting everything they've always wanted. And our new president has installed himself as the chairman of the Kennedy Center and filled the board with his cronies to usher in a great new era of American culture that will not include drag shows.

Musicology anyone? You hold in your hand what Susan McClary promises will be her last book of essays. But in a period of widespread official and unofficial silencing, Susan has no problem speaking out. I am sure we will hear more from her. In the meantime, this volume arrives on schedule, fully armed, endowed, inspired, and up to the task. For decades now, Susan has been the go-to writer who articulates music's capacity to unsettle, provoke, and to heal. For Susan, music is a site of resistance and secret and subterranean solidarities, anthems, proclamations, reclamations, re-enactments, hypotheticals. For Susan, music is prophecy, witness, outrage, hilarity, wildness, equilibrium, radiant beauty and devastating truth, collective conscience, social movement, and ongoing transformation with the astonishing power to hold intimate, private thoughts and feelings and all of public space simultaneously. Susan's lucid, brilliant, and courageous writing plunges into the heart of music's secret access to realms of gender, sexuality, ethnicity, race, class, ethics, and personal and political aspiration.

Susan has always had a breathtaking gift for structural analysis. Her vivid and instantaneous clarity lets her see and hear the shapes and materials of music with uncanny exactitude. Her deeper gift is her insight into invisible and unspoken realms, "the evidence of things not seen" that she shares with St. Paul and James Baldwin, the zone of pure intuition and feeling where music ultimately lives and breathes.

When Susan uses the expression "making sense of music," she really means using all of the senses, the inner senses and the outer senses, aesthetics, synaesthetics, but also all of our moral and sacred receptors.

In her early entries in this volume, Susan speaks as she has not fully spoken before, about where, in fact, she is coming from. Her honesty and retrospective understanding of her own family dynamics and the haunted, contradictory experiences of her childhood, together with her religious and musical formation bring to her writing a new humility and sense of personal struggle. Most writing about the history of music comes from self-fashioned omnipotences whose sense of their own invulnerability and unquestioned authority projects the aura of privilege and thoughtless presumption that we associate with white supremacy. Susan's autobiographical interpolations in this volume testify eloquently to how far she has come, how far she has yet to go, and to the quiet forces that motivate her extraordinary achievement.

And meanwhile, years after she titled one of her deepest and most foundational books *Desire and Pleasure in Seventeenth-Century Music*, we begin to sense how deeply those underground rivers of desire and pleasure run in her life and in her work. It is technically impossible to describe music in words, but Susan's sheer exhilaration, joy, crazy shifts of tone, shocking juxtapositions, recapitulations, codas, and second and third subjects are irresistible and intoxicating. The glee that invades her writing not only lets you know how deeply she loves this music, but it also becomes crucial survival equipment when she moves to explore carefully and seriously darker histories and painful truths.

Susan invites us to face the music and then to face ourselves. The unseen and the unspoken emerge from complicated feelings that we have inherited and that we still don't understand and that are still shaping our lives in ways that are difficult to acknowledge. Susan's quiet attention to those moments and repositories of recognition help clarify the things we have to do next.

Whatever worlds are being dismantled at the moment, I am grateful that the reimagining and the reconstruction will be in the hands of Susan's students, and we will reconstitute our world with much more compassion, imagination, and insight. Music is about motives and the ways thought becomes action. When Susan writes about "bodies of angels," she is inviting all of us to new levels of response and performativity.

As someone who is involved in performance, and every day has to contextualize and explore musical gestures, visual designs, and inner visions, movements, poetry, speech, architectures, and official and hidden histories, I am so grateful for the integrity and breadth of learning and curiosity that Susan has brought to our intricately layered fields. We are world building, looking again at where we are coming from, and attempting to create a place we want to live in now and in the future. That future is looking at us in the eye and asking some very hard questions.

Writing about her fifty years of engagement with Alessandro Stradella's 1681 oratorio, *La Susanna,* she says, " . . . understanding his music required me to dismantle everything I knew, to ask questions not native to the discipline." Thank you, Susan. What more can we ask for in this life? What more can we do? Susan McClary is a treasure and a necessary companion and example.

—Peter Sellars
March 4, 2025

About the Companion Website

www.oup.com/us/makingsenseofmusic

This book features a companion website that provides material that cannot be made available in a book, namely full-color versions of the manuscript facsimiles found in Chapter 19.

The reader is encouraged to consult this resource in conjunction with the chapter.

Fundamentals

An Introduction

All of us develop from multiple influences—a phenomenon we now call intersectionality. Most of this introduction will trace my intellectual development. But in other contexts, I might have produced very different narratives. Here is a glimpse at one:

I learned to sight-sing in the Church of Christ, the fundamentalist denomination to which my Oklahoma-raised parents belonged before they moved north to Illinois. The Church of Christ has two principal claims to fame: it helped spark the anti-evolution Scopes Trial in 1925, and it does not allow musical instruments, choirs, or anything other than the congregational singing sanctioned by the New Testament. During services, a designated song leader would call out a page number in the hymnal, then grab a random pitch out of the air to begin. We would all pile in.

Bored with just singing the tunes, I started puzzling out the voice parts printed (in shaped notes) below the melody—thus, my first experiences with sight singing. But the context within which I developed those skills influenced basic aspects of my musicianship permanently. For instance, we had to accept as tonic whatever pitch the song leader tossed out. Moreover, we not only had no fixed *do*, but we had an *infinitely sliding do*, as the congregation sagged on sleepy mornings or went sharp when over-caffeinated. In short, perfect pitch—a great boon to many musicians—would have left me dead in the water. (On the other hand, I developed pretty good relative pitch: no absolutes for me, here or elsewhere.)

As I grew a little older, I began to experience tensions between what I learned at church and some of my other interests. Like many grade-school kids, I became enamored of dinosaurs. Yet our preachers insisted that scientists manufactured the bones they dug up, precisely in order to destroy our faith. I would ask my father and mother (respectively a microbiologist and mathematician) about this troubling contradiction. They would tell me just to ignore what I heard from the pulpit. But then, how can you invest in a religion that seems intent on spreading misinformation? I remained perplexed.

At the same time, I was taking avidly to my piano lessons. I would listen to the hellfire-and-brimstone condemnation of the piano (fully in use at the Southern Baptist Church next door) as a tool of the Devil, then go home to practice Mozart sonatas and Bach fugues. Another cognitive dissonance, which my parents again advised me to ignore.

I got used to bracketing dinosaurs and the piano. But then I faced a conflict I could not circumvent. When those of us in our Bible study class hit age 12, we were all baptized. I had always enjoyed this class, which resembled a seminar: we would read a passage from the Bible, then discuss what it meant. To put it more accurately, the teacher and I would read the passage and discuss it. My fellow students showed no interest at all in contributing to this hermeneutic enterprise.

The Sunday after we all had been born again, we gathered as usual for Bible study. When I started to answer a question, the teacher admonished me that I could no longer speak in class because there were baptized men present. What?!!! These were the same scarcely literate boys who had been there for years, and being immersed the week before did not seem to have enhanced their ability to read. I was certain there was some mistake. Over and over again I tried to engage, only to have Saint Paul's directive to the Corinthians recited at me: "Let your women remain silent in the church." This time my parents' advice did not prevail. One day when crossing the schoolyard, I came to the firm conclusion that I could not accept a community within which my gender excluded me from participation or submit to a deity who made me in this body and then held it against me.

My students often ask me how I managed to become so brave, how I withstood the slings and arrows of my detractors in the 1990s. But after I had faced down Saint Paul and the Almighty at age 12, those later detractors were nothing. That moment in the schoolyard marks the beginning of my feminist consciousness.[1]

---

[1] I used to take comfort in the thought that this very marginal group would never achieve any kind of social authority, for I knew that my former congregants would happily reinstate witch burnings and the guillotine if they could do so. The preacher urged us to celebrate the assassination of Dr. King. And so I have watched in horror the ascendancy of conservative sects with their radical curtailing of women's, LGBTQ, and civil rights. I want to thank Suzanna Feldkamp for encouraging me to include this anecdote and to Arved Ashby for egging me on. I also thank all the elderly ladies in the my childhood congregation who tried to protect me from myself during that ordeal. Their efforts were futile but, in retrospect, much appreciated.

And also the end of my connection with organized religion. If nothing else, the Church of Christ had succeeded in convincing me that all other churches were gaping maws of falsehood and idolatry. Still, I've continued to draw on my fundamentalist background in surprising ways: I know all the verses of those hymns Charles Ives weaves into his music, and I can identify the oblique scriptural allusions in Bach cantatas. Moreover, I've been told that when I get wound up in my lectures I take on an unmistakably gospel cadence; I preach the efficacy of modes in the analysis of Renaissance music with hellfire-and-brimstone fervor, and my seminars continue to follow the format I learned in my Bible-study classes. You can take the girl out of the church but not, apparently, the church out of the girl.

But my father, Dan McClary—the same one who enjoined me not to worry about fundamentalist dogma—also deserves credit for planting me in classical music. On returning in 1945 from fighting in the European front, he entered graduate study at Washington University in Saint Louis; I was born the following year. Like many veterans on the GI Bill, he faced the hurdle of leaping from his impoverished childhood to the educated middle class, and he chose music as his principal route for acculturation. Over the course of the 1940s, he had discovered repeatedly that his favorite pop songs—for instance, Sinatra's "Full Moon and Empty Arms" and "Tonight We Love"—derived from Rachmaninoff and Tchaikovsky. He bought a record player and set out to acquire recordings of the originals for those songs, then broadened his repertory by asking colleagues to suggest other composers.

As a result, the standard repertory has always appeared transparent to me, largely because my father had sought to instill "culture" in me by playing the classics at me from earliest infancy. There was never a time when I didn't know all the Beethoven symphonies or the Mozart operas or the big Romantic concertos. Whatever one might think of this plan for upward mobility, my radical immersion in the canon certainly gave me a head start on a career in music. This was my vernacular, learned at the same time and in the same way that I gained fluency in English.

Or perhaps it was the other way around. I came to conversational speech quite late, and some of my elementary-school teachers suggested that my parents put me in special education. What my parents knew was that I was reading Dickens novels under my desk while my classmates were listening to *Winnie the Pooh*. When called upon, I was yanked abruptly from my dealings with Miss Havisham to find that I had no idea what Roo had been up to. In those years before we had terms such as "neurodivergent," my deer-in-the-headlights reaction clearly signaled some kind of intellectual deficiency. Nothing in school made sense to me.

Until I began piano lessons at age 9. Suddenly everything snapped into place. I insisted on skipping the John Thompson primers and advancing directly to unexpurgated Mozart sonatas. Three years later, my teacher passed me on to the piano faculty at Southern Illinois University, where my parents taught. Robert Mueller and Stephen Barwick threw increasingly difficult repertoire at me and allowed me to interpret as I liked as long as I could justify my choices when they challenged me. (I didn't know it was unreasonable to ask me to learn and perform Schumann's *Fantasiestücke* in a week, so I just did it.) My success in the realm of musicking also gave me confidence to speak; I went overnight from being the mutest kid in the room to the most loquacious.

When I started undergraduate study as a piano major at SIU, I took beginning music theory along with all my colleagues. And although I performed well in those classes and managed to absorb the terminology fundamental to professional musicians, very little of what I learned resonated with my understanding of music. I still do not grasp why we spent days on end in class memorizing the arbitrary names for augmented-sixth chords, especially since they seem to me products of contrapuntal lines. Meanwhile, outside of theory class, I was coaching a professional ensemble on Beethoven's Op. 131. Another cognitive dissonance: something like my collision between Miss Havisham and Roo in elementary school.

While at SIU, I accompanied all the choruses, played for most recitals, and provided piano and coaching for the voice studio of the legendary Marjorie Lawrence. My bailiwick was and has remained the mainstream canon. I could explain how anything from Bach to Brahms made sense, just as I could, as a native speaker, parse elements of a poem by John Keats or a novel by George Eliot. This is still how I teach.

Then one day in music-history survey, our teacher played a recording of Monteverdi's *Orfeo*. I was quite literally dumbstruck, for I had no idea how to account for how it worked. Because I assumed that musicologists dealt with the history of "the music itself" (silly me!), I set off for graduate study with the hope of learning how seventeenth-century repertories produced their extraordinary effects.

I quickly discovered that this is not what musicologists actually do, not then and not now. In other words, I signed on to musicology for all the wrong reasons. Harvard labored to discipline me, and I somehow managed to jump through hoops well enough that I got passed along through the program. But very little in my seminars resonated with anything that truly interested me. I mostly bided my time (as I had in music-theory classes), trying desperately to hold onto the things that had brought me to music in the first place while dutifully fulfilling tasks that seemed to me relatively meaningless. I nearly died of impostor syndrome.

Two members of the faculty did help to keep me afloat. Tony Newcomb accepted me into his madrigal group, which at least kept me engaged with actual music of the kind I hoped to study. I also served as Tony's assistant in music-history survey, where he constantly demonstrated the power of music with his extravagant bodily and facial responses.

And I had the opportunity to study analysis with composer Earl Kim. Earl's quirky questions (e.g., "Why are early pieces of music short and later ones long?") had become legendary among graduate students who regarded him as a caricature of the inscrutable Asian contemplating the sound of one hand clapping. One semester, his analysis seminar concentrated on two items: Samuel Beckett's television play *Eh, Joe* and Donna Anna's recitative in *Don Giovanni* leading up to her "Or sai chi l'onore" (we never went on to consider the aria). We spent hours in class reading the Beckett aloud, then trying to answer Earl when he asked if we would put a root-position or first-inversion chord with a particular word in the script. We then scrutinized "Don Ottavio, son morta!" puzzling over Mozart's strategic choices. All total nonsense to most of my colleagues, but the most explicit engagement with the concept of flow I had ever had. Tony and Earl have both passed on, but I owe them more than I can express.

When it came time for me to choose a dissertation topic, I homed in immediately on the seventeenth century, more specifically on Alessandro Stradella, whose music I had first encountered in Nino Pirrotta's seminar on *seicento* dramatic music. Stradella's music intrigued me almost as much as Monteverdi's had a few years earlier (see below, chapters 1 and 13). But my dissertation had to conform to the empirical demands of the field. I quickly discovered that I had zero interest in anything relating to the composer's biography—not even someone with the scandal-ridden life of this particular artist. I only cared about the music, which worked according to principles tantalizingly close to those I had learned to deal with, yet that somehow hovered slightly beyond my grasp.

At last I confessed to my adviser, David Hughes, that I wanted to devote my doctoral work to figuring out how seventeenth-century music worked.

He replied that this didn't make any sense whatsoever. But because I was married at the time and therefore already viewed as a lost cause, he relented. Rather, he said to me: "Here's a rope. Go hang yourself." He meant it as a put-down; I took it as license. And this is where the story gets interesting—what I did with that rope.

Although elated by my adviser's green light, I actually had no idea how to go about what I was proposing; I only knew that this was the only project that mattered to me. I began by reading what musicologists had written on related topics, but nothing I found had anything to do with what I wanted to know. I tried going back to the generation of composers before Stradella, only to realize that their music was even more opaque to me. Finally, I settled on Monteverdi, whose early career at least coincided with a robust literature by contemporaneous music theorists. My plan of attack was to study the formulations of Pietro Aron, Heinrich Glarean, and Gioseffo Zarlino and to see if I could perceive in the scores in front of me what they were describing.

But my entrenched analytical habits, instilled in me over years of theory training, kept getting in the way. And so I willfully *cauterized* that part of my brain that wanted to label chords (as an amputee, I use the word "cauterized" knowing all too well what that entails).[2] Recall that I had no other terminology upon which I could rely. Over time, I so successfully blocked out my tonal impulses and their attendant modes of verbal explanation that I lost my ability to speak—even to the UPS guy who came to the door to make a delivery. Deeply ashamed of what I was doing, I hid out in places where I thought no one would find me—in the Education Library and a Palestinian coffee shop on Brattle Street. There I would peruse my still-enigmatic scores and stare into space, sometimes drawing abstract patterns on napkins. I was terrified that someone would ask me what I was doing. I genuinely did not have a clue.

Gradually those patterns began to make a kind of sense to me. They were, in fact, the patterns that appeared in all sixteenth-century treatises, but I had not yet known how to implement them—nor, apparently had any of the musicologists who specialized in the Renaissance.[3] As my intuitions became more concrete, I began the process of translating what I had discerned back into language. Along the way, however, I feared that if I slipped and allowed

---

[2] A sarcoma claimed my right leg in 2021. I am forever grateful to Nathan Mesko and Jacob Scott, my doctors at the Cleveland Clinic, for saving my life.
[3] Indeed, those same musicologists became quite violent when I started claiming that the modal theories of Gioseffo Zarlino et al. offered insight into this music. The pushback against my modal analysis was as violent as that against my feminist criticism.

mental laziness to supply a Roman numeral under a vertical collection, then Euridice would be sucked back into the underworld. Painstakingly I developed means of verbalizing about this music and the way I thought it operated.

Only very recently have I found something to help explain what I was doing. In summer 2023, I plowed through Iain McGilchrist's enormous *The Matter with Things*—a book my husband, Robert Walser, had been recommending to everyone.[4] A psychiatrist, philosopher, and neuroscientist, McGilchrist has long advocated that we attend to the very different functions associated with the two hemispheres of the brain. His larger argument, which he presents with massive documentation as well as affective urgency, is that Western culture has increasingly privileged the left hemisphere, the side mostly responsible for calculation, data processing, tool manipulation, and language—the skills that made possible the Industrial Revolution, digital technologies, and other scientific advances that have shaped our modern world. But these advances have come at the expense of the kinds of insights provided by the right hemisphere: insights relating to perceptions of temporality, affect, the body, and intuition. Patients who have incurred damage in this hemisphere may continue to operate perfectly well intellectually, but they have difficulty recognizing any of those right-brain qualities as real. McGilchrist claims that our cultural predisposition toward left-brain activities has led to widespread dismissals of such elements as "subjective" and not worthy of scholarly attention. As a philosopher, he worries that we have systematically cut ourselves off from the questions of value and human experience that used to stand as the focus of the humanities, arts, metaphysics, and spirituality.

As I read *The Matter with Things*, I was struck by the ways his formulations resonated with my experiences as a musicologist and theorist, allowing me to understand crucial dimensions of my ideas and their reception in ways that have always baffled me. Most obviously, my work has always engaged with issues of temporality, gesture, and the body—those insights I had taken for granted in my performing and coaching—all explained by means of metaphor. And I have continually run up against critics who accuse me of arbitrarily bringing in topics that have no demonstrable relationship to the music I want to discuss. Because such elements leave no direct, visible trace on notated scores, I appear just to be making my arguments up out of thin air.

---

[4] Iain McGilchrist, *The Matter with Things: Our Brains, Our Delusions, and the Unmaking of the World* (London: Perspective Press, 2021).

Yet those are the aspects of music that have always mattered most to me, that seem to me fundamental to how music works, and this has led me to recognize in McGilchrist's book a kind of vindication. His myriad case studies invited me to reflect on the theoretical breakthroughs that lie at the center of my research; he has given me license to put aspects of my process into words.

McGilchrist only occasionally addresses music per se, but when he does so he raises very important issues that highlight some of our greatest challenges in music pedagogy. Like Henri Bergson and other phenomenologists who have wrestled with perceptions of time, McGilchrist turns for his examples to the experience of listening to music, as if readers would grasp the concept of flow immediately when thinking about their immersion in the temporal unfolding of a piece. When I read this, I had to laugh: this metaphor would work well perhaps for everyone *except* those musicians we have trained to exchange flow for the freeze-frame certainty of the chord.

Recall that he titles his book *The Matter with Things*—what happens when we break human practices and dynamic processes down into isolated, inert elements. Theodor W. Adorno often railed against "reification," which is the Latin term for the same crime. Jean-Philippe Rameau's chord-based methods received pushback as early as C.P.E. Bach,[5] who insisted instead that musicians maintain the practice of thoroughbass, within which the melodic integrity and mutual interactions of the voices remain paramount.

In his explanation of flow, McGilchrist offers this example from J. S. Bach:

> The best analogy is with music. Take this chord from the end of the *loure*, the sixth movement of Bach's French suite no. 5 in G major.

---

[5] Jean-Philippe Rameau, *Traité de l'harmonie* (1722). Rameau's formulations still occupy the center of music-theory pedagogy. For the critique by C.P.E. Bach, see his *Essay on the True Art of Playing Keyboard Instruments* (1787). Much later, Heinrich Schenker turned to C.P.E. Bach as he sought to replace chord-orientation with contrapuntal webs.

This constellation of notes makes no sense at all on its own and is a howling discord: the notes A, B, C, and D are sounded simultaneously. Try it, if you have a keyboard to hand. However, in the context of the flowing lines that harmonise together, it does not sound discordant, but takes its place in a pleasing resolution of lines designed to be heard together, and making sense only in relation to one another.

Once the left hemisphere has frozen its object in time, and decontextualized it in space, it is left with fixed, clear, distinct but inert parts, which then have to be reconnected and reanimated; the building blocks have to be put together again, and the power, as it were switched on. To the right hemisphere these 'objects' are already connected, animate, and in motion: the power was never switched off.[6]

This is precisely the way I deal with the so-called "*Tristan* chord": a problem if and only if it is isolated from the roiling intersection of lines that produces it, those metaphorical bodies and passionate subjectivities that constitute the subject matter of the opera. But it becomes a theoretical conundrum at the moment we call it a chord, at which point it becomes unsolvable. The same is true of attempts at writing off the raging dissonance in Monteverdi's "Cruda Amarilli" as a mere ninth chord instead of a strategic head-on collision of lines.[7]

In other words, McGilchrist would indict many of our educational approaches to training musicians as profoundly left-brain oriented and counterproductive. Why do we seek to demolish the qualities that most people seek in music? For the sake of objectivity? As a teacher, I can testify that it is nigh on impossible to get students who have been engrained

---

[6] McGilchrist, *The Matter with Things*, vol. I, 493.
[7] See my explanation based on modal practices in *Modal Subjectivities: Self-Fashioning in the Italian Madrigal* (Berkeley: University of California Press, 2005).

to hear only vertical arrangements to attend to the temporal dimensions of music. McGilchrist's brief discussion of Bach pinpoints how the censorious demands of the left brain close down the insights of the right in ways characteristic of and deeply injurious to the development of musicians.

An aside on metaphor. Decades ago, linguist George Lakoff and philosopher Mark Johnson presented the position that we can only understand anything about the world by means of metaphors grounded in bodily experience, and McGilchrist spends much of his book reinforcing this claim.[8] We can label items that appear in musical scores, the dots on the page. But those indications serve only as a kind of recipe for putting certain sounds together, falling very short of qualifying as "the music." The elements that make us dance or weep or feel overwhelmed by religious feelings do not show up on the page. We may choose to restrict our observations to those items we can see and manipulate, which prohibits any connection with the aesthetic; or we can use figures of speech to try to get at and convey the ways we understand what we hear or perform or compose. As McGilchrist argues, a craving for objective certainty will disallow the kinds of observations that depend on metaphor for their formulation and communication. But if we aim to *make sense* of music, then we have to accept the use of metaphor as a given.[9] Otherwise, we reduce this incomparably rich medium to chord labels, metrical signs, and pitch-class sets.

For a historian, this problem becomes an insuperable obstacle, for there is no way one can connect the notated data of a score directly with anything in the social context from which that score emerged. Thus, the long-standing split between pure archival research on the one hand and objectified analysis on the other, with virtually nothing in between. As Rob Walser has often reminded us, we puzzle over how to relate music and society only because we have separated them in the first place.[10]

---

[8] See, for instance, George Lakoff and Mark Johnson, *Metaphors We Live By* (Chicago: University of Chicago Press, 1980); and Mark Johnson, *The Body in the Mind: The Bodily Basis of Meaning, Imagination, and* Reason (Chicago: University of Chicago Press, 1987).

[9] The same is true of advances in the sciences, which often hinge on the replacement of one set of reigning metaphors with another. In his brilliant books *Un verdor terrible* (Barcelona: Anagrama, 2020; translated as *When We Cease to Understand the World*) and *MANIAC* (Barcelona: Anagrama, 2023), Chilean writer Benjamín Labatut has explained compellingly how Heisenberg, John von Neumann, and others had to undergo an excruciating process to advance from Newtonian principles to the counterintuitive metaphors of quantum physics in order to make sense of subatomic phenomena. *When We Cease to Understand the World*, trans. Adrian Nathan West (New York: New York Review Books, 2021); *The MANIAC* (Penguin, 2023).

[10] Robert Walser, "Analyzing Popular Music: Ten Apothegms and Four Instances," in Allan Moore, ed., *The Analysis of Popular Music* (Cambridge, UK: Cambridge University Press, 2003), 16–38.

This separation continues to haunt our timid attempts at acknowledging even such elements as affect in serious discussion. We allow ourselves to deal with the semiotic dimension of musical discourse only after it has been thoroughly formalized by the left brain: witness the reification of what used to count as basic cultural literacy in "topic theory," in which the mere labeling of units often becomes the principal goal. For all the extraordinary efforts of Joseph Kerman, Leonard Meyer, Charles Rosen, and the so-called New Musicologists, the cultural interrogations that lie at the center of art history and literary criticism still face resistance for the most part in music studies. We never have managed to cast off—or even seriously question—our disciplinary allegiances to positivism.[11]

I have been working explicitly with McGilchrist's insights into metaphor and temporal flow for several years; indeed, I made extensive use of his *The Master and His Emissary* in a talk I gave for a conference on academic writing in 2010 (see chapter 4).[12] But the myriad case studies in *The Matter with Things* have led me to reflect deeply on the unorthodox paths by which I reached the theoretical formulations that comprise the core of my research. I have told some parts of this story elsewhere, but others I have kept mostly to myself, aware of how absurd they would sound. With the implicit support of McGilchrist's new book, I want to take this opportunity to articulate fundamental aspects of my process in words.

To return to my work on seventeenth-century music, I had in effect managed to concentrate all my intellectual energies on my right brain, which had deliberately built a fire wall—what I referred to above as "cauterizing"—to prevent access to the methods and vocabulary I already knew. Only after I had arrived at what to me made sense did I permit my left hemisphere to begin doing what it does best: talking, writing, creating categories, analyzing.

He makes this particular claim on p. 27. Notice how this separation parallels the one McGilchrist describes above in his Bach example or what I mention as the *Tristan* "chord" dilemma. What the left brain has cut asunder is very difficult to repair.

[11] Of course, some musicologists have been decrying this division for a very long time. See, for example, Howard Mayer Brown, "Recent Research in the Renaissance: Criticism and Patronage," *Renaissance Quarterly* 40, no. 1 (1987): 1–10. Brown is responding to Joseph Kerman's *Contemplating Music* (Cambridge, MA: Harvard University Press, 1985), which he criticizes for overstatement but to which he somewhat reluctantly adds his own complaints. I wish to thank Louise Stein for calling this important article to my attention.

[12] McGilchrist, *The Master and His Emissary: The Divided Brain and the Making of the Western World* (New Haven, CT: Yale University Press, 2009).

If this sounds scary and crazy, that's how it felt as well. My friends and my then-husband, Daniel Garber, feared for my sanity, as did I. But when I emerged from this dark night of the soul, I was convinced that I could account for sixteenth- and seventeenth-century music to the same degree that I did with repertories from Bach to Brahms. That was the criterion I had held up for myself. I could now parse any Renaissance score and explain how it made sense—a kind of sense profoundly different from the one I had developed for my engagement with the standard repertory, yet one just as complex and capable of sustaining a wide variety of idioms.

When I tried to publish my findings, however, I received nothing but rejection slips from peer reviewers who could make neither heads nor tails of what I was doing. It was in the wake of that response that I decided I had to relativize "tonality," to demonstrate how musical procedures of the eighteenth and nineteenth centuries were also products of their own cultural moments; I had to deconstruct the canon and then put it back together according to very different principles. The rest is history. If having to think about the music of Bach, Mozart, or Brahms as documents of their own moment meant taking them down off some ineffable pedestal, then so be it. I prefer to hear my heroes grappling with the great questions of their day to maintaining a mystical aura. (Incidentally, I am the only member of my faculty who bothers to teach the German canon, still the very core of my quest to make sense of music; I have taught, for instance, a seminar on Beethoven quartets every second year since 1980 and at four different institutions. To my students, I'm the most enthusiastic cheerleader Beethoven has ever had.)

Those loony patterns I doodled in the Palestinian coffee shop finally made it into print twenty years later in *Modal Subjectivities: Self-Fashioning in the Italian Madrigal*. I am continually reminded, however, of the difficulty of rewiring the brain. I teach a seminar every two years on what we jokingly call pretonal theory and analysis, and I watch very bright students struggle to convert their listening habits from the vertical to the horizontal. They cling desperately to chords for dear life—they're the only tools their left brains have on offer. Even if they do not have to descend into the darkness with no idea of what might lurk there, they still find it painful if not impossible to follow my lead.

I have undertaken this process only one other time. I had long dreaded the unit on seventeenth-century French music in my history survey course. Of course I could lecture until the cows came home on the social context of Louis XIV's Versailles. But the music baffled me. I started by looking into what others had written, but nothing addressed the issues I found perplexing.

I did not even know how to articulate what stumped me. But I decided I could not face another class session on the dance suites of Froberger unless I came to terms with this problem.

Once again, I had only the vaguest notion of what I wanted to find out about this music. Because French composers all made full use of chords and followed a basic tonal schema, I realized that I could not locate difference in pitches. It had to be something else. So I spent the summer at the keyboard playing and replaying tiny dances by Chambonnières. Rob and the cats had to suffer through what seemed even to me like nonsense and must have been excruciating for them. But gradually I began to figure out how to distribute weight and timing, how to attend to the events in the score in ways that differed quite radically from those I would bring to, say, Bach's so-called French dances. The pieces began not only to make sense to me but also to bring me enormous pleasure, and I now spend most of my keyboard time with Jean-Henri D'Anglebert and Élisabeth-Claude Jacquet de la Guerre.

I am acutely aware of how subjective this enterprise sounds. What does it mean for something to "make sense" to me, and why should it matter to anyone else? Surely this is the most solipsistic "method" anyone ever put forward in a serious academic context. But after I had arrived at some notion of what I was seeking, I began the translation process, attempting to verbalize and theorize what I had gleaned from my right-brain immersion. At this point (but only after I had decided that experiences of temporality were at issue), I began looking at documents from seventeenth-century France— music treatises but also philosophy, visual art, theology, and literature—to find corroborations. And I found them in abundance, thereby buttressing my intuitions and, I hope, shedding light on French cultural practices.

In other words, I do care deeply at some level about grounding my right-brain intuitions somewhere in the real world. Why didn't I start by reading and then advancing to the music? Because, quite simply, I did not know what I was looking for. It was only after I had learned to register Chambonnières's music in my body that I could move on to more standard versions of research. And I am quite certain that I never would have made my discoveries if I had started with verbal documentation.

When musicologists speak of interdisciplinary research, they usually mean that they focus on the insights of other fields; the home base of music becomes little more than a launching pad for exploring something—*anything*—else, a process I regard as centrifugal. By contrast, my centripetal work never departs long from the music, even though I clearly engage with many other disciplines in my search for making sense of music. For I believe that musicking counts as a fundamental human activity, that studying its processes can shed light on aspects of histories, cultures, societies, subjectivities, and existence not available through other media. It exerts a force on me more powerful than anything else I experience, and I have always wanted to know why and how, even at the expense of diving so deep into its details that I risk losing normal channels of communication, at least temporarily.

I am not advocating that others adopt this approach and disappear down their own rabbit holes. I only know that I have twice felt *compelled* to do so in order to make progress in my work. My two trips to the underworld suffice for one career, and I do not relish the idea of doing it again. But McGilchrist's work has allowed me to understand a bit more about what I put myself through, to grasp that perhaps there was some modicum of method in my madness.

Making Sense of Music brings together some of my essays that have languished unpublished—or published in places many readers may not have discovered. They range in topic from repertories of the sixteenth century to compositions premiered quite recently, from problems in analysis to those raised by considerations of gender, sexuality, and race. In other words, a cluster of bagatelles representing the various tangents I have pursued over the course of my career.

All of them, however, engage seriously with the idées fixes introduced above: concerns with temporality and the body, methods based unapologetically on metaphor. This is why I reacted to McGilchrist's descriptions of right-brain activities much as Molière's M. Jordain did to the revelation that he had been speaking prose all his life. From my first experiences with performance and coaching, my work has relied heavily on those elements, even if I have attempted time and again (frequently in vain) to mask my idiosyncrasies through a self-protective translation process. In any case, this is how I have made sense of music.

I. Why I Do What I Do

My first cluster, "Why I Do What I Do," includes some of the self-justifications I have offered at various times over the years, attempts at explaining myself to both fans and detractors. I know that many people have in fact written me off quite simply as crazy: new graduate students even to this day delight in reporting to me that their undergraduate teachers characterize me thus. Crazy I may well be, but I always arrive at my positions after extensive thought and internal debate. I cannot deny that I have run afoul of my discipline's prohibitions by taking into account issues such as genders, sexualities, and bodies in my interpretations. But if we factor in those crucial dimensions of human life, the canon of great Western art music reads differently—no longer the transcendental escape so often sought in the concert hall but rather (or, at least, also) sonic artifacts from specific moments in history, filtered through the lenses of particular composers, performers, and audiences. Together with my late friends Richard Taruskin and Christopher Small, I believe that we should focus on the human agents who have engaged in musicking as an activity necessary for survival.

Yet I freely acknowledge dealing first and foremost with what musicologists increasingly scorn as "the music itself." I do so not because I regard analysis as an end in itself but because score study can promote far more effective performances and because musical texts can yield invaluable insights into fundamental assumptions of bygone eras. Most of my writing projects have emerged from coaching sessions or from the history-survey classroom in which I work with students to grapple with the past and its significance for the present and future.

In 2018, Philip Bohlman invited me to contribute an autobiographical sketch of my career to a series titled "A Life in Music" in *Acta Musicologica*. I was at the time working on a production of Stradella's *La Susanna* with my colleagues in the Historical Performance program at Case, and I realized that I could present an account through the lens of that lifelong obsession. "Stradella and Me" traces my institutional career, including my embrace of feminist and cultural criticism, in a narrative that perhaps resembles "When I Was a Lad." What I presented above in this introduction may resonate more with Coleridge's hallucinating "Kubla Khan" after he took opium—the dark side of the moon, as it were.

I have always maintained one foot in the discipline of music theory, and I had the honor of delivering the keynote address, "In Praise of Contingency," at the annual meeting of the Society for Music Theory in 2009. As I have repeatedly over the years, I call in this piece (published in *Music Theory Online*) for the necessary collaboration between historians and theorists, the inadequacy of analysis without context or of context without the music. Because some critics had sought to refute my interpretations of instrumental music by hurling the phrase "Why a goblin?" at me, I ended this talk by returning to E. M. Forster's treatment of Beethoven's Fifth Symphony in *Howard's End*.

Incidentally, the colleague who had once asked, "If feminist musicology, why not vegetarian?" was seated in the front row, laughing uproariously, evidently not recognizing his own quip.

UCLA, where I taught from 1994 to 2011, has a program called the Faculty Research Lectures, which features two presentations a year by a faculty member chosen by a senate committee. Only after I had agreed to deliver one of these in 2002 did I consult the university archives to learn about my predecessors. To my horror, I found that Arnold Schoenberg had offered his "My Music in Twelve Tones" in this series. Suddenly the pressure mounted. Who could follow that act? What could I possibly do in the face of that competition? I cannot pretend that "Evidence of Things Not Seen" operates in the same ballpark with "My Music in Twelve Tones" (long a classic of twentieth-century thinking about music). But I daresay my manifesto was more fun, as it ranged from Franz Schubert's String Quartet in G Major to Cipriano de Rore's "Da le belle contrade d'oriente" (performed live with me at the harpsichord as the hysterical lover in the middle section of the madrigal) to videos by Madonna. Because the Madonna videos involved copyright issues, UCLA decided it could not archive the video of my talk, though my script did appear later in a Festschrift for Derek Scott without the presentation's multimedia circus. In any case, "Evidence" argues for why music offers insights of cultural assumptions not only for musicologists but for historians in general.

My writing style has proven nearly as provocative as some of my ideas. Indeed, if I had expressed those ideas in anodyne prose, eschewing metaphors, I might have saved myself a good deal of grief. It's also possible than no one would have paid much attention to my work—or at least not mined it quite so often for outrageous quotations. A voracious reader, I have always cared deeply about the ways I put words together, especially with respect to flow and rhythm. Joseph Kerman and Charles Rosen stood as my models in musicology; I also studied the descriptions of music in Proust, Thomas Mann, and Richard Powers, all of whom can make you believe you are actually hearing passages from the fictional compositions they describe. In 2010 I was asked to speak at an interdisciplinary conference focused on academic prose, and my contribution appeared in *The Future of Academic Writing* as "Writing about Music—and the Music of Writing," a talk that drew heavily on McGilchrist's *The Master and His Emissary*. Among other things, this piece features a musical analysis of Derrida's prose strategies.

Central to my work is the significance of the body to all aspects of music— its creation, performance, communication, and reception. It informs our notions of rhythm, temporality, qualities of motion, desire, pleasure, and nearly everything else in the sonic medium. Yet a persistent squeamishness has prevented references to the corporal. "The Bodies of Angels," written for an interdisciplinary conference in Barcelona in 2009, deals with the taboos associated with recognition of the body in performance and scholarship, and it also presents some examples of embodiment in a range of repertories. When we exclude the flesh from our practices, we throw away the code to understanding. Or, as Wittgenstein put it, "Yes, a key can lie for ever in the place where the locksmith left it, and never be used to open the lock the master forged it for."[13]

Which leads me to another of my central themes, the resistance to interpreting what we call "absolute music"—a myth that took hold in the wake of the failed 1848 Revolution, which forced idealistic intellectuals and artists to flee or to pretend that nothing they did actually meant anything. Intended to elevate music above the realm of "mere" human experience, this doctrine stifles those who would venture beyond formalist observations.[14] In 1988 I published an essay titled "Terminal Prestige: The Case of Avant-Garde Music Composition," which dealt with the prohibition against interpretation specifically during the twentieth-century serialist binge (it was this piece—not *Feminine Endings*—for which I received the MacArthur in 1995). The ruckus produced by this article calmed down after a while, in part because composers themselves moved on to other aesthetic goals.

Much later, when I was a visiting professor in Oslo, I was invited by my colleague Erling Guldbrandsen to join him and Julian Johnson in a miniconference focused on the legacies of twentieth-century Modernism. My paper, "The Lure of the Sublime: Revisiting the Modernist Project," appeared in the collection they edited titled *Transformations of Musical Modernism* in 2015. Not quite an apology for "Terminal Prestige," this essay interrogated yet again reasons why intelligent, sensitive artists like the ones I lambasted earlier would have gone down that rabbit hole. I also considered the music of composers such as Thomas Adès, George Benjamin, and the late Kaija Saariaho, all of whom have continued to make full use of modernist techniques even while seeking to communicate with audiences. They allow us, in other words, to have our hermeneutics and our modernism, too—which was all I was requesting in "Terminal Prestige."

The centenary of Edvard Grieg's death coincided with the beginning of my five-year appointment at the University of Oslo, and I was invited to give

---

[13] Ludwig Wittgenstein, as quoted in McGilchrist.
[14] See my "Narrative Agendas in 'Absolute' Music: Identity and Difference in Brahms's Third Symphony," in *Musicology and Difference: Gender and Sexuality in Music Scholarship*, ed. Ruth Solie (Berkeley: University of California Press, 1993), 326–44.

a keynote for a conference in Bergen celebrating their most illustrious composer. I sweated bullets as I anticipated speaking in front of all the Grieg specialists in the world, especially since I had never studied his music or biography in any detail. But as I read feverishly through his writings, I realized how much he struggled with the relationship between his Norwegian place of origin and his music: to what extent should he try to make these aspects of his life speak to each other? He had had virtually no contact with indigenous musics, but had trained to compose in the unmarked idiom of Brahms and other musicians in the German-speaking world. Yet when Norwegian colleagues such as Ibsen decided to foreground national identity, Grieg considered what such a swerve might mean for him. In his letters, he wrestled explicitly with the dangers of identity politics, only gradually turning to writing the music for which we now remember him.

Grieg's dilemma resonated powerfully with my own situation as the child of a Cherokee father who grew up to specialize in the repertories of Italian courts. What if I had decided at a late date (my father told me of our lineage only when I was nearly forty) to shift the focus of my research to Native American practices? In my talk, I grappled with Grieg's personal and musical strategies and also with my own professional decisions concerning identity. If I never formally came out as Native, I did take the risk of stamping my work with my gender, something that would have horrified me when I was a graduate student. In short, although it was foolhardy to speak of Grieg in a hall full of Grieg devotees, "Playing the Identity Card: Of Grieg, Indians, and Women" did give me the opportunity to think about paths taken and not taken in my own career.

When George Floyd was murdered in Minneapolis in 2020, I, like many North American academics, had to think hard about what I was doing in the classroom. I had long split my accounts of twentieth-century music between the continuation of the European concert tradition and the African American genres that conquered the world with the advent of sound recording. But I had not dealt sufficiently with the music of Black *composers*. As I cobbled together my new syllabus, I realized that I was not sure how to approach pieces by Florence Price and others. To be sure, she made full use of her classical training; she had learned how to manipulate harmonies, forms, and counterpoint as well as any other conservatory musician. Yet I hesitated to impose my standard analytical techniques when I discussed her music in lecture. When the theory department at University of Michigan invited me to address their community, I decided to throw my qualms into their laps for discussion.

I have not published "The Object/The Objective of Analysis: The Case of Florence Price" because it seems like the beginning of a much larger project and, moreover, a project that probably is not mine to undertake. Instead, I contacted my colleagues Philip Ewell and Christopher Jenkins, urging them to organize an event at which theorists and musicologists of color could come together to brainstorm. The result was a conference, *Theorizing African American Music*, held at Case Western Reserve University in summer 2022—the first of an ongoing series, as well as the launch in 2024 of a new journal *Black Music, In Theory*. I am including my talk in this collection not so much as a proposed solution but rather as a challenge, a call to action. Diversifying the playlist is not enough. We also need, as Ewell has argued so forcefully, new methods for assessing and understanding even the formal dimensions of music. Of all music.[15]

II. Messing with Early Music

Most musicologists forget that I regard my work on early-modern musical procedures as my most important contribution. When critics interview me about my career, they never think to ask what it was like to try to puzzle out the modal grammar upon which the madrigal depends or the transformations of that grammar in the erratic repertories that followed before we settled down into something we celebrate as "tonality." No, my interlocutors only want to know about that infamous Beethoven sentence, which will be highlighted in my obits and may even appear graven on my tombstone. But I have not left early music behind, even if no one pays much attention to those publications. My second section, "Messing with Early Music," offers a batch of essays that address musics of the sixteenth and seventeenth centuries. They include some of my favorite pieces, and it was in part my fear that they might disappear without a trace that motivated me to compile this volume.

I received the title "Unwashed Masses" as a fortuitous gift from one of my undergraduates at UCLA. Invited to deliver a talk for a conference on Renaissance Conviviality, sponsored in 2009 by the UCLA Center for Medieval and Renaissance Studies, I had been wracking my brain for a topic. As I was lecturing in my history survey course on the often-scurrilous sixteenth-century

---

[15] See Philip Ewell, *On Music Theory, and Making Music More Welcoming for Everyone* (Ann Arbor: University of Michigan Press, 2023).

Parisian chanson, I said offhandedly that these were composed for the elite rather than the unwashed masses. One of the students asked what kind of masses those would be, then reminded me that we had studied cantus firmus, paraphrase, and imitation masses; so what would an unwashed mass be? I decided then and there that an "unwashed" variety of mass would be one based on a dirty chanson. I chose Orlando de Lasso's *Missa Je ne menge point du porc*, based on a shockingly scatological chanson by Claudin de Sermisy.

A short time later, I presented the same paper for a panel at the Renaissance Society of America. So successful was this talk (it is, I admit, a lot more fun than most conference papers) that I was asked to participate in a subsequent panel on Renaissance pornography. For this event, I wrote "Tumescence and Detumescence in a Monteverdi Madrigal," specifically his "Sì, ch'io vorrei morire" from Book IV. A Monteverdi specialist once explained to me that although the composer often chose sexually explicit verses, his music remained free of erotic imagery. I am quite certain that Monteverdi would have been gravely disappointed to hear this. What does a guy have to do, anyway? But then, this is a world in which some scholars like to claim that Wagner's *Tristan* and Strauss's *Salome* have nothing to do with sex. In any case, my series of smutty, Rabelaisian papers led to an invitation to give a keynote for the RSA in 2014. I've done my part; someone else will have to pick up the heavy burden of doing stand-up for this august group.

Like many of my publications, "Tumescence" deals with questions of performance. When I teach courses concerned with sixteenth-century repertories, I am always stunned by how little ensembles seem to know what they're singing about, as I try desperately to locate recordings that indicate any awareness of texts. Pervasive in commercial recordings is a homogenized quality of sound that signals sweetness and prelapsarian innocence, as if sex was discovered only in the 1960s, despite what the ribald lyrics would seem to suggest. Listen to the dozens of renderings of Lasso's "Matona, mia cara," for instance, most of which have no clue that the words are uttered by a coarse German mercenary trying to get laid by an Italian woman, with "I fuck you all night, butt like ram" as his parting shot. To say nothing of the train wreck of the first page of Monteverdi's "Cruda Amarilli," where the dissonances that Artusi ranted about are softened into nice escape tones with a slight, crooning slide leading into the offending high A, so as to apologize for it. If you're going to perform such pieces, please take the trouble to read and understand the texts.

I wrote "Doing the Time Warp" for a conference in honor of Christopher Hasty, a trailblazing theorist of rhythm and meter. It deals with the seventeenth-century obsession with bending time, with a Monteverdi madrigal from Book VII and an unmeasured prelude by Louis Couperin as its examples. I rarely use the word "baroque" in my classes, for the composers most people identify with that label—Vivaldi, Bach, Handel—all operated within the 1700s when diatonic tonality, the musical analogue to the philosophies during the Age of Reason, regulated harmonic practice. But if "baroque" means anything at all, it refers back to the eccentric artistic strategies that early eighteenth-century literary figures such as John Dryden found so abhorrent. Theorists have largely avoided the 1600s because its music defies order—in every way, but particularly with respect to temporality. Composers delighted in stretching and compressing experiences of time, often with radically different strategies in rapid succession. If the tonal model of time management won out by 1700, it did not even qualify as the most common or popular mode in the first half of the century. To understand this music, one must be prepared to do the time warp again . . . and again.

"In the Realm of *All* the Senses" may seem to those who remember that movie to be a continuation in this same domain. But in fact, it focuses quite chastely on two sarabandes for harpsichord by Élisabeth-Claude Jacquet de la Guerre. Written for the pioneering series *Oxford Analytical Essays on Music by Women*, edited by Brenda Ravenscroft and Laurel Parsons, it examines the ways this spectacular composer engaged with sight, hearing, touch, and even the olfactory in her music. Let me just say how thrilling it is to have the music—not just the biographies—of female composers now appearing. If they matter, it is because of the music they wrote.

As mentioned in the introduction to this collection, the music of Alessandro Stradella started me off on my wild musicological adventure, and I have never lost sight of him over the decades. When I was asked in 2011 to speak for the Voces Nostrates series at UCLA, I returned to his oratorio of 1675, *San Giovanni Battista*—a powerful work that focuses on the figure of Herod's stepdaughter, known to us as Salome. The mixture of seduction and wrath Richard Strauss brings to the murderer of John the Baptist scarcely surpasses what Stradella composed centuries earlier. "Salome in the Court of Queen Christina" examines some of the highlights of this *oratorio volgare*, which features the first use of concerto-grosso orchestration (Corelli played in the premiere), as it also considers the critical difference between arias that use a progressive ABB' format and those of the next generation that operate as ABA structures. I argue that the unpredictable, explosive energies of seventeenth-century practices get reined in, domesticated, in the da capo aria, designed to contain "baroque" excess on every possible level, making this a crucial moment of change in musical and cultural history.

I delivered "Adorno Plays the *WTC*" at an Analysis and Performance colloquium at Indiana University, with theorist Carl Schachter as the other guest presenter. It turned out that Carl and I had much more in common than we had anticipated: our comments to the student performers nearly always matched. (If you thought Cate Blanchett's master class in *Tár* was scary, you might imagine having the two of us responding to your playing!) In any case, I returned in my paper to Adorno (the late Richard Taruskin would have sighed in dismay) and his brilliant essay on Bach fugues in *Prisms*. Adorno locates the significant tensions in these pieces in Bach's allegiances both to complex imitative counterpoint and to the teleological model of temporality Vivaldi had made so compelling. Each fugue makes up its own détente between these incompatible forces, each associated with a different set of cultural investments. Needless to say, Adorno presented his analyses in prose that most readers find impenetrable. My presentation attempted to make sense of his diagnoses and to demonstrate how keyboardists might make those tensions audible. For too long, we have approached the *WTC* as a series of pedagogical exercises, ignoring how unlikely the genre of the Bach fugue truly is. (I might mention that the Bach chorale—an enterprise that seeks to make the modal tunes of the Lutheran liturgy appear as fully rational products of the Enlightenment—is similarly unlikely and largely misunderstood. But that's another project.)

III. Sex and Gender, Redux

Several of the essays in earlier sections of this collection have dealt with sexuality, in particular the X-rated pieces I delivered to the Renaissance Society of America. But in the wake of *Feminine Endings*, I have participated in countless events concerned with feminist and queer topics. "The Classical Closet" was written for a conference in which most of the other speakers were specialists in popular music. No one has to argue for the relevance of nonstandard gender identities and sexualities in that area: pop artists have foregrounded such issues in their performances for decades. But I wanted to take the opportunity to explore queer moments in classical music. I include this essay (published in a Festschrift for my dear friend and colleague at Oslo, Stan Hawkins) in my course packs at the Cleveland Institute of Music. It may have a greater effect on those young professionals than anything else I give them, and I often get emails from students who report that sexuality had never been mentioned at any point in their education. They feel "seen" when they read this.

"Soprano Masculinities" was long my road talk before it finally found a home in Phil Purvis's collection *Masculinity in Opera*. It addresses the cultural circumstances that have led artists such as Farinelli, Philip Bailey, Prince, and the new horde of countertenors now featured in productions of early music as well as new operas to sing in the soprano range. Like many teachers, I have always dreaded the moment in music-history survey when I have to break the news about castrati. But juxtaposing performances of Cavalli's *Giasone* with those of Michael Jackson at least reduces the automatic "ick" response. We too love to hear men sing in that range, even though we no longer demand the sacrifice paid by the male stars of the baroque stage.

When Phil invited me to contribute to a subsequent volume, *Music and Camp*, I wrote a piece on the heteronormative women who forge some of their most significant relationships with gay men. My essay, "Sister Campers," was perhaps a bit too self-revelatory, and I got cold feet before the volume was assembled. But I include it here in all its blazing glory—my tribute to Judy Garland, Cathy Berberian, Madonna, and many others who find the company of gay men so very meaningful.

My final two items return to classical music analysis. I wrote "Kaija Saariaho, Mater" as a tribute to the composer on her seventieth birthday in 2022. Long accused of essentialism when I write about the possibility that women might compose with gender-specific experiences in mind, I found that a few very prominent European composers—Olga Neuwirth as well as Kaija—responded enthusiastically to my writing about such issues. Like Grieg explaining why he began marking his music as Norwegian, Kaija has also articulated her journey from the abstractions of IRCAM to her operas that engage powerfully the subjects of abortion, pregnancy, and childbirth—topics now in the center of our attention since the revocation of Roe v. Wade in 2022. No one before had attempted to present such traumatic issues on the operatic stage, and certainly not with Kaija's ability to suture listeners into the interior contradictions mapped out in her orchestral writing. Kaija died in June 2023, and those of us who care about new music will long mourn her absence.

"Mahler Making Love" was written in response to an invitation to contribute to a collection focused on Mahler and sexuality. Like so many of the essays in this volume, it addresses the relationship of analysis to performance and history: what we can learn from historical recordings, in this case, Willem Mengelberg's account of the Adagietto from Mahler's Symphony No. 5.

As of spring semester 2025, I continue to teach full-time, though I am now literally on my last leg and cannot postpone retirement indefinitely. But I wanted to share these items—some of my favorites—while I still have the chance to do so. I hope they bring food for thought as well as delight. Like all my work, they careen unpredictably between cultural critique and hilarity, the greatest aesthetic goal to my mind. They shed light on how I wrestle to make sense of music.

Cleveland
2025

PART I
WHY I DO WHAT I DO

1
A Life in Musicology
Stradella and Me[1]

In October 2018, I had the privilege of leading my students in the Historical Performance program at Case Western Reserve University in a performance of Alessandro Stradella's 1681 oratorio *La Susanna*.[2] As I prepared the production, I had reason to reflect on the influence of this relatively obscure seventeenth-century composer (1639–1682) on the course of my entire career. At every turn in the last fifty years, Stradella's music has pushed me in new directions; he—not feminism, not critical theory, not postmodernist revisionism—has compelled me over and over again to challenge disciplinary wisdom. I can think of no better way of framing my unorthodox life in musicology than to trace my various encounters with Stradella.

In order to lay the groundwork for the initial encounter, I have to back up a bit. I came to undergraduate school already familiar with most of the standard eighteenth- and nineteenth-century concert repertory. My father, Dan McClary, had returned from World War II with funding from the GI Bill for graduate study in microbiology.[3] A Cherokee from an impoverished background in Oklahoma, he wanted his firstborn to grow up as a member of the cultured class, and he decided that classical music would be my route to upward mobility. Although I have grave doubts about what is called the "Mozart effect," my father did blast classical music at me every waking hour from my infancy onward. Classical music became my vernacular, its gestures and grammar firmly engraved in the innermost part of my brain. This peculiar immersion allowed me to advance very quickly in my piano training and to emerge as a professional coach of singers and chamber music during my

---

[1] Published in *Acta Musicologica* 91, no. 1 (2019): 1–16, in the Lives in Musicology series. Philip Bohlman graciously invited me to contribute this piece.
[2] A video of the production is available on the website of the CWRU Music Department.
[3] The GI Bill provided fellowship support that enabled soldiers who had served in the American military to enroll and complete studies in universities upon fulfillment of their military service. This program resulted in an enormous number of first-generation college students and the postwar expansion of the middle class.

undergraduate years at Southern Illinois University. I believed then that you could throw any score from the eighteenth or nineteenth centuries in front of me and I could tell you how it ought to go. As arrogant as that may sound, I still think that's a fairly accurate assessment.

But then I took the music-history survey and heard earlier music for the first time. Like many listeners, I was bowled over by Monteverdi's *Orfeo*; I thought it was the sexiest music I had ever heard, and I also realized I had no idea whatsoever how it worked. I went off to graduate school in 1968 to study musicology because I assumed that music historians knew how to understand early repertories the way I had learned to parse the musics of the standard canon.

Alas, musicologists at the time dealt scarcely at all with the music itself, except insofar as they prepared editions. With the exception of Anthony Newcomb, who even directed a madrigal group, my musicology professors at Harvard rarely engaged with scores. I continued to provide accompaniments for voice studios and to play organ at a Catholic church on the side, but my musical interests had to remain outside Paine Hall.

In 1970, I took a seminar on seventeenth-century opera with the brilliant Nino Pirrotta, whose work has opened up so many terrains. He assigned each of us a composer, and Stradella fell to me. I spent hours playing through facsimiles at the piano and was immediately swept up in the power of this music, which seemed to me somehow to unfold in ways that escaped my intuitions. When it came time to select a dissertation topic, I quickly settled on Stradella, with his oratorios as my announced focus. I acquired facsimiles of *La Susanna* and *San Giovanni Battista*, even though I knew I was expected to formulate some sort of archival project. Every day I would go to the library to ascertain where relevant materials might be found. But I would get bored and decide to take a break to play through some of his scores. Hours later, a tap at the practice-room door would advise me that they were closing the building. Once again, I had spent a day doing what counted as zero work and would go home ashamed, vowing to do better the next day—to no avail.

Around 1971, Ursula Gunther came to Harvard to speak on her discovery of materials relating to Verdi's transformation of *Don Carlo* for the Paris Opera. My mentors and colleagues gasped in amazement as she revealed long buried details and connections. As I listened, I too realized how extraordinary her discoveries were; I also realized that if someone placed the equivalent information concerning Stradella in a box across the street, I might not care enough to go fetch it.

I was devastated. All that programming from my father, all that training, now for naught. I spent a gloomy weekend in bed with the blinds drawn. When I emerged, I had decided to do what I had initially thought musicologists did: to understand how early music works. I announced my change of plan to my adviser. He did not think the new project made any sense, but he agreed not to stand in my way. (Well, what he actually said was: "Here's a rope. Go hang yourself.")

Armed with my rope, I headed off to the practice room with newfound determination. I played through my Stradella scores again but still found them somehow strange. Yes, I could label all the chords and formal outlines, which seemed "tonal" by all the criteria I knew. But something didn't quite match my expectations. I thought that if I went back a generation, to Carissimi, I would acquire the necessary perspective. But Carissimi struck me as even odder, again in ways I could not quite identify.

At last I backed up all the way to Monteverdi, for whose works I could at least refer to contemporaneous theorists. Now I spent my days reading modal theory and playing through madrigals, attempting to apply the guidelines of Gioseffo Zarlino to the scores in front of me. I tried to resist any temptation to think in terms of the concepts that had proven useful for Bach or Mozart, and in the process I temporarily even lost the ability to speak, so completely had I severed the links between my usual language and the task at hand. (I do not recommend this exercise.) But eventually I began to perceive Monteverdi's scores through the lens of Zarlino's precepts. Hiding in the dark recesses of a coffeehouse in Harvard Square, I drew shapes on napkins and eventually developed a way of verbalizing about those drawings. No one seemed particularly impressed by my Eureka! moment, but no one stopped me either.

The Stradella project set forth in my prospectus morphed into a theoretical account of how Monteverdi transformed his modal practices over the course of his career to procedures arguably identifiable as "tonal"; I traced the parameters that remained constant and those that changed. And I assumed in advance that successive styles during the seventeenth century would have made sense to those composing and listening. They were not waiting for the Godot of tonality to appear. I found the research in sociolinguistics especially helpful for understanding how languages shift in response to cultural exigencies. Style change in music, it seemed to me, worked in much the same way. I completed my dissertation, "The Transition from Modal to Tonal Organization in the Works of Monteverdi," in 1976 and headed out into the real world.

My attempts at publishing my work met with puzzlement, however, with readers' reports that stated flat-out that this music could not be analyzed because it didn't yet work. Recall that the music in question was that of Monteverdi, surely one of the giants of Western music history. What could it possibly mean to say that this music "didn't work"? As rejection slips piled up, I decided that I would have to demonstrate the cultural contingency of moments in the standard canon in order to explain the validity of seventeenth-century practices; I would have to show how presumably universal entities such as tonality and sonata form signified culturally. There followed a series of essays on Bach, Mozart, Beethoven, Schubert, and Brahms that sought to deconstruct processes long relegated to the realm of the absolute, provoking a hue and cry unparalleled in recent musicology.

My interrogation of those universals required my acquisition of tools from the cultural criticism and feminist theory then transforming the humanities and social sciences in North American universities. From my friend Rose Rosengard Subotnik, I learned of Adorno and Foucault, both of whom would become fundamental to my work: Adorno supplied ways of discerning ideologies in musical procedures, Foucault showed how presumably subjective dimensions of human life (e.g., genders, sexualities, the body) all had histories—histories that left traces in cultural artifacts such as music. From fellow members of the Center for Humanistic Studies at the University of Minnesota, especially Richard Leppert, I was introduced to the continental philosophies of Jacques Derrida, Roland Barthes, Michel de Certeau, Julia Kristeva, and Gilles Deleuze. From my colleagues in Women's Studies (Ruth-Ellen Joeres, Naomi Scheman, Amy Kaminsky), I came to recognize the necessity for feminist criticism in academic research. They encouraged me to introduce music into interdisciplinary conferences where, frankly, my contributions had always seemed a bit timid. When I assembled my feminist talks into a volume titled *Feminine Endings: Music, Gender, and Sexuality* in 1991, I thought that I was merely bringing established and by-then uncontroversial questions to bear on music.[4] Boy, was I wrong!

But back to Stradella. Although I had focused my dissertation on Monteverdi, I still had that box containing my facsimiles of Stradella's oratorios. Every year during music-history survey I would haul one of them into class to demonstrate how music around 1675 sounded, then return it

---

[4] *Feminine Endings: Music, Gender, and Sexuality* (Minneapolis: University of Minnesota Press, 1991).

to its box. And there they might have stayed except for an unlikely series of events in the mid-1980s.

While living in the Twin Cities, I had become a regular speaker for events sponsored by the Guthrie Theater and Walker Arts Center. In 1985, the Guthrie programmed a performance of Philip Glass's *The Photographer*, with a panel discussion featuring all the collaborators involved in that piece except for Glass, who could not attend. The Guthrie asked me to speak about the music in Glass's absence. My short presentation involved an attempt at explaining the ways in which Glass's shaping of time differed from that of the standard concert repertories. Few composers attended the panel discussion (Glass was still regarded as an affront to serious music), but most of the directors of the Twin Cities' avant-garde theaters were present.

Soon after this event, I received a phone call from Matthew Maguire, director of Creation Company, an experimental troupe based in New York. He was scheduled to perform his play *The Memory Theatre of Giulio Camillo* at the Walker, and he wanted me to serve as dramaturg. I had to look the word up in the dictionary, so foreign was the world of theater to me. But he insisted: he had heard me speak about time, and he needed someone for his play who could grasp temporal structures in the abstract. Maguire's play had no spoken dialogue but operated rather on the basis of objects and stylized motion onstage. I signed on out of curiosity and also because I had a light load that summer—I was otherwise only teaching an undergraduate course on women in the arts in Women's Studies.

By night I worked with Maguire on his dialogueless play; by day I introduced students and myself to the exciting feminist work then emerging in art history and literature. Among other items, I assigned the still-celebrated article by Mary Garrard on Artemisia Gentileschi, an article that focused on the genre based on Susanna and the Elders and Gentileschi's subtle subversion of the sexual dynamics that usually characterized such depictions.[5] I began to wonder if music could participate in sexist representations, then suddenly remembered that I had Stradella's *La Susanna* hidden away in its box. I played through the facsimile, now with different eyes and ears, asking questions I had never before entertained. Indeed, many of the issues Garrard raised concerning paintings leapt from the score: the eroticization of Susanna's body, the sexual shaming to which she is subjected, the male

---

[5] Mary Garrard, "Artemisia and Susanna," in *Feminism and Art History*, ed. Norma Broude and Mary Garrard (New York: Harper & Row, 1982), chapter 8.

bonding between the elders and the narrator who shapes the listener's point of view.

Back at Maguire's rehearsals, I realized that I was acquiring skills for producing theatrical works that operated principally on the basis of gesture, and I set about developing a postmodernist knockabout of *La Susanna*—a piece that would present Stradella's sensuous music intact but with staging that laid bare its dark side. Mike Steele, then theater critic for the *Minneapolis Star and Tribune*, and Patty Lynch, director of Brass Tacks Theater, aided me in transforming this odd idea into a viable play. In summer 1987, *Susanna Does the Elders* enjoyed a two-weekend run at the Southern Theater with the support of a grant from the Minnesota Composers Forum. Cindy Lambert performed the role of Susanna and the hapless musicologist who unleashes this oratorio; Joe Tambornino embodied Stradella as a swashbuckling cad singing the narrator's part; my colleagues in the Antiquarian Mofos provided the instrumental accompaniment.[6] This experience with staging found materials against the grain came in handy again most recently when I wrote a book on similar techniques in *The Passions of Peter Sellars: Staging the Music*.[7]

Although it qualified as a success (for experimental theater, in any case), *Susanna Does the Elders*—my very first feminist venture—also helped to undermine my position at the University of Minnesota. With the publication four years later of *Feminine Endings*, the tensions became overwhelming, and I left Minnesota, first for McGill University, then UCLA, and finally Case Western Reserve. Let's just say that I have lived in interesting times.

Stradella's scores have never stayed entirely within their box since that. In 1992 I delivered the Bloch Lectures at the University of California, Berkeley, and I led off the series "Conventional Wisdom: The Content of Musical Form" with a discussion of Susanna's first aria. By all rights, "Quanto invidio" ought to qualify as tonal. Yet some elements failed to jibe entirely with my understanding of tonal process, and I examined it as an example of the overlapping of what we usually regard as earlier and later conventions, both of which we need in order to grasp Stradella's strategies.

When I finally had acquired enough clout to publish my old dissertation materials in *Desire and Pleasure in Seventeenth-Century Music*, I turned

---

[6] A video of *Susanna Does the Elders* also may be viewed on the CWRU Music Department website, or at https://www.youtube.com/watch?v=PzqCBnFdJV4

[7] *The Passions of Peter Sellars: Staging the Music* (Ann Arbor: University of Michigan Press, 2019).

again to my box of facsimiles.[8] As I traced tonality's emergence in *Desire and Pleasure*, I argued that seventeenth-century style changes involve not pitch so much as temporal arrangements; I sought to demonstrate how pitches served as raw materials pushed into place to accommodate new structures of feeling and rhythmic shapes. I now had the benefit of work by Robert Gjerdingen, whose *Music in the Galant Style* allowed me to identify the building blocks Stradella was deploying for purposes of middle-level expansion.[9] My dissertation project finally saw print after a delay of nearly thirty years.

In the 2010s, my principal barnstorming talk—the one I gave at colloquia when no one specified a topic—dealt with Stradella more pointedly, now focusing on his depiction of La Figlia in *San Giovanni Battista* (1675). Although it mainly focused on musical characterization, "Salome in the Court of Queen Christina" also brings in the scandals for which this *seicento* libertine was celebrated by subsequent generations (see chapter 13). I owe a debt of gratitude to musicologist Carolyn Gianturco who actually undertook all that archival work I spurned fifty years ago; Gianturco has set the record straight on many issues concerning Stradella's life.[10] But just as I neglected the archives as a graduate student, I still find myself seduced by this music, at once familiar and yet not quite captured through common analytical methods.

Coming full circle, I finally had the opportunity to direct a production of *La Susanna*. My performers—graduate students in the Historical Performance program at Case—brought extraordinary technical skills and experience with repertories from before 1700 to the task, and they more than met the challenge. But time and again, what they had regarded as relatively simple music threw them, requiring hours of rehearsals. I confess that their struggles gratified me, for they were thrown off-balance by precisely the kinds of passages that first puzzled me and that drew me into a career-long obsession with Stradella.

Yet although I have returned at crucial moments to this composer, Stradella's influence on my career reaches far beyond his music, for he first led me to question the tenets of standard tonal analysis. If his chords and forms seemed familiar to me, something did not quite fit. I might have

---

[8] *Desire and Pleasure in Seventeenth-Century Music* (Berkeley: University of California Press, 2012).

[9] Robert O. Gjerdingen, *Music in the Galant Style* (Oxford and New York: Oxford University Press, 2007).

[10] Carolyn Gianturco, *Alessandro Stradella: His Life and Music* (Oxford, UK: Oxford University Press, 1994).

followed the example of many of my predecessors and just written off that failure to fit as evidence of his ineptness. Yet I could not bring myself to blame him for my inability to grasp his strategies; if I posited in advance that his music worked perfectly well on its own terms, then I had to fault myself and my inadequate analytical tools for my lack of understanding. If tonal process did not reside strictly within chords and forms, then what else did I need to attend to? What was the elusive difference between Stradella's language and that of his apprentice Arcangelo Corelli?

I cannot pretend to have solved this problem definitively. But the exercise of questioning this important moment just before our familiar hierarchy locked in encouraged me to regard tonality as a historical construct and to ask why it came into being when and as it did. "Tonality," for me, came to serve not as a default but rather as a particular group of arrangements prevalent at certain times and places. I became as interested in interrogating its covert values as in puzzling out those repertories that did not quite satisfy its criteria.

Ah, relativism! As Derrida might have put it, the supplement that was Stradella deconstructed the dominant paradigm. I did not set out with that as my goal.

I realize that my narrative so far little resembles the account most people would offer concerning my professional biography. And though reluctant to depart from my innocent Stradella-based idyll, I must turn to the rather more public side of my career in musicology.

When I left graduate school, I had few ambitions other than to get and sustain a good teaching job. I still receive my best ideas in the classroom, and I love the process of helping young musicians to perform more effectively and of teaching those without specialized backgrounds how to understand what they hear. Often the most extraordinary insights come from those who have clocked thousands of hours listening by themselves and who have not had their powerful reactions to music shamed out of them. As an academic, I knew I had to publish in order to hold on to my university position, but I calculated I would write just enough to get by.

As the inexorable tenure clock ticked on, I submitted drafts about Monteverdi madrigals and Dowland songs to journals. I mentioned above that I received only rejections. I might add that some of the responses to my work were curiously violent: at an AMS meeting in 1975 my paper on purely formal aspects of "Cruda Amarilli" provoked a quasi-riot, quelled temporarily by none other than Claude Palisca (my knight in shining armor), only to flare up again later in a restaurant at which one of my detractors assaulted me. My readers' reports did not address problems of evidence, argumentation, or writing so much as they expressed moral outrage at the fact that I thought sixteenth-century modal theory might help to explain music of the time.

Keep in mind that my interpretations involved neither feminism (I would not have been caught dead at the time dealing with "mere" women's issues) nor canon bashing. In retrospect, I recognize that this stormy reception had everything to do with my gender. A male scholar presenting the same ideas might have been labeled a young Turk, perhaps, but would not have experienced sexual assault. At that same meeting at which my modal analysis triggered an explosion, I was told by the search committee of a major research university that they could not consider my candidacy unless I submitted to sterilization. They did not want to waste a job on someone who would just poop out babies. And in response to the death and rape threats I received in the wake of *Feminine Endings*, the police once had to move me out of my apartment.

I regret having to include these sordid episodes in my narrative, but events of this sort deeply marked my career path and those of women of my age group. The history of our field does not reside solely in a list of publications or advances in knowledge. Those were the prices I had to pay for a life in musicology.

Mostly undaunted, I continued to work at getting my theories of modal strategy published. But I also developed important conversations with colleagues concerning other topics. First, I met Richard Leppert, a musicologist and art historian in the Humanities department at the University of Minnesota. Richard too sought to bring interdisciplinary methods to the study of music, and we both had found Rose Subotnik's pioneering publications on Adorno extremely stimulating.[11] In 1985, we organized an international conference, "Music and Society: The Politics of Composition, Performance and Reception"; the book of the same name that proceeded from the conference kicked off what came to be called (though not by us)

---

[11] See in particular Rose Rosengard Subotnik, "Adorno's Diagnosis of Beethoven's Late Style: Early Symptom of a Fatal Condition," *Journal of the American Musicological Society* 29, no. 2 (Summer 1976): 242–75. Leppert went on to edit the indispensable *Essays on Music by Theodor Adorno*, trans. Susan H. Gillespie (Berkeley: University of California Press, 2002). See also my "Adorno Plays the *WTC*: On Political Theory and Performance," *Indiana Theory Review* 27, no. 2 (Fall 2009): 97–112; chapter 14 in this volume.

The New Musicology.[12] Richard and I collaborated for about ten years, but we were soon targeted by Lynne Cheney, then head of the National Endowment for the Humanities and spouse of the Secretary of Defense, who was gunning for "tenured radicals." We seemed to fit the bill perfectly and were subjected to widespread ridicule; the university feared losing its defense funding, and we found ourselves in a precarious position. I left the Twin Cities, but Richard soldiered on, building an exceptionally strong and innovative humanities program, Comparative Studies in Discourse and Society.

Second, I became an informal adviser to members of the Minnesota Composers Forum, founded in 1973 by Libby Larsen and Stephen Paulus, both graduate students in composition at Minnesota. I had never composed. But my ideas concerning the historicity of tonality and the narrative that posited serialism as the only viable path forward for music resonated strongly with young composers who felt shackled by such ideologies, still very much in force. Starting with a few short essays in the *Minnesota Composers Forum Newsletter*, I gradually came to address tensions in the world of new music and newly minted theories of postmodernism. My article "Terminal Prestige: The Case of Avant-Garde Music Composition"—yet another cause célèbre—elicited more threats but also brought me to the attention of the MacArthur Foundation, which appointed me a fellow in 1995.[13] I attempt to keep up with the ever-changing terrain of new music in part through my seminar "Opera after *Einstein*," which I offer on a biennial basis.

Third, because I believe strongly that musicologists should know the music of their own time, I realized that I should also become conversant with popular music. In truth, I had managed to shield myself from pop genres during the 1960s, surely the zenith of the counterculture. My father had worked so hard to secure my allegiances to the canon that I feared I would destroy his aspirations if I listened to anything else. Only after he died in 1984 did I venture to imagine that the world would not end if I heard what

---

[12] Richard Leppert and Susan McClary, eds., *Music and Society: The Politics of Composition, Performance and Reception* (Cambridge, UK: Cambridge University Press, 1987). I am sometimes asked why I did not simply apply the methods of ethnomusicology to historical musicology, given that so many of the issues that concerned me had been addressed within that discipline. I can only answer that I did not have contact with relevant scholars when I was developing my work. I greatly admire the work of ethnomusicologists, and the majority of the books published in the Music and Culture series that George Lipsitz, Rob, and I edited for Wesleyan University Press come from those scholars. But they played a relatively small role in my earlier intellectual *Bildung*, and I ended up reinventing many wheels as a result.

[13] "Terminal Prestige: The Case of Avant-Garde Music Composition," *Cultural Critique* 12 (Spring 1989): 57–81.

everyone else on the planet was listening to so avidly. As it happens, I was assigned the twentieth-century part of the music-history survey at precisely that same time. And although I knew virtually nothing about blues, jazz, rock, and so on, I also knew I could not in good conscience teach the continuation of the concert repertory as if it alone constituted "Western music since 1900." I spent the summer cramming to learn about musics almost as remote to me as the thirteenth-century motet.

I had the good fortune of having as my assistant for this course Robert Walser, who shepherded me through these repertories and who became not only my collaborator in publications concerning popular music but also, later, my spouse. I cannot claim to have the depth of expertise in this area that he and many of my younger colleagues bring to their research. But my commitment to treating popular musics seriously resulted not only in the chapters on Madonna and Laurie Anderson in *Feminine Endings* or discussions of Prince and Public Enemy in *Conventional Wisdom*; it also has deeply influenced the ways I regard the early-modern music with which I had started my career.

Finally, my conversations with gay and lesbian students led me to contemplate queer music criticism. I arrived at an AMS meeting in 1986 hoping to ask colleagues if they knew the existence of any work in this area. On the bulletin board in the front entry, I found a flier announcing an open house for anyone interested in gay and lesbian issues. There, in a cavernous ballroom, I first met Philip Brett. No one else showed up, so terrified were they of being stigmatized in this age of AIDS. And so Philip and I compared notes and plotted. I had scarcely started to venture into feminist criticism yet. Without Philip's support and moral will power, queer musicology and several strands of its feminist analogue would have languished. The 1990 meeting at Oakland knocked the lid off the AMS, with panels devoted to women, to hip-hop, and to gay issues. Philip's panel included his work on Benjamin Britten, Gary Thomas's on Handel, Malcolm Brown's on Tchaikovsky, and mine on Schubert.[14]

I try to tell myself that I do not go looking for trouble. Yet each of these alliances, once brought back into musicology, proved explosive. The late Howard Mayer Brown once told me that I write too clearly, that the import of my arguments is far too self-evident. In truth, I write in order to communicate. After some editors of music journals urged me to strip my language back

---

[14] These as well as articles by Suzanne Cusick, Lydia Hamessley, Paul Attinello, and others appeared in *Queering the Pitch: The New Gay and Lesbian Musicology*, ed. Philip Brett, Elizabeth Wood, and Gary C. Thomas (New York: Routledge, 1994).

to the lifelessness of passive voice, I decided to move in the opposite direction. I had already so denatured my prose that I despised it. Having little left to lose, I chose to write with the vivid style I perceived in the literature and criticism I admired.[15] If musicologists still did not approve, I began to attract the attention of readers from a wide spectrum of disciplines.

My first publications—all post-tenure—appeared in interdisciplinary journals. One of the members of my tenure committee was the prominent scholar of French literature Tom Conley, who requested an article for *Enclitic*. Though quite technical (it dealt with sudden moves to the lowered sixth degree in nineteenth-century music), "Pitches, Expression, Ideology" first put my name in print.[16] *Cultural Critique* published two of my early pieces: an account of Mozart's Piano Concerto, K. 453, and the already-cited "Terminal Prestige";[17] *Genders* picked up my piece on Madonna, *Discourse* my article on Laurie Anderson.[18] I also received two commissions from the University of Minnesota Press for books I had read in French and recommended for translation: the afterword to Jacques Attali's *Noise* and the foreword to Catherine Clément's *Opera, or the Undoing of Women*.[19] My essay on Bach appeared in *Music and Society*, which I coedited with Richard Leppert.[20]

A word about interdisciplinarity. I bear much of the responsibility for introducing various kinds of cultural theory into musicology. At a time when conversations concerning gender, race, sexuality, class, subjectivity, and the like took place outside music departments, I had to locate useful sources in order to bring questions of this sort to my work. I want to emphasize, however, that I have always maintained my focus on music, and I hoped that the methods Larry Kramer, Rob Walser, and I brought into the field would bridge the long-standing gap between history and analysis.[21] With some

---

[15] See my "Writing about Music—and the Music of Writing," in *The Future of Scholarly Writing: Critical Interventions*, ed. Angelika Bammer and Ruth-Ellen Joeres (New York: Palgrave Macmillan, 2015): 205–14. Included as chapter 4 in this volume.

[16] "Pitches, Expression, Ideology: An Exercise in Mediation," *Enclitic* 7, no. 1 (Spring 1983): 76–86.

[17] "A Musical Dialectic from the Enlightenment: Mozart's Piano Concerto in G Major, K. 453, Movement II," *Cultural Critique* 4 (Fall 1986): 129–69.

[18] "Living to Tell: Madonna's Resurrection of the Fleshly," *Genders* 7 (March 1990): 1–21; "This Is Not a Story My People Tell: Time and Space According to Laurie Anderson," *Discourse* 12, no. 1 (Fall-Winter 1989–90): 104–28.

[19] "The Politics of Silence and Sound," afterword to Jacques Attali, *Noise*, trans. Brian Massumi (Minneapolis: University of Minnesota Press, 1985), 149–58; "Feminism, or the Undoing of Opera," foreword to Catherine Clément, *Opera, or the Undoing of Women*, trans. Betsy Wing (Minneapolis: University of Minnesota Press, 1988), ix–xviii.

[20] "The Blasphemy of Talking Politics during Bach Year," *Music and Society*, 13–62.

[21] See Lawrence Kramer, *Music as Cultural Practice: 1800–1900* (Berkeley: University of California Press, 1990), as well as the many books that have followed. See also Robert Walser and Susan McClary, "Start Making Sense: Musicology Wrestles with Rock," in *On Record: Rock, Pop, and*

dismay, I have watched as many younger musicologists have flaunted the interdisciplinary card as a way of avoiding dealing with "the music itself." I advise my students that others can explain Gilles Deleuze or Julia Kristeva more effectively, but that only they can bring music into interdisciplinary conversations. "Interdisciplinary" must not mean abandoning music.[22]

In the wake of my publications in these other sites, musicologists started to hear news of my gadfly operations. Some of my essays had circulated in samizdat fashion among music graduate students at Columbia and Berkeley. As my ideas received the stamp of approval from interdisciplinary journals and publishers, the discipline realized it could no longer ignore me. Joseph Kerman and Richard Taruskin both requested meetings with me, and this body of work, which had developed outside the purview of the field, suddenly became the emblem of notoriety. In the aftermath of the civil-rights movement, the phrase "They should have served that cup of coffee" emerged; echoing those wise words, my husband often suggests "They should have published that essay on modes." If the projects I had staked out in graduate school had received even minimal acceptance, I would have remained happily inside the tent. Left to my own devices, I quickly burned through many of the precepts still fundamental to musicology at the time.

If I had left graduate school with no particular interest in becoming a prolific writer, I suddenly found myself in great demand. I gave talks throughout North America and Europe, partly to explain my ideas. Many institutions asked me to speak because of my notoriety, and more than one of my hosts asked me if I had always been "that size." Imagining me a monster, they had read my prose with the vision of the gargantuan Barbra Streisand who sometimes stalks *South Park*, and they were taken aback when confronted by a small, standard-issue female academic. The talks I gave became publications, which generated yet further controversy and colloquium talks in which I sought to defend my honor.

---

the Written Word, ed. Simon Frith and Andrew Goodwin (New York: Pantheon, 1990), 277–92; and Walser, *Running with the Devil: Power, Gender, and Madness in Heavy Metal Music* (Middletown, CT: Wesleyan University Press, 1993).

[22] Historian and historiographer Hayden White has asked that musicologists not only borrow from historians and literary scholars but also that they pay back by offering information only available through music. See White, "Form, Reference, and Ideology in Musical Discourse," afterword to *Music and Text: Critical Inquiries*, ed. Steven Paul Scher (Cambridge, UK: Cambridge University Press, 1992).

My most notorious moment—the one that takes up most of the space in my Wikipedia entry, the one that will no doubt dominate my obituary—involved one of my little essays for the *Minnesota Composers Forum Newsletter*. Hoping to raise the public profile of the *Newsletter*, the board had invited Greg Sandow (then new-music critic for the *Village Voice*) to assume the role of guest editor for the 1987 edition. I wrote "Getting Down off the Beanstalk" in collaboration with Greg. Since nothing else I had written up until then had attracted any attention, we had no reason to believe that anyone would notice this piece.

My principal argument concerned temporality in music. As mentioned above, I had spoken about how Philip Glass's minimalist arrangements challenged the standard teleological vectors of tonal music, and I had repeatedly heard the objection that Glass's music "doesn't go anywhere." One of my students, Janika Vandervelde, was venturing into minimalism, spurred in part by her chagrin when elementary-school students began pumping their little fists in response to her growth-to-climax simulation of the magical vine's emergence in her *Jack and the Beanstalk*. She wanted to find other, less aggressive ways of shaping her music, which she pioneered in a series of *Genesis* pieces. Together with Greg, I sought in this essay not only to defend repetitive music but also to explain the ubiquity of that testosterone-laden imagery in much nineteenth-century music.

And Beethoven seemed the obvious example. I chose to address not the over-emphatic conclusion of the Fifth Symphony but rather a passage in which the teleological trajectory is thwarted: the point of recapitulation in the Ninth. Like so much of my work, my account of this passage came from the classroom. I had noticed that students (male as well as female) often cringed, clapping their hands over their ears, sometimes even running from the room when this recapitulation approached. As long as I could identify with that energy, which I usually could if wired up in teaching mode, I could share in the triumphant gestures we heard. But if I were listening passively, I too found myself cringing and feeling violated. In my women's-studies courses I had encountered the poetry and essays of Adrienne Rich, and I included her "The Ninth Symphony of Beethoven Understood at Last as a Sexual Message" in support of my argument.[23]

---

[23] Adrienne Rich, in *Diving into the Wreck* (New York: Norton, 1974), 205–6.

Critics have long noted the inordinate violence of that collision, some even in quasi-sexual terms.[24] But for a woman to observe the explosive failure of that moment, to make use of a metaphor that drew on an experience all too common to women, proved unforgivable. Somehow this essay in an innocuous, local newsletter made it into the hands of a few musicologists who ignored the essay's argument, excerpted the single sentence describing the passage as resembling rape, and used it to denounce me far and wide. It was this sentence that brought down the assault and death threats.

People often ask me if I regret having written this essay. I have lived with the consequences for over thirty years, and no matter how much I publish on modal theory or Kaija Saariaho, I will always be identified with this sentence, nearly always taken out of context. I hasten to mention that I have taught a course on Beethoven quartets every other year since 1980; unless a student has googled me and asks about the controversy, no one in my classes would have any inkling of my presumed hatred of this composer. But no, *je ne regrette rien*. I still stand by my argument and even my imagery after all these years.

I was not motivated by prurience. That overwhelming push for closure, even at the expense of violence, became the template not only of subsequent symphonists such as Mahler but also of action movies, in which we get car pileups and other kinds of mayhem before we can reach the end. Beethoven deserves a great deal of credit for inventing something that remains to this day a standard structure of feeling. Pointing this out should not get one lynched.

In the early 1990s, I received two extraordinary invitations. First, Cambridge University Press contacted me to ask if I would write a handbook on Bizet's *Carmen*. The editors of the series approached me not because of any expertise I might have had on this topic (in fact, I had none), but rather because my foreword to Clément's *Opera, or the Undoing of Women* had led them to believe that this opera might be best presented by a feminist. My account of *Carmen* addressed not only gender and sexuality but also Orientalism, class, prostitution, and mass culture.[25] At one point Cambridge asked me to delete any mention of Edward Said, which I refused to do. When I began the project, the going interpretation sided with poor Don José. My students now find that hard to believe. *Georges Bizet: Carmen* has never gone

---

[24] See Robert Fink, "Desire, Repression & Brahms's First Symphony," *repercussions* (Spring 1993): 75–103.

[25] *Georges Bizet: Carmen* (Cambridge, UK: Cambridge University Press, 1992).

out of print, and translations into Italian and Portuguese exist; directors consult me to discuss their ideas for staging. Even as late as spring 2019, I had to go on Irish and Australian radio to present my ideas about this, the most popular opera in the repertory. Quite a windfall! I never imagined I would become Miss Carmen.

The second invitation came from the University of California, Berkeley, when Joseph Kerman proposed that I deliver the Bloch Lectures in 1993. This was far too early in a distinctly unorthodox career for such an honor to occur. I accepted and then sweated blood for months. My eclectic curriculum vitae scarcely suggested a worthy topic. But I knew immediately that I wanted to do something that allowed me to deal with the concert repertory and popular music together, with similar methods and equal respect. Needless to say, issues of gender and sexuality would have to show up as well. Eventually I resolved to focus on the question of musical conventions, which undergirded all the musics I wanted to interrogate. After a lecture on myriad manifestations of the twelve-bar blues, I spoke about the highly standardized procedures of eighteenth-century music, examining tonality and its forms (sonata, da capo aria, etc.) as socially constructed patterns. In the final lecture, which brought together the postmodernisms of Philip Glass, John Zorn, k. d. lang, Public Enemy, and Prince, I sought to show how each of these artists continued to draw on long histories of conventions and traditions in the fashioning of new music. My audience members at Berkeley were not sure how to react to this bizarre narrative that stretched from (yes) Stradella to the shocking video of "Kiss," which nearly provoked a heart attack in one of the senior faculty members. *Conventional Wisdom: The Content of Musical Form* (2000) remains my favorite child, and I am grateful that Berkeley took that gamble.[26]

Thanks to the prestige of the Bloch Lectures and the MacArthur, the University of California Press finally allowed me to publish the work forged in my long-abandoned dissertation. *Modal Subjectivities* presented my reconstruction of sixteenth-century musical syntax, with analyses of madrigals ranging from Jacques Arcadelt and Philippe Verdelot to Gesualdo and Monteverdi. This was the same material that received scoffing rejection slips in 1980; it won the American Musicological Society's Otto Kinkeldey Prize in

---

[26] *Conventional Wisdom: The Content of Musical Form* (Berkeley: University of California Press, 2000).

2005.[27] Its sequel, *Desire and Pleasure in Seventeenth-Century Music*, traced the stages in the evolution of modal procedures to the full-blown tonality of Corelli.[28] Of course, the years between the completion of my dissertation in 1976 and the eventual release of these ideas in public had allowed me to acquire the methods of cultural criticism. These two books do not resemble in style the requisite dry prose of the thesis. But the theoretical models and basic analyses remain intact.

I thought I had finished with the writing of books. But fate—or my friends at the University of Toronto, Sherry Lee and Linda Hutcheon—kept putting me in proximity with Peter Sellars, first to view his Tristan Project, then for a day devoted to Sellars's production of Handel's *Hercules*. Moreover, like many others who teach courses in music of the last twenty years, I had found myself entranced by his stagings of John Adams's *Doctor Atomic* and Kaija Saariaho's *L'Amour de loin*.

I embarked on my Sellars project because he obviously attends so closely to the music. Few of us in musicology pay attention to the ways blocking and lighting shape what we hear, and Sellars seemed the perfect focus for dealing with the relationships among music, gesture, cultural criticism, and staging. Many of the skills I had developed throughout this strange career—coaching, dramaturgy, stage direction, and analysis of music, gender, and sexuality—came into play for *The Passions of Peter Sellars: Staging the Music*.[29]

I have greatly benefited over the course of my career from my encounters with too many colleagues and students to mention. When writing my dissertation in exile in Chicago, I joined up with an extraordinary cluster of graduate students at the University of Chicago—Bill Caplin, Ellen Harris, Louise Stein, Peter Burkholder, Jann Pasler—who have continued to be my cohort. Sometime in the mid-1980s I happened on a book by Christopher Small, *Music, Society, Education*, which encouraged me to pursue my interest in linking musical processes with social ideologies. Rob and I later met Chris and his partner, Neville Braithwaite, and we became close friends; we even began spending a month each summer in Sitges, Spain, in their company. Eventually, we acquired the rights to reprint Chris's books and commissioned his deeply influential book *Musicking*.[30] I cannot fail to

---

[27] *Modal Subjectivities: Self-Fashioning in the Italian Madrigal* (Berkeley: University of California Press, 2004).
[28] See again n. 6.
[29] McClary, *The Passions of Peter Sellars*.
[30] Christopher Small, *Music, Society, Education* (London: John Calder, 1977; reprinted, Middletown, CT: Wesleyan University Press, 1996); *Music of the Common Tongue: Survival*

mention as well George Lipsitz, Michael Cherlin, Pauline Yu, Peter Reill, and Georgia Cowart, all of whom have stimulated my mind and nurtured me during good times and bad.

As I slouch toward retirement, I look back at my life in musicology with some pain but also with considerable joy. Aspects of my work have influenced younger generations of scholars, who are carrying out investigations I never could have imagined. If nothing else, I have helped to inject into the field crucial debates concerning the place of music in society and its manifold meanings.

When I first arrived at graduate school, my cohort was told that all the important projects had been completed, that nothing remained for us but research on one or another *Kleinmeister*. It now seems to me that we have only begun, that the significant work lies ahead of us. I am fortunate to have been assigned Stradella as my *Kleinmeister*, for understanding his music required me to dismantle everything I knew, to ask questions not native to the discipline. Staging his *La Susanna* brought me full circle.

---

and Celebration in Afro-American Music (London: John Calder, 1987; reprinted, Middletown, CT: Wesleyan University Press, 1998); *Musicking: The Meanings of Performance and Listening* (Middletown, CT: Wesleyan University Press, 1997). See also the collection culled in part from the materials left at his death in 2011, *The Christopher Small Reader*, ed. Robert Walser (Middletown, CT: Wesleyan University Press, 2016).

2

In Praise of Contingency

The Powers and Limits of Theory[1]

When I first went on the job market in 1975, I advertised myself as both a musicologist and a theorist. Receiving offers in both fields, I chose musicology: I assumed I could do as much theory and analysis as I liked in my music-history courses but would spend all my time correcting parallel fifths if I pursued the other route. In the years since the Society for Music Theory broke away from the American Musicological Society, however, professional theorists gradually have moved closer to the humanities, while musicologists increasingly have gravitated toward the social sciences.

I plead guilty of having introduced cultural criticism into musicology. Yet at the same time, I believe firmly that *the study of music must also include the study of music*. And although I trust that the pendulum will eventually swing back toward the middle, musicologists have entered a phase in which analysis has become the butt of jokes—the business of gnostics straight out of Hermann Hesse's *The Glass Bead Game*.[2]

As I enter my last years before retirement, I find that I'd rather spend them wallowing in scores, sounds, and performances than worrying about what Pierre Bourdieu or Homi Bhabha might have to say. As a consequence, I moved my line in 2007 within the bizarrely balkanized territory contained within UCLA's Schoenberg Hall from Musicology to Music—from the Humanities to the School of the Arts, and I now work at least as much with the performers and composers at the Cleveland Institute of Music as with the musicologists at Case Western. So the die is cast: *Ich bin eine Musiktheoretikerin!*

But what precisely does this mean? Our Swedish colleagues Per Broman and Nora Engebretsen foregrounded the question "What kind of theory

---

[1] Keynote for the annual meeting of the Society for Music Theory, Montreal, 2009, published on *On-Line* (January 2010). http://www.mtosmt.org/issues/mto.10.16.1/mto.10.16.1.mcclary.html

[2] Hesse's *Das Glasperlenspiel* appeared in 1943. For critiques of analysis in musicology, see particularly Carolyn Abbate, "Music—Drastic or Gnostic?," *Critical Inquiry* 30, no. 3 (Spring 2004): 505–36.

is music theory?" as the title of their book.[3] In the other humanities, such as literary or film studies, the word "theory" refers to any enterprise concerned with general methods or approaches; it finds itself attached to specific modifiers such as "narrative," "feminist," "queer," or "postcolonial." I have often been identified by my colleagues in comparative literature as a "music theorist," because I bring the same sorts of questions to bear on music.

The individuals associated with the Society for Music Theory, however, have tended until recently to confine their purview more narrowly to the formal dimensions of music. Although linguistic theories that deal in the abstract with grammar and syntax also abound, they usually operate quite separately from activities focused on the interpretation of artworks. By contrast, music specialists lump pedagogical, grammatical, analytical, and speculative enterprises together within an uneasy category called "theory," which occasionally (but not often) also includes considerations of cultural history, aesthetic judgment, and meaning—the principal concerns of most other humanities disciplines.

Since at least the time of Pythagoras, music theorists have presumed to engage with much more than just the tunes humans invent; they have repeatedly aspired to mathematical objectivity and even to the metaphysical, to account for nothing less than the order of the universe.[4] Given those lofty aims, the consideration of repertories can seem pretty poor stuff. As philosopher Stanley Cavell once pointed out, "The absence of humane music criticism... seems particularly striking against the fact that music has, among the arts, the most, perhaps the only, systematic and precise vocabulary for the description and analysis of its objects." Yet, he cautions, "somehow that possession itself must be a liability."[5]

Cavell published that diagnosis in 1967, when taxonomic music theory was on the rise; Joseph Kerman echoed these sentiments ten years later when he wrote that "articles on music composed after 1950 ... appear sometimes to mimic scientific papers in the way that South American bugs and flies will mimic the dreaded carpenter wasp."[6] All in all, hyper-formalist music theory

---

[3] Per F. Broman and Nora A. Engebretsen, *What Kind of Theory Is Music Theory?*: *Epistemological Exercises in Music Theory and Analysis* (Stockholm Studies in Musicology, 2008).

[4] For an account of this aspiration over history, see Susannah Clark and Alexander Rehding, eds., *Music Theory and Natural Order from the Renaissance to the Early Twentieth Century* (Cambridge, UK: Cambridge University Press, 2001).

[5] Stanley Cavell, "Music Discomposed," in his *Must We Mean What We Say?*: *A Book of Essays* (Cambridge, UK: Cambridge University Press, 1976), 186.

[6] Joseph Kerman, "Who We Got into Analysis, and How to Get Out," *Write All These Down*: *Essays on Music* (Berkeley: University of California Press, 1994): 12. Originally written for the 1978–79

came in for quite a drubbing as individuals like Cavell, Kerman, and (yes) myself tried to clear a space for music criticism and interpretation.

Yet music theories—even those of the most esoteric stripe—have a legitimate place in the study of this most powerful and elusive of media. I wouldn't want to sound too much like Monty Python's Miss Anne Elk, who coyly touted "the theory that is MINE, it is MY theory, this theory that belongs to ME." But I too have developed abstract models for the analysis of early-modern music and have even proposed alternative ways of understanding the emergence of eighteenth-century tonality.[7] The human need to parse and organize information systematically into useful categories begins at infancy if not before. We cannot function or even survive without theories, whether explicitly formulated or not.

Let me turn again to linguistics. Most people acquire their native language without the assistance of grammarians. We toss gerunds around with aplomb without even knowing that such items have a name. When we confront another language, however, we turn to diagrams of declensions and conjugations—somebody's theories of how the still-opaque language is structured and how it relates to our own. It is usually only in the course of this arduous process that we learn to label those words ending with i-n-g as "gerunds," just as Monsieur Jordain in Molière's *Le Bourgeois Gentilhomme* first discovered late in life that he had always spoken prose. But as long as we stick with our native tongue, we can and do ignore the intricate theoretical apparatus that allows us to form sentences and comprehend the utterances of others. It is transparent.

A great many of the individuals who go around with iPods permanently affixed to their ears are innocent of music theory as we practice it. Such aficionados sometimes become productive musicians and even composers, still without the interventions of any formal theoretical training. Yet all of them have developed extremely sophisticated ways of receiving and making sense of musical configurations. They may not be able to identify a diminished seventh by that name, but they know to recoil in fear when one appears in a horror-movie soundtrack or to laugh when the chord is used

---

Thalheimer Lectures at The Johns Hopkins University; this text appeared first in *Critical Inquiry* 7 (1980): 311–31.

[7] See my *Modal Subjectivities: Self-Fashioning in the Italian Madrigal* (Berkeley: University of California Press, 2004), and *Desire and Pleasure in Seventeenth-Century* Music (Berkeley: University of California Press, 2012). The episode featuring John Cleese as Miss Anne Elk may be viewed at: http://www.youtube.com/watch?v=cAYDiPizDIs.

for purposes of mock terror. They can even explain the subtle implications of flat-six digressions when they hear one plugged unexpectedly into, say, "Amazing Grace."

One important strand of music theory brings the kind of parsing that individuals do by means of automatic pilot to a conscious level and systematizes the configurations that emerge as significant. Much of the work of the late Leonard Meyer pursued this goal, as he asked how listeners know what they know, why they experience heightened emotion in certain patterns, or how they perceive the hierarchies of strong and weak pulses that we call "meter."[8] My own work on sixteenth- and seventeenth-century repertories does something of this sort for what count as dead languages. In the absence of "native speakers," I have attempted to derive syntactical norms from the artifacts that survive.[9]

But how do we acquire basic linguistic and musical competence without pedagogical intervention? How does this automatic pilot operate? In the 1950s, Noam Chomsky posited the existence of an inborn grammar machine in the human brain—a theory that continues to generate heated debate among not only linguists but also specialists in cognition and neuroscientists.[10] Chomsky's still-controversial ideas made their way into music theory principally by way of composer Fred Lerdahl in collaboration with linguist Ray Jackendoff, who surmised that something of the same process must obtain with music cognition.[11]

Some of my composition students have grabbed onto affirmations of Chomsky's ideas and want to wield them as evidence that diatonic tonality, after all, is innate. But Chomsky did not argue that human beings have a predisposition for speaking twentieth-century English. Indeed, some of the strongest confirmation for his notion of a built-in grammar machine comes from linguist Derek Bickerton, who has demonstrated how the children of pidgin-speakers construct full-fledged creoles, complete with all

---

[8] See the special issue of *Musica Humana* 1, no. 2 (Autumn 2009), edited by Robert O. Gjerdingen and dedicated to the memory of Leonard Meyer.

[9] See my *Modal Subjectivities* and *Desire and Pleasure*.

[10] Noam Chomsky, *Syntactical Structures* (The Hague: Mouton, 1957). For recent arguments disputing Chomsky's Universal Grammar, see Nicholas Evans and Stephen C. Levinson, "The Myth of Language Universals: Language Diversity and Its Importance for Cognitive Science," *Behavioral and Brain Sciences* (Spring 2009). This article by Evans and Levinson has in turn proved quite controversial; the ongoing discussion may be followed on Google. My thanks to Lawrence Zbikowski for this reference—and for his words advising caution in this volatile arena!

[11] Fred Lerdahl and Ray Jackendoff, *A Generative Theory of Tonal Music* (Cambridge, MA: MIT Press, 1983).

the elements manifested by any other language. If a compulsion to organize comes with our standard operating equipment, the stuff that gets organized remains radically contingent upon the historical and social circumstances within which previous language groups collided to give rise to a creole. Bickerton titles his book *Bastard Tongues* to underscore the promiscuity of linguistic development.[12]

To return to music: even if we want to accept something like Chomsky's universal grammar for music cognition, we should be careful not to mistake that broader principle for the way "our" own music goes. We used to believe that Europeans alone discovered this way of organizing sound, much as they discovered how blood circulates, because of their intellectual superiority. But if Rameau's tonality were the expression of impulses inherent in human beings, then why did it underpin even European art music for little more than a century?

Linguists often differentiate between the synchronic—that is between the way a language operates at any given time—and the diachronic, which traces the changes in languages over time, owing to social contingencies. Much music theory (as well as linguistics) has focused on synchronic freeze-frames, which grant the impression of relative autonomy to the object of study. This is as it should be: If I want to learn to read Classical Latin, I turn to the systematized charts developed by grammarians. If I want to understand what I hear as consistencies in Mozart's music, I refer to the works of Schenker, Meyer, and many others. I do not wish to call the power of such theories into question.

I do, however, want to argue that these cannot be the only games in town. In the Iberian Peninsula, Classical Latin was filtered through populations of Visigoths and subsequently formed hybrids with the language of the Moors who ruled Spain for centuries. We cannot understand how that process occurred without recourse to a history of invasions, reconquests, and colonial expansion, all of which left their marks on modern Spanish. Nor can we understand any given piece of music or even a particular moment within the ever-evolving conventions we might call grammar without taking into account a wide range of extenuating circumstances. For culture proceeds sometimes by force of active will or imagination, but just as often by accidents,

---

[12] Derek Bickerton, *Bastard Tongues* (New York: Hill & Wang, 2008). Bickerton's work is also controversial. See, for instance, Salikoko Mufwene, *Language Evolution: Contact, Competition and Change* (London: Continuum, 2008). Again my thanks to Lawrence Zbikowski.

chance encounters, market pressures, or an unpredictable combination of these and other factors.

A few examples. The great flowering of polyphony in the Italian Renaissance courts collapsed not just because someone had discovered better ways of putting notes together but from want of male heirs.[13] Sometimes it's just that simple. What we call opera was kept on life support not by an elite (if dwindling) aristocracy but by traveling troupes of *commedia dell'arte* players. When it emerged again as a public entertainment in mid-seventeenth-century Venice, Francesco Cavalli figured out how to forgo the allegorical complexity of Monteverdi in order to set an entire play in a matter of a couple of weeks, much like a film composer. The result was a stripped-down standardized procedure that becomes the template for tonality.[14]

Another factor—the sheer perversity of the human imagination—can also shift the parameters we study, pulling the previously reliable rug out from under our feet. Jacques Attali proposes we consider music as residing on an axis between order and noise.[15] One could say that music theorists attempt to account for the orderly dimensions of musical practices, striving to distinguish between those elements subject to generalizable rules and those that count as dissonant with respect to the system. But one of history's delicious ironies involves the repeated upending of such hierarchies in favor of noise, which itself then becomes the object of theory.

Think, for instance, of how Nicola Vicentino grabbed onto the ancient Greek chromatic and enharmonic genera and thereby spawned several waves of virtually atonal experimentation in the late sixteenth and early seventeenth centuries; without that bizarre theoretical move, we would have no Gesualdo or Frescobaldi. Or the uncannily similar phenomenon in which Schoenberg justified unrelieved discord by means of serialism's unparalleled adherence to order. Or Messiaen's eclectic toolbox of Hindu mysticism, Catholic symbology, and bird calls, all of them systematized in such a way as

---

[13] Duke Alfonso of Ferrara presided over a court that nurtured the experiments of Giaches de Wert, Carlo Gesualdo, and many others. When he failed to sire a son, his court was confiscated by the Vatican. See my "Fetisch Stimme: Professionelle Sänger im Italien der frühen Neuzeit," in *Zwischen Rauschen und Offenbarung: Zur Kultur- und Mediengeschichte der Stimme*, ed. Friedrich Kittler, Thomas Macho, and Sigrid Weigel (Berlin: Akademie, 2002), 199–214. An English version appears in *Desire and Pleasure* as "Soprano as Fetish."

[14] Ellen Rosand, *Opera in Seventeenth-Century Venice: The Creation of a Genre* (Berkeley: University of California Press, 1991).

[15] Jacques Attali, *Noise*, trans. Brian Massumi, afterword by Susan McClary (Minneapolis: University of Minnesota Press, 1985).

to buttress his idiosyncratic work. Or John Cage's refusal of the fundamental dichotomy between order and noise. In these instances, human agency manages to change the subject, sometimes locally, sometimes internationally.

Not every individual proposition for stylistic transformation makes it to the Big Time, of course: the history of music theory is littered with one-offs, ideas that went nowhere. And not necessarily because they were less worthy than other ideas but also owing to mere contingency—who knew whom, who had access to widespread circulation or financial support, who happened to be living in a time and place that rewarded innovation. Such issues make the difference between what is received as avant-garde sophistication and what as incompetence or gibberish.

The disciplines of both music theory and musicology have long resisted acknowledging contingency. We refer disdainfully to whatever escapes the borders of theoretical control as "extramusical." Whether the Petrarch sonnets that inspired the chromatic twists and turns of Cipriano de Rore's madrigals or the program aligned with the formal eccentricities of Berlioz's *Symphonie fantastique*, these features are bracketed off as somehow irrelevant to "the music itself." If "the music" works properly in and of itself, then it doesn't need the training wheels of lyrics or narratives to help it; if it can only make sense by means of these props, then it fails to qualify as music per se. Or so the story used to go.

Fortunately, we have relaxed those borders considerably in recent years. For instance, analysts of Schubert songs—David Lewin and Yonatan Malin—have interrogated the ways in which the content of his chosen poems affect the structure, harmonies, melodies, rhythms, and temporalities of the final compositions.[16] To ignore the verbal component of songs is not even to grasp much of the music itself, which derives its basic metaphors and affective burden from the lyrics. Jim Hepokoski has demonstrated how the programs affixed to Strauss tone poems not only make the music intelligible to uninitiated listeners but actually allow the composer to imagine radically new formal strategies.[17] We cordon off these explicit "extramusical" factors at

---

[16] David Lewin, "Auf dem Flusse: Image and Background in a Schubert Song," in *Studies in Music with Text* (Oxford, UK: Oxford University Press, 2006), 109–33; Yonatan Malin, *Songs in Motion: Rhythm and Meter in the German Lied* (Oxford, UK: Oxford University Press, 2010).

[17] James Hepokoski, "Fiery Pulsed Libertine or Domestic Hero? Strauss's *Don Juan* Revisited," in *Richard Strauss: New Perspectives on the Composer and His Work*, ed. Bryan Gilliam (Durham, NC: Duke University Press, 1992): 135–75.

our peril as adequate interpreters. Even at the level of asking "Why this note rather than any other note?" we must take lyrics and programs into account.

Yet where do we draw the line? The circle we used to draw around the piece of music to define our object of study has expanded to include those components expressly signaled by the composers in multimedia works. But what of cultural or historical contingencies never mentioned by the artist? To what extent might those be admissible—or perhaps even indispensable—considerations in music analysis and theory?

Alas, this is where I always run afoul of the law, or at least the rules defining good behavior and decorum within our disciplines. For so tightly insulated from the outside world is the music (and a good many of its guardians, for that matter) that some of the parameters I have brought to bear on my analyses seem utterly arbitrary to certain readers. Why choose to map a symphony in terms related to the nineteenth-century ideal of *Bildung* rather than a story about someone going to the store to buy bananas? Why concentrate on issues of Schubert's sexuality? Why not depart from the fact that he was short and fat? "If feminist musicology, why not vegetarian?" asked one rather waggish skeptic (a query that we might take seriously if half the characters in operas were eggplants—and if the criteria for adequate closure demanded that the eggplant die). How far does contingency stretch?

This is, if I may say as much, a theoretical question—indeed, a *music-theoretical* question. For methodological issues can and should involve more than grammar and formal process, even if we still also want (as I do) to focus on considerations related to syntax. In the last few decades, music theorists have borrowed many of their models from mathematics and the hard sciences, with claims of objectivity prominent among their criteria. I have nothing against the ideals of "objective" analysis or research. But I do resist the implications of the word with which it is usually paired as an antithesis, namely "subjective." This binary opposition implies that anything not absolutely verifiable should be counted as groundless, as a purely personal impulse.

Yet even if certain aspects of music lend themselves to scientific or quasi-scientific approaches (especially in studies of acoustical properties), music has many more dimensions that can never yield to such criteria. Those who link music with the world outside the purely musical dimension of the score are not necessarily just making it up or imposing their own warped imaginations on this otherwise innocent object of study. To be sure, certain approaches may prove to be more productive of insights or better justified than others. But even some that may seem entirely arbitrary at first glance may turn out to have something substantial to add to the conversation, even if they require a fair amount of theoretical mediation to rescue them from the "extramusical."

Everyone's favorite example of a ludicrously ungrounded reaction to a piece of music appears in the 1992 film adaptation of E. M. Forster's novel *Howard's End*.[18] The central character, Helen Schlegel, is attending a music-appreciation lecture on Beethoven's Fifth Symphony. A supremely supercilious musicologist describes the Scherzo thus:

> I want to draw your attention to the third movement. We no longer hear the hero, but a goblin. A single, solitary goblin ... walking across the universe ... from beginning to end.

An elderly gentleman in the audience suddenly stands and voices an objection: "Why a goblin?" The lecturer responds condescendingly that his description is obvious. Yet his antagonist persists: "But why specifically a goblin?" As the speaker sputters back that "the goblin signifies the spirit of negation.... Panic and emptiness, that's what the goblin signifies," the impatient-looking Helen gets up and walks out of the hall. A truly hilarious moment that vindicates the position of those who like to scoff at far-flung interpretations. Indeed, the phrase "why a goblin?" has shown up in reviews of my own work.[19]

But I would like to engage seriously in this essay with the question "why a goblin?" First, I want to remind you that it's the postmodernist screenwriter who created this scenario rather than Forster in 1910. For the novelist ascribes the goblin interpretation to Helen herself as she attends a concert. I will quote Forster at some length because, as Greg Sandow has observed, this is one of the great descriptions of music in literature.[20]

---

[18] *Howard's End*, directed by James Ivory, produced by Ismail Merchant; screenplay by Ruth Prawer Jhabvala (1992).

[19] In particular, see Paula Higgins, "Women in Music, Feminist Criticism, and Guerrilla Musicology: Reflections on Recent Polemics," *19th-Century Music* 17 (Fall 1993): 174–92; Alex Ross, "A Female Deer? Looking for Sex in the Sound of Music," *Lingua Franca* 4, no. 5 (July/August 1994). Alex and I have long since made peace.

[20] Greg Sandow, *An Arts Journal Weblog* (Oct. 27, 2005): http://www.artsjournal.com/sandow/2005/10/forster_on_beethoven.html

"Look out for the part where you think you have done with the goblins and they come back," breathed Helen, as the music started with a goblin walking quietly over the universe from end to end. Others followed him. They were not aggressive creatures; it was that that made them so terrible to Helen. They merely observed in passing that there was no such thing as splendour or heroism in the world.... Helen could not contradict them for, once at all events, she had felt the same, and had seen the reliable walls of youth collapse. Panic and emptiness! Panic and emptiness! The goblins were right....

[A]s if things were going too far, Beethoven took hold of the goblins and made them do what he wanted.... He gave them a little push, and they began to walk in a major key instead of in a minor, and then—he blew with his mouth and they were scattered!... Oh, it all burst before the girl.... Any fate was titanic; any contest desirable; conqueror and conquered would alike be applauded by the angels of the utmost stars.

And the goblins—they had not really been there at all? They were only the phantoms of cowardice and unbelief? One healthy human impulse would dispel them? Men like ... President Roosevelt would say yes. Beethoven knew better. The goblins really had been there. They might return—and they did. It was as if the splendour of life might boil over and waste to steam and froth. In its dissolution one heard the terrible, ominous note, and a goblin, with increased malignity, walked quietly over the universe from end to end. Panic and emptiness! Panic and emptiness! Even the flaming ramparts of the world might fall.

Beethoven chose to make all right in the end. He built the ramparts up. He blew with his mouth for the second time, and again the goblins were scattered. He brought back the gusts of splendour, the heroism, the youth, the magnificence of life and of death, and, amid vast roarings of a superhuman joy, he led his Fifth Symphony to its conclusion. But the goblins were there. They could return. He had said so bravely, and that is why one can trust Beethoven when he says other things.

Helen does in fact leave the hall at this point, but only because she is so devastated by her understanding of what she has just witnessed.

I have no interest in persuading you of goblins per se—nor is Forster, for that matter. But his reading is no joke. And it is sufficiently rich in its implications that it will allow us to explore a wide range of contingencies.

Notice first that Forster's description is not devoid of music-theoretical references. In contrast with the pompous musicologist in the movie, Helen anchors her reading in specific pointers. She observes, for instance, that in the transition to the finale Beethoven deftly converts his motive from minor into major, and she strives to make sense of the return of the materials from the third movement in the middle of the finale. She responds to details in the symphony as it unfolds before her, and her references are sufficiently adequate that we can follow her reading without measure numbers. The professional analyst may miss many of the elements left unmentioned or at least underdeveloped in Forster's account: the dense web of thematic transformations that marks this entire symphony, or the background scaffolding that guarantees a quality of coherence despite surface discontinuities. Although I will not pursue these aspects of the symphony here, I want to reassure you that these projects matter deeply as well.

Helen is also responding, however, to other dimensions of the piece, and many of these have seemed at times to fall outside the permissible limits of analysis. Like many amateur listeners, she cares profoundly about affect. She hears splendor, panic, the ominous, glory, joy, and much more. Can music express emotions? So influential was Eduard Hanslick's denial in *The Beautiful in Music* that our disciplines still have not quite recovered.[21] Peter Kivy, in *The Corded Shell*, proposed that we are guilty of projecting feelings onto music in the way we might think a St. Bernard looks sad, regardless of the actual mood of the dog.[22]

But the dog, of course, is not the product of human artists striving to convey feelings, while music—at least music of Beethoven's era—is. Much of the music-theoretical ink spilled over the course of the eighteenth century concerned the ways in which composers could simulate affect through their choices of pitch, rhythm, timbre, tempo, and instrumentation. Theirs was a remarkably materialist project, nothing less than an attempt at explaining how to do cultural work with notes. If the Romantics preferred to imagine music as unmediated expressivity, their predecessors not only admitted their means of construction but happily shared their tricks of the trade in do-it-yourself manuals. Beethoven would have been scandalized had he foreseen

---

[21] Eduard Hanslick, *Von Musikalisch-Schönen* (1854). Recall, however, that Hanslick's own extensive corpus of music criticism engages extensively with such issues all the time.
[22] Peter Kivy, *The Corded Shell: Reflections on Musical Expression* (Princeton, NJ: Princeton University Press, 1980). Kivy's positions have changed considerably over the course of the last thirty years, as may be seen in his tribute to Leonard Meyer in the memorial issue of *Musica Humana*, but even his St. Bernard example played a significant role in reawakening discussions of affect in music.

listeners who refused to recognize glory when he hits them over the head with it. My god! What's a guy gotta do?

Gradually we are learning to overcome our disciplinary Asperger's syndrome, the autistic condition that prevents those afflicted from recognizing evidence of feeling in others. Our greater acquaintance with the *Affektenlehre*, the semiotic work of Raymond Monelle or Kofi Agawu,[23] and most recently the discovery of mirror neurons in the brain have made it increasingly acceptable to deal with affect as a part of the analytic enterprise.[24] For listeners do not grab onto any old emotional type when they hear a passage; they are responding to specific signs.

The finale of Beethoven's Fifth operates fully within the Triumphal March topic, and it would have been acknowledged as such at least a hundred years earlier: C major, ascending triadic theme, unswervingly diatonic harmony, four-square meter, emphatic accent patterns, brass and timpani, rising ornamental flourishes that become increasingly joyful, and utterly secure cadential confirmation. We could trace each of these elements back, explaining how they came to be associated with triumph; in fact, the movement seems to be modeled quite closely on the marches that proliferated in France during the Revolutionary period.

Recall, however, that the elderly man did not ask "Why a triumphal march?": that indeed is quite obvious to anyone willing to venture a connection beyond the notes themselves to some kind of signification. No, he asked about goblins. Leonard Ratner has no "goblin" topic in his book,[25] nor does Johann Mattheson include it in his *Complete Kapellmeister*.[26] If we shift our terms a bit and merely look for the topic of the "creepy," we don't fare much better. For this particular affect was quite new on the scene: a favorite zone for the Gothic novels just beginning to flood the market in the wake of the French Revolution, the Terror, and the Napoleonic Wars.[27] The framing sections of Mozart's *Don Giovanni* had begun to explore this terrain, as had his Symphony in G Minor and Piano Concerto in D Minor; Weber's *Der Freischütz* would soon unleash a whole vocabulary for the creepy.

---

[23] Raymond Monelle, *The Sense of Music* (Princeton, NJ: Princeton University Press, 2000); V. Kofi Agawu, *Playing with Signs: A Semiotic Interpretation of Classic Music* (Princeton, NJ: Princeton University Press, 1991).

[24] David Huron, among others, is pursuing the implications of this finding for music cognition.

[25] Leonard Ratner, *Classic Music: Expression, Form and Style* (New York: Macmillan, 1985).

[26] Johann Mattheson, *Der vollkommene Capellmeister* (1739).

[27] I owe much of my insight into the Gothic or fantastique revival to Marianna Ritchey. See her "Echoes of the Guillotine: Berlioz and the French Fantastic," *19th-Century Music* 34, no. 2 (Fall 2010): 168–85.

IN PRAISE OF CONTINGENCY   57

Forster's characterization strongly resembles that of E.T.A. Hoffmann—the great author of Gothic tales—who described the composer's effects in these words:

> Beethoven's instrumental music opens up to us also the realm of the monstrous and the immeasurable. Burning flashes of light shoot through the deep night of this realm, and we become aware of giant shadows that surge back and forth, driving us into narrower and narrower confines until they destroy *us*.... [His] music sets in motion the lever of fear, of awe, of horror, of suffering....[28]

Substitute whatever sinister apparition you like for "goblin," but the affect is in fact quite obvious. Less clear is why such material intrudes into a hero-oriented symphony, and this question becomes the burden of Helen's analysis.

Beethoven had to work much harder to produce this effect, for which he had few models. How to create an affect recognizable as creepy (or goblinesque) before it has coalesced into a convention? As Mark Johnson and Lawrence Zbikowski would explain, he depends heavily on his and our experiences as embodied beings and the bodily metaphors by which we make sense of virtually everything.[29] To be more specific, the insinuating melodic line that snakes up from the depths sounds quite literally dodgy. When the full orchestra enters with this movement's version of "Fate," it sounds downright malevolent: oppressive and unyielding, with sudden, apparently arbitrary key changes that render its force even more menacing. The opening C-minor tune returns but in B-flat minor—colonizing remote pitch relations and making its location difficult to predict. After a trio that offers a modicum of comic relief, the Gothic materials come back, now stripped down to barely audible pizzicato, now even creepier with tiptoe articulation.

OK, so why a goblin? I might prefer to call it a vampire or a dybbuk or another brand of specter. But surely there should be little question of the basic terrain Beethoven stakes out here.

---

[28] E.T.A. Hoffmann, "Beethoven's Instrumental Music" (1813); translated in Oliver Strunk, *Source Readings in Music History* (New York: Norton, 1950).
[29] Mark Johnson, *The Bodily Basis of Meaning, Imagination, and Reason* (Chicago: University of Chicago Press, 1990); Lawrence M. Zbikowski, *Conceptualizing Music: Cognitive Structure, Theory, and Analysis* (Chicago: University of Chicago Press, 2005).

More important to Forster's reading is his casting of this movement and the next in narrative terms. Citing Paul Ricoeur for theoretical support, Carolyn Abbate has claimed that music can narrate only under very rare conditions: only if there is an explicit narrator who speaks in the past tense of events already concluded. But in the passage she cites, Ricoeur actually argues *against* that position, and he deliberately includes any kind of process that involves emplotment: devices concerned with dramatic tension, obstacles, surprises, conflicts, delays, uncertain outcomes, and eventual closure.[30] These are precisely the same devices Schenker lists in *Der freie Satz*:

> In the art of music, as in life, motion toward the goal encounters obstacles, reversals, disappointments, and involves great distances, detours, expansions, interpolations, and, in short retardations of all kinds. Therein lies the source of all artistic delaying, from which the creative mind can derive content that is ever new. Thus we hear in the middleground and foreground an almost dramatic course of events.
>
> As the image of our life-motion, music can approach a state of objectivity, never, of course, to the extent that it need abandon its own specific nature as an art. Thus, it may almost evoke pictures or seem to be endowed with speech; it may pursue its course by means of associations, references, and connectives; . . . it may simulate expectation, preparation, surprise, disappointment, patience, impatience, and humor. Because these comparisons are of a biological nature, and are generated organically, music is never comparable to mathematics or to architecture, but only to language, a kind of tonal language.[31]

Patrick McCreless, Fred Maus, and myself, among others, have advocated the use of narratological models in the analysis especially of nineteenth-century instrumental music.[32] Scott Burnham's *Beethoven Hero* even spells

---

[30] See Abbate, *Unsung Voices: Opera and Musical Narrative in the Nineteenth Century* (Princeton, NJ: Princeton University Press, 1991), esp. 52–56. For Ricoeur's position, see his *Time and Narrative*, vol II, trans. Kathleen McLaughlin and David Pellauer (Chicago: University of Chicago Press, 1985), 68.

[31] Heinrich Schenker, *Free Composition*, trans. Ernst Oster (New York: Longman, 1979), 5.

[32] Patrick McCreless, "The Hermeneutic Sentence and Other Literary Models for Tonal Closure," *Indiana Theory Review* 12 (1991): 35–74; Fred Everett Maus, "Music as Narrative," *Indiana Theory Review* 12 (1991): 1–34; McClary, "Narrative Agendas in 'Absolute Music,'" in Ruth Solie, ed., *Musicology and Difference: Gender and Sexuality in Music Scholarship* (Berkeley: University of California Press, 1993): 326–44.

out how and why the composer dealt so intensively with this particular plot trajectory.[33]

The Fifth Symphony, along with the Eroica, has long been recognized as a *locus classicus* of Beethoven's heroic style, not only because of the triumphal-march topic of the finale but also because of the hyperdramatic struggle traced over the course of the first movement. Forster homes in, however, on the third movement, both within its own borders and with respect to its unexpected disruption of the finale's celebration. The creepy stuff ought to have been relegated to the boneyard with the finale's burst of C major. But, of course, that coffin had not been properly sealed up; the brilliant sleight of hand with which Beethoven pulls victory from the jaws of horror doesn't quite qualify as a silver stake driven through the heart of the specter. And so the revenant bubbles up again. And again.[34] In his recording of the Fifth Symphony, John Eliot Gardiner repeats the Allegro's trio, so that the listener becomes acutely aware of the tendency of the goblins to return: we have already heard them do so twice before the Finale even begins.

This is the crux of Helen's insight and the reason she flees the concert hall, deeply shaken by what she has just grasped. Beethoven, she claims, has revealed the deception behind triumphant closure; he has shown that evil always lurks below the surface, that it cannot be purged by a mere flip into a major key, even if announced emphatically with trumpets and timpani. He calls the lie, in other words, to his own heroic paradigm.

I might go even further: the goblin of the Allegro shares the obsessive rhythmic tattoo with the first movement's heroic struggle and the finale's march. If we regard thematic recurrence as more than simply a formal characteristic, we might hear the hero and the goblin—or at least the demonic—as inextricably intertwined: a kind of Jekyll-and-Hyde amalgam that makes ultimate triumph all the more questionable and even frightening. Recall, for instance, the career trajectory of Napoleon.

Again, I have no interest in perpetuating the specific label of "goblin" to describe this movement. When I teach the Fifth, I pray silently that no one in the class will mention the word. Nevertheless, the broader purpose of Forster's reading has several serious implications for music theorists. He

---

[33] Scott Burnham, *Beethoven Hero* (Princeton, NJ: Princeton University Press, 1995).

[34] A similar strategy occurs in Mozart's "Prague" Symphony: the menacing strains of the symphony's introduction return to disrupt the joyous proceedings of the finale. See my "Narratives of Bourgeois Subjectivity in Mozart's 'Prague' Symphony," in *Understanding Narrative*, ed. Peter J. Rabinowitz and James Phelan (Columbus: Ohio State University Press, 1994): 65–98.

leaves it us to do the theorizing, which is surely how it should be. But we should not dismiss out of hand the ever-widening circles of contingencies he indicates.

First, Forster addresses the meaning of form itself. What happens when Beethoven and his successors knock down the boundaries between presumably autonomous movements? What did the illusion of autonomy imply, and why did those boundaries suddenly seem so artificial and open to violation in the early nineteenth century? Leonard Meyer dealt with issues of this sort in his *Style and Music*—a book that brings together a powerful commitment to analysis with the insights of a humanist who had steeped himself in nineteenth-century poetry, cultural history, and ideological conflict.[35] I have tended to approach issues of formal convention from the other end: the seventeenth-century sonatas I study unfold without internal borders. What do the tidy structural units of the Enlightenment signify? What kinds of certainty do they promise? And why are the Romantics so eager to run roughshod over them? In other words, the return of the goblin in the finale of the Fifth Symphony ought to lead us to theorize why both the conventions and the transgressions matter. For even form and tonality themselves count as contingencies.[36]

Second, Helen experiences this chain of narrative events as undermining her sense of selfhood. The metaphysical security she had possessed when she entered the concert hall cannot recover easily from the crisis precipitated by the performance. Forster assumes that musical form usually carries with it certain guarantees concerning the way the world operates. Thus, much more is at stake here than the breaking of a musical expectation. Recall Edward Cone's article on Schubert's tiny *moment musical* that similarly denies the satisfaction of proper closure.[37] We may scoff at the metaphysical pretensions of the Pythagoreans or Giovanni Maria Artusi, both of whom regarded the violation of mathematically buttressed norms as threatening the balance of the cosmos. But the medium we study matters in part because it articulates so powerfully the ways a particular group of people understand themselves and their relationship to everything else. Musical form bears with it the weight of

---

[35] Leonard B. Meyer, *Style and Music: Theory, History, and Ideology* (Philadelphia: University of Pennsylvania Press, 1989).

[36] See my *Conventional Wisdom: The Content of Musical Form* (Berkeley: University of California Press, 2000).

[37] Edward T. Cone, "Schubert's Promissory Note," *19th-Century Music* 5 (1982): 233–41. See also my "The Impromptu That Trod on a Loaf: Or How Music Tells Stories," *Narrative* 5, no. 1 (January 1997): 20–35.

social contract. Might these issues be more often foregrounded in our theoretical discussions?

Third, Helen applies the lesson she has gleaned to her own moment in history, during the presidency of Theodore Roosevelt—sometime between 1901 and 1908. Roosevelt had recently been awarded the Nobel Peace Prize for negotiating a conclusion of the Russo-Japanese War, and he had brought a great deal of pride and confidence to America as it emerged as a world leader; all of Western Europe looked to the United States as the harbinger of a secure future. But the goblins Roosevelt had hoped to bury did indeed reemerge—and with a vengeance. We look back to this moment with knowledge of two world wars, the Holocaust, and the many other conflagrations that have proved Forster's point over and over again. The meanings of a composition may shift radically in accordance with successive world events, and this mutability may destabilize the work. But it also helps to explain why something like the Fifth Symphony continues to have relevance far past its own moment.

And Beethoven himself? He had experienced the exhilaration of the French Revolution, followed by the Terror; then the emergence of Napoleon Hero, followed by the Napoleonic Wars, as his erstwhile idol became the goblin that devastated all of Europe. Over the course of Beethoven's lifetime, no moment of triumphant glory lasted, each one gave way to conditions worse than the one before. Even if Helen and Forster impose their own point of reference upon this piece, they are not necessarily misinterpreting it.

Historians sometimes lament the fact that music scholars borrow from their work but rarely give them anything in return.[38] Yet here is a historical document premiered in 1808 that conveys in extraordinary detail a new post-Enlightenment version of the self, a subjectivity balanced precariously between hopes of glory and the clear awareness of pervasive and unavoidable horror. Stendhal's *Le Rouge et le noir* offers a similar sense of the age—but it was published in 1830, over twenty years after the Fifth.[39] Along with Hoffmann, Adorno, and Attali, I believe that music usually gets there first; it's

---

[38] See, for instance, Hayden White, "Form, Reference, and Ideology in Musical Discourse," afterword to *Music and Text: Critical Inquiries*, ed. Steven Paul Scher (Cambridge, UK: Cambridge University Press, 1992).

[39] For more on the relationships between plot trajectories and nineteenth-century ideological struggles, see Fredric Jameson, *The Political Unconscious: Narrative as a Socially Symbolic Act* (Ithaca, NY: Cornell University Press, 1981); and Franco Moretti, *The Way of the World: The Bildungsroman in European Culture* (London: Verso, 1998).

frequently the first medium to register the tensions that will only eventually find their way into verbal articulation.

The newspapers are full these days of laments over the Death of Classical Music. If it is indeed moribund, I'm afraid music professionals have had some hand in its demise. To the extent that we convert music's power into lists of biographical facts or into formalist jargon, we send a signal that people like Forster's Helen cannot possibly understand it, that it should be cordoned off as the exclusive purview of experts. Historian Lawrence Levine has demonstrated that American educators have been doing precisely this since the late nineteenth century, before which time people of the less elevated classes took Shakespeare plays, Italian opera, and Beethoven symphonies as their common cultural birthright.[40] What do we accomplish when we substitute chords and graphs for the shattering experience Helen and thousands of others have had with this symphony? What kinds of musicians are we training if they have learned to feel shame when they hear glory or terror in the music they play?

Below his title, *Howard's End*, Forster offers an epigraph: "*Only connect...*" To translate that into more familiar terms, "Only theorize," which is how we go about buttressing connections within the music but also between it and whatever else seems appropriate. Instead of drawing borders beyond which we dare not tread in our interpretations, we might liberate ourselves to trace lines linking the configurations in our scores with a wide range of possible readings. Contingencies need not threaten our area of specialization; they invite us to delve back into the music to find details we might never have noticed otherwise, to develop a richer understanding of how to do things with notes.

The discipline of music theory is increasingly broadening its vision. As is the case with any other field, ours has no single theory that can account for everything we might want to say about a genre or repertory or piece. But our ever-growing network of intersecting theories allows us to go both more deeply into the specifics of the notes themselves and more adequately into music's relationships with human experience and cultural history, into the intricate workings of the brain that permit us both to invent sound worlds and to derive pleasure and wisdom from them. I am honored to join you in this enterprise.

---

[40] See Lawrence W. Levine, *Highbrow/Lowbrow: The Emergence of Cultural Hierarchy in America* (Cambridge, MA: Harvard University Press, 1990).

3
Evidence of Things Not Seen
History, Subjectivities, Music[1]

Anyone familiar with the New Testament will recognize that my title grounds itself in scriptural authority. As Saint Paul wrote in his letter to the Hebrews: "Faith is the substance of things hoped for, the evidence of things not seen" (Hebrews 11:1). Upon that fairly flimsy rock he builds his sermon on spirituality; he is also, of course, asking his congregation to take his word for it, as in an ultimate-stakes confidence game. My essay will similarly explore experiences not visible to the eye, but—like Saint Paul—I hope to offer something of substance along with the leaps of faith I will invite you to take over the course of my discussion.

In his book *Eyewitnessing*, Peter Burke explains how the visual arts can contribute to historical knowledge. Although he cautions his readers about the epistemological limitations involved in mining artworks for reliable information, he demonstrates what we can learn from paintings about the clothing, living conditions, and even ideologies of other times.[2] Alas, music offers little concerning material culture, though the study of musical practices in their social contexts sheds some light on the people who made and enjoyed music. But the music itself? Mere sounds that vanish as soon as they appear? To an intellectual community that relies almost exclusively upon the visual and particularly upon verbal testimony, music takes a very distant back seat, even behind the plastic arts Burke so tenuously sets forth as viable sources for historical evidence.

Playing the fool to Burke's angel, I'll rush in nevertheless. For music engages with aspects of human experience that remain hidden from the eye: it can simulate emotions, give precise shape to conceptions of temporality, evoke gestures of the body, induce erotic pleasure, point beyond itself

---

[1] UCLA Faculty Research Lecture, 2002; published in *Critical Musicological Reflections: Essays in Honour of Derek B. Scott*, ed. Stan Hawkins (London: Ashgate, 2012): 21–38.

[2] Peter Burke, *Eyewitnessing: The Uses of Images as Historical Evidence* (Ithaca, NY: Cornell University Press, 2001).

to the transcendent. In short, it can reveal—and also teach us—what it feels like to be a self, as though from the inside.[3] Accordingly, it leaves traces of human consciousness that otherwise remain inaccessible to the cultural historian.

But if Burke threw up danger signs when he dealt with pictorial evidence, how much more must the musicologist beware the pitfalls that bedevil such a project. Our ears can perform amazing cognitive feats: we can recognize a friend's voice on the telephone from a single uttered syllable, and we can determine with great accuracy the direction of a sound source. Yet despite these skills, most of us would have considerable difficulty explaining *in language* how we make such discriminations. Moreover, although we can react physically to a dance groove within a second or two, it often seems as though the body picks up on the relevant signals without even consulting the brain; indeed, it proves very hard to puzzle out and verbalize how those infinitesimal divisions of time translate into a precise choreography of bumps and grinds. And if we respond as reliably as Pavlov's dog to the ambient music piped into restaurants, shops, and elevators to influence our moods, we usually do not even notice the stimulus responsible.

In other words, a sizable gap separates what we *know* concerning sound from what we *define as knowledge*. Whereas Peter Burke can describe the contents of a painting (common objects, colors, and so on) through ordinary language, the musicologist seems doomed either to make use of a specialized vocabulary intelligible to no one outside the field or to gesture vaguely through flowery images. As long as acceptable evidence depends upon the eye or the word, then the epistemological status of music interpretation is shaky at best.[4]

It gets worse. Before Edison's invention of recording technologies, music was preserved (if at all) in the form of graphic notation. The actual sounds made by musicians of earlier times no longer exist: we must reconstitute them from dots on a page, a task that necessarily entails the decisions of performers from a significantly different era. Imagine having to bring into being the vocal and affective nuances of, say, Bessie Smith if we had nothing to go on except a score of "St. Louis Blues" and a couple of ear-witness

---

[3] Derek Scott's work has contributed particularly to this discourse. See particularly his *From the Erotic to the Demonic: On Critical Musicology* (Oxford, UK: Oxford University Press, 2003).

[4] See Lawrence Kramer, *Interpreting Music* (Berkeley: University of California Press, 2010) for a thorough discussion of this topic and a brilliant rejoinder to those who would put limitations on such activities.

accounts.⁵ It's as if we had to approximate Leonardo's *Mona Lisa*, each time we wanted to see it, from paint-by-number diagrams that happened to have survived.

And yet. To anyone who came of age in the 1950s and '60s and who witnessed the vast sea change in sensibilities—physical, erotic, ethical— brought about in part by the influx of Black idioms into middle-class suburbia, the power of music to transform appears undeniable. Fundamentalist preachers thundered from their pulpits about how "the beat, the beat, the beat" was leading us all to perdition—and they were right to worry about the cultural ramifications of mere patterns of sound, for most of their dire predictions came to pass. Some tenured radicals have turned their attentions entirely to the popular musics that entered the academy as a result of this cultural upheaval: Robert Walser and Stan Hawkins led the pack in this important new terrain.⁶ Strangely enough, my own work has proven even more controversial, in that I have taken what I learned from the Sixties and sought prior moments in music history that similarly testify to ruptures in prevailing versions of subjectivity, that offer us experiential traces from the past of what Raymond Williams calls "structures of feeling."⁷

In this chapter I discuss three examples from very different periods. I concentrate on pieces that challenge sanctioned configurations of selfhood, but also discuss the conventions—the condensations of deeply held cultural beliefs—against which they rebel and thereby produce their meanings.⁸ Fortunately, some verbal testimony for those conventions exists, as do the controversies that followed in the wake of their violation. But the debates themselves cannot plunge us bodily and affectively into the pleasures and anxieties presented—as though with no mediation whatsoever—in the music.

Franz Schubert's String Quartet No. 15 in G Major, Op. 161 (1826), opens with a powerful assault on the very premises of musical rationality he had

---

⁵ Even scores so heavily marked as Mahler's Adagietto from his Symphony No. 5 have given rise to radically different understandings. See chapter 19, "Mahler Making Love."
⁶ See, for instance, Robert Walser, *Running with the Devil: Power, Gender, and Madness in Heavy Metal Music* (Wesleyan University Press, 1992); Stan Hawkins, *Settling the Pop Score: Pop Texts and Identity Politics* (Farnham, UK: Ashgate: 2002), and *Music, Space and Place: Popular Music and Cultural Identity* (Farnham, UK: Ashgate: 2005).
⁷ Raymond Williams, *Marxism and Literature* (Oxford, UK: Oxford University Press, 1977): 128–35.
⁸ For a fuller discussion of conventions, see my *Conventional Wisdom: The Content of Musical Form* (Berkeley: University of California Press, 2000).

Example 3.1a Franz Schubert, String Quartet No. 15, Op. 161, movement 1, mm. 1–5

inherited. As forecast in its title, it starts on a G-major chord. But as that sonority increases in volume, it flips abruptly into its opposite: a terrifying G minor, marked with aggressive, jerky rhythms, answered by a whimper (see Example 3.1a). Lest we miss this sequence, Schubert repeats it: major breaking off into minor, aggression, whimper. The whimper persists, holding on each time to its most plaintive element, the lamenting half-step.

The contrast between major and minor had served during the eighteenth century to encode opposite poles of the affective spectrum, with major generally aligned with positive emotional realms, minor with negative. The quintessential Beethovenian narrative schema progresses from grim minor, through heroic struggle, to glorious major (e.g., the Fifth and Ninth Symphonies). In his late years, Beethoven often gives us reason to doubt this optimistic fable in which effort and persistence guarantee success, but as a child of the Enlightenment he usually delivers it nonetheless, even if saturated with equivocations.

By contrast, Schubert chooses with some regularity to snatch tragedy from the jaws of triumph—to conclude blithe major-key pieces in minor-key despair.[9] But even he had rarely presented the alternatives so starkly as in this

---

[9] See, for instance, his Impromptu, Op. 90, no. 2, in E-flat Major, discussed in McClary, "The Impromptu That Trod on a Loaf: How Music Tells Stories," *Narrative* 5/1 (Jan. 1997): 20–34; and his *Moment musical*, Op. 94, no. 6, discussed in Edward T. Cone, "Schubert's Promissory Note," *19th-Century Music* 5 (1982): 233–41.

quartet. It is as if he cannot bring himself to enact the fiction his G-major title promises for more than a measure before he angrily rejects it—or, alternatively, before some other force enters to quash that gentle major-key beginning before it can even get started. At stake is basic musical identity, for not only a movement's themes but also its key count as the locus of selfhood, up against which the ensuing struggles will unfold and make themselves intelligible.

Ordinarily, the threat of rival keys enters only after the listener has had the chance to become acquainted with the protagonist. Not so in this quartet, which consistently denies us the security of unequivocal identity. Indeed, we might regard this ambivalence as the G-Major Quartet's defining characteristic, as its true key note; within its historical context, the quartet performs a refusal of the Enlightenment-era archetypes that reward linear reason and hard work with happy endings. Schubert casts serious doubt right from the outset on the viability—perhaps even the *desirability*—of such stories. A member of the Romantic generation that also produced skeptics such as Stendhal, Schubert peels back the veil that the eighteenth century had thrown over the less reassuring aspects of human experience, exposing us to the tribulations and uncertainties that beset even the most deserving of subjects.

But if Schubert assails us with unpredictable anxieties, he also grants us tastes of unearned, unanticipated bliss. For immediately following the protracted whimpers of the opening passage, he produces a hushed tremolo over which a prayerful melody in G major reaches toward consolation (see Example 3.1b). The materials themselves recall what Stuart de Ocampo has theorized as the subjunctive, the "as if" quality of so many of Schubert's secondary themes, all fated in advance to dissolve as mere illusions.[10] But this particular illusory moment counts as the first statement of the quartet's announced key, thus positioning undivided identity itself as fantasy.

Schubert's premature *deus ex machina* doesn't appear out of nowhere, however. He cobbles it together out of elements already heard: the melody's rhythms echo the jerky patterns of the opening, and the descent by half-steps in the harmonic bass transfigures the major-to-minor flip of the first gesture and the plaintive sighs that follow. In other words, he takes precisely those items marked earlier as signs of trauma and willfully pushes them to speak differently. Yet this cobbled-together complex never pursues the mandatory

---

[10] Stuart Ocampo developed these ideas in the course of his graduate seminars at UCLA. I am grateful to him for this and many other invaluable insights.

Example 3.1b Schubert, String Quartet No. 15, Movement 1, mm. 15–24

dynamic trajectory of becoming. Instead, it proceeds through a series of variations, each negotiating in a new way the chromatic moves that had so jeopardized tonal identity at the beginning.[11]

But now the movement risks stasis or even regression, for music and individuals at this time were expected to develop. Suddenly, without preparation or rational processing, Schubert imposes a change of key. Moreover, the major-key sonority upon which he arrives lies a half-step lower than our

---

[11] For more on the ways Schubert assembles materials as if they were facets of a crystal, see Theodor W. Adorno, "Schubert," in *Moments Musicaux* (Frankfurt: Suhrkamp, 1964).

tonic, as if the deviant semitone had seized the terrain. What follows this crisis is a courtly, slightly diffident little tune, which also features the half-steps but now as endearing personality traits (see Example 3.1c).

Occasionally the fury of earlier passages bursts through, only to give way again to the little tune, which uses its half-step component to slip furtively into unlicensed keys: the semitone that seemed an infirmity at the beginning thus becomes the means of survival and even agency. A cadence at the end of the exposition purports to celebrate the achievement of a conventional goal, only to unravel by means of half-steps in the cello back to the beginning, with its bitter refusal of major-key identity. All that effort was, apparently, for naught.

Example 3.1c Schubert, String Quartet No. 15, Movement 1, mm. 54–63

But the slippery semitones that have infiltrated each idea in the movement *enable* even as they destabilize, and in the extensive middle section of the movement they take center stage. By means of their unpredictable maneuvers, Schubert deposits us repeatedly on islands of melodic serenity, but with little apparent rhyme or reason along the way; he gives us either erratic motion or stasis. Yet his embrace of the semitone itself as his signature element allows him to push through the binary oppositions that still ground most of Beethoven's narratives.[12]

A formal recapitulation typically brings back the key and theme that opened a movement, but that consolidation of initial identity can qualify either as a triumphant return or (in cases where the piece has labored to escape its tragic beginnings) as an admission of defeat. The prospect of ending the struggle in this particular piece with a literal capitulation should inspire anxiety, and the lamenting quality of the passage leading up to the return bodes ill. But when the moment itself arrives, Schubert reverses his terms, for now a minor triad (which seemed to have prevailed) gives way to major and a graceful transformation of both jerky rhythm and whimper. To be sure, a split, self-contradictory identity still reigns, but the major-key element now has the upper hand (see Example 3.1d).

Example 3.1d Schubert, String Quartet No. 15, Movement 1, recapitulation

---

[12] See my "Constructions of Subjectivity in Schubert's Music," *Queering the Pitch: The New Gay and Lesbian Musicology*, ed. Philip Brett, Elizabeth Wood, and Gary Thomas (New York: Routledge, 1994): 205–33.

Nevertheless, when the movement approaches its conclusion, the half-steps re-materialize, dragging us back to the still-unresolved dilemma of the beginning, now if anything more concentrated, more undecidable. Minor gives way to major, major to minor, until a plastered-on cadence in G major arbitrarily simply ends the alternation by fiat (see Example 3.1e).

A word about interpretation. During the last century, "classical" music—whether liturgical chant or Mozart's *Requiem*—has come to stand for the reassurances of High Art. Subjected on a daily basis to the strains of the "Ode to Joy" in Starbuck's or Vivaldi concertos in Victoria's Secret, we learn not to pay attention to expressive detail but rather to hear any particular item

Example 3.1e Schubert, String Quartet No. 15, Movement 1, conclusion

from these repertoires as flat tokens of elite taste. My discussion of Schubert's quartet has sought to re-situate the piece within its historical context, in which his moves would have elicited shocked responses. Only if we do so can we learn from music about the cultural hopes and traumas it records.

Over the course of this extraordinary movement, Schubert simultaneously draws on the narrative paradigm of subjective *Bildung* characteristic of Enlightenment-era music and undercuts its very premises: this much seems certain. We cannot pin down with confidence, however, any external referents for the central ambivalence enacted in the quartet. Many possibilities present themselves—Schubert's struggle with aspects of his own identity, perhaps, or his inability to believe in sorrow-to-redemption fairy tales, given his impending death, or his refusal of the myth of political progress in view of the repressiveness of Vienna during his lifetime. If we go to this quartet for actual historical facts, we find ourselves disappointed by music's famed lack of specificity. Yet we *can* hear very clearly the challenge to cultural notions of identity formation treated by his contemporaries as fundamental, the critique of progress as mere illusion, and also the affective investment in working through the dilemmas moment by moment, even if the only viable conclusion is to openly embrace the terms of ambivalence.

Of course, people have always had to face mortality and have tasted disappointment instead of fulfilled aspirations. But Schubert's G-Major Quartet points to changes in the dominant fictions circulating within European culture concerning the relationship between individual striving and ultimate ends.[13] If Schubert finally grants us major-key closure, he packages it in irony or in a cautious subjunctive: instead of resolving the structural dissonance that drives the piece, he builds a new kind of tonal plot by making an active, versatile agent of the very semitone that usually serves to patrol the border between major and minor. Along the way, we experience moments of fervent hope, of iconoclastic rage against illusion, of provisional joy, of efforts rewarded temporarily if never permanently. Whatever the quartet meant to its composer, it offers us a remarkably vivid structure of post-Enlightenment feeling: the strategies of a subject who learns to embrace the contradictions of his condition.

---

[13] For more on the manifestations of such elements in nineteenth-century literature, see Franco Moretti, *The Way of the World: The Bildungsroman in European Culture*, 2nd ed. (London: Verso, 2000) and Fredric Jameson, *The Political Unconscious: Narrative as a Socially Symbolic Act*, 2nd ed. (London: Routledge, 2002).

My second example predates the Schubert quartet by 260 years, and although it counts as a masterpiece of Renaissance music, it also predates the repertories on which musicologists have a firm theoretical grasp. Consequently, our debates still focus on the extent to which its musical details can bear up under analytical scrutiny. I will not bore you here with the intricacies of modal grammar,[14] but I do hope to show you both how this madrigal produces its effects and how human subjectivity was construed during a very different historical period.

The text of Cipriano de Rore's "Da le belle contrade d'oriente" (published in 1566) operates within the generic bounds not only of the Petrarchan sonnet but also of the *auba*: a dialogue between lovers for whom dawn announces the dreaded moment of separation.

Da le belle contrade d'oriente	From the fair region of the East
chiara e lieta s'ergea Ciprigna et io	bright and joyful arose the Morning Star, and I
fruiva in braccio al divin idol mio	in the arms of my divine idol enjoyed
quel piacer che non cape humana mente,	that pleasure that defies human understanding,
quando sentii dopo un sospir ardente:	when I heard, after an ardent sigh:
"Speranza del mio cor, dolce desio,	"Hope of my heart, sweet desire,
T'en vai, haime, sola mi lasci, adio.	You go, alas! You leave me alone! Farewell!
Che sarà qui de me scura e dolente?	What will become of me here, gloomy & sad?
Ahi crudo Amor, ben son dubiose e corte	Ah, cruel Love, how false and brief are
le tue dolcezze, poi ch'ancor ti godi	your delights, for it even pleases you that
che l'estremo piacer finisca in pianto."	this extreme pleasure ends in weeping."
Nè potendo dir più, cinseme forte	Unable to say more, she squeezed me tightly,
iterando gl'amplessi in tanti nodi	repeating her embraces in so many knots
che giamai ne fer più l'edra o l'acanto.	that never made more ivy or acanthus.

The poet divides the dialogue against the grain of the sonnet's characteristic four-part structure: lines 1 through 5 belong to the principal speaker, who also delivers the concluding terzet, while lines 6 through 11 convey the utterances of his lover. In truth, however, all fourteen lines proceed from the speaker: his frame does not address his mistress in the heat of passion, but rather recalls the scene—complete with the ostensibly direct quotation

---

[14] See, however, my *Modal Subjectivities: Self-Fashioning in the Italian Madrigal* (Berkeley: University of California Press, 2005).

that testifies to his lover's travail—at a later moment for unspecified auditors. In keeping with that fundamental difference, the framing voice indulges at leisure in long, syntactically complex sentences, classical allusions, and extended metaphors. By contrast, his mistress's gasping phrases simulate the involuntary exclamations of lovemaking, and if her terzet all coheres as a single continuous thought, the effort ultimately melts down in the bodily secretions associated with what the Renaissance called euphemistically "the little death."

Whatever the intentions of the poet, the sonnet offers Cipriano the opportunity to explore and challenge the limits of his inherited musical language. But if he pits two discursive strategies against one another in this madrigal, he does so *not only* for the sake of pushing the boundaries of accepted musical practice, but *also* (and more important for our present purposes) as the means of configuring contrasting models of human subjectivity. Just as the sonnet's author employs a lofty register of speech for the male persona who addresses us directly, so Cipriano presents those lines within a style sanctioned by the scholastics who sought to regulate music.[15] Thus, the outer sections of the madrigal reside within a serenely diatonic F-Ionian, and they match the speaker's convoluted poetic syntax with studied, equal-voiced counterpoint (see Example 3.2a).

Thus far, this madrigal has given no indication that it harbors radical tendencies. But the opening of the second quatrain ushers in the flashback with a brief transitional phrase, at which point Cipriano hurls us across the threshold into an altogether different experiential world. If the opening section sustained a single mode for twenty-one bars, the next thirty measures suggest at least ten key orientations. Even these statistics fail to capture the degree of chaos conveyed by the passage setting lines 6 through 11; suffice it to say that we rarely get more than a couple of harmonies in a row that point to the same modal center.

Despite their deliberate assault on authorized rules of order, Cipriano's choices do not reduce to arbitrary cacophony. Rather, he relies on the experiences of the performer and listener as embodied beings to translate

---

[15] This is not to suggest an absence of imagination in this section. In mm. 6–7, the altus rises by step up a ninth, thereby depicting the rising morning star. This rise can scarcely be detected if a female alto, buried in the mix, sings the part. In my presentation of this talk, I had a male alto, Erik Leidal, perform the part, to ravishing effect. Erik now sings professionally in Vienna; he records his mash-up arrangements of medieval songs under the name Hieronymus Jackson. Available on YouTube.

Example 3.2a Cipriano de Rore, "Da le belle contrade d'oriente," mm. 1–9

the resulting patterns into meaningful gestures, for those patterns that strain upward only to break off precipitously, that sink to unfathomed depths, or that accelerate or hover in suspension all map onto the body. The solo voice yearns and despairs, heaves and thrashes like someone in the throes of passion. Cipriano can thereby break all the rules of grammar and render feelings we have never before heard articulated and yet remain intelligible (see Example 3.2b).

Observe, for instance, the setting of lines 9 and 10. The quatrain had concluded on a hopeful (though questioning) preparation for an arrival on D. But on the words "Ahi, crudo Amor!" the woman lashes out with a C-minor triad that bears no relation to anything that had preceded it. Pursuing its own aberrant but inexorable logic, the passage penetrates deeper and deeper into the dark region on the flat side, until it halts with an enigmatic D-flat-major triad on "dolcezze." Those false and brief delights appear here as the site furthest from the discursive clarity of the male lover's social realm, that mysterious locus of female pleasure. Time stands still for a moment of unfathomable bliss. Then Cipriano retraces the process that had brought

Example 3.2b Cipriano, "Da le belle contrade d'oriente," mm. 33–48

us to this nadir, and the woman finishes her speech with a conventional questioning formula. Only that D-flat remains as unknowable as it was when it occurred.

The woman's concluding gesture goes unanswered. Another musical ellipsis... and we find ourselves back in the male lover's time, place, and mode. The flashback completed, he continues to narrate his erotic adventure—in the past tense, with himself once again in the picture. The exquisite counterpoint that prevails from here to the end admits not a single chromatic alteration. F-Ionian serves as the sufficient terrain for the representation of the embraces, and although an occasional extravagant melisma can be heard to register the speaker's passion, he resists indulging in the unbridled ecstasy of his mistress. He operates always in the public domain, within the strictures of musical decorum shared by his cultivated male peers.

And what about Cipriano, the ventriloquist who stands behind all these musical details? Clearly the D-flat is no less a product of his imagination than the elaborate counterpoint of the final section. No woman actually speaks here—let alone grants us access to her most secret recesses, where she experiences that brief delight as a pause on D-flat. Like the persona who relates the sonnet, Cipriano maintains his grounding in the realm of reason while purporting to convey directly the non-rational feelings that attend female *jouissance*. Yet we remember Cipriano for the middle part of the madrigal—the woman's speech; this radical experimentation constitutes his bid for the status of genius. Any of his contemporaries might have composed the framing sections of "Da le belle contrade d'oriente," which stick resolutely to the musical language of common practice. But in order to inscribe the interiority of the Other—she who by definition evades conventional language—he must venture outside the bounds of accepted (male) discourse.

Cipriano takes us into modality's dark continent and proposes a tentative answer to the age-old question: "What does Woman want?" What is the nature of female pleasure, the invisibility of which continues to pose technical problems for pornographers? How can the artist represent the unrepresentable, offer evidence of things not seen?

The exclusion of women from cultural production until very recently left this mystery and its possible solutions in the hands of male artists. Moreover, most female composers—wary of participating in a game that locates the essence of Woman in her sexuality—have chosen to turn their talents to nearly any other topic than the one for which Cipriano so eagerly sought the answer. Fortunately for my purposes, Madonna took up the challenge in a song titled "What It Feels Like for a Girl."[16] Her spoken introduction sets the terms:

> Girls can wear jeans
> And cut their hair short,
> Wear shirts and boots
> 'Cause it's OK to be a boy;
> But for a boy to look like a girl is degrading,
> 'Cause you think that being a girl is degrading,
> But secretly you'd love to know what it's like,
> Wouldn't you?
> What it feels like for a girl.

Cipriano would be there, all ears, in the front row!

Madonna's lyrics dwell for the most part on the images that made her appear to critics in the early 1980s as a mere boy toy: "Silky smooth/Lips as sweet as candy; Hair that twirls on fingertips so gently." Yet the occasional protest rumbles just beneath the surface ("Strong inside but you don't know it, /Good little girls they never show it"), and especially in her sardonic allusion to that most detestable of love songs, "My Funny Valentine," when she sings "When you open up your mouth to speak, Could you be a little weak?"

The lyrics tell us little about the musical setting, however. Faced with producing music for such lyrics, Courtney Love would no doubt exploit the contrast between sweetness and irony to explode in snarling rage whenever feasible. But anyone seeking that kind of punk sensibility in Madonna's song will be disappointed, for her musical choices put "What It Feels Like for a Girl" in league with that old hymn to wifely submissiveness, "The girl that I marry has got to be / as soft and pink as a nursery." Drawing on musical stereotypes of "the feminine" that range back to early opera, Madonna produces a reassuring, passive, repetitive melody, supported by static harmonies, with only obliquely shifting inner lines granting a modicum of movement toward the sighing refrain: "Do you know / what it feels like for a girl in this world?" Freud (had he had the courage to listen to music at all)

---

[16] Madonna, Guy Sigsworth, and David Torn, "What It Feels Like for a Girl," *Music* (Maverick Records, 2001). Audio: https://www.youtube.com/watch?v=yN1aV4ZwAg8

would be relieved at this response: Woman, in fact, does not want anything at all!

A child of the MTV era, however, Madonna frequently produces her meanings dialectically between the apparent implications of her music and her *mise-en-scène* in performance. Sometimes she offers visualizations that reinforce the affective burden of the song (as in, for example, "Like a Prayer"); other times the song acts as foil, surprising those who thought they knew what to expect. As it turns out, "What It Feels Like for a Girl" serves as the pretext for at least three radically divergent video interpretations.

The implicit anger of the lyrics, which never disturbed the placid surface of the song, erupts ferociously in the first of these. The official video release (over a pumped-up club remix) stages a revenge fantasy, as Madonna and an elderly lady sidekick turn the tables on gender prerogatives and embark on a joyride and shooting spree.[17] Madonna's then-husband, Guy Ritchie, famous for his film *Lock, Stock, and Two Smoking Barrels*, directed this video. No less focused on random violence than the video for Madonna's song, the movie garnered widespread critical acclaim, while the video was withdrawn from circulation on MTV. She asks: Do you *really* want to know what it feels like for a girl? No, I thought not.

Madonna mounted not one but two presentations of this song for her *Drowned World Tour* in 2001, each putting yet another spin on what those lyrics might mean and, not coincidentally, destabilizing the interpretation offered in the nihilistic video you just saw. The first juxtaposes elements of the song with footage taken from Japanese animation, and it targets the violence against women celebrated so graphically in much popular culture.[18]

The last performance, by contrast, exploits the erotic serenity of the original song, but places it within an all-woman context in which Madonna plays femme to a multiethnic array of butch dancers. Not coincidentally, she also upgrades her question from "What it feels like for a girl" to the Spanish "Lo que siente la mujer": what a *woman* feels.[19] No longer victim or harpy on the rampage, Madonna here luxuriates in the self-possession the musical materials of the song imply. But this romantically inclined persona exists in a realm where no men need apply. Is *this* what Woman wants? I suspect that some find this rendition even scarier than Guy Ritchie's cartoon mayhem.

---

[17] https://www.youtube.com/watch?v = qYwgG2oyUbA
[18] http://www.youtube.com/watch?v = r-Je_lIR-Xo
[19] https://www.youtube.com/watch?v = W9X6aOOBoGg

Madonna's performative reworkings of her song threaten to undermine everything I set out to argue today, for my reading of the music fails to find consistent corroboration when put alongside hard visual evidence. Yet the original song grounds these surprising—even shocking—renditions, all of which draw on the gap between the apparent docility of her recorded performance and her transgressive visualizations. Would I want to guess that Madonna's "true" subjectivity resides in any one of these versions? Not for an instant, for like so many female artists before her who have grappled with the cultural roles available to women, she recognizes the danger of actually revealing her interiority. She gives us masks—an endless array of masks. What does it feel like for a girl? You may as well ask Cipriano; Madonna's not telling, nor am I.

In a cultural world that prizes "authenticity" in art, that turns most especially to music to experience genuine feeling, Madonna's chameleon aesthetic often gets dismissed as superficial. By contrast, our string quartet seems to wrestle with deep existential problems, to surrender its conflicted persona nakedly for our examination; even Schubert's friends read his later music as betraying his innermost condition. But if the Romantic invites us to perceive his art as a direct manifestation of his being, Schubert also operates through masks: Does the "true" Schubert reside in those moments of bliss or in the rage? Does the "real" Cipriano correspond to the male speaker in his madrigal or to the far more daring female voice he invents? And if there are no actual subjectivities in any of this music, then what are we talking about here?

All our examples (as, for that matter, all of literature and cinema) count as fictions—not as documentation concerning any particular individual who ever lived. But that is not where I would want to locate historical evidence with respect to music. Rather, I would focus on the tensions performed between socially tolerated versions of personhood at any given moment and the music that would fly in the face of those conventional assumptions.

Schubert rebels against the tidy pairs of binary oppositions and the affirmative narratives of the Enlightenment, Cipriano against the Neoplatonic proprieties of scholastic authority, Madonna against a centuries-old etiquette that regulates the behavior of "good little girls." Neither Schubert nor Cipriano could have invented his particular scenario at an earlier point in history: indeed, their immediate successors backed off from the radical implications of their accomplishments, leaving formal philosophical treatments for future generations. Thus, Schubert's refusal of the antinomies that had sustained Enlightenment thought recurs in Kierkegaard or

Nietzsche, while Cipriano's denial of scholastic tradition comes to a head in Descartes's much later "Cogito." As Jacques Attali has argued, music is frequently there first, offering to those who will listen a foretaste of what will only eventually be verified in words.[20]

As for Madonna—well, time will tell. But cultural theorists have long hailed her as someone who has an uncanny grasp of the stakes of female representation and who concocts ever more dazzling performances of resistance, self-acceptance, and who knows what next. Feminists have scrambled to keep up, for she always seems to bound forward to the next, still-unexplored phase.[21] As we look back at the last twenty years of gender negotiations, Madonna provides a veritable archive for historical structures of feeling: a specific set of options for each point in time of what it felt like, what it can feel like, and sometimes even what it *will* feel like for a girl.

When each of these musicians plays their fictional changes on our bodies and emotions, we experience to some degree the confusions, the antagonisms, the pleasures, the anxieties from some moment in the past. Multiply mediated, to be sure, through musical conventions, through the necessary act of performative reconstruction, yet still offering insights not available through other media. If contemporaneous verbal confirmation fails to corroborate their bold enterprises, it may be because we have to wait for words to catch up. Until then, we have to accept what we can hear in the music on Faith, which is—as we know from Divine Authority—the evidence of things not seen.

---

[20] Jacques Attali, *Noise: The Political Economy of Music*, trans. Brian Massumi, afterword by Susan McClary (Minneapolis: University of Minnesota Press, 1985).

[21] See my woefully outdated "Living to Tell: Madonna's Resurrection of the Fleshly," first delivered at a talk for the Feminism and Mass Culture conference at SUNY-Buffalo in 1988, then published in *Genders* 7 (1990). It finally appeared as chapter 7 in my *Feminine Endings: Music, Gender, and Sexuality* (Minneapolis: University of Minnesota, 1991). Even now, at age 66, Madonna continues to reinvent herself.

4

Writing about Music—and the Music of Writing[1]

I came to this project as something of an outsider. My distinguished colleagues who participated in the conference titled *The Creative Possibilities of Academic Writing* represent fields that take the verbal medium for granted, even if their particular modes of expression differ enormously according to discipline and individual preference. Musicologists also traffic in words, of course, when they are conveying information concerning history or sources. Many of them, however, flatly deny the ability of words to engage productively with music; some of them even call into question as unethical the practice of writing about what they like to exalt as having transcended speech.

The first part of my essay will explain why I persist in violating this prohibition, merrily rushing in where if not angels then at least most music historians fear to tread. To a great extent, this part rehearses what I have necessarily written time and time again in defense of the projects I have pursued throughout my career. Such in-house arguments may not offer much beyond prurient curiosity to scholars in other fields, though they may shed light on an unfamiliar ideological world for an interdisciplinary readership—rather the way a native informant may explain a custom that could sound bizarre to outsiders but that qualifies to insiders as knowledge fundamental for survival.

Consequently, I will spend the second part of the essay turning these terms around: I want to offer the kinds of principles I have absorbed from a lifetime of theorizing about music to anyone who happens to engage in the act of writing. Indeed, my inclusion in that conference stemmed from a chance conversation I had with convenor Angelika Bammer, in which she asked me if I ever think about rhythm when I write. The fact that she responded

---

[1] Presented as "Effing the Ineffable: Why and How to Dance about Architecture," at the conference *The Creative Possibilities of Academic Writing*, Emory University, May 2010. This version appeared in *The Future of Scholarly Writing: Critical Interventions*, ed. Angelika Bammer and Ruth-Ellen Joeres (New York: Palgrave Macmillan, 2015): 205–14.

Making Sense of Music. Susan McClary, Oxford University Press. © Oxford University Press 2025.
DOI: 10.1093/9780197779798.003.0005

to my affirmative reply with relief made both of us realize how crucial such elements might be to effective prose.

Most humanists fear talking or even reading about music. As Stanley Cavell explained years ago, the elaborate technical vocabulary developed for music analysis prevents or limits critical engagement with this genre of artistic expression.[2] Even musicologists worry about those within the discipline who deal directly with compositions, and they often ridicule offenders with the old canard, "Writing about music is like dancing about architecture."[3] As a result, "the music itself" continues in most quarters to maintain its status as ineffable, immune from the kinds of debates that take place as a matter of course within literary, film, or art-historical studies.

But I contend that music is far too important a cultural enterprise to float unexamined in the ether. And if it proves difficult to account precisely for musical experiences in words, it is no less difficult to explain on paper how a poem produces its effects or, for that matter, how my coffee tasted this morning. Instead of throwing up barriers to prevent discussions concerning music, I believe that we should find ways of using verbal discourse—for better or worse, the medium through which human beings exchange ideas and compare differences in perception—that would allow us to bring sonic artworks into conversations with historians, humanists, and the wider public. Doing so may well violate certain codes of academic prose, but it may also help to loosen the strict rules of writerly decorum we have learned to observe. In short, if music has been cordoned off as "ineffable," it's time we figured out how to eff it.

In his brilliant book *The Master and His Emissary*, Iain McGilchrist explains how the two hemispheres of the brain function in processing information. While the right side tends to pay attention to the outside environment, with its constant changes and relational contingencies, the left side focuses in analytic fashion by means of established structural abstractions. McGilchrist posits that humans—and other animals, for that matter—need both in order to survive and flourish. But he also presents the case that, over

---

[2] Stanley Cavell, "Music Discomposed," in his *Must We Mean What We Say? A Book of Essays* (Cambridge, UK: Cambridge University Press, 1976): 186.

[3] The source of this put-down is much contested, as the ongoing debates on Google demonstrate. Elvis Costello certainly said it in an interview in 1983, but it is also attributed to Thelonious Monk, Frank Zappa, Laurie Anderson, and many others. By this point, it has become something of a truism hurled at would-be transgressors—like me.

the course of European history, left-brain activities (the "emissary" of his title) have increasingly censored or sought to inhibit the input of the right hemisphere, and he sees us as living in an imperiled condition as a result.[4]

This conflict and the asserted dominance of the left hemisphere coalesce in the opposition between the "objective" and "subjective." A product itself of the analytical predisposition, this binarism has the effect of acknowledging as valid only those observations that can be verified regardless of the researcher's particular investments; anything else is relegated to the scrap heap of the "merely" subjective. Our educational processes train students to strive for the objective and to recoil in shame from all other kinds of perceptions, which are labeled variously as childish, emotional, soft, feminine, or self-indulgent.

McGilchrist's argument touches on a vast number of important concerns, among them the very issues addressed in the collection *The Future of Scholarly Writing*. In many academic disciplines, the premium put on objectivity has strangled not only prose style—the exclusive emphasis on documentation and a deliberately drab vocabulary—but also methods: the questions we may ask and the ways we go about trying to engage with those questions.

We all have horror stories. A friend of mine who writes in a powerfully dynamic fashion recently received his manuscript back from an editor who had rendered his sentences virtually unrecognizable—and certainly unreadable—with the insertion of parenthetical citations. The references had taken priority over his arguments. In the premier journal in musicology, *Journal of the American Musicological Society*, the most celebrated articles have four to eight lines of text at the top of the page with the rest taken up by footnotes in small print. The text itself becomes a pretext for the display of erudition. I have had editors who have converted all my sentences into passive voice and systematically stripped out all the metaphors, thereby (presumably) making my texts safer for public consumption.

I have no quarrel with the kinds of endeavors that require such approaches. If I am seeking to ascertain Alessandro Stradella's baptismal date or to identify the singers performing in the first production of Handel's *Messiah*, I too want to see the evidence set forth as clearly as possible (though I resist the notion that clarity even in factual matters requires bad writing). But the problem arises when the discipline recognizes only those endeavors that

---

[4] Iain McGilchrist, *The Master and His Emissary: The Divided Brain and the Making of the Western World* (New Haven, CT: Yale University Press, 2009). See also the introduction to this book, which deals with McGilchrist's more recent work.

lend themselves to the dry delivery of information. I have spent my entire career trying to open music studies to discussions of cultural meaning. For although most people outside musicology do not care much about baptismal records or original performers, they do respond powerfully and viscerally to the music they hear. All of the facts amassed from historical sources will get us no closer to understanding why and how music produces those effects in the real world of performers and listeners.

As a musicologist, I talk and write about music for several reasons. First, I am concerned with the ways music has functioned at various moments in history: how it entrains the body in dance and gesture, how it simulates particular structures of feeling, how it articulates and transmits notions of gender, sexuality, racial identity, and selfhood.[5] A good Foucauldian, I believe that of these all have histories, and I also contend that music offers us insights not available through other media. We may, of course, cull some of this information from archival sources: descriptions by eye-/earwitnesses of their own reactions, expressions of intention by composers, performers, or patrons. But to rely exclusively on those (note!) *verbal* accounts is like trying to account for the nineteenth-century novel while fastidiously refusing to read any of them. Historians necessarily put their evidence and arguments into words, and music historians should be no different.

Second, I talk about music for the sake of performers who often need assistance in order to make their performances as effective as possible. Some advocates of ineffability have defined themselves as devoted to the "drastic" effects of performance, as opposed to "gnostics" like me who play glass-bead games with scores.[6] I regard this as a false opposition, rather the way Saint James resisted the choice between faith and works when he wrote that "faith without works is dead." In fact, few of the "drastics" actually perform or engage with performers; several of us "gnostics," on the other hand, work actively as singers, players, composers, and coaches.

Why this need to intervene verbally in the music-making process? Performers spend much of their time polishing technique—training their bodies to enact delicate motions with the accuracy and speed required for professional careers. For the most part, they rely in their interpretations

---

[5] See, for instance, my *Feminine Endings: Music, Gender, and Sexuality* (Minneapolis: University of Minnesota Press, 1991).

[6] The term comes from Hermann Hesse's *Das Glasperlenspiel*, which appeared in 1943. For this particular controversy in musicology, see particularly Carolyn Abbate, "Music—Drastic or Gnostic?," *Critical Inquiry* 30, no. 3 (Spring 2004): 505–36; and the response in Lawrence Kramer, *Interpreting Music* (Berkeley: University of California Press, 2011).

on something called "musicality," a set of unexamined intuitions absorbed through listening and private lessons. Needless to say, many artists have superb instincts, and we like to listen to them as if their sound patterns were entirely unmediated. But standard musicality has limits: it can override "drastic" moments in scores in the interest of just sounding "nice," and it can create performances that come to sound more or less alike. Humanists who specialize in literature or art supplement what readers or viewers notice on their own, pointing out additional dimensions of texts or paintings through their extensive knowledge and experience. When I work as a coach (as I have for half a century), I call attention to the unusual features of pieces—those elements that may not fit the common notion of the "musical"—and encourage performers to dramatize these instead of trying to suppress them. And this activity demands language.

Notice that I am not suggesting that we substitute verbiage for the sonic experience of the music itself. Just as I wouldn't trade in my caffeine-laden cup of coffee for a description of its taste, however exquisite, nor for an accurate chemical analysis of its constitution, I don't want words to replace sounds. I do recognize a very few literary figures who can describe imagined music with such deftness that we may feel that we've heard it: Marcel Proust, Thomas Mann, and Richard Powers come immediately to mind. But that is not why academics write about music.

I have already discussed two of my reasons for doing so: namely in my engagement with history and performance coaching. But it is the third—music criticism—that matters most to a broader humanistic readership.

If music means nothing, then cultural criticism has no role to play, and we can simply let the sounds wash over us. Those who hold music as ineffable often insist upon the impossibility of linking mere notes to anything outside themselves; they hold that the composer him- or herself may have embraced noxious beliefs, but that the music can and should be enjoyed without reference to those "extramusical" issues. Such debates break out whenever Wagner's operas are programmed: a devoted anti-Semite and author of *Das Judenthum in der Musik*, whose *Der Ring des Nibelungen* features the eponymous greedy, misshapen goldsmiths, Wagner is loathed—but also worshipped uncritically by those who try to maintain a firewall between these inconvenient truths and the undeniable affective power of his music. I think of this as the "ain't nobody here but us notes" defense.

Yet critics ranging from Plato to John Calvin to Stalin's cultural henchman Andrei Zhdanov have believed so fervently in the ability of music to shape us ethically that they have sought to impose social control over it. In reaction against such attempts at curtailing its free circulation, many individuals in liberal democratic contexts hesitate to talk at all about meanings in music; their reluctance stems not only from the difficulty of writing effectively about music but from their fear that reactions might lead to censorship or—in extreme instances—even to the gulag.

Is it possible to debate the meanings discerned from art without sliding all the way over to totalitarian squelching? Is there something special about music that predisposes us to guard it more zealously than we do literature or film? Might it be because we have greater trouble accounting for why music affects us so powerfully that we both subject it to constraints and demand to give it a free pass?[7]

I pose these questions because they lie at the root of whether or not I can risk engaging in serious interdisciplinary work at all. My feminist critiques of standard operas and symphonies brought forth vehement denunciations that compared such writing to Nazi abuses and even the Holocaust.[8] I do not recall that degree of hysteria breaking out in response to feminist criticism in other disciplines.

Fredric Jameson once wrote that history is what hurts,[9] and sometimes music—which qualifies, I believe, as a crucial part of the historical tapestry—might also make us uncomfortable, especially if we prefer to derive unalloyed pleasure from our listening. When I teach the history of music, I aim not at appreciation but rather at the debates that have shaped the course of its development. And I teach my students how and why to debate meanings with each other and also with me. In my experience, such discussions cause the music to come to life, to matter more to those of us wrestling with values of other times and places in conjunction with our own.

For all that advocates of musical ineffability present their positions as the defense of innocence, such prohibitions have always seemed to me the

---

[7] For a book that grapples provocatively with these issues, see Richard Taruskin, *The Danger of Music and Other Anti-Utopian Essays* (Berkeley: University of California Press, 2009).

[8] See, for instance, Leo Treitler, "Gender and Other Dualities of Music History," *Musicology and Difference: Gender and Sexuality in Music Scholarship*, ed. Ruth Solie (Berkeley: University of California Press, 1995), 23–45. Solie edited out some of the more extreme accusations from the original draft. See also Pieter C. van den Toorn, *Music, Politics, and the Academy* (Berkeley: University of California Press, 1996). For a rhetorical analysis of these critiques, see Barbara Tomlinson, *Feminism and Affect at the Scene of Argument: Beyond the Trope of the Angry Feminist* (Philadelphia: Temple University Press, 2010).

[9] Fredric Jameson, "On Interpretation," *The Political Unconscious: Narrative as a Socially Symbolic Act* (Ithaca, NY: Cornell University Press, 1981), 102.

shielding of powerful interests. Is it really coincidental that all the repertories so protected come from the mythical Dead White Males? That none represent the voices of women or minorities? I cannot imagine a piece of music I truly would want to banish from the face of the earth. But I do want to claim the right to talk back and to envision other possibilities.

Thus far I have written about how writing about music might benefit musicians and perhaps readers from other disciplines as well. But I promised at the beginning of my essay to deliver some music lessons for writers themselves. The reader will have noticed that I use a wide variety of images and figures of speech in my writing. I developed this prose style through my attempts at writing about music, for which very few straightforward, objective statements make sense to anyone outside the priesthood of professionals armed with a secret code of technical terms. Over the years, I have learned that most listeners respond not to the pitch relationships music theorists agonize over but rather to gesture and temporal shapes, neither of which shows up directly in notated scores. To the extent that we restrict our observations to dots on the page, we can never address emotion, physicality, or meanings of any sort. Nor have I ever accepted the charge that those effects reside exclusively in my own fevered imagination.

If I started out my career borrowing the kinds of verbal tools I discerned in literary criticism, I hope to bring back to writers some of the insights I have gleaned from my immersion in music. Both language and music operate rhetorically in the sense that choices of ingredients and strategies of combination influence their effectiveness. If writers usually focus on finding "le mot juste" (as Flaubert put it), musicians pay greatest attention to notes, harmonies, and structures. Yet in both media, rhythmic qualities may ultimately count more than particular items, even though we don't always recognize temporal relationships as such.

Let me begin with the relatively simple principle of upbeats and downbeats. Often presented purely as a matter of variety, the choice of starting a sentence with its subject (with a downbeat) versus leading up to that subject with a dependent clause (with an upbeat) can make an enormous difference to the meanings conveyed. Downbeats tend to assert confidence, a willingness to get directly to the point. On the other hand, upbeats can seem gracious and inviting, leading the reader to flow gradually toward the core of the statement.

Understanding the rhythmic impact of such choices helps writers to manipulate this dimension of their prose as effectively as their word selections. In ordinary good writing, such structures alternate quite freely. If more than a couple of each kind occurs in a row, our long-ingrained habits of style intervene: experienced writers will begin scanning their prose, looking for sentences they can flip around to the other structure. But this principle did not come into being arbitrarily. In the right situation, an unbroken chain of downbeat sentences may sound forceful and emphatic, as each statement hammers its point home unequivocally, and concluding a polemical essay in this way can register a powerful charge. But if left unattended, a chain of this sort can become inert—as it does in the hands of those who simply neglect to observe variety—or sometimes brutal, like the overinsistent, pounding conclusions of far too many nineteenth-century symphonies.

Conversely, an overabundance of upbeat structures may sound tentative and hesitant, as if the writer can only creep into each statement gradually, always sticking in a toe to test the waters before plunging in. Yet in the hands of masterful writers, extended upbeats can produce astonishing effects: recall, for instance, how Milton manages to compress the entire history of humanity into the anacrusis stretching from "Of Mans First Disobedience" all the way to "Sing, Heav'nly Muse!" As the virtuosic upbeat gathers increasingly more dynamic energy, pulling into its vortex both Genesis and the Revelations of John, it urgently demands release. When the delayed moment of resolution finally arrives, the pent-up weight of the upbeat explodes onto the imperative. Milton charges the heavenly Muse to take it from there and generates the fuel for her to do so.

> Of Mans First Disobedience, and the Fruit
> Of that Forbidden Tree, whose mortal tast
> Brought Death into the World, and all our woe,
> With loss of Eden, till one greater Man
> Restore us, and regain the blissful Seat,
> Sing Heav'nly Muse. . . .

Compare this with the beginning of Beethoven's Ninth Symphony, which similarly emerges from nothing and eventually hurls its accumulated power into the first statement of the movement's titanic theme. But recall that the wild Scherzo movement of the Ninth as well as the Finale's "Ode to Joy" remain resolutely downbeat in orientation. A piece that opens in the void, then hurtles forward into violence, has to ground itself somehow—a task that becomes ever more difficult as Beethoven's sustained upbeats challenge even his ability to release all that energy. Which may lead us back to *Paradise Lost*: how does Milton deal with his large-scale rhythmic effects, once he has them launched? I'll leave that to the rhythmically aware reader to discover.

Writers might also consider the phenomenon of the deceptive cadence, whereby a musical phrase prepares for resolution—then harmonizes the melodic arrival in a way that denies the anticipated closure. This device has appeared in Western music since at least the fifteenth century, and it never fails to deliver a rhetorical punch. Although Wagner's *Tristan und Isolde* qualifies as exceptional in its obsessive concentration on this technique, it operates both musically and metaphorically according to the principle of delayed, failed, or interrupted cadences, for within that opera's framework, a full cadence must equal figurative and even literal death. The single moment of genuine closure in the five-hour-long opera appears with the very last sonority.

My example of a verbal equivalent of this technique may come as a surprise: the prose and also the methodology of Jacques Derrida. Derrida's writing often frustrates English-speakers, who tend to expect a bottom line to arguments. But Derrida seeks to destabilize that particular mode of expression and thought through what he calls "différance." Much like a composer, he will lead the argument to the point where the attentive reader will be leaping forward mentally to grasp some nugget of truth—only to back off at the last moment to pursue another tack. For he wishes not so much to articulate a set of principles as to instill the habit of always refusing the comfort of a secure resting point. Within the framework of his thought, such resting points always count as a kind of death, the cessation of restless thought.[10]

In other words, it helps to read Derrida as if listening to *Tristan*. A great many graduate students who fall under the spell of deconstruction came away thinking that they have to make their prose as obscure as possible; something of the same sort happened with composers after Wagner, many of whom disappeared without a trace into a thicket of gnarly, purposeless harmonic relations. But Derrida's (and Wagner's) elegant, carefully calculated writing never loses its clarity. In order for it to work properly, it must always have directionality, always pointing to possible solutions before withdrawing from or erasing that certainty.

---

[10] See, for instance, Jacques Derrida, "Freud and the Scene of Writing," chapter 7 in his *Writing and Difference*, trans. Alan Bass (Chicago: University of Chicago Press, 1978), which discusses writing in terms such as deferring closure, orality, temporality, periodicity, and even qualities that unwittingly simulate death.

In his "Translating the Untranslatable," Samuel Weber takes a similar approach in explaining Theodor Adorno's prose, which also frustrates many English-speaking scholars.[11] The dialectical patterning of Adorno's writing appears confused and self-contradictory to those who expect unequivocal, concrete propositions. But, as Weber argues, the Frankfurt School critic demands that we hold mutually incompatible ideas together in our minds until the verb at the end of the sentence tilts in one direction or the other.

In my experience as a theorist of early-modern music, I encounter the same kinds of strategies in the sixteenth-century Italian madrigal, which holds multiple key identities in tension until the cadence. Musicians accustomed to the linear eighteenth-century practices of, say, Mozart complain about why it took so long for composers to indicate their pitch center at all times; they demand a sonic GPS to minimize uncertainty. But the repertories developed for the Renaissance courts strove to maintain a high degree of ambiguity, continually revealing and concealing meanings, often even within the very last chord.[12] That way of thinking persisted until J. S. Bach and was taken up again in Beethoven's late works. Both these composers deeply influenced Adorno's philosophy and—I would argue—even his way of fashioning prose.

In closing I want to address one more concern that brings writing and music together: namely, performativity. In the days when poets sang their epics or families read novels out loud in the evenings, readers treated texts as if they were scores that demanded to be rendered into dramatic sound. Effective writing therefore had to have a strong musical component.

Although the growing genre of audio books promises to bring back some of those aural pleasures, most of us do not approach writing with the assumption that our texts should be effective to the ear, even when we know we will have to get up in front of a hotel ballroom packed with conference attendees to present our papers. It should go without saying that we ought to attend to the musical dimensions of our writing when we plan to put it into actual sound. Alas, this usually occurs only at the moment of performance, when the author trips over an unwieldy construct that not even she or he

---

[11] Samuel M. Weber, "Translating the Untranslatable," introduction to Theodor W. Adorno, *Prisms*, ed. and trans. Samuel M. Weber and Shierry Weber (Cambridge, MA: MIT Press, 1981), 9–15.

[12] See my *Modal Subjectivities: Renaissance Self-Fashioning in the Italian Madrigal* (Berkeley: University of California Press, 2004).

can render as credible speech. And nothing indicts a clunky sentence more surely than reading it aloud in a public forum.

But I want to argue that we should attend no less to such elements when we are writing strictly for the page. For sonic rhetoric does not disappear when prose addresses the eye alone. As we read, we respond powerfully—even if not entirely consciously—to qualities such as flow, rhythm, and affective structure. I once realized only after I had fallen asleep several times reading a book manuscript that it contained nothing but passive sentences.

Always remember: the great prose stylists—whatever their subject matter or discipline—present their ideas partly in song.

5

The Bodies of Angels[1]

In fall 2008, I taught a graduate seminar in Baroque Performance Practices at UCLA, where I was employed at the time. The fifteen participants—most of them already concert artists working toward the Doctor of Musical Arts degree—included not only North Americans but also individuals from Korea, China, Japan, Turkey, Armenia, and Germany: an astonishingly international group representing vastly different cultural backgrounds, all dedicated to developing their ability to perform seventeenth- and eighteenth-century European art music.

Regardless of the conservatory in which they had previously studied, however, they agreed upon one thing: that serious music should have nothing to do with the body. When I asked that they pay attention to dance rhythms or to physical gesture, they wrinkled up their noses in displeasure. Over the course of the semester, I worked to change their attitudes: assigning them readings from historical documents, showing them paintings and sculptures, playing and singing for them, conducting and sometimes even dancing in my own feeble way. By the end of the course, they were advising each other to engage physically with their performances. But it was a long and difficult process that brought them to that point.

I recognized this syndrome all too well, in part from the writing of prominent aestheticians. Roman Ingarden, for instance, wrote: "We may doubt whether so-called dance music, when employed only as a means of keeping the dancers in step and arousing in them a specific passion for expression through movement, is music in the strict sense of the word."[2] But I also had

---

[1] Written as keynote for an international conference on the body, *El Cos: Objecte i subjecte de les ciències humanes i socials* (Barcelona, January 2009). Published in *Desvelando el Cuerpo: Perspectivas desde las Ciencias Sociales y Humanas*, ed. Josep Martí et al. (Barcelona: CSIC, 2010), 137–44. Also presented as the Edith V. Curry Lecture (University of Michigan); as keynotes for conferences *Music and the Body* (University of Cork) and *Sirens: Festivalen för ny musik* (University of Göteborg, March 2011); and as an invited lecture at Amsterdam Conservatory and the Royal College of Music in Stockholm.

Instead of music examples I have included only links to recordings in this chapter. I want the reader to experience the bodily states I describe in specific performances.

[2] Roman Ingarden, *The Work of Music and the Problem of Its Identity*, trans. Adam Czerniawski (London: Macmillan, 1986): 46.

experienced this prohibition against the body in music firsthand. When I first began studying piano as a child, my teacher would whack me across the wrist if he detected that I was moving to the music—an experience shared by nearly all my recent students. Any reminder that the body was responsible for producing sound was greeted by corporeal punishment.

Most musicians respond to this kind of training by suppressing their awareness of the body, by trying to erase its embarrassing (if necessary) presence. I reacted in the opposite fashion: I have spent a great deal of my professional life as a musicologist, music theorist, performer, and coach demonstrating how fundamental the body is to all aspects of what Christopher Small has termed musicking.[3] And I have found particular support in the work of philosopher Mark Johnson, who argues that all human cognition operates on the basis of body-based metaphors.[4]

It is not difficult to find evidence in early-modern documents that the body served then as the basis of musicking. When codes for simulating various affects started to appear in the sixteenth century, theorists usually explained the correspondences in terms of kinetic experience. In 1597, for instance, Thomas Morley wrote: "If the subject be light you must cause your music to go in motions which carry with them a celerity or quickness of time . . . ; if it be lamentable the notes must go in slow and heavy motions. . . ."[5]

Over the course of the sixteenth century, musicians found it possible to delineate very complex combinations of physical gestures,[6] all of them intelligible so long as the body remains the understood referent not only for listeners but also for performers, since performers have the responsibility of translating the dots on the page into plausible simulations of corporeal experiences. I would argue that most music operates according to this set of assumptions, which is why we can make a certain kind of sense of unfamiliar repertories and traditions. We even call the subunits of extended compositions "movements," because they offer diverse qualities of motion: in the conventional Italian, "andante," "allegro," "lento," and so forth. Music invites us to imagine our embodiment in radically different ways.

---

[3] Christopher Small, *Musicking: The Meanings of Performing and Listening* (Wesleyan University Press, 1998).
[4] Mark Johnson, *The Body in the Mind: The Bodily Basis of Meaning, Imagination, and Reason* (Chicago: University of Chicago Press, 1990). For more on metaphor in my work, see again the introduction to this book.
[5] Thomas Morley, *A Plaine and Easie Introduction to Practicall Musicke* (London, 1597).
[6] See my *Modal Subjectivities: Self-Fashioning in the Italian Madrigal* (Berkeley: University of California Press, 2004).

As in my seminar, I want to start with music of the seventeenth century: a period that witnessed a crucial split between modes of composition that foregrounded the body and those that appeared to break away from it. In my years as a coach of early music, I have found that students resist in particular the French repertory, precisely because it demands careful attention to the body. Dance occupied the pinnacle of cultural production at the French court; all courtiers spent hours each day rehearsing with dance masters to ensure their perfect self-presentation before the king, who often took the leading role in court ballets. As a result of this grounding in dance, French Baroque music and its details—its ornaments, its bowing patterns, even its ways of setting words for vocalists—depend upon a powerful sense of the disciplined body moving in accordance with stylized choreography. The music presents a temporality focused on the present: on the shifting of feet, on the rhythmic parsing of words, on the nuances that pull the ear into the subtle interplay of each moment.[7]

A couple of examples. First, a keyboard chaconne from Louis Couperin's Suite in D Major. In this performance by Edward Parmentier, the proud bearing of the aristocratic body is made palpable, not only through the measured groove but also by the carefully situated embellishments, which serve to locate each step and hand gesture with energy and precision.[8]

But French music not designed for actual dance also shares this grounding in the body. I first grasped this when I saw the film *Tous les Matins du monde* in the early 1990s and became entranced with Jordi Savall's performances of compositions by Marin Marais. The *Tombeau pour Mr de Sainte Colombe* is, as the title announces, an elegy, written by Marais in homage to his late teacher. In keeping with its funereal topic, the *Tombeau* is slow, in a minor key, and characterized by the kinds of sorrowfully drooping melodic lines Thomas Morley would have prescribed. And yet the physicality of dance can still be discerned, in the exact gradations of weight assigned to each pitch and the ornaments that refuse stoically to give in to undisciplined grief.[9]

My title, however, refers to a very different cultural ideal: the fantasy of weightlessness, of the possibility of transcending the constraints of human

---

[7] See my "Temporality and Ideology: Qualities of Motion in Seventeenth-Century French Music," in my *Desire and Pleasure in Seventeenth-Century Music* (Berkeley: University of California Press, 2012). See also chapter 12 of this volume.

[8] Louis Couperin, Suite in D Major, Chaconne. Edward Parmentier, harpsichord.
https://www.youtube.com/watch?v=v2-HqaVFmXc

[9] Marin Marais, *Tombeau pour Mr de Sainte Colombe*. Jordi Savall, viol.
https://www.youtube.com/watch?v=XkRUTUYBua0

reality, whether the constraints of physical motion or the materiality of words.[10] The polyphony of the Renaissance often manages to produce such effects, through the overlapping of many voices. Music of this sort invites the listener to escape the gravitational pull to which human beings are subject on this earth and to identify instead with a "virtual" angelic body. Listen, for instance, to Jean Mouton's motet "Nesciens mater virgo virum," which celebrates the paradox of Mary's incorporeal conception, labor, and lactation as she delivers the "king of angels." Mouton creates an allegory through his musical process, in which four notated lines effortlessly give birth through a secret formula to four others, culminating in an eight-voice ensemble. Because this motet unfolds through four simultaneous canons, the voices cannot arrive at the same place for cadences, thereby attenuating any sense of closure. Mouton invites us to hover in a mystical place in which even childbirth causes no discomfort.[11]

Nesciens mater virgo virum peperit	Without knowing man, the virgin mother gave birth
sine dolore Salvatorem saeculorum,	without pain to the Savior of the ages;
ipsum regem angelorum,	to this same king of angels
sola virgo lactabat	the virgin alone gave suck
ubere de caelo pleno.	with breasts filled by heaven.

But several ideological movements in the later sixteenth century sought to bring music back to earth, to ground it in the more commonplace phenomena of talking and dancing. As I already mentioned, the French court

---

[10] See my "Fetisch Stimme: Professionelle Sänger im Italien der frühen Neuzeit," in *Zwischen Rauschen und Offenbarung: Zur Kultur- und Mediengeschichte der Stimme*, ed. Friedrich Kittler, Thomas Macho, and Sigrid Weigel (Berlin: Akademie, 2002): 199–214. Available in English as "Soprano as Fetish: Professional Singers in Early Modern Italy," chapter 3 in my *Desire and Pleasure in Seventeenth-Century Music*.

[11] Jean Mouton, "Nesciens mater virgo virum." I fell in love with this motet when the BBC sent me a CD, *Christmas Choral Music*, Monteverdi Choir, cond. John Eliot Gardiner (BBC, 2007), and it was this performance I played when giving this talk. Gardiner takes a very slow tempo, producing a kind of trance state in the listener.
https://www.youtube.com/watch?v=_hZHKKD5ahk.
But listen also to the recording by Ensemble Jacques Moderne. Joël Suhubiette conducts with the tactus, creating a quality of physical motion. This YouTube link includes the score, allowing one to see how Mouton produces his eight voices out of four. https://www.youtube.com/watch?v=M7crqD8xurA.
In truth, if I were conducting this motet, I would probably choose a tempo closer to that of Suhubiette because of my training in Renaissance performance practices. But I can't let go of the Gardiner. Note that both performances relate to the body, though in profoundly different ways. I return to the issue of the body and performance tempo in the final chapter of this collection, "Mahler Making Love: Mengelberg's Adagietto."

made ballet its principal idiom. In Italy, Vincenzo Galilei (father of the astronomer) condemned counterpoint for obscuring verbal meaning; his arguments contributed to the emergence of monody—the stripped-down speech-song that made early opera possible. Something similar happened in the church, as the Council of Trent pressured Palestrina to sacrifice for the sake of uniform declamation the kind of dense polyphony that allows Mouton's motet to produce its simulation of spiritual transcendence.

Yet if the pragmatic side of the Counter-Reformation sought to legislate plain expression, another side cultivated imagery inspired by Spanish mysticism, and many artists excelled at both. Recall that Gian Lorenzo Bernini was responsible for both the monumental piazza of St. Peter's, which gave weighty material presence to divine authority, and also for the sculpture of *Saint Teresa in Ecstasy*, in which those same supremely heavy elements of metal and marble offer the illusion of airborne hovering: Teresa seems lifted to the heavens in the throes of blissful union with her Lord.

In the realm of composition, Bernini's contemporary Claudio Monteverdi manifested a similar split. He demonstrated his mastery of the new monodic style in his opera *Orfeo* of 1607, and his own polemical writings insist that words should control music. Yet he found it difficult to abandon altogether his ability to make music take flight. In his *Vespro della Beata Vergine* of 1610—a collection mostly devoted to monumental psalm settings for multiple choirs—he inserted a small piece representing two angels soaring around the throne of God intoning the Sanctus. The solo voices begin high above a slow-moving bass that provides a minimal grounding. As they proceed to the singing of the Sanctus, they liquidate their words, dissolving them into an ecstatic ululation that surpasses mere language. Finally the two play a game in which they depart from the present moment and catapult themselves forward in their orbit, refusing any temptation to stop even to breathe as they race by.[12]

Now, I would not claim that Monteverdi's seraphs lack bodies. Indeed, it is because we can identify with their virtual bodies that we are able to experience vicariously what it would feel like to be able to slip the leash that tethers us to the earth. And although I have chosen not to focus unduly on the sexualized body in this paper, it seems quite apparent that our angels engage in highly erotic activity as they go about their business of praising God.

---

[12] Monteverdi, "Duo seraphim," *Vespro della Beata Virgine*, as recorded in *Un Concert spirituel*, René Jacobs, dir. (Harmonia Mundi, 1980). https://www.youtube.com/watch?v=tdbqWFqjBFM. I have written on this performance in "Soprano as Fetish," chapter 3 of my *Desire and Pleasure*.

It is not only the seventeenth century that saw such tensions between an explicitly body-oriented mode of musicking versus one invested in transcendence. One could structure a history of Western music by tracing allegiances to one of these poles or the other. A constant struggle occurs between those who regard music properly as a means of sustaining dance or amplifying language and those committed to exploring what music can do when released from those mundane obligations.

Those obligations, of course, do not really qualify as mundane, even if they are very much tied to this world. Historian William H. McNeill has argued that human beings have an evolutionary need to participate in activities in which they keep together in time.[13] Most small children learn to move rhythmically to music quite early on in life, and they derive great pleasure from the measured interactions between their bodies and external sound. In other words, the music designed for dance, marches, or exercise plays a fundamental role in our development as individuals within social networks.

Consequently, there are good reasons why certain people may fret when music strays too far from these extremely important functions, and some of the most important style changes involve deliberate attempts at making music serve these purposes. I have already mentioned that the emergence of what we now call opera around 1600 was the result of a concerted effort to strip music of its complex polyphony and ornate embellishment for the sake of verbal intelligibility; words moved into the foreground, with the music providing minimal support. Calvinist reformers similarly ordained a syllabic mode of singing hymns, viewing as repugnant the ornamentation or instrumental riffs that threatened to distract congregants from the theological substance of their texts.[14]

We don't have to look very far back in history for manifestations of this point of view. The rise of alternative rock in the early 1990s can be understood in part as a reaction against the virtuosic display of heavy-metal guitar solos. Rock critics condemned with impunity the melismatic exuberance of singers such as Mariah Carey. The less polished the voices and the cruder the instrumental backups, the more indie rock seems to be relaying unadorned truth instead of merely showing off.

---

[13] William H. McNeill, *Keeping Together in Time: Dance and Drill in Human History* (Cambridge, MA: Harvard University Press, 1997). See also Kate van Orden, *Music, Discipline, and Arms in Early Modern France* (Chicago: University of Chicago Press, 2005).

[14] See again the introduction to this book for an account of my own early grounding in Calvinism.

But those who feel hampered by language and earthbound bodies also have their reasons, many with ancient pedigrees. The mystical quality of wordless melismatic singing sustains the joyful Alleluia in both Jewish and Christian liturgies, and it also animates the Muslim Call to Prayer; all of these dissolve their texts into evanescent simulations of unbridled ecstasy worthy of Monteverdi's seraphim. Ludwig Wittgenstein wrote: "Whereof one cannot speak, thereof one must be silent."[15] But it may be that when we lack words to express the ineffable, then we leave language behind and return to melodic practices that may predate our verbal abilities, that trace patterns of feeling without recourse to mere speech.

Most musicians work one side of this fence or the other, locating themselves either within communities that expect dance and the clear presentation of words or else within those that favor the exploration of other possible realms. J. S. Bach consistently evoked both—though not always as mutually compatible modes of being. As an artist whose career unfolded largely on the periphery of cosmopolitan centers of cultural activity, Bach was left to experiment with anything he could pick up from the Italianate opera house in Dresden, from the dances slavishly imitated in Francophile German courts, from the dusty manuscripts of Renaissance motets heaped in the backs of churches, or from the latest Scarlatti keyboard sonatas imported from Spain. And he made innumerable combinations of these throughout his career.

But he also loaded his combinations ideologically, especially with respect to France, which was increasingly identified with superficial, aristocratic *Civilisation* in contrast with what pre-Romantic Germans were coming to value as the more profound qualities of *Kultur*.[16] If French music grounded itself in the dancing body, Bach took those patterns and either demonstrated their inherent oppressiveness or else taught them how to break free.

An example of each. Bach's Chaconne for solo violin qualifies as one of the most difficult pieces in the repertory, not only because of its technical demands, which are formidable, but because Bach asked the violinist simultaneously to present a dance pattern and to struggle to escape its demands. He chose not just any dance type, but rather the one Louis XIV ordered his

---

[15] Ludwig Wittgenstein, *Tractatus Logico-Philosophicus*. "Wovon man nicht sprechen kann, darüber muss man schweigen."

[16] The terms "Civilisation" and "Kultur" come from Norbert Elias, *The Court Society*, trans. Edmund Jephcott (New York: Pantheon, 1983). See my account of Bach in *Conventional Wisdom: The Content of Musical Form* (Berkeley: University of California Press, 2000), Chapter 3.

courtiers to perform in a circle around him, thereby causing them to simulate planets in orbit around the Sun King.

Bach asks his violinist not only to keep the repeating pattern of the chaconne's ostinato bass continually present, but also to attempt through increasing agitation to throw off its inflexible constraints. The very long composition finishes with neither side conceding to the other: the obstinate chaconne pattern cannot be shaken loose, and the energies battling against it refuse to surrender. They emerge as bloodied but undefeated opponents.[17]

Not all Bach's confrontations with French dance end with such pessimistic results, however. The opening of his Cantata 140, *Wachet auf*, presents a very different scenario. A cantata based on the New Testament parable of the Wise and Foolish Virgins, *Wachet auf* takes us from the announced appearance of the bridegroom, through amorous bride-and-groom duets between the Soul and Jesus, to a communal celebration of the wedding.[18] Bach begins his opening movement with the strutting rhythms of the French overture, the kind of music to which Louis XIV would process into royal events. Within a couple of measures, Bach has identified the topics of royalty and kingly procession with the Second Coming of Christ.

Yet Bach never wants to remain locked in French codes any longer than necessary. Already in bar 5, an Italianate mode of activity begins to wrestle against the predictability of the march groove and to strain forward. This time, in contrast to the standoff between tensions in the violin chaconne, the struggle here is rewarded: by bar 9, the top melodic line has broken through and can soar unimpeded toward its own utopian goal. To be sure, Bach eventually pulls everything back and reinserts us into the processional rhythm. But he also shows us over and over again how to convert French currency into Italian or German, how to escape the constraints of courtly dance.

I am not suggesting that Bach dispensed with the body here or in any of his music; indeed, his son Carl Philipp Emanuel claimed that his father's body was so expressive that one could tell by watching him perform what affect

---

[17] J. S. Bach, Ciaccona, from Partita II for Unaccompanied Violin. The performance that comes closest to what I am describing is by Nemanja Radulović. https://www.youtube.com/watch?v=MS1ATruO7f4

For a more detailed account of this piece and the history of the chaconne as a genre, see my "The Social History of Groove: Chacona, Ciaccona, Chaconne, and THE Chaconne," chapter 7 of my *Desire and Pleasure*.

[18] For a fuller discussion of this cantata, see my "The Blasphemy of Talking Politics during Bach Year," *Music and Society: The Politics of Composition, Performance and Reception*, ed. Richard Leppert and Susan McClary (Cambridge, UK: Cambridge University Press, 1987): 13–62.

he was trying to convey. But he did work hard to produce collisions between very different notions of the body: the one bound by dance patterns imposed from the outside and the one that could fly with the weightlessness of the imagination itself toward distant goals. And his dramatic scenarios leave little doubt concerning which side he preferred.

Earlier in this essay I linked Bach with the German Romanticism that was to build increasing momentum through the eighteenth century. Although Bach would not have recognized this aesthetic movement, he served as a powerful example for theorists of German nationalism in the early nineteenth century. Moreover, the Romantics shared Bach's grounding in Lutheran mysticism, however much they cloaked their writings with secular explanations. German idealist aesthetics shaped the instrumental music of the nineteenth century, not only in its homeland but everywhere the Gospel of Beethoven offered what E.T.A. Hoffmann called "a kingdom not of this world": music that was valued precisely because it transcended "mere" human values, including most particularly the body.[19]

And that brings me back to my seminar students. Whether from Istanbul or Singapore, they had been trained to become staunch German idealists and to shun the body as if it were the Devil Incarnate. Such training served them well enough as long as they stayed with the music informed by the nineteenth-century German aesthetic position. But it prevented them from comprehending repertories from before Bach—or even from recognizing the carefully constructed collisions of body-types in the music of Bach himself. Theirs was not an intellectual objection; it was grounded so deeply in their identities that suggestions concerning kinetic activity raised palpable emotional anxiety. Having learned to assume the bodies of angels, they were loath to descend into the frivolity that the German Romantics once associated with Versailles.

I will conclude with another example that juxtaposes dramatically these two modes of being. In his Ninth Symphony, Beethoven often grounds his music powerfully in the body; recall the Dionysian dance of the scherzo movement, for instance, or the marchlike settings of the "Ode to Joy." And at other times he produces passages that attempt to transcend human reality. In the final movement, Schiller's poem allows Beethoven to portray twice the desire to ascend to face God (at the words "und der Cherub steht vor Gott,"

---

[19] See Stephen Rumph, "A Kingdome Not of This World: The Political Context of E.T.A. Hoffmann's Beethoven Criticism," *19th-Century Music* 19, no. 1 (Summer 1995): 50–67. For more on the connections between German Romanticism and Lutheranism, see Carl Dahlhaus, *The Idea of Absolute Music*, trans. Roger Lustig (Chicago: University of Chicago Press, 1989).

"muss ein lieber Vater wohnen"); but both times the music presents those aspirations as unanswered questions before relocating us back in the earthbound hymn.

In the concluding section, Beethoven pushes for closure to this symphony of unprecedented length. Quite abruptly, however, he interrupts his trajectory with a vocal quartet. As they sing once again the ideal that all men can become brothers wherever joy spreads its gentle wings, the solo voices begin to soar heavenward with ever more extravagant embellishment, offering one last glimpse of Elysium. These are Monteverdi's seraphim translated into the idiom of the nineteenth century.[20]

But in the final analysis, Beethoven is too much a realist to allow the symphony to evaporate into sheer evanescence—and, moreover, in a key other than the tonic that defines the real world for this symphony. He makes the quartet's conclusion sound like an ellipsis, thereby reinterpreting as provisional the celestial vision we have just shared, then forges ahead to the end. Voices and orchestra—including the exotic Janissary instruments featured in the Turkish segment of the finale—unite forces to drive home the words "werden Brüder." No longer the provisional (if heavenly) fantasy of the quartet, this sentiment is now located in the insistent, stomping, even headbanging body. The concrete energy Beethoven brings to this conclusion demands the physical response of listeners, nearly always bringing them to their feet in a standing ovation.

Earlier I mentioned that I would not focus on the erotic dimensions of the body as they inform musical procedure. But, of course, many of the examples I have played resonate profoundly with our experiences as sexual beings. Fundamentalist ministers used to condemn the pulsating beat of rock 'n' roll because they heard it—and quite rightly so—as simulating the rhythms of intercourse. I will risk the wrath of my longtime critics by pointing out that few rock songs can compete with the end of Beethoven's Ninth.[21]

Yet the images of the body delineated by the opposite extreme—all those melismas and instrumental arabesques—are no less grounded in erotic experience, even if they emerge from a different metaphorical base. Musical virtuosity depends upon extreme physical discipline: to be able to sing or play those rapid scales and flourishes requires years of practice. But the intended

---

[20] Beethoven, Symphony No. 9; John Eliot Gardiner, Orchestre Révolutionnaire et Romantique. https://www.youtube.com/watch?v=DuDFyigVcXw, at 57:00.
[21] The controversy was sparked by my essay "Getting Down off the Beanstalk," which appeared in *Feminine Endings: Music, Gender, and Sexuality* (Minneapolis: University of Minnesota Press, 1991).

result of all that physical labor is the sensation of airborne motion, just as the body strives in sexual activity to arrive at the moment when the real world—including the very body that has brought us there—seems to fall away in a flash of timeless ecstasy. Of course, the world comes back soon enough, and the illusion quickly fades. As the Romans used to say, "Post coitum omne animal triste est": all creatures are sad after sex.

But such knowledge rarely prevents us creatures from trying it again. And that foretaste of heaven—*la petite mort*, the French call it—also inspires the kind of music that seems to transcend reality and even the body itself to simulate weightlessness and effortless soaring. Such music gives material presence to mystical ideals, allowing the listener to be caught up in a state of rapture. It invites us to inhabit, at least temporarily, the bodies of angels.

6

The Lure of the Sublime

Revisiting the Modernist Project[1]

In 1988 I delivered a paper titled "Terminal Prestige: The Case of Avant-Garde Music Composition" at a conference titled *The Economy of Prestige*. This interdisciplinary conference, held at the University of Minnesota, sought to explore the ways in which prestige operates as a system of reward and recognition. At the time, this topic seemed particularly relevant to music studies, which still vaunted "non-commercial" but institutionally supported artists and held popular success and even communication in contempt. My paper appeared in print for the first time the following year in a special issue of *Cultural Critique* dedicated to that conference, and it has been reprinted in English and other languages several times since then.[2]

An early salvo against the stringent version of postwar Modernism still dominating many North American music departments, the article stirred up considerable controversy. It also contributed to the emergence of a self-aware Postmodernism among composers, many of whom had been exploring eclecticism and neo-tonal sonorities in their music without using this label. A careful reading of that article will reveal that I was not attacking Modernist music per se but only some of the ideologies that had upheld its hegemony: in particular, an institutionalized prohibition against address meaning in music (imposed not only on new compositions but even on repertories from previous eras) and an insistence that serialist procedures comprised the necessary future for genuine music.[3]

---

[1] Published in *Transformations of Musical Modernism*, ed. Erling Guldbrandsen and Julian Johnson (Cambridge, UK: Cambridge University Press, 2015): 21–35.

[2] "Terminal Prestige: The Case of Avant-Garde Composition," *Cultural Critique* 12 (Spring 1989): 57–81; for reprints, see *Keeping Score: Music, Disciplinarity, Culture*, ed. David Schwarz, Anahid Kassabian, and Lawrence Siegel (Charlottesville: University Press of Virginia, 1997): 54–74; and my *Reading Music: Selected Essays* (Aldershot, UK: Ashgate, 2007): 85–109.

[3] Joseph Straus, among others, has claimed that no such imperative existed. See his "The Myth of Serial 'Tyranny' in the 1950's and 1960's," in *The Musical Quarterly* 83/3 (Fall 1999): 301–43. He must not have been there at the time. I know dozens of composers who left the field as a result. Paraphrasing Allen Ginsberg, I saw the best minds of my generation destroyed by compulsory

Now, over thirty years later, many things have changed. First, what had appeared then as the nearly unbreakable stranglehold of academic serialism suddenly weakened and vanished, leaving scarcely a trace. In the United States, former metal guitarist Steve Mackey replaced Milton Babbitt on the Princeton composition faculty, John Zorn receives major prizes for his fusions, and the *Norton History of Western Music* (if not so much the *Oxford*) includes blues, jazz, and rock in its account of music since 1900. A flood of serious scholarly research on popular idioms has made genres such as hip-hop respectable topics for intellectual inquiry. If "Terminal Prestige" now seems antiquated, it is largely because the battles in which it engaged have long since been won.

Yet something else has occurred in the intervening years, namely the rise of a new, twenty-first-century version of Modernism. For the avant-garde of the 1950s now has—in addition to its oedipal rebels—some highly productive and successful progeny. Composers such as Kaija Saariaho, Salvatore Sciarrino, Thomas Adès, Olga Neuwirth, and George Benjamin, unwilling to throw out the baby with the bathwater, have returned to techniques and sonorities pioneered by Messiaen, Boulez, and others. In contrast to some of their predecessors, however, these artists openly acknowledge the expressive and rhetorical power of their strategies. It is no coincidence that many of them gravitate toward opera—a genre largely abandoned in the years of absolutist autonomy. Because staged works necessarily include actors, voices, and lyrics, such music humanizes its post-tonal idiom, making its power intelligible to audiences.

The recent resurgence of Modernism now appears less like the terminal stage of a fatal disease than the repurposing of earlier resources for innovation. It invites us to think again about postwar Modernism—not as the way European music was predestined to develop organically from within itself or as a reaction formation against popular idioms but rather as an array of relationships between artistic expression and cultural contexts. At this point in time, in other words, it has become possible to treat postwar repertories as just another chapter in history.

But a strange chapter it is. We have grown so accustomed in the academy to recognizing Boulez's *Marteau sans maître* and Stockhausen's *Gesang der Jünglinge* as mid-century masterworks that we may no longer perceive how

---

serialism. See, for instance, the testimonies of Philip Glass concerning Princeton and John Adams concerning Harvard.

radical they were when they emerged. The requisite perspective is easily restored, however, as soon as one tries to introduce them to a class of canon-devoted conservatory students. So strong is their sense of indignation that one sometimes fears suffering the fate of all messengers bringing bad news when reaching this point in the syllabus.

For, in fact, such music *does* communicate to the uninitiated, though perhaps in ways that differ significantly from its modes of self-justification. The soundtrack compiled by Robbie Robertson for Martin Scorsese's 2010 film *Shutter Island*, for instance, featured music by György Ligeti, Morton Feldman, John Adams, and John Cage, among others, all of which were meant to sound like manifestations of the insane asylum in which the film took place. To today's filmgoer, this soundtrack may register quite simply as bughouse music. And this would have made sense to Expressionists such as Schoenberg (*Erwartung*) and Berg (*Wozzeck*), both of whom developed their musical languages in part to convey psychological disorder. If we do not simply try to cudgel our students into obedient acceptance (the pedagogical strategy of decades past), their indignation when confronted with this repertory might lead us to consider fundamental questions concerning the purposes of this music—or, indeed, of music in general.

What would have motivated sensitive artists to take up the positions they maintained so fiercely in the 1950s and beyond? Audience appeal certainly does not spring to mind as an explanation. Although the alienation between composers and listeners intensified after World War II, the problem dates back at least forty years before that. For a while, people in the academy and isolated sites such as IRCAM and Darmstadt tried to ensure the continuation of Modernist music even if—especially if—no one else much cared. If we discount the argument of historical necessity, how do we explain this moment to our students or even to audiences, who might give the music another chance under the right circumstances?

Several important factors come to mind. First, the world was still reeling from the shock of what had transpired during the war itself. Both the Nazis and the Soviets had harnessed the arts to their political programs, censoring whatever seemed not to accord with their purposes and appropriating anything that suited them as propaganda. One need only watch the film footage of Wilhelm Furtwängler conducting Beethoven's Ninth in front of Goebbels and other Nazi brass to witness how musical energies can be channeled to support and animate insidious agendas. To be sure, societies have sought to control music and the other arts from Plato's *Republic* to Louis XIV's absolutist monarchy. But the new media of sound recording, amplification, radio, and film raised the stakes immeasurably during World War II.

It is no great wonder, then, that serious artists reacted by writing music that refused the heated rhetoric that made so much of the traditional canon vulnerable to totalitarian abuses. They preferred to withdraw their work to a place where music would address the cool intellect rather than the emotions, which had proven all too easily swayed by propaganda machines. The nationalist fervor that had fueled so much art in the previous hundred years had also led to unspeakably inhumane atrocities. In the face of this unprecedented level of catastrophe, the very notion of conveying meanings seemed tantamount to manipulation. Better then to operate within the cerebral sphere of electronic experimentation or high degrees of abstraction or even chance. In retrospect, this ethical position appears not only understandable under the circumstances but laudable.

Second, the traditional centers for musical production—Vienna, Berlin, Paris, Moscow, Rome, London, New York—found themselves on fiercely opposing sides during the war, and modes of communication across that abyss had disintegrated. But there arose the hope that if music were cleansed of ideological trappings, then it could serve as a conduit for healing. One of the first international communities to emerge from the ashes of the war comprised composers who shared with each other the excitement of developing new musical procedures. For this reason many government agencies, including the US State Department, actively encouraged institutes for experimental music. And surely this climate of international cooperation, with sites such as Darmstadt and later IRCAM, represented genuine progress.[4]

Third, the unparalleled advances in technology during the war, capped by the dropping of atomic bombs on civilian populations, created an emphasis on the hard sciences. Institutions of higher learning—even sleepy liberal-arts colleges previously dedicated to the life of the mind—suddenly changed their priorities to focus on physics, mathematics, and engineering. Because faculties devoted to philosophy and poetry had no claim to economic productivity or technological advancement, they found themselves increasingly on the margins of the educational process. Federal funding poured into the development of computers, and the Cold War race to compete with

---

[4] See the heated debate between Richard Taruskin and Charles Rosen over the extent to which this support affected cultural production. Taruskin, "Afterword: *Nicht blutbefleckt?*," *Journal of Musicology*, Vol. 26, no. 2 (2009): 274–84; and Rosen's response, "Music and the Cold War," *New York Review of Books* (7 April 2011).

Sputnik or to put humans on the moon transformed even elementary-school curricula.

Music, of course, has always had a precarious perch within mainstream education, especially in the puritanical English-speaking world. Whereas most schools in North America boasted a band, a chorus, and perhaps even an orchestra, few offered courses beyond those in music appreciation designed to add a thin veneer of culture to the hordes of first-generation college students who showed up after the war, courtesy of the GI Bill. Some universities had a music historian on staff or someone who could teach basic musicianship, but these tended to be lightly trained amateurs; only with the wave of Jewish refugees from Central Europe did more rigorous versions of musicology and music theory take root in North America.[5]

Within the new postwar academy, we suddenly had composers such as Milton Babbitt, Vladimir Ussachevsky, and Otto Luening who were able to speak the language of laboratories, experimentation, and advanced technologies. They brought unprecedented prestige and outside funding to their departments, for they made their projects appear closer to the objective sciences than to the slipshod humanities. Of course, the question of whether to locate music with mathematics or with the rhetorically based arts goes back as far as Pythagoras. And after the war, for both pragmatic and philosophical reasons, composers opted for allegiances with the Quadrivium rather than the Trivium. A sympathetic reading of Babbitt's "Who Cares If You Listen" (which he himself had titled, much less aggressively, "The Composer as Specialist") reveals this argument quite clearly. Music was now to be one of the sciences, comprehensible—like the advanced physics of Babbitt's colleagues at Princeton, Albert Einstein or John von Neumann—principally to other experts.[6]

My last point concerns popular music. With the rapid development of sound recording and broadcast media, popular music had taken center stage in Western music history. The apparatus connected with (what do we call it?) classical music bears some of the responsibility for its own eclipse. Our museum-oriented enterprises, our symphony orchestras and opera houses,

---

[5] For an account of this transformation and its consequences, see Joseph Kerman, *Contemplating Music* (Cambridge, MA: Harvard University Press, 1985). See also David Josephson, "The German Musical Exile and the Course of American Musicology," *Current Musicology*, nos. 79/80 (2005): 9–53.

[6] Milton Babbitt, "Who Cares If You Listen?," *High Fidelity* (February 1958). For insight into Babbitt's intellectual context at Princeton, see Benjamín Labatut, *The MANIAC* (Penguin, 2023). See also Louis Menand, *The Free World: Art and Thought in the Cold War* (New York: Farrar, Straus & Giroux, 2021).

have continued to cater to nineteenth-century tastes. Historians have shown that this calcification of the repertory began to occur soon after Beethoven, with fewer and fewer composers added to the rosters as the decades passed.[7]

And it wasn't even that audiences learned how to listen to the content of the canon; many of them became familiar with the principal melodies and tuned out the rest. Performers themselves have restricted their function to executing the notes on the page as accurately as possible, inflecting them indiscriminately with what is termed "musicality," and most conservatory students still object vehemently to any discussion of musical values or interpretation. I hope that Julian Johnson's *Who Needs Classical Music?*, Larry Kramer's *Why Classical Music Still Matters*, my own *Reading Music*, and Greg Sandow's blogging campaign to salvage classical music can turn the situation around, but I fear it may be too late.[8]

Indeed, long before the war, Theodor Adorno had warned that easy-listening habits and automatic-pilot performances were inviting many cultivated Germans to lower their critical guard. As he explains, the music that might have accustomed his contemporaries to thinking seriously about moral tensions came to be perceived merely as elite entertainment or to be rejected altogether for the easier demands of a debased form of dance-hall jazz. This slippery slope, according to Adorno, led inexorably to the rise of the Nazis in Germany and, eventually, to the Holocaust.[9]

Adorno's jeremiads indicate that the battle for listeners had already been lost. After the war, people of my parents' generation were still encouraged at least to pretend to like classical music; they learned to attend symphony concerts if they aspired to professional careers. But by the time I started my undergraduate studies in the 1960s, many intellectuals were finding greater stimulation and even greater ethical fiber in the jazz of John Coltrane or the protest rock of Bob Dylan. The old browbeating methods that had shamed educated people into acquiring a modicum of music appreciation no longer had any effect.

---

[7] William Weber in particular has painstakingly traced the history of concert programming. See his *The Rise of Musical Classics: A Study in Canon, Ritual and Ideology* (New York: Oxford University Press, 1992).

[8] Julian Johnson, *Who Needs Classical Music? Cultural Choice and Musical Value* (New York: Oxford University Press, 2002); Lawrence Kramer, *Why Classical Music Still Matters* (Berkeley: University of California Press, 2007); McClary, *Reading Music*; Gregory Sandow, www.gregsandow.com/blog.

[9] Adorno elaborated these arguments throughout his career and in many places. See the compilation of some of his major pieces in *Essays on Music*, ed. Richard Leppert, trans. Susan H. Gillespie (Berkeley: University of California Press, 2002). For a pointed indictment of casual listening, see Adorno, *Introduction to the Sociology of Music* (1962), trans. E. B. Ashton (New York: Seabury, 1976).

Given the unbridgeable gap between "serious" music and the popular music that had long since become dominant, the valiant attempts by the postwar avant-garde to uphold and continue the development of an ever-more complex and uncompromising canon appear heroic. In statement after statement, Boulez, Babbitt, Roger Sessions, and many others posited as their goal nothing less than the survival of music *tout court*. The analogue is the Fall of Rome to the barbarians, when a handful of scholars like Boethius fought to hold onto a few remnants of their civilization's former glory. And who could blame them for that?

So here I am, relatively late in my own career, becoming something of an apologist for Modernism—or at least attempting to see matters from its defenders' point of view. I suppose this is something like the process that occurs to us all when we get old enough to view our parents not as tyrants of discipline but as vulnerable human beings who made the best choices they could, given their array of options. The postwar Modernists did not create the cultural circumstances in which they found themselves as they embarked on their careers, any more than people of my generation invented the Cold War or the Vietnam War, to which we have responded throughout our conscious lives. Given the resources, conditions, and aesthetic assumptions of the postwar era, what they accomplished was truly remarkable.

But many of those aesthetic assumptions and social priorities went unstated or, worse, were stated in ways that provoked more animosity—especially among musicians of my generation—than sympathy. In "Terminal Prestige" I called not for the silencing of Milton Babbitt's *Philomel* (which I greatly admire) but rather for a discussion of its meanings. The late music theorist David Lewin more than satisfied my challenge with his beautiful humanist account elucidating the relationships between Babbitt's thorny *modus operandi*, its allegorical significance, and the affective force of the piece performed so memorably by Bethany Beardslee.[10] In countless stimulating theory conversations that often lasted for hours, Michael Cherlin has labored since the 1980s to help me understand the positions held by Babbitt, one of his most-loved teachers.[11] And contact with Erling Guldbrandsen

---

[10] See his discussion of *Philomel* in his *Studies in Music with Text* (New York: Oxford University Press, 2006).

[11] See, for instance, Cherlin's attempt to trace Schoenberg's development from his tonal roots instead of back from serialism in his *Schoenberg's Musical Imagination* (Cambridge, UK: Cambridge University Press, 2007). His arguments depart quite radically from historical narratives that interpret Schoenberg's serialism as a necessary stage between late-Romantic tonality and the total serialism of the 1950s.

and his seminar students in Oslo, 2007–11, have engaged me in stimulating discussions of Boulez and Ligeti.[12] These conversations continue with my Israeli friends Assaf Shelleg and Yoav Sadeh.

So allow me to ask once again: Why was it so difficult for the composers of such works to speak eloquently about what they were doing? Why did they seek to deny cultural meanings, choosing instead to assert their agendas as the next necessary stage in the evolutionary trajectory of Western music? Why did formal complexity itself and the deliberate shunning of listeners seem like badges of honor?

I want to suggest that they had succumbed—like so many of their predecessors and like not a few of their Postmodernist successors—to the lure of the Sublime. A product of the new public sphere emerging in eighteenth-century England and, later, German-speaking domains, aesthetic theory posited a binary opposition between the Beautiful and the Sublime. The Beautiful emphasized pleasure, symmetry, and order, while the Sublime reached beyond such domesticated sensations to simulate the wild, untamable forces of nature and human interiority. In Goethe's *Sorrows of Young Werther*, for instance, the eponymous hero leaves Charlotte's genteel garden to brave the savage storm; a river that had previously provided the backdrop for their lovely outings now rages beyond its banks, uprooting trees and dragging everything along in its wake.

As long as music operated under the patronage and tastes of aristocratic courts, most of it aspired to the status of the Beautiful. But the postrevolutionary undercurrents that soon burst through that placid surface with the Gothic novel, the rantings of William Blake, and the horrific paintings of Goya all gave vent to other impulses. In his descriptions of this binarism, Kant identified the Beautiful with feminine qualities, the Sublime with the masculine. No longer would art cater to the merely pretty and congenial. It also would break out of those bounds and, like Prometheus, defy the very gods. In music, Beethoven stood as the hero who threw off the fetters of balanced formal procedures and inherited harmonic practices, thereby challenging the social contracts represented by convention. Many of his compositions feature the explicit dismissal of Beauty by the erupting Sublime: think, for example, of the move from the exquisite slow movement

---

[12] See Erling Guldbrandsen's interviews with Boulez in *Tempo*, 65, nos. 255–58 (2011); and Peter Edwards, "Tradition and the Endless Now: A Study of György Ligeti's *Le Grand Macabre*" (PhD dissertation, University of Oslo, 2012).

of the Ninth Symphony to the finale's cruelly dissonant opening, which shatters that carefully wrought island of bliss. We celebrate him for having had the courage to do so.

Beethoven's example set the tone for the artists of subsequent generations. Thereafter, any idea already in circulation would qualify as a domesticated element that had to be superseded. Over the course of the nineteenth century, composers shredded conventions as soon as they began to coalesce. They created extraordinary masterworks in doing so, but they also quickly exhausted the options available to them—at least the options that could still communicate with listeners. Any whiff of convention—in other words, the social contract that allowed listeners to follow the logic of the music they heard—had to be resisted. By the early twentieth century, only unrelieved dissonance would do.[13] Not a few pieces played out their transgressions with topics that featured violence against women: Strauss's *Salome*, Stravinsky's *Rite of Spring*, Berg's *Lulu*, and Hindemith's *Murderer, Hope of Women* come immediately to mind.

To be sure, some composers still aspired to the Beautiful. In the twentieth century, Sergei Rachmaninoff and Benjamin Britten continued to write gorgeous melodies much loved by listeners. But they received their reward in the form of audience popularity rather than within the institutional economy of prestige; they don't get to count among the Big Boys, for the chroniclers who traced the path of music history largely ignored or belittled them.[14] It was the Sublime or nothing at all.

When I first started writing about Postmodernist music in the 1980s, I believed that we might be witnessing a break away from the Modernist trajectory. Critiques of what Jean-François Lyotard called the Master Narrative and a swerve away from the ultracomplex machinations of postwar composers held out some hope for a different set of aesthetic priorities.[15] But art historian Maggie Nelson's *The Art of Cruelty* traces a lineage from Antonin Artaud that has valued greater and greater transgressions.[16] The fetishizing

---

[13] See McClary, *Conventional Wisdom: The Content of Musical Form* (Berkeley: University of California Press, 2000), chapter 4.

[14] See Christopher Chowrimootoo, *Middlebrow Modernism: Britten's Operas and the Great Divide* (Berkeley: University of California Press, 2018). For a historical analysis of this phenomenon, see Peter Franklin, *Reclaiming Late-Romantic Music: Singing Devils and Distant Sounds* (Berkeley: University of California Press, 2014). Franklin responds directly to Chowrimootoo in *Britten Experienced: Modernism, Musicology, and Sentiment* (London: Routledge: 2024).

[15] Jean-François Lyotard, *The Postmodern Condition: A Report on Knowledge*, trans. Brian Massumi (Minneapolis: University of Minnesota Press, 1984).

[16] Maggie Nelson, *The Art of Cruelty: A Reckoning* (New York: Norton, 2012).

of violence even escalated: recall the case of Chris Burden, who once had someone shoot a bullet into his arm as part of a performance-art piece.

Of course, performance art of this sort qualifies as Postmodernist; indeed, Lyotard himself wrote of a "Postmodern Sublime." And it is in such circumstances that aspects of Modernism become indistinguishable from those of its oedipal successors, which often felt the need to push the already distended envelope yet further in order to claim the right of ascendancy. What nineteenth-century French poets such as Rimbaud celebrated with the slogan "Épater la bourgeoisie" turned into the imperative to spit on just about everyone in the interest of a progress narrative that demands a scorched-earth treatment of all previous values. Nor is popular culture immune from this pattern, as escalating levels of violence and sexual transgression appear in films, music videos, internet sites, and computer games. The prestige of the Sublime reigns as soon as it makes an appearance within a new genre.

So what are the alternatives? A large part of the problem I have been describing goes back to those two eighteenth-century categories, one of which was always already fatally tainted by associations with the feminine. Aesthetician Alexander Nehemas tries to revitalize that category in his *Only a Promise of Happiness: The Place of Beauty in a World of Art*.[17] But the Beautiful has long since been demoted to the merely pretty, and few serious artists dare pitch their tents in that terrain for fear of ridicule.

There could and should be other categories, however. When I teach Berlioz, I always lament the fact that the Fathers of Aesthetic Theory failed to recognize the Hilarious among their types, thus condemning us to unrelieved earnestness in the arts. Occasionally a serious composer ventures over into hilarity—think of Stravinsky's *Renard*, for instance—but this option by and large got consigned to the trash heap. We may acknowledge the playfulness of Erik Satie or Virgil Thomson from time to time, but we refuse to locate those artists within our principal canons. Note that all the composers I have just mentioned operated within the orbit of French culture. Is it possible that C.P.E. Bach was the last hilarious German composer? How sad is that! And why did we all allow the Germans to set the rules?

Spirituality also makes appearances now and then in postwar music. It is no accident that our eighteenth-century philosophers avoided listing this among their categories, for they sought to establish secular alternatives to

---

[17] Alexander Nehemas, *Only a Promise of Happiness: The Place of Beauty in a World of Art* (Princeton, NJ: Princeton University Press, 2010).

systems based on Christian precepts. Among the religious masterworks written by twentieth-century composers ordinarily associated with the Modernist Sublime are Stravinsky's *Symphony of Psalms* and Schoenberg's *Moses und Aron*.

In the postwar era, Olivier Messiaen stands out as an artist whose experiments all revolved around his deep commitment to Roman Catholicism. A father figure for Boulez and Stockhausen, as well as Saariaho and Benjamin, he fashioned a musical language grounded not on defiance but on his love of birdsong, his interest in non-Western musical procedures, and his mystical contemplation of the Divine. Because of this grounding, his music has continually reached out to include listeners and to move them. Think of the extraordinary scene in his *Saint Francis of Assisi* in which the saint heals the leper by kissing him, gradually leading us back into blissful triadic harmonies for the end of the opera's first act. The so-called Holy Minimalists who emerged from the collapse of the Soviet bloc also participated fully in the aesthetic category of the Spiritual. In the United States, Steve Reich has returned to his Jewish heritage for sustenance; in the UK, John Tavener, Jonathan Harvey, and James MacMillan have turned unapologetically to spiritual themes. A few musicologists, for instance Marcel Cobussen, have begun to theorize the relationships between music and spirituality.[18]

At a more basic level, we have the long-dismissed category of Pleasure, which eighteenth-century Germans resisted in part because of its strong associations with the absolutist French court. Pleasure never has disappeared from music, of course. Whenever artists begin to pursue the Sublime, whether in classical or popular culture, many music lovers just turn to ballads, dance music, and other forms of entertainment. Historian Andreas Huyssen has shown how such activities came to be linked in the nineteenth century not only with the feminine but also with the lower classes and despised races, with austere Modernism set up as a bulwark against cultural contamination.[19] But popular taste often ignores arguments based on cultural hierarchies. Recall how poor Don José in Bizet's *Carmen* tries to carry the banner of serious music in the face of the much catchier habaneras, seguidillas, and toreador songs of the indigenous population. Even after José

---

[18] Marcel Cobussen, *Thresholds: Rethinking Spirituality through Music* (Aldershot: Ashgate, 2010).
[19] Andreas Huyssen, "Mass Culture as Woman: Modernism's Other," in his *After the Great Divide: Modernism, Mass Culture, Postmodernism* (Bloomington: Indiana University Press, 1987): 44–63.

resorts to Sublime violence to stifle the sounds of those Others, we leave the opera house humming Carmen's tunes.[20]

In the twentieth century, the songs of Irving Berlin, Cole Porter, and George Gershwin celebrated a version of urban Modernity with which Ivory Tower composers could scarcely compete. Cerebral bebop and cool jazz got displaced by R&B, rock, and soul. When rock musicians decided to experiment with strange meters in the name of progress, many people just switched to disco, which still invited its listeners to dance.[21] An old cliché opposes the Sublime and the Ridiculous. But maybe the Sublime itself, with its self-importance, exudes more of the Ridiculous than we like to admit.

Perhaps more than anything else, we have forgotten that we are in the business of what my late friend Christopher Small termed "musicking."[22] Chris moved after the war from New Zealand, where he had composed scores for ballets and other full-length works, to study formally in London. But faced with the choice between serialism and teaching in a high school, Chris opted for the latter. Within that context he wrote the books that have transformed musicology, music education, ethnomusicology, and music criticism.[23] Although he preferred playing Mozart and listening to Sibelius, he became so disgusted with the narrow perspectives of many of his professional colleagues that he set about finding a way of putting the activity of music-making back in the center of attention. Instead of fetishizing works, he argued, we should be observing how and why human beings engage in producing and sharing meaningful sounds. And in a world so fraught with anxieties and dangers, we surely cannot afford to sneer at pleasure, as if "our" music were self-evidently morally superior. We all require music in our lives, perhaps for purposes of survival itself. Otherwise, why would human societies have persisted in investing their limited energies in this enterprise?

It is for such reasons that I cannot bring myself to regret the arguments in "Terminal Prestige" concerning popular music. With the advent of sound

---

[20] See my *Georges Bizet: Carmen* (Cambridge, UK: Cambridge University Press, 1992).

[21] Elijah Wald, *How the Beatles Destroyed Rock and Roll: An Alternative History of American Popular Music* (Oxford, UK: Oxford University Press, 2009).

[22] Christopher Small, *Musicking: The Meanings of Performing and Listening* (Middletown, CT: Wesleyan University Press, 1998).

[23] Before he wrote *Musicking*, Small had published *Music, Society, Education* (London: John Calder, 1977; 2nd ed., Middletown, CT: Wesleyan University Press, 1998) and *Music of the Common Tongue: Survival and Celebration in African-American Music* (London: John Calder, 1987; 2nd ed., Middletown, CT: Wesleyan University Press, 1998), both of which deal insightfully—critically yet with evident love—with the canon and twentieth-century Modernism. He even published a monograph on Schoenberg (London: John Calder, 1978).

recording, the history of Western music became a radically different story from the one still too often presented in our textbooks and curricula. For all the undeniable brilliance of Richard Taruskin's *Oxford History of Western Music*, it stumbles when it reaches the twentieth century.[24] Not even most composers today, many of whom channel pop musics in their own work, would restrict "Western music" to the continuation of the Schoenberg legacy.

In any case, Postmodernism supplanted postwar Modernism beginning perhaps as early as 1957 with Bernstein's *West Side Story* and continuing in the 1960s with Berio's *Sinfonia* and George Crumb's *Ancient Voices of Children*. Minimalists such as Philip Glass and Steve Reich moved as far away from abstract Modernism as they could, in explicit defiance of the Modernists' stern prohibition against repetition. We're now in a phase some call Post-minimalist, though the prefix "post-" in all these labels points more to rejection of what came before than to new directions. Indeed, the concept of "Modernity" itself announces that process of radically splitting off from the past. We seem destined to live in an infinite series of "posts."

Consequently, it may seem strange, after so many episodes of eradicating connections with tradition, to inquire into the long-term cultural contribution of Modernism. Did the postwar generation leave a legacy besides that of reaction? Or, better, does anyone—other than the odd serialist still rattling around inside an academic department—now choose to claim that legacy? And how is that legacy understood?

I want to close by dealing briefly with three contemporary artists who draw heavily from the Modernist tradition yet have attracted a relatively large and enthusiastic following. Finnish composer Kaija Saariaho picks up the spectral harmony and electronic sound sources associated with IRCAM and the sonorities associated with Messiaen. I am interested in Saariaho in part because she emerged as perhaps the the most successful women composing in the twenty-first century but even more because I find her music ravishing. Until her death in 2023, she was also by far the best-known Nordic composer on the international stage.

Saariaho often chose female characters and points of view in her operas: think, for instance, of *L'Amour de loin*, *Adriana Mater*, *La Passion de Simone*, *Émilie*, and (most recently) *Innocence*. But she went far beyond simply marking her subject matter as woman-oriented; she also developed a

---

[24] Richard Taruskin, *The Oxford History of Western Music*, 6 vols. (Oxford, UK: Oxford University Press, 2005). See my review-essay in *Music and Letters*, vol. 87, no. 3 (2006): 408–15.

musical vocabulary designed to simulate a very different quality of desire by means of what I call smoldering intensities: a dense fabric of low drones and spectral harmonies, extended trills, and static ostinatos disrupted occasionally by violent eruptions or rushes of passion. Before she went to Darmstadt and IRCAM, Saariaho studied composition in Helsinki along with Esa-Pekka Salonen (former conductor of the Los Angeles Philharmonic) as a fellow student, and that connection no doubt gave her greater access to concert programming and recording than may have been feasible otherwise. But it is surely her music's lush, sensual version of Modernism that attracts and holds listeners.

Although Saariaho occasionally made use of sounds familiar to traditional audiences, her music operates outside the sphere of tonal practice. The open fifths that resonate with her troubadour, Jaufré Rudel, in *L'Amour de loin* serve to anchor his *chansons* in the Middle Ages, but his own utterances refuse the comfort of triadic convention. Yet the opera communicates powerfully with audiences through its gestures, its brilliant orchestration, and its ability to produce moods. For all that Saariaho chooses her pitches through spectral devices, she explicitly refuses to write what she calls "paper music": music designed for cerebral analysis. It is no coincidence that she came to operatic composition through the urging of Peter Sellars—the longtime collaborator with John Adams—and the model of Messiaen's *Saint François d'Assise*, which Sellars staged. He also staged the extraordinary first production of *L'Amour de loin*.[25]

My second composer, George Benjamin, similarly descends from Messiaen, with whom he studied. Benjamin's *Written on Skin* took the opera world by storm. Simultaneously austere and opulent, this work shares with *L'Amour de loin* a story taken from the troubadour tradition, in this case the tale of the eaten heart. And like Saariaho, Benjamin makes his music immediately comprehensible through his deployment of gesture and mood. The menacing quality of The Man, the repressed sexuality of The Woman, the uncanny quality of The Boy, who doubles as an angel: all of these seize listeners and pull them inexorably toward the opera's grisly end.[26]

---

[25] Kaija Saariaho, *L'Amour de loin* (2000), libretto by Armin Maalouf, DVD of Sellars production (Deutsche Grammophon, 2005), with Gerald Finley and Dawn Upshaw, cond. Esa-Pekka Salonen; CD cond. Kent Nagano (Harmonia Mundi, 2009), with Daniel Belcer and Ekaterina Lekhina. See the chapter on Saariaho in my *The Passions of Peter Sellars: Staging the Music* (Ann Arbor: University of Michigan Press, 2019); see also chapter 18 of this volume, "Kaija Saariaho, Mater."

[26] George Benjamin, *Written on Skin* (2012), libretto by Martin Crimp, DVD with Barbara Hannigan and Bejun Mehta, cond. Benjamin (Opus Arte, 2013). Available on mediciTV.

It bears mention that both *L'Amour de loin* and *Written on Skin* eschew the usual male/female dichotomy by featuring an important intermediate figure: Saariaho's Pilgrim, who is given no gender in the libretto, and Benjamin's The Boy, sung by a countertenor. A mere twenty years ago, countertenors still sounded repellent to many audiences. But we have witnessed a boom in recent years, thanks to the historical-performance movement and the development of virtuoso singers dedicated to falsetto singing. If Benjamin Britten made use of this voice to convey the queerness of Oberon in *Midsummer Night's Dream* and Philip Glass to signal a kind of deformity in *Akhnaten*, countertenors now allow for a more complex array of gender types.[27]

Salvatore Sciarrino drew his inspiration for *Luci mie traditrici* from Carlo Gesualdo's murder of his wife and her lover, but he takes his source music from a highly chromatic Renaissance chanson by Claude Le Jeune rather than from Gesualdo. The chanson runs through the opera, presented first as just a tune and later—as the drama becomes more fraught—in distortions that render it all but unrecognizable. Sciarrino has his characters whisper menacingly at each other, as if reluctant to sing at all. Whenever they begin to give a word full voice, they soon distort it to a raspy hiss or else break off as if a hand had been clamped down over the mouth. In the context of the extended-performance-techniques movement, these sounds are right at home. But to move them onto the operatic stage is quite another matter. Yet Sciarrino's deft control of temporality and mood make this work a gripping experience.[28]

In an article on the resurgence of Richard Strauss, *New York Times* critic Anthony Tommasini quipped: "The polemical era when brainy uptown composers battled downtown exponents of postmodernism is, thankfully, past."[29] Indeed, no one pays much attention any longer to the preponderance or absence of triads in scores. What matters now is musical and dramatic effectiveness. Thus, although I have been tracing composers who would identify themselves with a kind of Modernity, I might well also have considered works by Thomas Adès or John Adams, who may at one time have seemed aligned with the swerve away from Modernism but who freely engage as well

---

[27] For a fuller discussion of this issue, see "Soprano Masculinities," chapter 16 in this volume.
[28] Salvatore Sciarrino, *Luci mie traditrici* (1998); DVD with Nina Tarandek and Christian Miedl, cond. Marco Angius (EuroArts, 2011).
[29] Anthony Tommasini, "Drifting Back to the Real World," *New York Times* (8 June 2014).

with devices and sonorities from the postwar era. For all these composers, the whole world of sound is their oyster.

Adolescents often feel the need to break violently with their fathers and mothers; recall not only the Postmodernists lashing out against their postwar predecessors but also Boulez's savage "Schoenberg est mort" pronouncement. Yet close affinities sometimes emerge between grandparents and grandchildren, helping to knit ruptured families back together into some semblance of continuity. My young composition students these days are avid fans of Boulez, Ligeti, and Feldman. They don't care about the old arguments concerning the survival of music and the necessity of toeing the Modernist line; they simply love the compositions for their own sakes, for the ways they put sounds together. And they mine them for ideas, as composers have done forever. For the return of this particular prodigal daughter to the fold, I owe a particular debt of gratitude to my former student Ethan Braun, who has continued to correspond with me concerning these issues even after both of us moved on to other institutions.

In the public realm, composers such as Saariaho, Benjamin, and Sciarrino have done a great deal to guarantee the Modernist legacy by taking up elements from postwar composition and fashioning pieces that communicate powerfully with large audiences. No one studying their music can avoid reflecting upon the works of those who developed so many of the materials with which they operate. As their operas send us back to Messiaen, Ligeti, or Boulez, they invite us to hear the postwar Modernists again with new ears. Our post-Postmodern Modernists thereby remind us of the aesthetic richness in the music of their forebears, especially the emotional qualities they tried by and large to deny but that now glow unapologetically in their music.

7

Playing the Identity Card

Of Grieg, Indians, and Women[1]

The English have the expression "bringing coals to Newcastle," which means offering something as a gift to the people who are themselves renowned for that very item. Nothing could express better my sense of inadequacy as I appeared at a conference celebrating Edvard Grieg, hosted in his hometown. Most of the musicologists who specialize in the life and works of Grieg—those who have the linguistic and cultural expertise required for such study—already lived there. I could not imagine myself saying anything about Grieg that most of them did not already know far better than I. But the conveners of this symposium were surely aware of this when they invited me to participate, for they titled their event *Music and Identity* in part so as to make the occasion truly international and not an in-house discussion among Norwegian musicians and scholars. So there we were in Bergen to commemorate the centennial of Greig's death in 1907. And however unworthy I may have been to discuss his legacy with all those specialists, I hoped to contribute at least some insights into the aesthetic and political dilemmas he confronted so very brilliantly over the course of his career.

I first encountered Grieg's music as the result of a very different response to the issue of identity. My father, Dan McClary, determined that he would raise his daughter in such a way as to shield her from any knowledge of her Native American ancestry. With the assistance offered by the US government to World War II veterans, he managed to acquire an advanced degree and become a professor of microbiology in a northern state, where our straight black hair would not automatically provoke the racism he had suffered as a child. He chose music as his principal strategy for mainstreaming me; in the

---

[1] Delivered as keynote for *Music and Identity: Symposium for 100th-Year Commemoration of the Death of Edvard Grieg* (Bergen, Norway, September 2007). Published in *19th-Century Music* 31, no. 3 (2008): 217–27.

1940s, he had loved the popular songs based on music by classical composers, and in graduate school he tracked down the originals on recordings, which he played for me night and day as I lay in my crib.

Among the crossover hits from classical music at that time were the tunes cobbled together from Grieg's melodies for the Broadway musical *Song of Norway*.[2] Suffice it to say that my father liked this show well enough that he bought not only the soundtrack (which I still own) but also the Piano Concerto and the *Peer Gynt Suite*. As the result of his efforts, I became a pianist and then a musicologist, with classical music as my only musical vernacular. Indeed, he so inculcated me with his cultural project that I could only bring myself to listen to any kind of popular music after he died in 1984, when I was nearly 40.

It was only shortly before his death that my father told me for the first time that we were of Cherokee descent. He had to repeat his statement at least twice before I could register what he was saying. By then I was a tenured musicology professor specializing in the music of Italian Renaissance courts. My father's legacy of Grieg concertos, Mozart operas, and Beethoven symphonies had shaped my identity, leaving no trace whatsoever of the culture associated with my genetic heritage. In fact, my sole impression of the music of what turned out to be "my people" was restricted to the thumping tom-toms and shrill whoops in Hollywood westerns.

As American universities began to push for ethnic diversity, however, many individuals discovered that they had some Indian blood, which made them eligible for special scholarships and gave them certain privileges when they applied for jobs. Occasionally someone will discern my ethnic background and persuade me to lend my support to a center for Native American studies. But given my absolute ignorance of Indian customs, I have never done much more than to try to help out minority students or junior faculty struggling to make their way in an alien environment; I have never been able to bring myself to play the identity card.

Or, at least, not that particular one. For I was not invited to Bergen to speak on matters concerning identity arbitrarily, though I doubt that the conveners had any inkling of my Indian ancestry. My claim to fame, of course, involves not race but gender. If my father could succeed in mainstreaming my musical tastes, he could not very well disguise the fact that I was a girl, no matter how

---

[2] *Song of Norway*, music adaptation by Robert Wright and George Forrest; book by Milton Lazarus (1944).

much he instilled in me professional ambitions more appropriate to males. When I went off to graduate school, I tried desperately to downplay the fact that I was a woman—much as my father had tried to pass as white or Grieg to pass as a native proponent of German music. But in Leipzig, Grieg's fellow students treated him as a diminutive exotic, and at Harvard, I was, for all my efforts, just a small female whom the departmental custodian nicknamed "Squaw."

And here we come to the crux of the matter. Racism, sexism, and other prejudices are with us always, even unto the ends of the earth. Yet some individuals—at particular times and circumstances—decide to respond not by attempting just to fit in but by embracing and inventing an identity around the very element regarded by others as a defect. In the 1940s, my father would not have succeeded if he had flaunted his Cherokee blood; fifty years later, his grandchildren might have expected university scholarships if they had done so.

Grieg happened to be developing his musical voice at the very moment when cultural identity was the focus of attention among Norwegian intellectuals. Nothing less than national autonomy was at stake, and some of Grieg's closest associates participated passionately in the debate over the forging of a standard language for Norway. Writers such as Ibsen drew on regional folklore, and collectors went searching out the songs and dances of rural people.

In his youth, Grieg was relatively innocent of firsthand acquaintance with Norwegian indigenous music. His own training had allowed him to absorb as his own the Germanic style then (and still) dominant in concert music, and he continued to pride himself throughout his career on the cosmopolitan dimensions of his work. Yet he gradually became convinced of the importance of marking some of his music as specifically Norwegian. And he had to do considerable homework in order to undertake this project: he consulted ethnographic collections, visited regional folk festivals, and even commissioned colleagues to make transcriptions he could use for his settings. Nowhere does Grieg claim an essentialist connection to these folk-songs and dances; indeed, his letters and essays make clear the labor that went into his invention of his Norwegian-inflected idiom. He sought to bridge between the international style and community, on the one hand, and Norwegian national-identity formation, on the other, and he never stopped contesting critics who wanted to deny him his claims either to cosmopolitanism or to Norwegian musical culture.

But playing the identity card—however carefully theorized—comes with a price tag. If marking his music as specifically Norwegian put Grieg on the map as a distinctive musical voice, it also had the effect of pigeonholing him. As Grieg knew, the nationalist trick had worked magically once: the early German Romanticists had trafficked in folklore in constructing their own style, which separated them from the Italian and French idioms that had long dominated European music. But the Germans somehow managed to persuade the international community of the universality of their own nationalist project and then defined all other nationalist agendas as parochial. Consequently, the mainstream happily consumed Grieg's folk-based music as they might collect postcards from exotic sites and minimized the significance of his unmarked music; the same community also seems to have determined that one Norwegian in the collection sufficed, making other composers from this country superfluous for purposes of the canonic repertory. Meanwhile, on the home front, Grieg had to battle chauvinists who wanted to restrict Norwegian musicking to Norwegians alone, as when he found his invitation to the Concertgebouw Orchestra blocked. More recently, some ethnographers have taken him to task for his exploitation and distortion of authentic folk materials. The most Norwegian of composers became by turns too Norwegian and not Norwegian enough.

I would like to make a brief comparison between Grieg's experience with identity politics and my own. Like Grieg, I received my training in the mainstream and had no intention of deviating from that. As a woman and the daughter of Depression-era Okies, I felt quite privileged to be admitted into the hallowed halls of a major university. I was far too busy studying abstract music theory to participate in marches for women's rights or in consciousness-raising groups; I aspired to be a genderless intellectual. But in the 1970s and '80s, the women's movement gave rise to an explosion of feminist theory: an explosion that radically transformed most disciplines in the humanities and social sciences. The most significant work produced in North American universities during this period involved examining the ways gender and sexuality informed artistic expression, social arrangements, and even language itself.

I was operating, in other words, within a larger academic culture when I started to pose questions concerning gender and sexuality in music. I had come to identify my work as feminist with considerable reluctance at first: as a graduate student I would have been shocked to learn that I would eventually move in this direction. But when feminist criticism became the leading intellectual current in other disciplines, I started trying to bring together the musicological mainstream and interdisciplinary work focused on gender.

As I wrote in 1991 in *Feminine Endings*, however, musicology was managing to pass from pre- to post-feminism without feminism itself having left much of a trace. What now qualified as a mainstream in other disciplines came to be identified in musicological debates largely with . . . me. Some colleagues have accused me of essentialism, of producing work—however painstakingly theorized—that flows directly from my chromosomes, and they have largely failed to notice the fact that I mostly write on topics related only tangentially to gender. And, on the other hand, some female musicologists have taken my insistence on continuing my work as a music analyst as evidence of a basic lack of commitment to sisterhood. Pigeonholed as just a woman on the one hand, pilloried as not sufficiently feminist on the other: what's a girl to do? But I would scarcely have been speaking at the Grieg symposium or lecturing in Oslo the next week if I had not played this card. Nor, perhaps, would most people outside of Norway have heard of Grieg if he had not chosen to make some of his music deliberately identified with his homeland.

Grieg was extremely sensitive to the ethical complexities involved in his use of folk materials, and he tried to acknowledge his sources (unlike Stravinsky, for instance, who claimed to have used no folk materials in his *Sacre du printemps*).[3] To be sure, Grieg did—as did most of his contemporaries—romanticize the purity and "spiritual vitality" of the Norwegian folk. As he wrote:

> Anyone who has a feeling for these sounds will be entranced by their great originality, their juxtaposition of fine and delicate graceful beauty and bold power and untamed wildness, melodically and especially rhythmically. They bear the stamp of an imagination that is as audacious as it is bizarre—relics from a time when Norwegian peasant culture was isolated in remote mountain valleys from the outside world and precisely for that reason have preserved their authenticity.[4]

---

[3] For a thorough treatment of Stravinsky's use of folk materials in this score, see Richard Taruskin, *Stravinsky and the Russian Traditions: A Biography of the Works through Mavra* (Berkeley: University of California Press, 1996).

[4] Grieg, preface to original edition of *Slåtter* (C. F. Peters, 1903); as translated in Finn Benestad and Dag Schjelderup-Ebbe, *Edvard Grieg: The Man and the Artist*, trans. William Halverson and Leland B. Sateren (University of Nebraska Press, 1988): 370–71.

But he also wrestled explicitly in his writing with the relationships between the music he drew on and his own creations. When first studying the transcriptions of Hardanger fiddle tunes he had requested from his colleague Johan Halvorsen, he confessed: "At present it is a sin for me to adapt the tunes for piano. But sooner or later I will commit this sin. It is too tempting."[5]

Despite the fact that Grieg terms his decision to set these folk materials "a sin," he also saw his mission as translating the folk ballads of his native land into idioms accessible to the broader, international cultural community. As he put it: "The music of each nation proceeds in the course of time from the folk song through the small forms and then into the larger, richer, more complex forms."[6] He also recognized the value of occupying a position in the margins of European culture: "the representatives of the small countries have an inestimable advantage vis-à-vis those of the large countries in that we, the former, who have to know everything, acquire a wider horizon than those who get stuck in the middle of their own one-sided [i.e., German] culture."[7] In his view, the rest of the world needed the clean astringency of Norwegian sounds: "The Norwegian artists still have the capacity to deliver naive, healthy, straightforward art if only it is formed out of the national temperament and not out of the foreign one. And now even the music of the Germans has strayed so far afield from the healthy nature [of their art] that their modern interpreters deliver an utter caricature of their own masters."[8] And Norwegian musicians needed the recognition that could come only from a mediator like Grieg, who could speak both languages.

Without question, Grieg's was a project of translation. Anyone seeking genuine Norwegian folk music here will meet with disappointment. But he never pretended to be doing anything different from translation in his folk-music settings. A more productive question than that of authenticity involves the nature of his translations: what elements from each side—the folk and the German mainstream—did he select for intersection?

I want to spend the remainder of this essay considering "Røtnams-Knut" from Grieg's Op. 72, Slåtter: the collection composed from Halvorsen's transcriptions—the pieces that resulted from that irresistible temptation to commit the sin of translating Hardanger-fiddle tunes onto the piano. There

---

[5] Grieg in a letter to Johan Halvorsen, 6 December 1901. Translated in liner notes to recording of Slåtter by Einar Steen-Nøkleberg, piano, and Knut Buen, Hardanger fiddle (Pro Music, 1988).
[6] Grieg in his eulogy for Halfdan Kjerulf, in Edvard Grieg: Diaries, Articles, Speeches, ed. and trans. Finn Benestad and William H. Halverson (Columbus, OH: Peer Gynt Press, 2001), 219.
[7] Grieg, diary entry, 17 February 1906, in Edvard Grieg: Diaries, Articles, Speeches, 111–12.
[8] Grieg, diary entry, 20 January 1907, in Edvard Grieg: Diaries, Articles, Speeches, 162.

exist several recordings that juxtapose Grieg's piano settings with fiddlers playing the tunes in a traditional manner. I will not get into the controversy concerning authenticity here, but the recording of "Røtnams-Knut" by Knut Buen gives some impression of what Grieg might have heard at folk festivals and what Halvorsen might have been listening to when he produced his transcriptions.[9]

In Buen's recording, one first hears an insistent turn figure holding discordantly over the drone characteristic of the Hardanger fiddle; then, a varied version of the turn proceeds down toward a cadence; later, the opening figure appears down an octave, creating a different set of clashes against the drone. The materials are highly repetitious, and they might seem quite resonant with the minimalist or hip-hop idioms of more recent years. Indeed, a hyper-athletic performance by the Snuff Grinders at the Norwegian Extreme Sports Week in June 2007 merged the fiddle, aggressive rhythms, and leaping gestures of the *halling* with the percussive moves of African American breakdancing.[10]

Grieg focused in his writing on issues of pitch. Testifying to Halvorsen that he was particularly fascinated by what mainstream music theorists would hear as a raised fourth scale degree, he mused (again, like a somewhat naughty anthropologist) that:

> It was this "strangeness" which you seek by using G-sharp in D major, that drove me crazy in 1871. I naturally stole it immediately and used it in my "Scenes from Rural Life." This sound is something for the explorer. This augmented fourth can also be heard in the peasant's song. It is the ghost from one or another old scale. But which one?[11]

Most musicologists associate this "strange" interval with Lydian, the old church mode based on F. But in fact, the Lydian scale with the high fourth degree almost never occurred in medieval plainsong or in Renaissance polyphony: it was always "corrected" down in practice, producing the common major scale.[12]

---

[9] Grieg, *Slåtter*, Einar Steen-Nøkleberg, piano, and Knut Buen, Hardanger fiddle.
[10] See the video at http://vids.myspace.com/index.cfm?fuseaction = vids.individual&videoid = 16559417
[11] Letter to Halvorsen, 6 December 1901 (see n. 3).
[12] See my *Modal Subjectivities: Self-Fashioning in the Italian Madrigal* (Berkeley: University of California Press, 2004). Beethoven experimented with Lydian in the "Heiliger Dankgesang" movement of the A-minor Quartet, but he exploited principally the mode's characteristic inability to produce a dominant-seventh rather than the raised fourth degree in his melodies.

I am suggesting, in other words, that Grieg was quite right not to leap at the obvious solution of labeling these pieces as "Lydian." If many of them seem to conform to the textbook definition of Lydian, they happen to fill an otherwise nearly empty category: unalloyed Lydian of this sort is rarely found in the captivity of the Western canon, and the Hardanger fiddlers Grieg heard certainly had no intention of channeling a mode theorized centuries before by medieval monks. If it is "the ghost from one or another old scale," it is an indigenous one. And it posed a fascinating challenge to Grieg's thoroughly German training: in his words, it drove him crazy when he first heard it.

Like anyone trained in Leipzig, Grieg regarded harmony as the basis of music. In the eighteenth century, Rameau had famously argued that fundamental harmonies generate melodies, and Grieg approached his task from this vantage point. As he wrote:

> The realm of harmony has always been my dream-world, and the relations between my sense of harmony and Norwegian folk music has always been an enigma to me. I have found that the obscure depth in our folk melodies has its foundation in their undreamt-of harmonic possibilities. In my arrangements... I have tried to give expression to my sense of the hidden harmonies in our folk tunes. I have been rather especially fascinated by the chromatic lines in the harmonic texture.[13]

This statement expresses particularly well what seems to me to be at stake in Grieg's setting of "Røtnams-Knut," for as he makes his way through the transcription supplied by Halvorsen, he tries out as many of these "hidden" and "undreamt-of harmonic possibilities" as he can muster. In contrast to his earlier approach to folk-song settings, in which he sought to accommodate the tunes to the exigencies of standard harmonic syntax, in the *Slåtter* and other later pieces Grieg moves back and forth—sometimes dressing up indigenous melodies with chord changes familiar to continental audiences, sometimes allowing the peculiarities of the original materials to suggest sounds far outside the bounds of common practice. He listens carefully and tries to let the tunes lead the way. He wrote: "one doesn't know whether they

---

[13] Letter to Henry Theophilus Finck, 17 July 1900, in *Edvard Grieg: Letters to Colleagues and Friends*, ed. and trans. Finn Benestad and William H. Halverson (Columbus, OH: Peer Gynt Press, 2000), 229.

Example 7.1a Edvard Grieg, "Røtnams-Knut" (*Slåtter,* no 7), mm. 1–12

were conceived in major or minor. Some of them are incredibly beautiful. In any case, I have set some hair-raising chord combinations on paper."[14]

Grieg opens his setting of "Røtnams-Knut" with his most hair-raising combination, with the raised fourth degree superimposed over the drone a major seventh below. For the first strain, neither side relents: Grieg gives us this astringent dissonance in highly concentrated form for several measures. It is more astringent, in fact, than the fiddle performance we just heard, in part because of the percussiveness of the piano and in part because Grieg wanted to produce an in-your-face clash. As his section unfolds, however, the left hand begins to move as if in search of a way out of this apparent impasse: a middle voice stalls by reproducing the raised fourth, leaving it to the bass to perform a turn that resolves decisively onto the tonic (see Example 7.1a).

These maneuvers point to a central dilemma for our translator: Grieg's musical language was profoundly teleological, whereas the music he sought to adapt (like most dance music) fostered a temporality focused on the body in the present moment. As Daniel Grimley has argued so persuasively, Grieg wrestles with this conflict in temporal states as he assigns his harmonies, usually resolving in the direction of the goal-orientation his classical training regarded as a basic criterion for excellence.[15] Or, as we might say today, he had to make the music "go somewhere." I have discussed the ways in which this dilemma plays out in various repertoires: in French baroque dances,

---

[14] Letter to Julius Röntgen, 22 August 1896, in *Edvard Grieg: The Man and the Artist*, 335.
[15] Daniel M. Grimley, *Grieg: Music, Landscape and Norwegian Identity* (Woodbridge, UK: Boydell, 2006), chapter 4.

Example 7.1b Grieg, "Røtnams-Knut," mm. 12–18

in Bizet's *Carmen*, in rap and minimalism, in music by women.[16] But although Grieg almost always resorts to teleological game plans in the end, just as Mahler and Debussy usually end their pieces on triads, he does sustain these moments of dissonant hovering much longer than many of his contemporaries found tolerable. A mere ten years later, Stravinsky and Bartók would allow their peasant materials to kick the props out from under goal-oriented temporalities. They might not have done so quite so easily, however, if Grieg had not already pointed the way.

For his second section (mm. 12–18), Grieg takes the already cadence-directed material from the transcription and gives it a more or less tonal harmonic setting, even concluding the strain with a hilarious circle of fifths (see Example 7.1b).

Next he chooses to interpret the melodic fragment as if it were in F-sharp minor (mm. 21–24), thus affording a contrasting island of calm before he revs up for a dramatic return. As the bass spins its wheels on the ever-present turn figure (mm. 30–33), the right hand tries to spring up—rather like a young man attempting to kick the hat off a stick in a *halling* (see Example 7.1c). Only when the right hand concedes to assume the raised fourth degree once again does it succeed in launching back to the boisterous opening tune

---

[16] See, for instance, my "Temporality and Ideology: Qualities of Motion in Seventeenth-Century French Music," chapter 9 in my *Desire and Pleasure in Seventeenth-Century Music* (Berkeley: University of California Press, 2012); *Georges Bizet: Carmen* (Cambridge, UK: Cambridge University Press, 1992); "Rap, Minimalism, and Structures of Time in Late Twentieth-Century Culture," in *Audio Culture: Readings in Modern Music*, ed. Christoph Cox and Daniel Warner (New York: Continuum/The Wire, 2004), 289–98; *Feminine Endings: Music, Gender, and Sexuality* (Minneapolis: University of Minnesota Press, 1991).

Example 7.1c Grieg, "Røtnams-Knut," mm. 19–24

Example 7.1d Grieg, "Røtnams-Knut," mm. 30–34

(m. 34), with the left hand now performing athletic dissonant leaps on the offbeats. If this leads back to the cadential materials with a normalized fourth degree securely in place, it sounds almost like a joke—albeit a satisfying one—after the unapologetic rowdiness that precedes it (see Example 7.1d).

In contrast to most of the *Slåtter*, "Røtnams-Knut" features a middle section in the minor. Formally this seems quite familiar: ABA pieces often hinge on major/minor contrasts. Recall, however, that Grieg delighted in his inability to peg certain folk tunes as either major or minor, and in this section he puts the original materials through a new series of transformations. First, he exoticizes the turn figure by marking it with the augmented second characteristic of music from the Middle East, an association he knew perfectly well when he wrote "Anitra's Dance" for *Peer Gynt* (see Example 7.1e). Next, he harmonizes the cadence-oriented part of the original with heavy Romantic suspensions and the full, overblown sonority of the piano we might associate with Rachmaninoff (see Example 7.1f).

But when the smoke clears, he offers another contrasting island of calm, this time as a pure Lydian hymn (see Example 7.1g). Jazz theorist George Russell has argued that the Lydian mode eliminates the domineering dominant-seventh chord that compels tonal music always to declare allegiance to its tonic, and he inspired a generation of bebop musicians to improvise modal fragments over implicit pedals instead of maintaining the jazz standards that maintained what he regarded as the oppressive ideological

Example 7.1e Grieg, "Røtnams-Knut," mm. 53–57

Example 7.1f Grieg, "Røtnams-Knut," mm. 73–81

temporality of European culture.[17] In this short passage, Grieg sets his little turn figure in a way that avoids both tonal reference and also the wild dissonance of the principal setting. As George Russell might have put it, see how nice life can be when you forgo the dominant-seventh? This passage leads back inevitably, perhaps reluctantly, to the materials that opened the middle section, which in turn give way to the A section: we have here a structure of nested symmetries, making the piece very easy to grasp on the formal level.

Grieg's predilection for small forms has received much criticism. In a world in which size matters, in which the ability to compose extended, complex symphonic movements demonstrated one's prowess, Grieg has often been relegated to the demeaning category of the "little master": a category that carries pejorative implications related to both masculinity and ethnicity. This means that Grieg frequently receives a condescending pat on the head

---

[17] George Russell, *Lydian Chromatic Concept of Tonal Organization* (New York: Concept, 1953).

Example 7.1g Grieg, "Røtnams-Knut," mm. 87–94

and the reduction of his nationalist endeavors to the merely cute.[18] Hubert Foss wrote, for instance: "[N]ever touched in his manhood by the *kolossal*, Grieg was determined, content, to be a small master: his deliberate smallness is one of his greatest virtues."[19] Even when Grieg takes on the powerful rhythms and dissonances of the Norsemen and simulates the aggressive kinetic moves of the *halling*, to some he still seems to lack the phallus of formal authority wielded by his German mentors.

Literary theorist Henry Louis Gates, Jr., and Nobel laureate Toni Morrison have eloquently addressed the ways in which such criteria continually marginalize subaltern voices. Gates argues that Black writers and musicians deliberately hold to preestablished forms in order to maximize communication and the cementing of community, concentrating their efforts instead on what he calls "signifyin(g)" on shared cultural themes. Morrison explains that her novels sometimes opt for magic-realist conclusions rather than the tragedy demanded by critics because she and her readers need to be able to imagine a better world, even if only in fiction.[20]

I want to propose that Grieg's penchant for small conventional forms counts as part of his nationalist—or perhaps better, his *postcolonial*—strategy. Gayatri Spivak altered her writing style when she discovered that the South Asian women whom she wished to represent could not decipher what she was trying to say. Self-conscious language games and deliberate structural obfuscation can seem powerful for intellectuals persuaded that modes of

---

[18] He is often simply ignored, as if interchangeable with Dvořák or as if he contributed nothing important to the repertory. In his recent six-volume *Oxford History of Western Music*, Richard Taruskin mentions Grieg a mere once—and that only to compare his use of folk materials with Gershwin's use of jazz in *Rhapsody in Blue!*

[19] Hubert Foss, "The Orchestral Music," in Gerald Abraham, ed., *Grieg: A Symposium* (London: Lindsey Drummond, 1948), 16. Quoted in Grimley, *Grieg: Music, Landscape and Norwegian Identity*: 4, note 7.

[20] Henry Louis Gates, Jr., *The Signifying Monkey: A Theory of African-American Literary Criticism* (Oxford, UK: Oxford University Press, 1988). Toni Morrison, *Playing in the Dark: Whiteness and the Literary Imagination* (Cambridge, MA: Harvard University Press, 1992).

expression have become too implicated in dominant authority. But this was never Grieg's subject position. If he had composed in ways that appeared obscure to the mainstream, he would have been taken as incompetent and never would have achieved the acclaim that allowed his music to circulate internationally. Instead, he threaded a path between gestures that made evident his knowledge of "the way music is supposed to go" and gestures that pushed the envelope in the direction of Norwegian identity.

In the *Slåtter*, written at the end of his career, Grieg intensified this process of hybridization nearly to the breaking point. To the bourgeois Norwegians most likely to attend recitals or to perform his music in their homes, these peasant dances apparently seemed too raw, too closely allied to a dimension of Norway they could not or did not want to recognize as themselves. The continental mainstream, on the other hand, had long since stockpiled all the domesticated lyric pieces and folk arrangements they thought they needed.

If he had lived another decade, Grieg would have witnessed the rise of a Modernism that would embrace precisely the "primitivist" elements that make the *Slåtter* still sound so startling. But those same Modernists were likely to have condemned those aspects of a piece like "Røtnams-Knut" that reached out for comprehension by the mainstream. And, of course, an even later generation would accuse him—a composer attempting to speak as a postcolonial subject of Danish, Swedish, and German domination—of himself having colonized rural traditions in delivering these dances up for consumption by European audiences. But Grieg, like the rest of us, could only operate within the historical context in which he found himself, and his ability to perform in both his prose and his music as what Gramsci calls an organic intellectual beggars the efforts of many better-known artists and cultural theorists.

Earlier I referred to my own Cherokee ancestry. It turns out that Grieg served as a model for a cluster of American composers who produced and published song arrangements of Native American tunes.[21] There was little market for these, however, perhaps because advocates such as Arthur Farwell did not have the translation skills Grieg had acquired through his Leipzig training and also because of the greater problems with race in the United

---

[21] Henry Theophilus Finck, "An interesting application of Grieg's method to the tunes of the North American Indians may be found in some of the songs of the talented American composer Harvey Worthington Loomis." *Edvard Grieg* (1905; repr., Uxbridge, UK: Cambridge Scholars Press, 2002): 131, note 19. See the various entries on Arthur Farwell and the Wa-Wan Press on Google for more information concerning this venture.

States: recall the cold response Dvořák received when he recommended that American composers draw on African American and Native American musics (see chapter 8). When Charles Ives and Virgil Thomson—both painfully aware of their colonial status with respect to the world of serious music—attempted to invent an identifiably American music, they drew exclusively on white Protestant sources.[22] For better or worse, Native American music was left to ethnographers and to Hollywood, which invented those thumping tom-toms and shrill whoops for its fantasies concerning the Wild West.

At least Grieg did not have to contend directly with the issue of racial difference when he decided to channel the music of his folk traditions. Still, in writing music marked with regional characteristics, he risked exoticizing himself—marking himself as an Other in a world in which questions concerning Difference were becoming quite lethal. Later on, the very bad finale of German nationalism in National Socialism made every bid for identity seem like another potential fascism. Indeed, when I "came out" as a woman in musicology, some critics linked even that version of identity politics back to the Nazis.

And yet. A fastidious refusal to raise the issue of Difference leaves the mainstream unchallenged, its hegemony unquestioned. It seems to me that the voices of those marginalized on the basis of ethnicity, nationality, gender, or sexuality can only increase the sum total of human expression and mutual comprehension. Although he had to struggle not to be pigeonholed for his efforts in hybridization, Grieg clearly enriched us all when he played the identity card.

---

[22] On Ives, see Lawrence Kramer, "Cultural Politics and Musical Form? The Case of Charles Ives," in his *Classical Music and Postmodern Knowledge* (Berkeley: University of California Press, 1995), chapter 7.

8
The Object/the Objective of Analysis
The Case of Florence Price[1]

In addition to all the other traumas of 2020 (the COVID pandemic, protests over police violence, political division), the usually insular discipline of music theory entered a phase of unprecedented and widely publicized upheaval. To those who spend most of their classroom time warning of parallel fifths, training students' ears to recognize intervals, or navigating the complexities of post-tonal styles, Philip Ewell's "Music Theory's White Racial Frame" may seem to have come out of the blue.[2] How could anyone perceive those innocuous enterprises as reinforcing an agenda most of us would claim to abhor? The ensuing debate has pitted students, professors, and even university administrators against one another. I can think of only one other occasion in which music studies experienced such turmoil, and I'm afraid I was the center of that episode.

Ewell's argument, as well as the racial strife sparked by the murder of George Floyd in summer 2020, has challenged all of us to reexamine the premises of our courses and research projects. Most academic societies, including the Society for Music Theory, have issued policy statements encouraging diversity, and music departments now spend a good deal of time in strategizing for curricular changes and recruitment of future students and faculty slots. As someone who principally teaches music history, I have a relatively easy time dealing with inclusion: I can begin by acknowledging the debt we owe to North Africa and Moorish Spain for our musical instruments,

---

[1] Delivered in my capacity of Distinguished Lecturer 2020–21, University of Michigan Department of Music Theory in March 2021.

[2] See Philip Ewell, "Music Theory and White Racial Framing," presented at the 2019 meeting of the Society for Music Theory, published in *Music Theory Online*, vol. 26, no. 2 (September 2020). The responses appeared—without peer review or an invitation to Ewell to respond—in *Journal of Schenkerian Studies*, vol. 12 (2019). I will leave to the reader to locate the dozens of reactions in the mainstream media.

As evidence of the discipline of music theory taking up Ewell's challenges, I would point to a special 2024 issue of the *Journal for Music Theory*, for which Richard Cohn solicited and edited a series of responses to Jason Yust's essay "Tonality and Racism." Ewell and I are among the respondents.

the New World procedures that gave us the *ciaccona* and sarabande—as well as the fact that, after the advent of sound recording, African American genres became the mainstream of music worldwide.

But my colleagues who teach music theory in conservatories or schools of music face a much greater problem. Their curriculum has long focused on the European canon that most of their students strive to present on the concert stage, and the analytical models developed to account for this repertory are, by definition, Eurocentric—indeed, appropriate mostly for musics from Bach to Brahms, with some extended techniques added for more experimental styles.

Before proceeding, I want to point out that Ewell was scarcely the first musician to declare the premises of standard European procedures politically repressive. George Russell, author of *The Lydian Chromatic Concept of Tonal Organization,* cited the imperative for the tritone in the dominant-seventh to contract onto the tonic as deeply coercive, and he advocated that jazz musicians adopt modal configurations for liberation from its strictures.[3] Closer to home, none other than Arnold Schoenberg indicted tonality in his *Harmonielehre* in these heavily politicized words:

> Of course the idea of closing with the same tone one began with has something decidedly right about it and also gives a certain impression of being natural. Since indeed all the simple relationships derive from the simplest natural aspects of the tone (from its first overtones), the fundamental tone then has a certain sovereignty over the structures emanating from it just because the most important components of these structures are, so to speak, its satraps, its advocates, since they derive from its splendor: Napoleon, who installs his relatives and friends on the European thrones. I think that would indeed be enough to explain why one is justified in obeying the will of the fundamental tone: gratefulness to the progenitor and dependence on him. He is Alpha and Omega. That is morally right, so long as no other moral code obtains....
>
> Thus it can also be imagined how the chance occurrence of a dissonant passing tone, once established by the notation, after its excitement had been experienced, called forth the desire for less accidental, less arbitrary repetition; how the desire to experience this excitement more often led to taking possession of the methods that brought it about. But, should the

---

[3] George Russell, *The Lydian Chromatic Concept of Tonal Organization* (New York: Concept, 1953).

excitement of the forbidden lead to uninhibited indulgence, that essentially despicable compromise between morality and immoderate desire had to be drawn.... Dissonance was accepted, but the door through which it was admitted was bolted whenever excess threatened.[4]

Schoenberg went on to imagine "a fluctuating, unending harmony, a harmony that does not always carry with it certificate of domicile and passport carefully indicating country of origin and destination" (129). Recognizing that he and other ethnic minorities counted as dissonances in an increasingly anti-Semitic Europe, he heard in tonality the logic of racial genocide— one of the reasons he chose to jump ship. That collision of "morality and immoderate desire," resolved only by the demise of the source of that excitation, also accounts for all those prima donnas whose dead bodies still litter the opera stage.

We rarely talk about such issues when we introduce students to tonal voice leading or explain to them why early-twentieth-century composers departed from age-old practices. Within our progress-oriented narrative, we have learned to regard serialism as the necessary next step in the evolution of our musical language. (Recall the convoluted arguments we have pursued with the goal of naturalizing that very bizarre eventuality!)[5] One way of addressing Ewell's challenge is to grasp the cultural contingency of our theoretical methods—not only Schenker's but also Schoenberg's, Rameau's, Glarean's, Guido's, and Plato's.[6]

I have spent all of my professional career trying to lay bare the underlying ideological assumptions of standard tonality, not because I despise the canon but because the apparent airtightness of its theoretical arguments allows for virtually nothing else—not even the music produced before Corelli. I certainly did not mean to upset the applecart when I decided to take the works of Monteverdi seriously. Isn't he a canonic composer, after all?

But no, not really, as it turns out. Isn't he still confused about when to use leading tones? In order to analyze Monteverdi or Cipriano on something like their own terms, I decided I had to bracket my tonal impulses and teach myself to listen in an entirely different way.[7] Their sense of coherence

---

[4] Arnold Schoenberg, *Harmonielehre* (1911); translated by Roy E. Carter as *Theory of Harmony* (Berkeley: University of California Press, 1983), 128–29.
[5] See chapter 6 in this volume.
[6] See chapter 2 in this volume.
[7] See McClary, *Modal Subjectivities: Self-Fashioning in the Italian Madrigal* (Berkeley: University of California Press, 2004). See also the introduction and chapter 1 in this volume.

differs radically from the one that consolidated around 1700. But once I learned to live within that alien terrain, I found a treasure trove of fascinating questions: If the advent of tonality was not inevitable, then why and how did it develop over the course of the seventeenth century? Why those procedures instead of the myriad alternatives explored by superb composers such as Girolamo Frescobaldi or Giacomo Carissimi or Louis Couperin? In refusing to treat tonality as a foregone conclusion, I also pointed to its consolidation as a fascinating area for theoretical and historical inquiry. Tonality itself becomes a much richer phenomenon when we trace its cultural development.[8]

But the fact that we don't extend the courtesy of full inclusion even to our own European forebears indicates profound parochialism. The problem deepens when we try to consider the musics of Others. We might try to address this issue by adding compositions by Clara Schumann or Joseph Bologne, the Chevalier de Saint-Georges, to our anthologies for analysis classes. Yet because Schumann and Bologne composed within familiar idioms, their music may serve to reinforce the procedures we already know without really changing the conversation. Do we include other voices if and only if they abide by the conventions we too often hold as universal?[9]

A more radical approach would begin the theory curriculum with a course that deals with a range of procedures—Arabic *maqams*, South Asian ragas—within which European ones could appear as cultural choices rather than just the way God meant music to go. We would greatly enhance our approach to fundamentals by backing up and allowing for a much wider range of how human societies arrange rhythms, pitches, formal procedures, and aesthetic priorities.

Yet we still face the problem of teaching the analysis of European concert music in ways that do not reinforce (however unwittingly) white-supremacist assumptions. I fervently believe in the need to instill analytical skills in students; I developed a course titled Analysis for Historians, required of all musicology graduate students at CWRU—a course that has

---

[8] See McClary, *Power and Desire in Seventeenth-Century Music* (Berkeley: University of California Press, 2012).
[9] See Christopher Jenkins, *Assimilation v. Integration in Music Education* (Routledge, 2023). Jenkins is Associate Dean for Academic Support at Oberlin College; recently completed simultaneously a DMA in viola from the Cleveland Institute of Music and a PhD in musicology at Case Western Reserve University. See also his "Signifyin(g) within African American Classical Music: Linking Gates, Hip-Hop, and Perkinson," *Journal of Aesthetics and Art Criticism* (January 2020). In 2024 Jenkins and Philip Ewell launched a new journal, *Black Music, In Theory*.

included units on the *Eroica*, a keyboard suite by Élisabeth Jacquet de la Guerre, Josquin's *Miserere mei Deus, Swan Lake, Tristan und Isolde, Quartet for the End of Time*, Robert Johnson's and Cream's recordings of "Crossroad Blues," *Bluebeard's Castle*, Toru Takemitsu's *November Steps*, Monteverdi's "Ah, dolente partita," a responsory by Hildegard von Bingen, the soundtrack to *The Power of the Dog*, Kendrick Lamar's Pulitzer Prize-winning album, *Damn*. At the beginning of each unit, I remind students that they must always start by considering the OBJECT of analysis and the OBJECTIVE of analysis. In other words, what is this thing, and what do we want to know about it?

It takes a while to dislodge the one-size-fits-all approach to analysis my students bring with them from their undergraduate theory programs. The *Eroica* does, in fact, submit to traditional methods of tracking themes, forms, harmonies, and modulatory schemas, and even to Schenkerian modeling, though this undeniably rich cultural artifact also raises discussions concerning sonority, rhythm, temporalities, the channeling of violence, the legacy of French military bands, and much more. Tap almost any moment in this score and ask a question. It may well lead you outside the symphony itself and into the thickets of cultural reference or the ideological assumptions that undergird Beethoven's compositional choices. But then it should lead you back into the piece and allow you to hear it in new ways. (I never dwell long outside the music, which is always my focus: my version of what acquired the label New Musicology aimed mainly to find ways of connecting the music itself with historical context. Theorists have been more willing to help me bridge this gap than historians who still shy away from the dreaded "music itself.")

Besides the *Eroica*, nothing else on the syllabus for this course even begins to yield to traditional analytical methods. Jacquet de la Guerre requires that we acquire notions of temporality quite foreign to those we bring to Bach; *Swan Lake* demands some grasp of choreographic conventions; Monteverdi forces a reckoning with modal organization (don't get me started on how difficult it is to disabuse students of the notion that Dorian pieces have to have consistent B-naturals!); Kendrick Lamar insists that we develop a radically different skill set. The procrustean bed of tonal premises proves not only ineffective but even counterproductive for all of these. I still want students to focus on the music rather than simply on lyrics—though the latter are crucial for grasping strategies. But the very concept of "music" shifts as we move from unit to unit, and so do parameters for analysis.

We don't have to look hard to find a repertory for which we ought to ask, "What is this thing?" even if it has long stood in the very center of our teaching of fundamentals: the Bach chorale. Although we often use these to teach students about tonal harmony, they are, in fact, very odd hybrids: Bach took old modal tunes he had inherited and labored to demonstrate their compatibility with modern procedures, hoping to maintain his Lutheran faith in the midst of a secular revolution.[10] This was not an easy fit: witness the convolutions required to convince us that Phrygian configurations like those in "O Sacred Head" qualify as tonal. Tremendously interesting endeavors, but paradigms of tonal process they ain't. I doubt that many instructors of beginning harmony inform their students how bizarre these little artifacts really are. Moreover, such training actually proves antithetical to the realization of basso continuo, as keyboardists come to believe they have to clomp along, granting every note in the left hand a four-voiced chord. C.P.E. Bach warned that the vertical orientation of Rameau's theories would lead musicians to ignore the melodic integrity of the bass line, and to his great credit, Schenker returned to C.P.E. Bach for his own formulations. In neglecting to ask of a Bach chorale "What is this thing?" we miss out on the fascinating answers that can come of asking "What do we want to know about it?"; it also potentially damages our very goal for immersing students in this repertory. To study how Bach wielded tonality, we would be better served to turn to nearly anything else he wrote—or, better yet, to Handel.

We analyze music for many different reasons. In the undergraduate classroom, we teach students how to recognize and manipulate basic grammatical norms, to parse structures, and to gain familiarity with the jargon musicians have developed for referring to sonic events. At a more advanced level, young composers study scores to pick up strategies for their own future use; performers ponder details in order to shape more effective renditions; musicologists derive materials for understanding a composition's relationships to cultural context; critics ground their interpretations in what they hear and see; theorists bounce their hypotheses off real pieces to test the viability of their abstractions. But when analysis becomes the means for measuring aesthetic worth, as it does quite explicitly in Schenker, then we run into trouble.

---

[10] Compare this project with that of Grieg, as discussed in chapter 7, or to the hybridization apparent in Florence Price, discussed later in this chapter.

Many of us have added pieces by Black composers to our syllabi as a result of recent events. But inclusion alone does not suffice. We have to take these additions seriously, which means dealing with the music itself to the same degree we afford the pieces long ensconced in the canon—a task made much easier if we have already dealt with representatives of the standard repertory as cultural entities that similarly braid together inherited procedures and historical contexts, that need to be interrogated with respect to content as well as form.[11]

As a musicologist, I have long included units on blues, jazz, rock, soul, funk, and hip-hop on my syllabus. Beginning in 1986, when I first received the assignment to teach the twentieth-century segment of the music-history sequence, my courses have dealt with such African American genres almost as much as with those with European pedigrees. But such choices risk perpetuating a sort of apartheid. For there are, of course, myriad Black composers of concert music whose works also made invaluable contributions to highfalutin Western culture, however we want to define the opposite of "popular." And that means examining these too-often-neglected repertories as well.

As a scholar who passes for white, I have to take care to not speak for composers of color, heedlessly imposing my own vantage points on musics for which we do not yet have shared methods. One of Phil Ewell's critics enjoined him to teach the rest of us how to analyze these repertories,[12] and every theorist and musicologist of color I know is busy responding to that challenge. I anticipate a radical paradigm shift in the discipline as a result of this important agenda.[13] But meanwhile, I had to figure out how to present such works in my music-history survey.

---

[11] See Philip Ewell, "Erasing Colorasure in American Music Theory, and Confronting Demons From Our Past," https://musictheoryswhiteracialframe.wordpress.com. (10 March 2021). See also his *On Music Theory, and Making Music More Welcoming to Everyone* (Ann Arbor: University of Michigan Press, 2023).
[12] David Beach, "Schenker—Racism—Context," *Journal of Schenkerian Studies*, vol. 12: 128: "My suggestion to Philip Ewell is that he stop complaining about us white guys and publish some sophisticated analytical graphs of works by black composers. I, for one, would welcome into the analytical canon works by both black and women composers." Sorry not to include any graphs in my discussion of Florence Price, but we also need other kinds of analysis as well.
[13] Christopher Jenkins has already moved forward with the project I recommend here. See his "'Everything but the Heartbreak': Recognizing Coleridge-Taylor Perkinson," Ph.D. dissertation, Case Western Reserve University, 2024. Jenkins assisted me in courses, and I served as co-advisor for the dissertation. I am happy to acknowledge that he, Ewell, and others are quickly rendering this chapter a bit obsolete.

When I first considered a topic for my talk at Michigan in 2021, I planned to spend time dealing with Julius Eastman, whose music I find astonishing. But I have little to add at present to the flood of analyses that have appeared since his work was rediscovered only a few years ago. A member of the avant-garde, with colleagues such as Morton Feldman and a prize-winning performer with Peter Maxwell Davies and Meredith Monk, Eastman quickly caught the attention of theorists who heard in his newly available pieces a degree of social engagement and intellectual complexity often absent from the process music of the 1970s and '80s. I would direct you to a superb article by Ellie Hisama and an entire book of detailed readings edited by Renée Levine Packer and Mary Jane Leach, the woman credited with rescuing the scores we now treasure.[14] I often tell my students in history survey that the canon can be transformed, and I point to the attention now lavished on Eastman as an extraordinary example of such recovery. The fact that he highlighted his Black and queer identities in his titles and in his music means that we will be wrestling with his legacy for the foreseeable future. I will leave for now the question of how even music of this caliber almost disappeared. Recall that anti-Semitism tried and nearly succeeded in erasing Gustav Mahler from music history.

I want to spend the rest of this essay with another Black composer—one who has some name recognition but who has received insufficient analytical attention. In 2020 I included Florence Price's 1935 String Quartet No. 2 for my unit titled "America in Concert Music" (along with Ives and Copland), after I heard a gorgeous performance of the second movement online, played by the ensemble Castle of Our Skins, a group committed to performing the music of marginalized composers.[15]

A bit of background. While he was in the United States at the National Conservatory of Music, Antonín Dvořák became familiar with African American idioms (still often called "slave songs") through a Black scholarship student at the NCM, composer and performer Harry T. Burleigh; Burleigh supplemented his stipend by working as a part-time handyman at the NCM. Under Burleigh's influence, Dvořák famously proclaimed that this music should become the basis of North American concert music, and he led

---

[14] *Gay Guerrilla: Julius Eastman and His Music*, ed. Renée Levine Packer and Mary Jane Leach (Rochester: University of Rochester Press, 2015); Ellie Hisama, "'Diving into the Earth': The Musical Worlds of Julius Eastman," in *Rethinking Difference in Music Scholarship*, ed. Olivia Bloechl, Melanie Lowe, and Jeffrey Kallberg (Cambridge, UK: Cambridge University Press, 2015), 260–86.
[15] Gabriela Diaz and Mina Lavcheva, violins; Ashleigh Gordon, viola; Seth Parker Woods, cello.

the way with his *New World Symphony*. Douglas Shadle has demonstrated that America already had several of its own composers of symphonies who had incorporated such references into their scores.[16] Yet that fortuitous encounter with Burleigh made Dvořák's work the emblem of indigenous concert music. For different reasons but with similar results, George Gershwin channeled Black idioms into his songs, orchestral works, and his opera, *Porgy and Bess*.

But the hybrids of Dvořák and Gershwin, though rightly celebrated, sucked up all the oxygen in the room. My students dismiss William Grant Still as just sounding like Gershwin. And in response to a performance of William Dawson's *Negro Folk Symphony* in 1934, one critic wrote: "the influence of Dvořák is strong almost to the point of quotation, and when all is said and done, the Bohemian composer's symphony stands as the best symphony 'à la Négre' written to date." In other words, been there, done that—no need for any more music that draws on spirituals. Grasping the colonialist dimension of Dvořák's project, Dawson replied: "Dvořák used Negro idioms. That is my language. It is the language of my ancestors, and my misfortune is that I was not born when that great writer came to America in search of material."[17]

It was in this cultural environment that Florence Price composed her works.[18] For a composer of classical music of any ethnicity, Price had an enviable career: education at the New England Conservatory and University of Chicago, a premiere by the Chicago Symphony and a prestigious Rodman Wanamaker Prize for her Symphony No. 1, friendships with Langston Hughes and Marian Anderson.[19] Not too shabby for a woman who had to

---

[16] See Douglas Shadle, *Orchestrating the Nation: The Nineteenth-Century American Symphonic Enterprise* (Oxford, UK: Oxford University Press, 2015), and *Dvořák's New World Symphony* (Oxford, UK: Oxford University Press, 2021).

[17] As quoted in Shadle, "Let's Make the Future That the 'New World' Symphony Predicted," *New York Times* (March 17, 2021). Compare these dilemmas with Grieg's project (chapter 7). Spanish composers faced the same problem after Bizet's *Carmen* established what "Spain" sounds like. Bizet did not even consult the equivalent of Burleigh; he invented his "Spanish" idiom from Afro-Cuban cabaret songs and other sources that had little connection with Spain. See my *Georges Bizet: Carmen* (Cambridge, UK: Cambridge University Press, 1992).

[18] For more detail on Price's life, see Rae Linda Brown, *The Heart of a Woman: The Life and Music of Florence B. Price* (Urbana: University of Illinois Press, 2020). Brown was Price's most stalwart advocate. Her book was issued posthumously.

[19] Samantha Ege has examined the network of women who supported Price in Chicago and who helped to create the conditions for this premiere. See her *South Side Impresarios: How Race Women Transformed Chicago's Classical Music Scene* (Urbana: University of Illinois Press, 2024). Composer Margaret Bonds also benefited from this network. A virtuoso pianist, Ege has recorded much of Price's piano music. Listen, for instance, to her *Fantasie Nègre: The Piano Music of Florence Price* (Lorelt, 2021).

flee from Arkansas when the Ku Klux Klan explicitly targeted her daughter. Yet her work (like Eastman's) nearly disappeared; some of it was discovered by accident only in 2009 in a rundown house in St. Anne, Illinois.[20]

At first hearing, Price's music may recall that of Dvořák, with its spiritual-infused melodies. But to write her off as a Dvořák wannabe would be like accepting *Huckleberry Finn* as representative of Black literature, rejecting the novels of Zora Neale Hurston as somehow less innovative.[21] Like Hurston, Price locates her voice not in a nostalgic past but in the dynamic intersection between that past and twentieth-century modernity—the same intersection Daphne Brooks discerns in the technological advances in sound recording and the rural traditions brought north by the blues queens during the Great Migration.[22] W. E. B. Du Bois called the effect of this intersection of cultures on Black individuals "double consciousness":

> this sense of always looking at one's self through the eyes of others, of measuring one's soul by the tape of a world that looks on in amused contempt and pity. One ever feels his twoness,—an American, a Negro; two souls, two thoughts, two unreconciled strivings; two warring ideals in one dark body, whose dogged strength alone keeps it from being torn asunder.[23]

Listen to the very opening of Price's second string quartet, for instance, with its edgy, mechanical figure and colliding lines suddenly giving way to a blues tune before returning to the maelstrom of expressionist dissonances.[24] Price thereby reveals her knowledge of and skill at composing concert music of her own moment while also inserting an explicitly Black identity into the scenario. The tension between African American and European idioms, between traditional and modernist proclivities, will mark this quartet, as they did Price's life, the aesthetics of the Harlem Renaissance, and, indeed, the

---

[20] Christine Jobson has recorded many of the songs found in this cache on *Nearly Lost: Art Songs by Florence Price* (CD Baby, 2019).

[21] Percival Everett has taken on the challenge of retelling Huckleberry Finn's adventures through the voice of Jim. In his novel, the Black characters speak standard English when by themselves, though they have to switch to dialect for self-protection when whites are around; the white characters still speak as Twain presents them. See his *James* (New York: Doubleday, 2024).

[22] Daphne Brooks, *Liner Notes for the Revolution: The Intellectual Life of Black Feminist Sound* (Cambridge, MA: Harvard University Press, 2021).

[23] W. E. B. Du Bois, "The Strivings of the Negro People," *The Atlantic* (August, 1897).

[24] Price, String Quartet no. 2, Movement 1: https://www.youtube.com/watch?v = 5dReunYXQz 8&t = 20 1s

artworks of every genre developed by Black Americans up to the present moment.

But it was the second movement of this piece that I first fell in love with. Price aligns the melodies in her Andante Cantabile with the pentatonic collections and hymn-like harmonies characteristic of spirituals, and we might hear her writing as transparent and simple. Yet some unusual strategies appear even in her opening gambit. First, the second violin initiates a two-note ostinato that wavers between E and F-sharp, producing a kind of slow moan in the background. And this moan continues without alteration even as Price moves from the principal key of A major to A minor, then from E major to E minor, turning repeatedly from potential hope to sorrow (see Example 8.1).[25,26]

Price foreshadows this problem in m. 9 when the melody's uplifting C-sharp (scale degrees 1-2-3) is met not with the A-major chord she leads us to expect but with C-sharp minor: a startling harmonization that halts the action and opens out onto a gap. The moans persist through the duration of the ensuing silence, marking time until the next phrase initiates a lament in A minor on an emphatic C-natural. (Price's pentatonic melody here, especially with its rhythmic figure, may recall the line "Tell old Pharaoh" in the iconic spiritual "Let My People Go.") Yet throughout that passage of A-minor lamentation, the ostinato persists with its F-sharp, adding a kind of astringency to what might otherwise signal unmitigated grief. At m. 25, a bright arrival on E major appears, as if to assuage the grief of the previous strain. But when a new melody appears in m. 29, it returns to E minor; the comfort forecast by the arrival in m. 25 vanishes.

The opening section operates, in other words, within an uneasy modal terrain in which the various elements prevent any real stability. The old major/minor dichotomy of Schubert and Mahler certainly functions here, but Price deploys it in ways that allow her to stake out her own narrative as each glimmer of hope in turn collapses. If she cadences in m. 43 on E, she reaches that destination ambiguously and remains locked in E minor. A bit of closing material (m. 45) restores the G-sharp of the E major, though it quickly falters, giving way to the fatalistic G-natural. In her closing gambit, she situates that problematic G-natural within a

---

[25] Price, String Quartet no. 2, Movement 2: https://www.youtube.com/watch?v = Opp4YlUmyfA
[26] Used by permission of G. Schirmer.

146 MAKING SENSE OF MUSIC

Example 8.1 Florence Price, String Quartet No. 2, II, mm. 1-52

Example 8.1 Continued

sunny C-major context; it is as though the strategies of repetition and reharmonizing might produce a different outcome. Alas, the section ends in m. 52 in a decisive E minor.

A middle section in E major brings some relief. While maintaining aspects of the spiritual (especially the cadential figures), the melodies now reach upward, and the moaning ostinato disappears. Romantic composers taught us to hear such interludes as memories of past happiness, and so it seems here. Yet in her interlude, Price continually breaks off as if uncertain how to sustain this fantasy, leaving arpeggios hanging, then descending twice through the mournful augmented second to Phrygian cadences that bottom out through F-natural onto a desolate E (mm. 75 and 76).

But a final arpeggio rising from the viola through the two violins concludes with a trill on a high E, preparing the way for one of two reprises (m. 78). The first presents the opening materials again, but with a shimmering, halo effect replacing the ostinato. As before, the melody traces its path from A major through the shocking pause on C-sharp minor. When Price arrives at the moment when she ought to return to A minor, however, she signals that she will not again go gentle into that place of lamentation. Instead, she throws down an agitated diminished sonority over the cello's open fifths of A and E. Fragments of the theme we had expected get tossed around the ensemble, ending in another truncated arpeggio.

A second reprise begins at m. 99, introduced by the ostinato. Now the violin plays its hymn an octave higher, doubled by the cello—a voicing detail that creates a sense of mutual support by two vulnerable individuals, in contrast with the more communal texture of the opening. This iteration goes through the same sequence of events we have now heard twice, complete with the enigmatic C-sharp-minor chord in m. 111. But in a coda, Price finally grounds that C-sharp with an A-major triad (mm. 133–34), and in mm. 140–42 she allows the melodic ascent (1-2-3, in A major) its longed-for resting place. The ending extends hope, though it does so by embracing C-sharp, that same pitch that has so often swerved into minor. A fragile, tentative hope, indeed.

I first listened to this movement shortly after the murder of George Floyd, and it seemed to me that radio stations ought to have been playing it on repeat. It bears witness to the unending cycle of tragedy and violence through which Price and so many others have had to persevere, often with little more than spirituals to sustain them. Her work brings to mind Christopher Small's book *Music of the Common Tongue: Survival and Celebration in African American Music*, which traces the crucial role music has played during the horrors of the diaspora.[27] Price goes on in this quartet to present a juba dance, conveying the joyous African-based rhythms that have ignited all our popular-music genres of the last hundred years. But this Andante Cantabile will not let me go.

So, what is my objective in analyzing this movement? That would vary with context. In keeping with my usual agenda, I want to know what cultural work it does, how it brings to the ear the tensions experienced by individuals like Price during the Great Migration, how it articulates in the medium of a string quartet Du Bois's double consciousness. Hence my references to Zora Neale Hurston and other luminaries of the Harlem Renaissance and Harry Burleigh's powerful influence on Dvořák.

But I am also interested in how Price's compositional strategies make such a deep impression on me as she draws on both African American and European resources. I would not under any circumstance use standard analysis as a device for assessment of basic aesthetic worth, for Price deliberately bends rules of common expectations; that is how she produces her effects, and it is also, for that matter, how composers have *always* produced their effects.

I might also consider in discussion the intersection of race and gender in Price's work. That she had to struggle against misogyny as well as racism has been amply documented by her biographer, Rae Linda Brown. I have focused for now on racial identity, but this does not preclude any number of other readings.

I should not have to add that Price does not include materials that recall spirituals because of some essence, as if she couldn't help herself. A few years ago, a musicologist asked if I thought Prince knew what he was doing when he put his songs together, as if all those thousands of brilliant songs just got secreted out of some special gland Black musicians are endowed with. So, no: she could have written any way she liked, as her myriad compositions demonstrate. She could have composed something like Ruth Crawford's ultramodernist String Quartet. But she chose to mark much of her work with Black idioms, just as Nobel laureate Toni Morrison chose to write about the experiences of Black women.

In class discussion, I might ask why Price composes this movement with two reprises. Doing so allows her to display her exquisite use of her

---

[27] Christopher Small, *Music of the Common Tongue: Survival and Celebration in African American Music* (London: John Calder, 1987; rev. ed., Middletown, CT: Wesleyan University Press, 2012).

instruments through the very different affects she simulates with each iteration, and sonorities ought to matter to analysis. But her double reprises also operate on the level of musical narrative: if the first breaks off inconclusively in gestures of refusal, the second suggests a provisional "magic realism" ending of the sort Toni Morrison sometimes used when she wanted to convey a hope not of this world, or that Reverend King signaled in his "I Have a Dream" speech.

I could add as well that similar equivocal moments of closure occur throughout the nineteenth century, beginning with Beethoven. In other words, querying Price's formal plan could lead us back to rethinking his Op. 95, Schumann's *Dichterliebe*, Brahms's Third, and most of Mahler. And of course I would want to examine Price's harmonic palette: the ways she weaves together pentatonic gestures and tonal harmonies. In many instances, her strategies remind me of Bach's chorale-harmonization enterprise, as he—like Price—sought ways to reconcile modal traditions steeped in spiritual devotion with practices aligned with a urban modernity. In fact, I have long argued for hearing a kind of double consciousness in Bach; W.E.B. Du Bois can help us even with classics.

Florence Price does not need my ramblings so much as I need her works to nudge me in new directions analytically, aesthetically, and culturally. It should not have taken the murder of George Floyd to make me think seriously about Florence Price, William Grant Still, William Dawson, Julius Eastman, Blind Tom Wiggins, Coleridge-Taylor Perkinson, and countless other Black composers. Black musicologists have long been producing elaborate bibliographies and websites devoted to these repertoires.[28] The wealth of such contributions cannot be ignored in our concert programming, research, and pedagogy without perpetrating, well, systemic racism.

I do not wish to preempt Black theorists and analysts in this essay; we need as many voices and insights as possible as we finally engage with these neglected repertoires, and I hope only to add a bit to the conversation. But when offered a platform for my music-theory lecture at Michigan, I wanted to spend my time and energies addressing this crucial issue, which is foremost in our minds these days. In short, we need many more objects for analysis and a much wider range of objectives.

---

[28] Scholars such as Eileen Southern and Samuel A. Floyd, Jr., published extensively on Black composers. For more recent bibliographies, see, for instance, Christopher Jenkins, "Exploring the Aesthetics of African-American Classical Music: An Annotated Bibliography," *American Society for Aesthetics*, and Darryl Taylor, American Art Song Alliance (online). Many other resources exist.

PART II
MESSING WITH EARLY MUSIC

9

Unwashed Masses

Music for the Morning After[1]

In January 2009 I assumed stewardship of the UCLA music-history survey, which had reached the year 1500 by the end of the previous quarter. I opened my lectures on the sixteenth century with secular music. As I was introducing the often ribald Parisian chanson, I mentioned that the composers of these pieces—like their contemporary Rabelais—wrote for the elite classes, even if they often pretended to emulate the unwashed masses.

At this point in my exposition, a hand shot up. "What do you mean by 'unwashed masses'?" asked Abhik Banerjee, a student whom I soon came to recognize as the most tenacious interlocutor in the room. Always wary of being caught out in a politically incorrect stance, I stumbled through a reply to his challenge: "Well, *I*, of course, don't mean to denigrate the lower classes, blah, blah, blah." He would not let me off the hook. "But what *kinds* of masses are 'unwashed masses?'" I stood looking puzzled and fell uncharacteristically mute. He helped me out: "Last quarter, we learned about cantus-firmus masses and paraphrase masses. What kinds of masses are 'unwashed masses?'"[2]

Finally, I understood. I explained that I had used the term to refer to the common people. But I also mentioned that something that might qualify as "unwashed masses"—in the sense of liturgical music based on dirty or obscene sources—also existed and that we would get to that phenomenon a couple of weeks later. As it happened, the conveners of a conference on conviviality were asking me just then for a title. I went to my office and sent in my title, featuring the phrase "unwashed masses" Abhik made available to me.

---

[1] First presented at an international conference, *Courtly Conviviality and Gastronomy in Early Modern France and Italy*, UCLA Center for Medieval and Renaissance Studies, April 2009. Also presented at the University of Leuven (2010) and at the Renaissance Society of America (2013).

[2] A "cantus-firmus mass" bases its musical process on a melody ("cantus")—either sacred or secular—that provides the basis, in long notes, for the setting of the liturgical text. In a "paraphrase mass," the preexisting melodic material is manipulated to serve as the melodic substance of the new composition.

Making Sense of Music. Susan McClary, Oxford University Press. © Oxford University Press 2025.
DOI: 10.1093/9780197779798.003.0010

Nothing would please me more than to see his felicitous label become part of the standard technical vocabulary in musicology.

In any case, the concept (if not the expression) "unwashed masses" appears explicitly in the decrees concerning church music released by the Council of Trent in 1562. Convened twenty-six years earlier in 1536, the Council sought to clarify doctrine and to introduce reforms from within Catholicism in response to the critiques launched by Luther and Calvin, which threatened to fracture the unified church.

Many of the Trentine principles concerning music seem relatively straightforward. Music in the worship service was to be uplifting, and the words sung were to be made intelligible to congregants. But the Council also stipulated that liturgical music, whether for organ or voices, was to exclude elements deemed "lascivum aut impurum"—that is, lascivious and impure. What could they have meant by this? Was inappropriate music inserted into the worship service so frequently that a specific law prohibiting such items had to be promulgated? Maybe they had a lower threshold for what counted as "lascivious" during those (no doubt) more innocent times; recall, for instance, that John of Salisbury in the twelfth century heard *all* polyphonic music, with its interweaving voice parts, as simulating pederasty. He wrote:

> Music sullies the Divine Service, for in the very sight of God, in the sacred recesses of the sanctuary itself, the singers attempt, with the lewdness of a lascivious singing voice and a singularly foppish manner, to feminize all their spellbound little followers with the girlish way they render the notes and end the phrases. Could you but hear the effete emotings of their before-singing and their after-singing, their singing and their counter-singing, their in-between-singing and their ill-advised singing, you would think it an ensemble of sirens, not of men.... The ears are almost completely divested of their critical power, and the intellect, which the pleasureableness of so much sweetness has caressed insensate, is impotent to judge the merits of the things heard. Indeed, when such practices go too far, they can more easily occasion titillation between the legs than a sense of devotion in the brain.[3]

---

[3] John of Salisbury, *Policratus* (1159); as quoted in William Dalglish, "The Origin of the Hocket," *Journal of the American Musicological Society* 31 (1978): 7.

This amazing passage manages to combine misogyny, homophobia, and castration anxiety into its attack on what came to be regarded as Europe's great contribution to the musical art. We can but stand bewildered when reading such a diatribe, which imputes moral violations to what we would regard as quite innocuous phenomena.

The Council of Trent knew whereof it spoke, however. Anyone who has ever played the organ for the church can think of countless occasions in which musicians try to sneak profane references past an unsuspecting clergy. A friend of mine composed a solemn-sounding chorale prelude based on the old standard "Put Another Nickel In," which he played during the Offertory. I used to tease a Wagner-besotted priest in my congregation by ending my Communion improvisations with the final cadence of *Tristan und Isolde*; sometimes I could see his shoulders quivering with scarcely contained giggles as he struggled to launch into the next portion of the mass.[4] As it turns out, church musicians have been doing this forever, and sometimes the worst offenders were themselves men of the cloth.

Some of the Renaissance church music with secular models has been explained by way of allegory. Guillaume Du Fay, for instance, composed a cycle for the ordinary of the mass—the Kyrie, Gloria, Credo, Sanctus, and Agnus Dei—based on his own love song "Se la face ay pale" (If My Face Is Pale). But musicologist Anne Robertson has revealed that Du Fay wrote his *Missa Se la face ay pale* when he was in residence in Turin, right when the famous shroud first made its appearance.[5] The discipline heaved a collective sigh of relief when it learned that this extremely influential cantus-firmus mass had its heart in the right place; at long last, it had been shown to be above reproach.

Throughout the fifteenth century, many musicians produced mass cycles that deployed the melodies of secular songs as the compositional point of departure. It is not always easy to detect the scurrilous scaffolding in the resulting pieces, any more than my friend's congregation recognized "Put Another Nickel In" creeping through his bass line in lugubrious slow motion. But professional singers in the Renaissance, many of whom performed both

---

[4] This may seem startling if you've read my introduction concerning the demonization of instruments in my own religious background. But in graduate school, I was hired to play the organ for Sacred Heart Church in Waltham, Massachusetts. My fundamentalist parents were so upset when they learned of my side hustle that I think they would have preferred me to be working as an exotic dancer. I did learn to play the organ on the job, however.

[5] Anne Robertson, "The Man with the Pale Face, the Relic, and Du Fay's Missa Se la face ay pale," talk presented at the annual meeting of the American Musicological Society, November 2008; published in *Journal of Musicology* 27, No. 4 (October 2010): 377–434.

chansons at rowdy festivities on Saturday night and masses in church the next day, were much more likely to be in on the joke, for they would find themselves on Sunday morning singing the same tunes, however cleverly camouflaged by the thicket of surrounding voices. That same complex polyphony that made the words hard to distinguish also served to conceal the illicit contraband that gave a particular mass its structural coherence and musical materials.

Consequently, the Council of Trent put the kibosh on this ill-advised practice in 1562. Or so they thought. The historical record would indicate otherwise, for it was as though formally prohibiting this custom only poured fuel on the fire.

Many of the transformations from profane to sacred received the blessing of ecclesiastical critics. The songs chosen by Johannes Ockeghem and Josquin des Pres as models, for instance, usually boast a certain *gravitas*: it does not take a leap of imagination to transform a melancholy love ballad into a melancholy piece of church music. In fact, Martin Luther created many of the chorales crucial to his indoctrination of converts by taking familiar melodies and giving them new words: Heinrich Isaac's "Innsbruck, ich muss dich lassen" (Innsbruck, I Now Must Leave You), for example, became "O Welt, ich muss dich lassen" (O World, I Now Must Leave You). As one great reformer is supposed to have quipped: "Why should the Devil get all the good tunes?" This technique of merely changing the lyrics (called *contrafactum* by music historians) was around long before George Harrison turned the Chiffons' girl-group hit "He's So Fine" into his gospel rip-off addressed to Krishna, "My Sweet Lord."

But the sixteenth century also witnessed the circulation of masses by leading composers based on materials far more problematic than "Se la face ay pale" or "Innsbruck"—or even "He's So Fine," for that matter. The very day that Abhik Banerjee asked about unwashed masses, we were studying a couple of chansons that shocked even the hip-hop-jaded sensibilities of my undergraduates. Since we had these particular songs close at hand, I quickly demonstrated how one of them might be made into a mass.

For example, the lyrics of Jacques Arcadelt's "Margot labourez les vignes," with its abrupt imperatives, suit the acclamations of the Kyrie especially well

Example 9.1a Jacques Arcadelt, "Margot, labourez les vignes," mm. 1–7

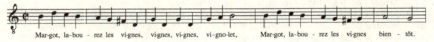

(see Example 9.1a). For those of you not acquainted with her, Margot is a woman pressed into the servicing of soldiers—or, as the euphemistic words of the chanson put it, into "working the vineyards." But she has her revenge, as the three captains she encounters realize that she is responsible for spreading the camp fever, the sexually transmitted disease that afflicts them all. Only gradually does the listener come to associate the bouncy rhythms and bobbing melody on "vigne, vigne, vignolet" (later presented in all voices) with the mechanical actions Margot is ordered repeatedly to perform.

Margot, labourez les vignes,	Margot, go work the vineyards,
vigne, vigne, vignolet,	vin, vin, vineyards,
Margot, labourez les vignes, bientôt.	Margot, go work the vineyards, right now!
En ruement de Lorraine	On the road from Lorraine
Margot rencontrai trois capitaines,	Margot encountered three captains,
vigne, vigne, vignolet,	vin, vin, vineyards,
Margot, labourez les vignes, bientôt.	Margot, go work the vineyards, right now!
Ils m'ont saluée vilaine, Margot,	They hailed me with bad humor, Margot,
Je suis leurs fièvres quartaines,	I'm their camp fever,
vigne, vigne, vignolet,	vin, vin, vineyard,
Margot, labourez les vignes, bientôt.	Margot, go work the vineyards, right now!

I thought I was making up my Kyrie as a *reductio ad absurdum* when I sang the sacred plea for mercy to this profane little ditty in class (see Example 9.1b).

Example 9.1b McClary, contrafactum of "Margot" as Kyrie

But then I discovered that one of the brightest lights of Renaissance sacred music, Orlando di Lasso, had composed a Magnificat based on his own setting of this very same chanson. Lasso surely could not have had an allegorical motive in mind when he set the words of the Virgin Mary to a tune everyone would have recognized as "Margot, labourez les vignes." On the other hand—what was he thinking?!!!

It seems, however, that no one could resist this catchy little tune. Even Calvinist Huguenots appropriated it (see Example 9.1c). With only a sleight of hand, they changed it to this: "Qui laboure champ ou vigne / Est heureux, si humblement / A la volonté divine / S'attent" (Whoever works in field or vineyard is happy to attend, if humbly, to the divine will).

Example 9.1c Calvinist contrafactum of "Margot"

Well, just go work those vineyards, whatsoever they be, say I!

But not even I could have anticipated that the other, far more outrageous Parisian chanson on that day's syllabus had also served as the basis for a mass setting. Once again, the culprit was none other than Orlando di Lasso. The model he chose for this particular mass, Claudin de Sermisy's "Je ne menge point de porc," must qualify as the most vividly scatological piece in the entire history of music, outdoing even Mozart in the realm of coprophilia.[6] Those of you who know your Rabelais will recall that Claudin figures as one of the immortal musicians in Book IV of *Gargantua et Pantagruel*, merrily singing smutty songs in Jupiter's heaven. Claudin, like many of his Rabelaisian companions, was himself a cleric.

Je ne menge point de porc.	I don't eat pork.
Le porc a condition	The pig has a condition
Telle que je vous dire,	And I'll tell you why,
S'il a mengé cent estrons,	If he has eaten a hundred turds,
Il ne s'en fera que rire.	It will only make him laugh.
Il les tourne, il les vire,	He turns them, he twists them,
Il leur rit et puis les mort.	He grins at them and then nibbles them.
Je ne menge point de porc.	I don't eat pork.
Le porc s'en alloit jouant	The pig went playing
Tout au long d'une rivière.	Along the bank of a river.
Il veit ung estron nouant,	He saw a turd float by,
Il luy print a faire chere,	He scooped it out to regale himself on it,
Disant en ceste maniere:	Saying the following:
"Estron nouant en riviere,	"Turd floating on the river,
Rend toy ou tu es mort."	Surrender or you're dead."
Je ne menge point de porc.	I don't eat pork.[7]

---

[6] On the latter, consult any biography or collection of letters. These documents inspired Peter Shaffer's *Amadeus*.
[7] Listen to https://www.youtube.com/watch?v=DzNi2jBgKeU. I want to thank Daniel Goldmark for introducing me to this chanson long before it found its way into this project.

It is not hard to locate Orlando di Lasso's *Missa Je ne menge point de porc*: it holds a place of honor in his Collected Works—the very first item in the very first volume of his complete masses. I had assumed on the basis of a musicological article that it would be camouflaged under the title *Missa brevis* or *Missa sine nomine*.[8] But no: the Venetian print from 1570 proudly proclaims the mass as having been composed from "Je ne menge point de porc."

Lasso's *Missa Je ne menge point de porc* is an imitation or parody mass,[9] which means that the composer takes a polyphonic source (rather than just a tune) as its model; he considers the entire musical entity he has borrowed and figures out how to employ textures, sonorities, and intact passages in his setting of the liturgical text. This technique requires considerable ingenuity, given that the composer restricts his choices in advance to the materials made available by the model.

Lasso clearly reveled in this challenge: to paraphrase Claudin's lyrics, he took portions of the chanson and he turned them, he twisted them, he grinned at them and nibbled them. An extraordinarily convivial artist, celebrated by his contemporaries such as Pietro Aretino for his hilarious improvisations as a *commedia dell'arte* actor, for his abilities as an amusing raconteur, for his unusually intimate relationship with his noble patron, for his letters that freely punned in a dazzling and often obscene scramble of French, German, Italian, Latin, and Spanish, Lasso no doubt anticipated precisely this joke when he was writing this mass. He self-consciously made a silk purse from something quite a bit less dignified than a sow's ear, and he rejoiced in the activity like a proverbial pig in shit.

So imagine that you were celebrating Oktoberfest one night (this being Munich!), and your friends became so inebriated that you all decided to sing Claudin's "Je ne menge point de porc." However gross its lyrics, this is not a particularly easy chanson to sight-sing, even when you're stone-cold sober. Just as Rabelais delighted in juxtaposing his classical erudition and his ribald jokes, so Claudin brought complicated musical strategies to bear on his setting of this scatological text. Each individual singer, with his individual part book containing nothing more than his own individual melodic line, would have to work very hard to hold up his strand within the complex. Otherwise, it would all fall apart—and there's nothing quite so pathetic or humiliating as a failed attempt at singing about pigs and turds! (see Example 9.2).

---

[8] James Haar, "A Wedding Mass by Lasso," *Journal of Musicology* 17, no. 1 (Winter 1999): 120.

[9] As used in Renaissance musicology, the word "parody" is not intended to bring with it any sense of irony. We all wring our hands in frustration over the fact that we have inherited this unfortunate term, which always requires long explanations and still causes great confusion. "Imitation" is so bland that it scarcely helps at all. But those are the available labels.

Example 9.2 Claudin de Sermisy, "Je ne menge point de porc," refrain

Several passages would no doubt stand out. First, the refrain itself. Claudin sets the words of the title in imitative counterpoint: the four voices enter one after the other on the same tune fragment, though on different pitches. Our singers would have to be counting like mad in order to come in at the right time. To make it more difficult yet, Claudin starts on a pitch other than the stable notes of the G-Hypodorian mode, the identity of which only becomes clear at the cadence on "porc." It's as if he sneaks only gradually into his topic or sidles in sideways, which makes it even harder for the singers to find their bearing.

If this creates a sly beginning, it also sets up a very clever formal strategy. Note how the refrain comes back each time just after a disgusting description of or quotation from the pig. Claudin always has the pig-oriented sentences end triumphantly, his exclamations landing on a bright, stable B-flat-major chord. And each time, the refrain enters in its off-balance way and pulls us firmly back to a G-Hypodorian cadence on "porc." With each iteration, the refrain sounds more emphatic: if it starts out as an off-the-cuff comment—"I don't eat pork"—it seals its argument with a causal hinge between the pig's activities and the increasingly fervent vow never again to eat pork. No one singing this chanson is likely to forget either the challenges or the rewards of performing the refrain well.

So there you are, somewhat hung-over at mass the next morning. You open your part book to begin the mass ordinary, only to find precisely the same music. But now the jaunty tune that you remember all too well as "Je ne menge point de porc" has become "Kyrie eleison," complete with the snarl of complexities that made it such a trial to coordinate the night before (see Example 9.3).

Example 9.3 Orlando di Lasso, *Missa Je ne menge point de porc*, Kyrie, mm. 1–6

Your choirmaster—the same person who last night was cutting obscene capers as Pantalone in his *commedia* scenario and who, incidentally, also composed this mass—stands solemnly directing your ensemble, daring you to laugh. Conviviality has spilled over into the worship service. Or at least into the choir loft.

Once you've recognized Lasso's game ("Yes, he really has gone and composed a mass on 'Je ne menge point de porc'"!), you fast-forward mentally through the chanson. What parts stand out in your memory? Two passages, probably: the one where the pig is described as turning and twisting and nibbling his delicacies and the one where the pig cries out: "Rend toy ou tu es mort!," made all the more emphatic by a switch in meter and homophonic text declamation from the whole ensemble. "Oh my God!" you say to yourself. "What parts of the mass is he going to set to *those*?" As you sing, you begin to worry just a little bit about the Inquisition. I'll stick with the second of these passages, since it counts as the most striking moment in the chanson (see Example 9.4).

Lasso flirts here and there with elements that recall the pig's ultimatum, but it emerges most unequivocally in the Credo. The text is identifying the Holy Spirit as the third member of the Trinity, along with the Father and the Son. Suddenly, on the words "simul adoratur" (together is adored), the pig's entire musical statement—meter change and all—sounds forth intact (see Example 9.5). You wheeze with stifled guffaws, trying desperately not to meet the eyes of your fellow musicians. Lasso stands poker-faced, though Wilhelm V, his patron, appears to smirk slightly. The officiating priest may or may not be clueless.

162   MAKING SENSE OF MUSIC

Example 9.4 Sermisy, "Je ne menge point de porc," mm. 37–end

Example 9.5 Lasso, *Missa Je ne menge point de porc*, Credo, mm. 80–87.

What do we make of this? Why would a musician of Lasso's stature do such things, and how did he get away with it? We do know that Dr. Walram Tumler, a representative of the German College in Rome, was sent to Munich in 1581 to implement certain Roman reforms. A chronicler of the German College mentions that there was some resistance at the Bavarian court:

> Indeed Orlando, who acted as chapel-master and had, moreover, published shameful music prints, took offence and with his accomplices—some of whom were married, some of whom were accustomed to wear swords and thus resembled mercenaries more than pious servants of God—conspired in anger against Walram. But the anger that took hold was vain and powerless.[10]

An article by David Crook analyzes an edict from 1575 concerning appropriate music for a new Jesuit College in Munich, as well as lists of approved and prohibited repertoire; not surprisingly, Lasso—by far the most significant composer in that city—figures heavily in both lists.[11] And as Duke Wilhelm became increasingly more pious, especially with regard to Marian worship, he may have put something of a damper on Lasso's usual fun and games.

Lasso was scarcely hiding from ecclesiastic authorities, however. He had dedicated his book of masses containing "Je ne menge point de porc" and other flagrantly indecent songs to Pope Gregory XIII himself. Four years later, the pope honored Lasso by naming him a Knight of the Golden Spur. Bear in mind the fact that the clergy at this time held quite contradictory moral standards. Pope Gregory not only had sired an illegitimate son, but he had appointed him to elevated positions in the church. In the next century, Pope Clement IX would write opera libretti that prominently featured *commedia* characters and shticks.[12]

Yet musicologists have tended to be more Catholic—or at least more prudish—than the pope with regard to Lasso and the other artists they study. No one with any acquaintance with Lasso's letters or his secular music can fail to have noticed his fondness for raunchy language and imagery. But

---

[10] From a seventeenth-century history of the German College in Rome by Wilhelm Fusban, as quoted in David Crook, *Orlando di Lasso's Imitation Magnificats for Counter-Reformation Munich* (Princeton, NJ: Princeton University Press, 1994), 36.

[11] David Crook, "A Sixteenth-Century Catalog of Prohibited Music," *Journal of the American Musicological Society* 62, no. 1 (Spring 2009): 1–78.

[12] A production by William Christie of the future pope's *Sant' Alessio* has appeared on DVD.

scholars often go to great length to explain that this great composer of the Counter-Reformation could not possibly have intended the lewd meanings his puns often imply. A friend of Aretino, and a renowned *commedia* actor, isn't aware that his carefully crafted statements might be construed as double entendres? Is this even remotely plausible?

Concerning Lasso's unwashed masses and Magnificats, David Crook wrote in 1994:

> Magnificats on worldly chansons served to elevate the spirit and sublimate the original musical material. Purification of the music could be brought about through the substitution of its text. . . . Whereas Trent sought to banish secular music from church, Munich strove to elevate and purify it through its association with a more holy text. And what greater testament to a composer's skill and piety than his ability to gather the most varied expressions of his art and apply them to the Virgin's most perfect song of praise? It was not in their avoidance of the secular but in their redirection of it toward more holy ends and, above all, their thoughtful reaffirmation of the Church's traditions—her liturgy, her saints, her musical adornments—that Lasso's Magnificats embraced and embodied the spirit and ideals of the Counter-Reformation.[13]

Let me get this straight. I want to honor "the Virgin's most perfect song of praise." I know! Why don't I start with "Je ne menge point de porc"?!!! The idea that Lasso sought out such tunes in order to purify them makes him sound a bit like a Jesuit actively searching for particularly recalcitrant savages to convert.

Although Lasso himself freely admitted his predilection for basing his sacred music on ribald sources, he sometimes presented whitewashing explanations as well. In his dedication of his 1570 mass collection to the pope, he points conventionally to the power of music to lift the spirit, then slyly refers to the lascivious materials (elevated, of course, by their accordance with musical law) through which he hopes to help the pontiff celebrate God. Even playful music, it seems, can manifest God's order through its adherence to Pythagorean ratios.

There remains the possibility that Lasso intended his setting of this moment in the Credo to signify theologically. In both Claudin's chanson and

---

[13] Crook, *Orlando di Lasso's Imitation Magnificats*, 81–82. Crook's position has shifted over the course of the last fifteen years. See note 9.

Lasso's mass, this passage stands out for its sudden declamation of the text in all voices at the same time, thus (in Lasso's case) underscoring the word "simul." The voices drop their bids for individual expression and instead sing here of one accord. As Brian Copenhaver has pointed out, this is the section of the Nicene Creed that had been subject to the most intense debate, for it insists unequivocally upon the divinity of Christ and upon the equivalence of the Father and the Son.[14] The emphatic quality Claudin brought to his pig's ultimatum can be heard here as an acclamation of orthodox faith (especially if the listener is ignorant of the source materials).

In closing, I want to suggest that a great deal of Lasso's work, including his dedication in this collection of masses and the particular masses themselves, falls between the cracks of our eighteenth-century aesthetic theories, which offer us only the sublime and the beautiful as possible categories. To be sure, Lasso wrote a lot of extremely beautiful, often utterly sublime music: Peter Sellars's staging of Lasso's *Lagrime di San Pietro* has left audiences in Disney Hall in tears. But Lasso also trafficked incorrigibly in the hilarious: a category not commonly recognized in musicology, even though Rabelais, Aretino, Claudin, Monteverdi, and many other Renaissance artists also worked that particular vineyard.

Surely we should acknowledge the extent to which Lasso's penchant for innuendo-laden letters, *commedia* shticks, and dirty songs also informs his delight in bringing the most tawdry of tunes to the sacred music he was required to compose as part of his job. It does not diminish his greatness to recognize the ways in which this irrepressible jokester sought to provoke laughter and conviviality in nearly everything he touched. For insiders who can identify his sources, follow his maneuvers, and share in his sometimes off-color sense of humor, Lasso's unwashed masses can be flat-out hysterical. Just deal with it—the pope did!

---

[14] Professor Copenhaver offered his insight during the discussion following the presentation of this paper at the conference.

10
Tumescence and Detumescence in a Monteverdi Madrigal[1]

What can historians of erotica (to avoid the loaded word "pornography") learn from music? Unlike some of the most celebrated documents from the sixteenth century, such as Giulio Romano's engravings, music of this time presents no pictures of body parts. It may have lyrics with obscene words of the kind tossed around with such aplomb in, for instance, Pietro Aretino's *sonetti lussuriosi* (or licentious sonnets);[2] but the guardians of music have tried to sustain the idea that their chosen medium remains neutral, untouched in its essence by texts or contexts. Instead, they cordon it off with fearsome graphs and specialist jargon that truly seem to have nothing to do with the world, erotic or otherwise. These attitudes have constructed a firewall that prevents historians from venturing in and that even hamstrings musicologists who might wish to communicate aspects of what they know.[3]

My object for this chapter is Claudio Monteverdi's "Sì, ch'io vorrei morire," published in his Book IV of Madrigals in 1603 but in circulation some years before that. Some of the pieces in this collection raised the ire of music theorist Giovanni Maria Artusi, who published an attack in 1600 concerning the unacceptable transgressions of what he called "modern" music. Yet what scandalized Artusi was not the erotic content of some of these madrigals,

---

[1] Invited paper for the session "Music and Pornography" for a meeting of the Renaissance Society of America, 2014. This was the follow-up after "Unwashed Masses" (chapter 9) the previous year.

[2] For a translation of Aretino's sonnets and reproductions of Romani's images, see Bette Talvaccia, *Taking Positions: On the Erotic in Renaissance Culture* (Princeton, NJ: Princeton University Press, 1999). When I teach Monteverdi madrigals in my seminar on the analysis of early music, I pass this book around so that students know what we're dealing with in this repertory. Yet I have had debates with Monteverdi scholars who insist that the composer—even with all his rhetorical skills—never would have lowered himself to simulate anything sexual, regardless of the content of some of the poems he chose to set.

[3] Esteban Buch plows through this firewall in his *Playlist: Musique & sexualité* (Paris: Éditions MF, 2022). See my review in *Revue de musicologie* (2023). Arved Ashby has just completed an even more explicit study in his *My 1980s Gayboy Playlist*. I have had the privilege of reading Arved's extraordinarily courageous book in manuscript.

but rather the ways they ran roughshod over time-honored rules of voice leading and dissonance control. They offended, in other words, his purely musical, formalist principles. As Monteverdi responded in his brief defense, he aligned himself with what he dubbed the Second Practice, to distinguish it from the First Practice *modus operandi* of composers such as Palestrina. By contrast, Second Practice composers allowed the lyrics to dictate important aspects of the music's unfolding, even if that required the breaking of Artusi's cherished rules.[4]

"Sì, ch'io vorrei morire" doesn't show up on Artusi's hit list, though, as we shall see, it might well have appeared there among the other culprits. Its text, probably by Maurizio Moro, begins and ends with the ubiquitous Renaissance pun on "to die," and it includes several images that point explicitly toward lovemaking: kissing mouths, wet tongues, white bosoms. It traces growing excitement, propelled forward by an inventory of the beloved's attributes. But if metaphoric death occurs here, it transpires after the close of Moro's poem. There's nothing here that would drive Aretino out of business or lead Walmart to remove it from its shelves.

Sì, ch'io vorrei morire	Yes, I would like to die
ora ch'io bacio, Amore,	now that I am kissing, Love,
la bella bocca del mio amato core.	the beautiful mouth of my beloved sweetheart.
Ahi, cara e dolce lingua,	Ah, dear, sweet tongue,
datemi tant'umore,	give me so much wetness,
che di dolcezz'in questo sen m'estingua!	that I faint from sweetness upon this breast!
Ahi, vita mia, a questo bianco seno,	Ah, my life, to your white bosom,
deh, stringetemi fin ch'io venga meno!	yes, crush me until I lie exhausted!
Ahi, bocca, ahi, baci, ahi, lingua, torn'a dire:	Ah, mouth, ah, kisses, ah, tongue, I say again:
"Sì, ch'io vorrei morire!"	"Yes, I would like to die!"

The *music* of this madrigal, however, offers astonishingly explicit simulations of sexual arousal, climax, and subsequent deflation. For all Monteverdi claimed to be following the exigencies of his lyrics, he tracks quite a different set of trajectories from the relatively provisional one suggested by the text. Instead, he takes advantage of every mention of death, fainting, or depletion to present a collapse into detumescence, each one requiring another quick buildup. Note that this is not how Monteverdi

---

[4] Giovanni Maria Artusi, *L'Artusi overo delle imperfettioni della moderna musica* (Venice, 1600); Monteverdi's extended response—written by his brother Giulio Cesare—appeared in his *Scherzi musicali* (1607). See chapter 8 in my *Modal Subjectivities: Self-Fashioning in the Italian Madrigal* (Berkeley: University of California Press, 2004).

depicts mature lovemaking, which he simulated in music with great care throughout his career. No, this more closely resembles the experiences of a fourteen-year-old with what the Australians call a wank mag. Over the course of a piece that lasts less than three minutes, Monteverdi offers no fewer than five cycles, as if with time-lapse photography. In words taken from "Those Magnificent Young Men in Their Flying Machines," it goes uppity-up-up, it goes downdity-own-down. A cartoonish rendering of male sexual performance, deliberately hilarious in its exaggerations. (See full score at the end of this chapter.)

All representations, of course, reach us through multiple layers of mediation, even one that seems so very transparent. Monteverdi's most obvious device involves ascending and descending scales, the former producing the sensation of rising tension, the latter of deflation. When the words suggest self-exhaustion, the lines limp downward. Four times—once on "Ahi, vita mia!" and thrice on "A questo bianco seno"—he attains the peak and allows the protagonist to crow before toppling. One does not have to be a music theorist to hear these, especially if the passages are performed well.[5] In order to make these gestures more compelling, Monteverdi breaks Artusi's rules with gleeful abandon. Taking advantage of the repeated love cries of "Ahi!," the composer hoists us up with biting dissonances on each step. At times, three adjacent pitches of the scale occur at the same moment, creating a hitherto unmatched rendering of the pleasure/pain principle.

I have left for last the setting of the first and final lines of the poem: "Sì, ch'io vorrei morire" (see Example 10.1). The music Monteverdi gives this refrain would have puzzled not only Artusi but any of his colleagues who cared about voice-leading principles. Leading tones—the most urgent component in the penultimate chord in cadence formulas—had existed in Western music since at least the fourteenth century. They usually occurred, however, at moments of closure, to maximize the listener's desire for the implied resolution. Only in the second half of the seventeenth century do leading tones begin to appear consistently throughout a piece as part of the foundational scale, the "ti" that inevitably goes to "do."

---

[5] I am not happy with most of the commercial recordings of this or most madrigals, which nearly all present chaste readings, rendering Monteverdi's carefully crafted imagery moot. Listen, however, to the recording by Les Arts Florissants conducted by Paul Agnew: https://www.youtube.com/watch?v=5qLn_2fXzlU

TUMESCENCE AND DETUMESCENCE   169

Example 10.1 Claudio Monteverdi, "Sì, ch'io vorrei morire," mm. 1–6

Example 10.2a Aeolian cadence formula

Example 10.2b Mock-up of "Sì, ch'io vorrei morire," mm. 1–6, with standard resolution

Monteverdi sticks a leading tone into his very first measure, as well as each subsequent measure. Those leading tones throw out of whack the standardized progression that sixteenth-century listeners would have expected with the opening bar; Example 10.2a shows the normal version of the Aeolian mode's principal defining gesture. Example 10.2b shows the way the leading tones are supposed to resolve upward.

But Monteverdi's leading tones contort every moment of the sequence. Instead of resolving upward, these press forward only to collapse, their acute vectors broken. In the grammar of the time, the canto's D-sharp in m. 1 ought not yield melodically to A in m. 2: the moment of most intense desire has the rug yanked out from under it. Performers alert to this strategy need to respond to that abrupt break with something that sounds like a sucker punch. As he advances through his passage, Monteverdi reiterates the same pattern with its failed leading tone at successively lower pitch levels. Only the third statement brings about closure, but in a register an octave lower than anticipated (see again Example 10. 1).

The image of "dying" is quite clear here, with the incremental descent. But Monteverdi choreographs something even more specific with his unorthodox voice leading. If each of those leading tones strains upward until it collapses, then we have the simulation of shuddering, sputtering release—the very gesture that got Nijinsky into trouble when he mimed masturbating into a scarf at the end of *Afternoon of a Faun*. Erotic climaxes are simulated all the time in classic ballet, but they're highly stylized; Nijinsky's was far too real in its juddering physicality. In Monteverdi's madrigal, the images of tumescence and detumescence mostly operate within the bounds of stylization. But not this one. And it was this refrain line that required the composer to exercise his technical ingenuity to its fullest extent.

Pornographers used to refer to this gesture as the money shot. One might say in response to Monteverdi's carefully construed sonic representation: "Well, that's just the way it is." But lots of other musical money shots exist, with very different dimensions of the experience inspiring a wide variety of simulations. I want to argue, following Foucault, that even this apparently universal act—necessary for the conception of every single one of us since Adam and Eve—has a cultural history.

The earliest explicit representation of sexual climax *in music* occurs at the end of Jacques Arcadelt's "Il bianco e dolce cigno," the madrigal responsible for the popularity and marketability of the genre as a whole. The white swan of the title sings once for its "swan song" and then dies; our interlocutor, who compares himself to the bird, also dies, but with such intense pleasure that he would gladly die a thousand times a day. Arcadelt constructs this orgasm by taking a simple cadential pattern that rushes toward closure, then layers it with the other three voices, each of which similarly presses toward resolution. The resulting wave motion produces a kind of bliss, prolonged as long as subsequent waves continue to ebb and flow. The voices finally come together, as it were, in an Amen cadence, allowing the pent-up energies gradually to subside in bliss. No sputtering, no incremental cranking up of excitement; just the serene release of fluids.[6]

Arcadelt may well have drawn his model from the intense contrapuntal activity that often occurs in Josquin's settings of the Kyrie, where presumably it has nothing whatsoever to do with sexual activity but rather with religious ecstasy. But the madrigalists did not invent their images out of nothing. Musical images simulating *jouissance*, sacred or secular, often sound exactly the same, and composers can slip them promiscuously back and forth across that porous border at will.

Repertories from the first half of the seventeenth century in particular trafficked in this ambiguity in their heated depictions of Divine Love, inspired by the ecstasies of Saint Teresa of Ávila.[7] Implausible as it may seem, the music of "Sì, ch'io vorrei morire" appeared in print in 1609 with an altogether different text, "O Jesu, mea vita," with all its musical and poetic imagery of self-induced arousal intact.

O Jesu, mea vita,	O Jesus, my life,
in quo est vera salus,	in whom there is true salvation,
O lumen gloriae, amate Jesu,	O light of glory, beloved Jesus,
O cara pulchritudo,	O blessed beauty,
tribue mihi tuam	give me your
dulcedinem mellifluam gustandam.	mellifluous sweetness to taste.
O vita mea, O gloria coelorum,	O my life, O glory of the heavens,
ah restringe me tibi in aeternum.	ah, bind me to you eternally.
O Jesu, lux mea, spes mea, cor meum,	O Jesus, my light, my hope, my heart,
do me tibi.	I give you myself.
O Jesu, mea vita.	O Jesus, my life.

I'll leave the performance of this contrafactum to your lurid imaginations. But just consider loving Jesus so much that the mere mention of his name set you going on Monteverdi's onanistic roller coaster! Today only gospel churches continue to mine this rich vein of erotic intensity for sacred purposes.[8] But J. S. Bach did so every time he got an excuse to write a duet for Jesus and the Soul.

The locus classicus for money shots, the pornographic film, also necessarily features music to buttress the repetitive and ultimately banal action on screen

---

[6] See *Modal Subjectivities*, chapter 3.
[7] For more on this phenomenon, see "Libidinous Theology," chapter 5 of my *Desire and Pleasure in Seventeenth-Century Music* (Berkeley: University of California Press, 2012).
[8] Listen, for instance, to "Something about the Name Jesus," Kirk Franklin, *The Nu Nation Project* (1998): https://www.youtube.com/watch?v = NxksjhN1Qv4

with sonic continuity, designed to hook the viewer in and sustain interest. Most often, such movies make use of disco-style tracks that maintain a high and unwavering level of urgency, thus suggesting the fantasy of the ever-erect, invincible penis, always eager to keep pumping tirelessly.

But classical music, too, is rife with such images. The ideologies that protect so-called absolute music disdain the idea that representations of any sort might occur within this sacred realm. Consequently, theorists can toss around terms such as "climax," or "masculine" and "feminine" (describing themes) with impunity, secure in the knowledge that no one will take any of these words literally. But, of course, I have done precisely that in my book *Feminine Endings*. Anyone willing to read the gestures spread out for all to hear in instrumental music can easily recognize them when they occur. In fact, I would argue that listeners need special training *not* to recognize them.

I'll begin with what has to be one of the great money shots of all time, from the final movement of Rimsky-Korsakov's *Scheherazade*. OK, so the title he gave this movement marks this as a ship breaking up against a cliff. Whatever. Nobody invests particularly in seas crashing, but few can resist this climactic moment.

The buildup to that moment stars a bank of trumpets, simultaneously tonguing a sequence of very fast repeated notes in a row. Because *Scheherazade* is so popular with audiences, orchestras have to deliver on this extraordinary lingual feat, and trumpet auditions invariably demand that aspiring musicians execute those tongue twists—the only place in the entire repertory anything like this occurs. With those staccato trumpet patterns, Rimsky pulls the active level of meter down to the eighth note, creating a quality of almost unbearably pent-up energy. But suddenly they explode out into a vast realm in which the level of meter now operates at the level of the megameasure. The long-withheld theme from the opening movement (based on the Sultan's motive) reappears and soars over the undulating strings associated with Scheherazade. Waves crashing? Yes, but in precisely the same sense that Arcadelt produced wave formations.[9]

I'd like to call this the Blaze of Glory money shot. A great deal of effort was expended in holding it back (think of all those tongue cramps in the brass section!), but most listeners have difficulty keeping their eyes from rolling

---

[9] Nicolai Rimsky-Korsakov, *Scheherazade*. You may as well listen to the Maestro, Leonard Bernstein, play this with shameless flamboyance: https://www.youtube.com/watch?v = _ IPgwwoxSbU, at 40:40.

back in their heads when the resolution finally arrives. This is one reason why *Scheherazade* doesn't get included in the official canon, why it still counts as a guilty pleasure. A *very* guilty pleasure.

So let's return to "Sì, ch'io vorrei morire," which now must seem pretty innocuous. Indeed, Monteverdi meant it as a joke, something like Justin Timberlake's brilliant "Dick in a Box" skit on *Saturday Night Live*. Designed to be sung by five men (a Renaissance boy group), this madrigal displays the kind of bawdy, unapologetic attitude toward body parts and fluids featured in Aristophanes, Chaucer, Rabelais, and Shakespeare, as well as our early-modern pornographers *par excellence*, Giulio Romano and Pietro Aretino. What Monteverdi brought to the table was the musical technology of leading tones—musical pricks—that allowed him to engineer such sonic representations.

In 1603, these devices—unless situated at cadences—still counted as special effects, and Monteverdi deployed them with playful virtuosity. What he presents here is nothing other than the penis, with its momentary delusions of grandeur, its somewhat abject deflations, and the fantasy of repeated, surefire erections. It is *not*, however, the phallus. Later composers learned how to dam up the desire mechanism of the leading tone, thereby postponing expected moments of arrival to create extended teleological trajectories. Resolutions when they finally occur are all the more explosive. It became possible to go through these paces of incited desire, delayed gratification, and climactic fulfillment even without texts attached.

We call this technology tonality: the musical logic that underpins the vocal and instrumental repertories of the eighteenth and nineteenth centuries. Hidden as it is behind the veil of the "purely musical," this desire-driven mechanism shapes opera plots: think of the way it predisposes us to yearn for Carmen's or Salome's deaths or to hope for some kind of release from the five-hour-long agonies of Tristan and Isolde. It also propels the heart-pounding scores for Hollywood action movies. And it produces transcendental moments like the one in *Scheherazade*, the finales of Beethoven's symphonies, the place in Mahler's Second where orchestra and pipe organ join the chorus as it screams "Auferstehn!"—I will rise again!

As is obvious, these pieces are not about the penis. But they are profoundly phallic in that they borrow what began as ejaculatory imagery and deploy it as the abstract, governing postulate upon which all tonal music relies. When we find that premodern, postmodern, or world musics "lack" something, it is precisely this mode of temporality based on the long-term manipulation of desire we are missing. And when, on occasion, the mechanism fails to deliver the promised goods—in the opening movements of Beethoven's Ninth or Tchaikovsky's Fourth, for instance—the effect is nothing less than catastrophic.

Music was not alone in taking on ideologies that elevated attributes of a body part to the status of a transcendental principle; just think of the Washington Monument. But because music operates on us—structures our sense of time and even affects our pulses—without our fully conscious knowledge, it was among the most important for shaping modern subjectivities. Literary genres continued to proceed in epistolary mode until the novel took on the temporalities and sensibilities developed in the symphony. Only experimental films (the kinds that flop at the box office) escape its imperative.

Monteverdi offers us a toy model, still acknowledging its grounding in common physical experience. He could never have imagined how his Little Engine That Could would become The Way Music Is Supposed to Go.

TUMESCENCE AND DETUMESCENCE 175

TUMESCENCE AND DETUMESCENCE 177

178 MAKING SENSE OF MUSIC

11
Doing the Time Warp in Seventeenth-Century Music[1]

Toward the end of his pioneering book *Meter as Rhythm*, Christopher Hasty includes analyses of a couple of early-seventeenth-century pieces.[2] Like many composers of that era, the artists Hasty discusses—Monteverdi and Schütz—often indulged in wildly contorted temporalities, with pieces that careen between simulations of rational speech, paralyzed stasis, free-falling spirals, and extravagant teleological trajectories. Although *seicento* composers had available to them the combination of devices later consolidated as "tonality," they clearly preferred to exploit such rapidly changing qualities of motion.

This essay considers the predilection of seventeenth-century composers for what I will call "the time warp." Our desire to see the incremental development of tonal harmonic grammar has sometimes led us to push many such pieces to the side as unfortunate throwbacks or else to minimize their strangeness. Yet for a good fifty years after the hierarchical arrangement of harmonic tonality had become viable, many composers chose to approach the shaping of time in very different ways. They did so in the service of cultural priorities—simulations of Divine Love, performances of quirky and spellbinding virtuosity, expressions of abnormal affective states such as erotic trance or madness—quite alien from those for which eighteenth-century tonality was designed.[3]

The *seicento* vexes not only music historians but also those who study virtually any of its cultural practices, even—or particularly—the sciences. For if this period witnessed the appearance of many concepts we regard as progressive, contradictory impulses often manifested themselves within the

---

[1] Delivered at a conference in honor of Christopher Hasty at Harvard, 2013; published in *Music in Time: Phenomenology, Perception, Performance: A Festschrift in Honor of Christopher F. Hasty*, ed. Suzannah Clark and Alexander Rehding (Cambridge, MA: Harvard University Press, 2016), 237–56.
[2] Christopher F. Hasty, *Meter as Rhythm* (New York: Oxford University Press, 1997), chapter 14.
[3] See my *Desire and Pleasure in Seventeenth-Century Music* (Berkeley: University of California Press, 2012).

same individual: think, for instance, of Isaac Newton's (to us) embarrassing pursuit of alchemy alongside his celebrated advances in physics and optics. The activities that flourished between the glory of the Renaissance and the brilliance of the Enlightenment qualify to some as a second Dark Age; indeed, eighteenth-century intellectuals branded this interregnum period "baroque," which was not meant as a compliment.[4]

Crucial to most of these enterprises is the phenomenon of change. Whereas many of our theories rely on steady-state, quasi-universal principles, the seventeenth-century penchant for simulations of instability resists uniform methods. In part as a consequence of the radical upheavals in the political, religious, and intellectual domains of the time, artists and thinkers in all media found themselves drawn to concerns such as discontinuity, decay, acceleration, and fluctuating affects. It is no coincidence that the mathematics required to account for change—the calculus—was invented simultaneously by Newton and Leibniz, so urgent was the need for such a tool.

In his odd yet influential book *Noise*, Jacques Attali has argued that musicians often take the lead in cultural transformations, in part because sound is so much more malleable than the materials with which, say, architects work.[5] A composer can quickly fan through myriad possibilities for a new device: recall, for instance, the fecundity of Joseph Haydn in the 1780s or hip-hop in the 1980s, and the speed with which their innovations became common practices in a wide variety of genres.

Similarly, musicians in the first half of the seventeenth century took the idea of temporal fluctuations and ran with it. They relied on a number of new techniques, especially monody and basso continuo, which relieved voices or solo instruments of their traditional task of articulating modal functions.[6] This is not to suggest that this music counts as "tonal," for in some ways its logic becomes even more tenuously related to the procedures of eighteenth-century repertories. But the security of the newly developed bass line makes possible the acrobatics and radical shifts in qualities of motion that have puzzled analysts even as they have delighted listeners.

---

[4] See the interdisciplinary collection *Structures of Feeling in Seventeenth-Century Expressive Culture*, ed. Susan McClary (Toronto: University of Toronto Press, 2013).

[5] Jacques Attali, *Noise: The Political Economy of Music*, trans. Brian Massumi (Minneapolis: University of Minnesota Press, 1985); foreword by Fredric Jameson, afterword by Susan McClary.

[6] For an extensive explanation of modal practice, see my *Modal Subjectivities: Self-Fashioning in the Italian Madrigal* (Berkeley: University of California Press, 2004).

Monteverdi first started publishing his experiments with basso continuo halfway through his Fifth Book of Madrigals (1605) in a setting of Giovanni Battista Guarini's rime "Ahi, com'a un vago sol." In highly mannered and convoluted verse, our baroque Amfortas here laments his long-standing and incurable affliction, even as he seeks to rip off the bandages and renew his anguish. Monteverdi's setting seems at first no less convoluted: he bisects some lines and runs others together, extenuates some words and chatters through others.

Ahi, com'a un vago sol cortese giro	Ah, how at a single kind and lovely glance
de due belli occhi, ond'io	of two beautiful eyes—from which I
soffersi il primo, e dolce stral d'Amore,	suffered the first and sweet arrow of Love—
pien d'un nuovo desio,	full of a new desire,
sì pronto a sospirar, torna il mio core.	so ready to sigh, my heart turns back again.
Lasso, non val ascondersi, ch'omai	Alas, hiding is fruitless, for by now
conosco i segni, che'l mio cor m'addita	I know the signs that my heart shows me
de l'antica ferita,	of the old wound,
ed è gran tempo pur che la saladi.	which I thought I had long since cured.
Ah, che piaga d'Amor non sana mai!	Ah, a love wound never heals!

But he punctuates his piece with a homophonic refrain on the rime's final line, "Ah, che piaga d'Amor non sana mai!," thus imposing upon it an overarching architecture, similar to the Alleluia that punctuates Giovanni Gabrieli's *In ecclesiis* (see Example 11.1a) Moreover, he gives his refrain the most powerful of modal progressions, the Romanesca, and it moves in typical sixteenth-century fashion, with each bass note supporting each pitch in the mode-bearing voice on a one-to-one basis, thus providing the stable temporality most familiar to Monteverdi's listeners[7] (see Example 11.1b). Only the occasional change in voice-leading or slight embellishment moves

---

[7] The Romanesca was one of several formulas (Passamezzo antico, Passamezzo moderno) based on the descent from the fifth scale degree to the modal final. Musicians in the sixteenth and seventeenth centuries made use of these in improvisation and as building blocks in composed music, as in the example at hand.

The word "Romanesca" has acquired a completely different meaning since the publication and widespread adoption of Robert O. Gjerdingen's *Music in the Galant Style* (Oxford, UK: Oxford University Press, 2007). I have asked Bob why he chose as a label a theoretical term that already existed, in contrast with, say, his invention of the term "Meyer," named in honor of his mentor, Leonard Meyer. He admits that his decision was arbitrary. Because of the centrality of the Renaissance Romanesca to much of my own work, I now struggle with students to disambiguate, which they seem unable to do. I greatly admire Bob's ideas; I just wish he hadn't grabbed onto "Romanesca."

Example 11.1a Claudio Monteverdi, "Ah, com' a un vago sol giro," refrain

Example 11.1b Romanesca

this part of the madrigal beyond the bare presentation of the formula itself (though I might mention the wonderful extenuation of the second scale degree on "non sana," made possible by the unexpected appearance of a C-natural that has to be corrected upward).

In its first two iterations, the refrain features two treble voices plus a bass; later the entire five-voice ensemble will join in the admonition. As the refrain enters over and over to wag its moralistic finger at our subject, it may recall the choral platitudes interjected throughout *Orfeo*, for, like the character Orfeo, our subject is enjoined to buck up and develop some discipline. But, as Saint Augustine would say, "Lord, not yet."[8] Otherwise we would miss out on all his delicious backsliding. Only toward the end do the tenors dutifully recite the refrain, thereby admitting the consequences of the failure to resist temptation.

As he often does in his continuo madrigals, Monteverdi renders his subject with two equal voices, which affords him the clarity of diction and dramatic immediacy of monody while allowing for the intertwining of lines so crucial to the simulation of divided interiorities and erotic *frisson*. And with the support of his basso continuo, he is able to produce the jagged or ornamented melodies he wants to foreground—the kinds of melodic figures that would be unintelligible within a strictly modal logic.

---

[8] Saint Augustine, *Confessions*, 8:7.

A tonal musician may see the first few measures of the madrigal as tracing a circle of fifths and will feel relatively safe. But this is not a Vivaldian circle, and although the progression moves systematically by fifth, it should not be trusted (see Example 11.2a). Rather than heeding the bass alone, I would suggest understanding it as a secondhand response to a modal line moving slowly through the Dorian species of fifth: from A to G (sustained by G and C) to F, where it stalls, listing back and forth between G and F. This passive descent and its desultory wavering lull us into a false sense of security, for, along with the subject, we are suddenly brought up short with the words "belli occhi." The generating line, which had stretched out in such a leisurely fashion, abruptly reverses course, dumping us unceremoniously on B-natural and a very hard hexachord.

Note that Dorian usually makes use of the flatted version of the sixth degree when operating within the diatonic diapente (see Example 11.2b).[9] For although the Dorian scale does indeed include B-natural, that pitch comes into play primarily when a piece is exploring its subregions. Consequently, the B-natural here comes as a very rude shock. I am reminded of the moments in *Being John Malkovich* (1999) when individuals ejected from Malkovich's mind get plunked down beside the New Jersey Turnpike. Yet that chain of fifths is so compelling that Monteverdi simply returns to it, leading us down the garden path once again, only to spike us back to B-natural at "desio" (see Example 11.2c).

A third chain of fooling occurs, but this time the twice-tricked heart acknowledges its unwilling acquiescence with an extended cadential preparation to the long-delayed cadence on D. Notice that the composer has not yet really revealed his mode, for the slippage by fifth required that each sonority include the leading tone to the next, causing even the chords based on the final to include F-sharp rather than the F-natural upon which this mode will ultimately depend. An interpreter who sticks with the concept of madrigalisms can easily explain the elaborate intertwining melismas preceding the cadence as painting the word "turn." I would not deny this, but I would also argue that the strategy up until this point has presented a

---

[9] Problems with pedagogical practice arise here as well, as theory teachers instruct students to understand D-Dorian as always identified with B-natural. But tonal minor actually descends from Dorian, with its flexible sixth degree, rather than Aeolian, which brings with it unusual limitations and compositional strategies. Aeolian, for instance, cannot tonicize its fifth scale degree, which Dorian does as a matter of course. Because "modes" are taught in the first week of fundamental theory classes, the association of Dorian with a necessary high sixth scale degree is carved in stone, a tenet nearly impossible to shake loose.

Example 11.2a Monteverdi, "Ah, com'[a?] un vago sol giro," mm. 1–24

condition of lazy complacency disrupted twice by that wound the subject has tried to forget. The flurry of ornamental pitches before the cadence simulates a last-ditch effort at denial, delaying his surrender to the inevitable.

It is here that our stern, chordal refrain enters for the first time, not only with its no-nonsense, unexpanded statement of truth but also with the hitherto missing F-natural planted firmly in the bass. For the rest of the madrigal, the subject tries repeatedly to fabricate that carefree zone that drifts by in fifths. Now, however, it is faced with a B-flat that will not allow it to reconstitute its previous condition. When it does manage to achieve a cadence

Example 11.2b Dorian diapente descent

Example 11.2c Monteverdi, "Ahi, com'[a?] un vago sol giro," mm. 1–6, reduction

away from reality, the refrain hauls it back, even replicating itself at the level of the fifth degree in order to block all exits. The soloists' attempts become truncated: thirteen measures, then only two phrases of a mere four measures each. The cautionary refrain takes over the piece, reducing the subject to a whimper. Indeed, the final iteration of the refrain even appropriates the *seconda prattica* harmonic violence that would seem to have belonged to the soloists, crushing the breath out of any last protests.

What Monteverdi grasps in this and his other continuo madrigals is his newfound ability to work time as if with a zoom lens. He can still wield the one-to-one relationship with each pitch in the modal line, as in his refrain, but he can also allow the bass thus generated to maintain a single function while the melodic lines frolic luxuriously over it—most clearly in the five-measure extravaganza on "core." This temporal elasticity becomes, then, one of his principal techniques for expression.

I hasten to emphasize that this expressivity operates not only at the service of his texts but, more importantly, as a new and increasingly pervasive "structure of feeling"—a term I borrow from Raymond Williams, one of the founders of Cultural Studies. Williams sought through this concept to connect dimensions of human experience often regarded as unique or subjective with scholarly methods of formal analysis and archival research. In his words:

> For what we are defining is a particular quality of social experience and relationship, historically distinct from other particular qualities, which

gives the sense of a generation or of a period. The relations between this quality and the other specifying historical marks of changing institutions, formations, and beliefs, and beyond these the changing social and economic relations between and within classes, are again an open question: that is to say, a set of specific historical questions. . . . We are talking about characteristic elements of impulse, restraint, and tone; specifically affective elements of consciousness and relationships: not feeling against thought, but thought as felt and feeling as thought: practical consciousness of a present kind, in a living and interrelating continuity.[10]

I would argue that Monteverdi chooses texts like "Ahi, com'a un vago sol," precisely because they allow him opportunities for time warping. In the first years of the *seicento*, the certainties of the late Renaissance became attenuated to the point of no return. And even if they continued to serve as points of reference, they stood at the same time as wearisome reminders of parental discipline. The glee with which Monteverdi and his contemporaries transgressed sixteenth-century notions of time is palpable, especially when they launched off into queasy-making territories. These composers were in no hurry to embrace another standard brand of temporal regulation, which would begin to solidify only decades later.

But experiments such as Monteverdi's become perceptible to listeners only if performers know how to respond to his indications. In fact, I have located no recordings that do what I have suggested in my comments.[11] One of my teachers once told me that composers of this period did not really care very much about where they cadenced; they just got to the end of their texts and stopped. Several commercial recordings do just this—they coast along with little differentiation between the chains of fifths and the move to B-natural or between the drawn-out melismas and the tight progression of the refrain. Others grasp the idea of time warping but use it indiscriminately all the way through, even slowing the pace of the refrain so that it sounds as languid as the passages surrounding it. Performers need to develop analytical skills not so that they distance themselves from the music that they

---

[10] Raymond Williams, *Marxism and Literature* (Oxford, UK: Oxford University Press, 1977), 131–32.

[11] At the Hasty conference, I had to substitute another Monteverdi madrigal, "Non vedrò mai le stelle," so that I would have a recording that backed up my argument. I had already published an account of that madrigal, however, in *Desire and Pleasure*, and I did not want to duplicate that discussion here. I hope that enterprising performers can use my discussion of "Ahi, com' a un vago sol" as a guide.

sing or play (a common complaint in theory classes) but because familiarity with the grammar of these early repertories can invite or even demand much more shocking renditions than an all-purpose sense of "musicality" will admit. Just as the first page of Monteverdi's "Cruda Amarilli" should sound like a head-on collision rather than the wispy ninth-chord heard in most recordings, so "Ahi, com'a un vago sol" should alternately cajole and jolt listeners, repeatedly slapping us upside the head.[12]

Temporal elasticity appears in nearly all Italian genres of the time, including sacred music. Recall Monteverdi's "Duo Seraphim," which begins with excruciatingly deliberate modal unfoldings and nearly impossible feats of ornamentation, then progresses to wildly careening spirals, simulations of angels circling weightless around the throne of God.[13] Heinrich Schütz caught the bug during his sabbaticals with Giovanni Gabrieli and Alessandro Grandi in Venice, and he brought the contagion home to Germany with him. As Christopher Hasty's rhythmic analysis of "Anima mea liquefacta est" reveals, the principle of time warping deeply influenced Schütz, who used it to simulate fluctuating states of mystical ecstasy.[14]

Moreover, composers of instrumental music made full use of such devices, producing the same kinds of phenomenological experiences without the assistance of verbal texts. Dario Castello's sonatas frequently depart from linear exposition to the kind of lavish, protracted spiraling developed by Monteverdi for his explorations of space.[15]

My title alludes to *The Rocky Horror Picture Show* (1975), where the "Time Warp" led by Riff Raff seems tame and even stodgy next to these seventeenth-century experiments. But not all of Europe embraced these erratic qualities. The French famously resisted transalpine influences, sometimes even going so far as to prohibit the playing of Italian music. They did so not only because of nationalist chauvinism, however, but also because such willful eccentricities offended the Neoplatonic ideals that regulated most aspects of Louis XIV's court, which greatly preferred the discipline of orderly dance.

Yet the *seicento* time warp did manage to infiltrate France in the guise of a uniquely French genre: the unmeasured prelude. Indeed, the first of these,

---

[12] See the discussion of "Cruda Amarilli" in *Modal Subjectivities*, 181–88.

[13] See my discussion in *Desire and Pleasure*, 165–68 and in chapter 5 of this volume.

[14] Hasty, *Meter as Rhythm*, chapter 14. I deal extensively with this piece in *Power and Desire*, 148–58.

[15] Many excellent recordings of Castello's sonatas now exist. Listen, for instance, to Andrew Manze and Nigel North on *Phantasticus* (Harmonia Mundi) or to Quicksilver on *Stile Moderno* (Acis Productions).

produced by Louis Couperin around 1650, were explicitly modeled on the toccatas of Johann Jacob Froberger, who learned this part of his craft from Girolamo Frescobaldi in Rome. French lutenists and keyboardists had long preceded their dances with relatively free improvisations, some of which survive as sketchy or fully fleshed-out scores. But capturing temporal elasticity in notation posed both technical and conceptual problems. The Italians chose to write out their improvisations in extremely intricate rhythms, with frequent thirty-second notes, and then to indicate in their prefaces that performers were to play freely, avoiding at all cost a rigid reproduction of the note values that appeared on the page. Good Italian that he was, J. S. Bach followed this precept in his toccatas and fantasias. Performers were expected to bend the meticulously indicated rhythms indicated on the page.

Louis Couperin and his successors, including most prominently Jean-Henri d'Anglebert and Élisabeth-Claude Jacquet de la Guerre, chose a radically divergent means to a similar end: they simply tossed mostly undifferentiated pitches onto the page and invited players to arrange them in whatever shape they liked. This encouragement of a kind of performative anarchy seems antithetical to the usual French modus operandi; recall that this was a moment when ornaments and dance steps were being codified and controlled to an unprecedented degree.[16] Yet performers get to exercise extraordinary, nearly unparalleled agency in the *prélude non mesuré*.

Not everyone regards this kind of license as welcome. My harpsichord students, most of whom hesitate even in the face of fully realized French dances, cannot be coaxed to venture into the preludes. At least the Italians provided precise sets of instructions for their extravaganzas; Louis Couperin leaves only a vague trace of his own noodling and then invites us to make it up for ourselves.

Never less than perverse, I love wallowing in these things, for they demand all that I know concerning voice leading, formal backgrounds, and everything in between. During the first read-through, I try to locate the centers of relative gravity—the places where the restless energies seem (or can be made to seem) to land. This was the period in which Galileo and Kepler attempted to calculate the orbits of the planets, with Newton later supplying the mathematical means to account for and measure the phenomena of attraction,

---

[16] See my discussion in *Desire and Pleasure*. For a broader cultural analysis of this moment in French history, see also Michel Foucault, "Docile Bodies," in his *Discipline and Punish: The Birth of the Prison*, trans. Alan Sheridan (New York: Vintage, 1979), 135–69.

repulsion, and acceleration, what he called "the science of fluxions."[17] We already saw that Monteverdi was drawn to lyrics concerning circling stars and angels for some of his most dazzling experiments, though he indicates with great precision how to go about realizing his effects.

But when one plays an unmeasured prelude, one gets to invent an entire cosmology. It is as if we are there before Time began, before the Big Bang, confronted with mere blobs of unarticulated matter, and we have to determine the extent to which each potential point of release exerts a gravitational pull, the ways the surrounding pitches submit to or resist that magnetic force. And what could be more fun than playing God?

I want to turn now to Louis Couperin's Prélude in what I would term G-Hypodorian. The score presents us only with bunches of whole notes and lines that indicate something about voice leading. That is all. (The facsimile appears at the end of this chapter, Example 11.3.)

Like most such pieces, this one opens with an unfolding over a tonic pedal. Notice how nicely Couperin points up the tenor line's Schenkerian unfolding from G to A to B-flat, as the top line moves through anguished intervals. Just as it seems that the opening peroration has ended with G in the bass, the top line substitutes the triadic D with E-flat, thereby blocking closure. Although the next cluster replaces that pitch with E-natural as part of a secondary dominant, the E-flat returns unresolved for most of the next system. For all the apparent stability afforded by the sustained pedal on G in the bass, it is not entirely clear where the next pillar in this suspension bridge is located. Whenever a cadence on G seems within grasp, something happens to skew the harmonic vectors.

I see two plausible places for at least momentary repose on the first page. The first occurs in the second system just after the second low G. The right hand's C stands alone, and if it is marked in performance as preparatory to the B-natural, then B-natural can serve both as a quasi confirmation of the G final and a new impulse forward. If this does not allow for release, it may allow us to catch a breath.

A more complicated situation appears in the fourth and fifth systems, and I can propose two possible solutions. Most of system 4 is taken up with written-out pre-cadential ornaments—something one sometimes finds in Frescobaldi and Froberger toccatas. But however emphatic this buildup

---

[17] See Isaac Newton, *The Method of Fluxions and Infinite Series*, trans. John Colson (London: Henry Woodfall, 1736); the translation was from a posthumously published Latin text.

might be, it is not entirely clear where to put its arrival. We can treat the D in the bass that occurs seven pitches from the end of the line as a downbeat, thus eliding arrival with a new forward-moving gesture. Or we can perform that D as continuing the upbeat quality that precedes it and allow the lower G at the bottom of system 5 to serve as the arrival, nicely sealed up with the ornamented B-flat in the right hand. That solution allows the E-natural to begin a new impulse.

The point is not that one of these is somehow correct and the other not; rather, it is precisely these sorts of quandaries that make unmeasured preludes so challenging and also endlessly variable. If Couperin had wanted to require one of these or the other, he could have indicated as much—as he does, perhaps (or perhaps not), with the bar line halfway through the second page. With that bar line he may signal a discontinuity following the upward sweep in the right hand and also make explicit a link between the C in the bass with the B-flat in the preceding system. But some expert performers just barrel through that spot, basing their decisions on other patterns or other musical impulses.

This particular moment presents another set of questions as well. At the end of system 5 of the first page, the right hand has a seven-pitch configuration that unfurls some kind of seventh chord against the bass, and this figure persists throughout the next page. Should one play these as if they are not related? Or make their similarities audible through rhetorical emphasis? Or perhaps even create a rhythmic pattern that gives them a motivic profile? I happen to like emphasizing the dissonances of each cocktail chord (i.e., the fifth note in the figure), holding it quite a bit longer than the surrounding pitches. Again, it is up to the performer to decide whether such features should emerge from the surrounding chaos as continents rising from the sea or planets from the firmament.

The prelude never strays far from G, its point of reference, but it manages to touch briefly on C minor, D minor, and F major before ending on G. And then Couperin switches to something completely different, announced in the score as a *Changement de mouvement*. The eccentric energies of the opening give way to the Neoplatonic order of social dance. After a page of regular rhythms, the dance disintegrates and lapses back into unmeasured conundrums for the conclusion. The stable metric foundation offered during this reassuring section is withdrawn, the rug unceremoniously yanked out from under the feet of our simulated dancers.

In a parting shot, Couperin stages a passage of dissonant stagnation near the end of the *prélude*. A pattern in the right hand gets stuck at the top of page 4, becoming increasingly strident against the bass. Here voice leading is paramount: Which pitches link with which others to provide a plausible contrapuntal framework? How might the performer harness the energies of the various linear vectors in order to achieve the greatest dramatic effect?

Our ability to deal effectively with seventeenth-century music has been hampered by its considerably different sense of harmonic syntax—an obstacle we can overcome if we take the trouble to learn about late-sixteenth-century modal procedures. But the greater obstacle is its very alien constructions of temporality. Of course, these two dimensions are tightly related to one another. Yet if we concentrate too much on the pitches, we will miss the reasons these composers deployed them in such erratic ways.

I prefer to understand pitch *in all musical repertories* as raw material to be pushed around and arranged in order to produce particular qualities of motion and experiences of time. The pitches give us something concrete to analyze, but it is finally the construction of temporality that matters culturally and aesthetically, that offers us traces of bodies, emotions, and subjectivities from other moments in history.

For it is not only seventeenth-century music that foregrounds radical transformations in temporality. Indeed, this erratic treatment of time occurs throughout music history, especially in moments of extreme style change. Think, for instance, of how Leonin shifts back and forth so thrillingly between free organum and measured discant, of the dizzying superimpositions of rhythmic layers in cantus-firmus motets, of the eccentricities of Beethoven's late quartets, of Mahler's montages, of the shocking simplicity of Miles Davis's "So What" or early Philip Glass, or even of the metric experiments of prog rock.

My decision to concentrate in my own career on how seventeenth-century music works has required me to focus on this inescapable element. But we should all, regardless of the repertories we study, pay much more serious attention to temporalities, especially those whose radical fluctuations stymie our well-behaved linear theories. Even if we want to understand the cultural work associated with the emergence of eighteenth-century tonality, we have to recall the great age of the Time Warp, against which it was reacting. So let's do the Time Warp again.

192 MAKING SENSE OF MUSIC

Example 11.3 Louis Couperin, Prélude in G minor

Example 11.3 Continued

Example 11.3 Continued

Example 11.3 Continued

12

In the Realm of *All* the Senses

Two Sarabandes by Élisabeth-Claude Jacquet de la Guerre[1]

Music theorists usually restrict the senses used in the process of analysis to the auditory and the visual. Although we work to develop skills through our courses in ear training and sight singing, the other sensory organs would seem to have no place in our idealized medium. And that may be why we have such difficulty with repertoires of seventeenth-century France. This music often appears simplistic and banal to the eye and—if it is not performed well—also to the ear, and we tend to write it off as unworthy of detailed scrutiny.

Yet the problem resides not so much in the music itself as in our neglect of channels of communication that involve much more than ears and eyes. For French music of this period appeals to and by means of the tactile, the kinetic, the spatial, and perhaps even (albeit through synesthesia) the olfactory, all of which pass through the filter of taste: that elusive *goût* celebrated by Francophiles. Qualities such as color and timbre, usually pushed to the side in the interest of objective analysis, become primary parameters in these repertoires. This essay focuses on two works of Élisabeth-Claude Jacquet de la Guerre: the sarabandes from her keyboard suites in A minor and D minor.[2] My comments could apply equally, however, to many other French composers of her era and of others as well.

Like other French composers of this time, Jacquet de la Guerre grounded much of her music in the social dance so central to life at court. I have written elsewhere about how this close allegiance to dance produced a kind of temporality quite different from the musics of other parts of Europe. In particular, it

---

[1] Published in *Analytical Essays on Music by Women Composers*, ed. Brenda Ravenscroft and Laurel Parsons (Oxford, UK: Oxford University Press, 2018), 109–28.

[2] Élisabeth-Claude Jacquet de la Guerre, *Les Pièces de Claveßin de Mad.elle De la Guerre*, Premier Livre, facsimile, ed. Catherine Cessac and Arthur Lawrence (New York: Broude Trust, 2009). The sarabande in D minor appears on pp. 11–12, the one in A minor on pp. 30–31. A transcription by Steve Wiberg appears on IMSLP. The music examples here are my editions.

focused the attention on a succession of moments, each one in turn offering a sense of plenitude. This way of parsing time corresponded not only with the physical actions of the dancing body but also with widespread ideological precepts in French philosophy, theology, and governance.[3] It was within this ideological context that Jean-Philippe Rameau developed his freeze-frame approach to harmonic analysis, whereby each vertical collection receives its own independent label, a Roman numeral.

By contrast, Italian and Italianate musics of the seventeenth century worked to create forward-striving trajectories by interrupting and delaying expected points of arrival, creating qualities of motion antithetical to those of the French.[4] To the very large extent to which musicians today are trained in the Italian fashion by way of the German composers who made it their own, we often find it hard to locate the content of French dances. Even musicologists who claim to specialize in this area sometimes apologize for the music's thinness. In a volume dedicated to Jean-Baptiste Lully, for instance, Paul Henry Lang wrote:

> The music all these [French seventeenth-century] composers cultivated was in the sign of the dance, so congenial to the French, with its neat little forms, pregnant rhythms, great surface attraction, and in tone and structure so much in harmony with the spirit of the age. This music, though slight and short-breathed, was elegant and so different from any other that the whole of Europe became enamored of it.[5]

Performers insufficiently attuned to the *délices* of French dance work often blunder obliviously through pieces and then scurry back to the guaranteed greatness of Bach.

Seventeenth-century French court dance involved much more than a set pattern of steps per measure, repeated by the dancers for the duration

---

[3] See my "Temporality and Ideology: Qualities of Motion in Seventeenth-Century French Music," in *Desire and Pleasure in Seventeenth-Century Music* (Berkeley: University of California Press, 2012), 241–57. But see also chapter 11 for a discussion of the *prélude non mesuré*, the exception that proves the rule.

[4] See the discussions of Monteverdi, Cesti, Frescobaldi, Stradella, and Bach in *Desire and Pleasure in Seventeenth-Century Music*. My analysis of the Allemande from Bach's French Suite in D minor in "Temporality and Ideology" points particularly to the ways in which his music differed from that of his French models.

[5] Paul Henry Lang, introduction to *Jean-Baptiste Lully and the Music of the French Baroque: Essays in Honor of James R. Anthony*, ed. John Hajdu Heyer (Cambridge, UK: Cambridge University Press, 1989), 1. See my extended discussion of feminizing tropes of this sort in *Feminine Endings: Music, Gender, and Sexuality* (Minneapolis: University of Minnesota Press, 1991).

of the piece. If it had been so simple, Louis XIV's dance masters would not have had such control over the daily regimen of courtiers. But in part as a way of preventing his nobles from fomenting revolution, the king kept them busy with lessons and rehearsals, leading to the evening's exam in which his subjects would have to perform two by two in front of him. Those who excelled might receive his favor and bounty; those who did not risked banishment from court and financial ruin. The stakes were high.

Dancers faced several levels of complexity in executing these choreographies. First, the couple had to execute a sequence of geometrical maneuvers with respect to one another: sometimes shaping a figure eight together, then separating out from each other in an arch form, and so on. The choreography of a single dance might demand a dozen such patterns, each one corresponding to a mere four or eight bars of music. See, for instance, this period notation for a mere eight bars of a passepied (see Figure 12.1).[6]

Second, the dances engaged not only the feet but also the arms, hands, and face, which responded to different metric levels, sometimes even producing cross-rhythms with the steps themselves. It was on the basis of these other factors that the king would distinguish a superlative performer from a mediocre one, with all the rewards and demotions those distinctions entailed. One could go through all the motions, in other words, and still fail to execute an aesthetically pleasing result.

Finally, the desired qualities of motion for these dances depended almost entirely on minuscule discrepancies of timing in the music—the kinds of discrepancies immediately perceived and relayed to the body as what we now might call groove but which can be measured only with the aid of recent digital technologies.[7] If, in the words of William Butler Yeats, we cannot tell the dancer from the dance, we also cannot separate the music from the player, who either succeeds or fails in buoying up the festivities in precisely the right way.

Think, for example, of the invention of a groove called the jerk. On May 12, 1965, producer Jerry Wexler approached some studio musicians during a recording session and said, "Why don't you pick up on this thing here?"

---

[6] This example comes from Raoul Auger Feuillet, *Chorégraphie, ou l'art de décrire la danse* (Paris, 1700), 26. Many other examples may be viewed online.
[7] See the discussion of participatory discrepancies in Charles Keil and Steven Feld, *Music Grooves: Essays and Dialogues* (Chicago: University of Chicago Press, 1994), and the theorizing of rhythm in Anne Danielsen, *Presence and Pleasure: The Funk Grooves of James Brown and Parliament* (Middletown, CT: Wesleyan University Press, 2006).

IN THE REALM OF *ALL* THE SENSES   199

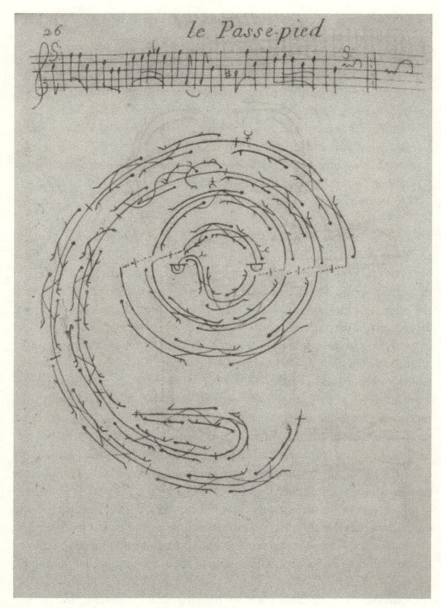

Figure 12.1 Dance notation for a passepied

He then executed a brief physical gesture for the musicians. Guitarist Steve Cropper later explained:

> [Wexler] said this was the way the kids were dancing; they were putting the accent on two. Basically, we'd been one-beat-accenters with an afterbeat, it was like 'boom dah,' but here this was a thing that went 'un-chaw,' just the reverse as far as the accent goes. The backbeat was somewhat delayed, and it just put it in that rhythm, and [drummer] Al [Jackson] and I have been using that as a natural thing now, ever since we did it. We play a downbeat and then two is almost on but a little bit behind, only with a complete impact. It turned us on to a heck of a thing.[8]

A heck of a thing, indeed! This groove gave rise to a new style of soul music and provided Stax Records with the boost it needed to make it a viable presence within the industry. Millions of kids picked up "on this thing here," and they still respond in late middle age with precise physical motions within a bar of Wilson Pickett's "In the Midnight Hour": the track produced during that recording session.

Analyzing Jacquet de la Guerre's (or Lully's or D'Anglebert's) dance music requires developing devices similar to those just discussed. The reductive strategies typical of our usual methods predispose us to eliminating ornamental levels so as to get down to the real substance of a piece. For musics that thrive on expansion, this approach makes a good deal of sense; we scrape the embellishments off so as to discern the broader picture. But this method does not work at all for the repertories at hand, which actually require that we scrutinize and immerse ourselves in the minute details of the surface—just the kinds described by Steve Cropper.

Or, indeed, by François Couperin, when he seeks to theorize this phenomenon. He writes that if "*Mesure* defines the number and equality of the beats, . . . *Cadence* or *Mouvement* is properly the spirit and soul that it is necessary to add." Bénigne de Bacilly further explains these important qualities thus:

> *Mouvement* is . . . a certain quality that gives soul to the song, and . . . it is called *Mouvement* because it stirs up, I may say it excites, the listeners'

---

[8] Steve Cropper, quoted in Ed Ward, Geoffrey Stokes, and Ken Tucker, *Rock of Ages: The Rolling Stone History of Rock & Roll* (New York: Rolling Stone Press, 1986), 293–94. For a fuller discussion, see my "Music, the Pythagoreans, and the Body," in *Choreographing History*, ed. Susan Leigh Foster (Bloomington: Indiana University Press, 1995), 82–104.

attention, in the same way as do those who are the most rebellious in harmony.... it inspires in hearts such passion as the singer wishes to create, principally that of tenderness.... I don't doubt at all that the variety of *Mesure*, whether quick or slow, contributes a great deal to the expression of the song. But there is certainly another quality, more refined and more spiritual, that always holds the listener attentive and ensures that the song is less tedious. It is the *Mouvement* that makes the most of a mediocre voice, making it better than a very beautiful voice without expression.[9]

If we know how to parse out *mesure* (i.e., meter), we do not even have a term in our vocabulary for *mouvement* ("groove"? "swing"?), which Bacilly rightly compares in effect with transgressive harmonic practices—the feature we typically regard as evidence of progressive and imaginative genius.

Although Jacquet de la Guerre's music may appear "tonal," it operates so closely to the background structure handed down from sixteenth-century modal practice that I find it more productive to examine the ways she expands on an age-old formula. For as far back as we have notated scores to dances such as estampies, we can observe a very simple mechanism: the first strain opens in the home key and achieves its first point of arrival on a place that sustains the modal fifth degree (most commonly the second degree poised to resolve back to the final, but sometimes what we hear as the relative major or even a plagal cadence that returns us to our starting position); the second strain reaches closure on the final. So automatic was this formula that it underwrites all those improvisatory patterns—the Romanesca, the Passamezzo Antico, the Folia—that flourished from at least the mid-1500s. Example 12.1 shows the two most common harmonizations of the descent through the mode's diapente or species of fifth (from the fifth scale degree to the final): the Passamezzo antico and the Romanesca.[10]

Moreover, it provides the framework for tonal schemata, with its generating lines pushed further and further into the background by middle-ground strategies that sustain the points along the way as brief key areas. My charts may resemble Schenker graphs, in part because Schenker discerned this process from the other end: through increasing stages of reduction.

---

[9] The quotations of both Couperin and Bacilly are taken from the translations in Beverly Scheibert, *D'Anglebert and the 17th-Century Clavecin School* (Bloomington: Indiana University Press, 1986), 40–41.

[10] See again chapter 11, note 7, for the problems that have arisen with the term "Romanesca" in music theory.

Example 12.1 Diapente descents

By contrast, my approach builds from the principal unit of modal syntax, the descent through the modal diapente from the fifth degree to the final, examining the means by which seventeenth-century composers worked to expand and animate that pattern in their new practices.[11]

I shall begin with the sarabande from Jacquet de la Guerre's keyboard suite in A minor, a piece that seems quite transparent at first glance (see Example 12.2a). Its opening strain comprises a mere eight bars, which break down into 2+2+4 measures. As is characteristic of the sarabande genre, each bar features a strong agogic accent on the second beat. And although we pass briefly through C major in mm. 3–4, we return to the tonic in m. 5 and continue through a scalar descent to a half cadence pointing back toward A at the bar line.

If I were introducing French dance types to a class, I could do worse than to use this as an example, so precisely does it satisfy the conventions of the style. Moreover, it could serve as an example for an introductory Schenker class, so obviously does it establish the fifth degree, then harmonize it with C, then move down by step to the half cadence, as shown in Example 12.2b. Yet that very sense of adhering to established conventions is what may diminish the value of the piece in our eyes and ears.

As we shall see when we compare it with the second strain and also with the next example, this opening strives strategically to present itself as simple. Yet it is far from *simplistic* if we take into account the physical impulses

---

[11] See again my *Desire and Pleasure*, especially the first two chapters concerning expansion, as well as chapter 8, which focuses on the development of binary dance forms.

Example 12.2a Elisabeth-Claude Jacquet de la Guerre, Sarabande in A minor, pt. 1

Example 12.2b Jacquet de la Guerre, Sarabande in A minor, reduced

registered in the score. The two eighth notes in the first beat, for instance, launch the dancer aggressively toward beat two, at which point the motion might well hang in suspension under the right hand's dotted-quarter. Similarly, the string of eighths in m. 2 implies the option of continuous action toward the downbeat of m. 3, where the unstable harmonization of the upper auxiliary, F, tilts us forward to the C major of m. 4. Now nothing remains but the descent in the top line from the fifth degree by step down to the half cadence supported in tenths in the bass. But not so fast! Notice the sneaky suspension in the tenor that links mm. 4 and 5 and the flurry of motion at the eighth-note level from m. 6 to the cadence—all carefully balanced between hesitations and fluid advancement.

Identifying oneself with the dancing body calls attention to all those minute details and the crucial differences they make to possible choreographies. Here, for instance, is a description from 1671 of a gentleman dancing a sarabande solo:

At first he danced with a totally charming grace, with a serious and circumspect air, with an equal and slow rhythm, and with such a noble, beautiful, free and easy carriage that he had all the majesty of a king, and inspired as much respect as he gave pleasure.

Then, standing taller and more assertively, and raising his arms to half-height and keeping them partly extended, he performed the most beautiful steps ever invented for the dance.

Sometimes he would glide imperceptibly, with no apparent movement of his feet and legs, and seemed to slide rather than step. Sometimes, with the most beautiful timing in the world, he would remain suspended, immobile, and half leaning to the side with one foot in the air; and then, compensating for the rhythmic unit that had gone by, with another more precipitous unit he would almost fly, so rapid was his motion.

Sometimes, for the pleasure of everyone present, he would turn to the right, and sometimes he would turn to the left; and when he reached the very middle of the empty floor, he would pirouette so quickly that the eye could not follow.

Now and then he would let a whole rhythmic unit go by, moving no more than a statue, and then, setting off like an arrow, he would be at the other end of the room before anyone had time to realize that he had departed.

But all this was nothing compared to what was observed when this gallant began to express the emotions of his soul through the motions of his body, and reveal them in his face, his eyes, his steps and all his actions.

Sometimes he would cast languid and passionate glances throughout a low and languid rhythmic unit; and then, as though weary of being obliging, he would avert his eyes, as if he wished to hide his passion; and, with a more precipitous motion, would snatch away the gift he had tendered.

Now and then he would express anger and spite with an impetuous and turbulent rhythmic unit; and then, evoking a sweeter passion by more moderate motions, he would sigh, swoon, let his eyes wander languidly; and certain sinuous movements of the arms and body, nonchalant, disjointed and passionate, made him appear so admirable and so charming that throughout this enchanting dance he won as many hearts as he attracted spectators.[12]

Several excellent performances of French dance may be found on YouTube. I recommend in particular the footage of my colleague Julie Andrijeski and our mutual students dancing a chaconne (www.youtube.com/watch?v= ywCnejJUSjg), especially Andrijeski's solo at the beginning of the track. Like the performer described in the quotation, she sometimes allows the meter to guide her, then hovers, then shifts the attention down to the level of the eighth note for a flurry of steps. And like him, she responds to the music with her entire body: face, arms, and hands feature as prominently as do the actions of the feet.

Many of the nuances in these performances depend on notated ornaments in the music, which call upon the player not merely to alternate with the note below (as with the *pincé* or mordant on the first beat) or above (as with the *tremblement* or trill on beat two) but to focus intently on touch. Romance languages refer to the activity we call "play" and the Germans call *spielen* with their terms *toucher, toccare, tocar*—and thus François Couperin's celebrated *L'Art de toucher le clavecin*. He intended his treatise to cover all dimensions of performance, but he paid special attention to the interplay among rhythmic nuance (*mouvement*), ornaments (*agréments*), temporality, and physicality. It is this, he argues, that makes French music so difficult for foreigners to appreciate and to master; indeed, such elements may fly below their radar, not even noticed by the kinds of performers who concentrate on other features that are more easily viewed on the score and thus acceptable as genuine information.

Of all repertories, that designed for the French harpsichord may be least amenable to translation to other instruments—the piano, for example. It has been demonstrated by comics that much of the content of Bach's music comes across even if played on garden hoses.[13] But a dance by Chambonnières, D'Anglebert, or Jacquet de la Guerre reduces to little more than nonsense if performed on the wrong instrument. Touch, sonority, and that complex *je ne*

---

[12] Father François Pomey, "Description d'une Sarabande dansée," in *Le Dictionnaire Royal Augmenté* (Lyons, 1671), translated in Patricia M. Ranum, "Audible Rhetoric and Mute Rhetoric: the 17th-Century French Sarabande," *Early Music* 14, no. 1 (1986): 22.

[13] Performances featuring such antics appeared on recordings released by the Hoffung Music Festival in 1958 and 1961.

sais quoi to which Couperin gestured comprise the musical substance and should, therefore, be the purview of the analyst.

For good reason, theorists have usually counted color as a secondary parameter, ranking in importance behind matters of pitch. Although we can identify instrumentation in scores, we could not until recently measure the shades of difference wielded by expert performers or the subtle qualities of sound exploited by, say, Rameau, Berlioz, Fauré, or Messiaen. Not coincidentally, a French laboratory, IRCAM, has bequeathed us spectral analysis, though the ability to quantify a sonority does not bridge the gap between the phenomenon and its experiential or aesthetic resonance. As Leon Wieseltier has argued with respect to the relationship of the sciences and humanities:

> Imagine a scientific explanation of a painting—a breakdown of Chardin's cherries into the pigments that comprise them, and a chemical analysis of how their admixtures produce the subtle and plangent tonalities for which they are celebrated. Such an analysis will explain everything except what most needs explaining: the quality of beauty that is the reason for our contemplation of the painting. Nor can the new "vision science" . . . give a satisfactory account of aesthetic charisma. The inadequacy of a scientistic explanation does not mean that beauty is therefore a "mystery" or anything similarly occult. It means only that other explanations must be sought, in formal and iconographical and emotional and philosophical terms.[14]

Or, to return to the matter at hand, I could create a graph with the right equipment of the sound made by one of my harpsichord strings, but doing so would advance my project very little.

Although Wieseltier writes concerning painting, his words "subtle and plangent tonalities" resonate exceptionally well with the matter at hand. Keyboardists still tend to uphold the piano as their standard and find other instruments wanting: clavichords too soft, synthesizers cheesy and artificial, harpsichords lacking in sustain and sensitivity to touch. Within this Goldilocks world, only the piano is "just right."

But let me turn this around. The piano lacks the aggressive percussive quality, the "subtle and plangent tonalities," of the harpsichord, which

---

[14] Leon Wieseltier, "Crimes against Humanities," *New Republic* (3 September 2013); http://www.newrepublic.com/article/114548/leon-wieseltier-responds-steven-pinkers-scientism

produces something like what organists call chiff not only at the moment of attack but also of release. Because of the noise of the mechanism, the performer must control that sound (not unlike that of a high-hat cymbal in a drum set) as carefully as the pitches. When the harpsichord operates as part of the continuo/rhythm section of an ensemble, its pitches nearly cease to matter, but the impulses it conveys through that percussive element have the responsibility of driving the whole group.[15]

Even when the instrument plays solo, as in the dances under consideration, the noise factor contributes all-important precision as well as a kind of sonic arrogance. Not for nothing was the piano—with its exquisite palette of *Empfindsamkeit*—the keyboard embraced by an emerging bourgeoisie. Pianists sometimes try to simulate the sound of the harpsichord by playing softly and with consistent staccato. In fact, the older, aristocratic instrument is far brasher and has access to color combinations and percussive qualities not available to the piano. It also has a surprising amount of sustain, which allows for melodic pathos as well as the transparent articulation of contrapuntal webs.

With all this in mind, let us return to those eight seemingly transparent measures in Jacquet de la Guerre's A-minor sarabande. The right hand begins with a biting *pincé*, a figure repeated on the downbeats of mm. 3 and 5 and in all three cases sharply fixing the note it inflects and grounding the physical weight of the dancer. But how to approach the second pitch? Like other such graces, this one has melodic content, for it brings the line down by step from the initial E through D to C. Note that it thereby produces a striking discord, hidden from view in a notation that purports to adhere to prevailing notions of dissonance control yet readily apparent to the ear.

The degree to which this discord resonates is left to the performer's touch. I would lift the hand after the sarabande's opening salvo and land with deliberation on the D of the second beat, only gradually moving into the alternation, milking the dissonance for all it's worth. And the third pitch? Well, clearly the hand has to lift at the bar line to prepare for the alternation between B and A that begins the second measure. But should one also lift before the last pitch in m. 1? Raising the issue may seem pedantic, but one's choice

---

[15] When harpsichordists forget this and try to show off their improvised figuration, their clattering can come off sounding like a garbage can being dumped out; it registers as nonsense with respect to both rhythm and pitch. I coach continuo players to listen carefully to strategies used by excellent jazz drummers, to pay attention to how they establish groove, how and when they bring in fills.

will greatly influence the quality of motion presented to the listener and/or dancer. In fact, the hands themselves must dance.

In m. 2 the interest shifts to the left hand, which fills in the gap of a seventh from C down to D. The string of eighth notes invites the deployment of *notes inégales*, though how unequal is the prerogative of the performer. If presented as a string of undifferentiated eighths, a dancer might be inclined to hover at beat two; if presented as three pairs, the dancer likely would more likely move with each beat toward the downbeat of m. 3. Now look at mm. 5–6. The tenor voice breaks the two bars into hemiola: three half notes against the two dotted halves in the right hand and bass. Accented properly, such a passage might provoke a pattern of cross-rhythms in the dancer.

When Jacquet de la Guerre composed these pieces, she may or may not have intended them to accompany actual social dance. But just as, say, Earth, Wind & Fire simulates bodily activity in their sound, even on their recordings, so a performer of this music must make palpable the qualities of motion to which a dancer could respond. Our virtual bodies should be able to imagine those shifts in weight, languid hesitations, or sudden bursts of energy, all of which depend on delicate gradations in touch.

I am posing here the question why we analyze music. If we do so in order to demonstrate that a piece satisfies the conditions we demand for tonal coherence, then Jacquet de la Guerre's sarabande passes muster, though little more. But surely establishing that foregone conclusion is not the reason we subject the works we care about to such scrutiny. Approached properly, analysis should benefit performers by making them aware of the salient features of the music they hope to convey. As my demonstration thus far indicates, I firmly believe in this goal.[16]

But the historian also should find analysis fruitful or even necessary as she attempts to understand how music operated as a mode of expression at a particular time, to explain how it manifested crucial cultural values by means of sound, to justify the inclusion of certain pieces in an anthology or syllabus. In her own lifetime, critics frequently praised Jacquet de la Guerre as the most accomplished of female composers, and her triumphs at court and in the opera house fully support that reputation. Yet qualifying as the best girl on the block should not suffice. We need to figure out how to enter into her artistic universe and to glean how she engaged with her medium.

---

[16] I have benefited greatly from observations of and discussions with my colleague Julie Andrijeski—an exquisite performer of French Baroque music on violin and dance.

I suggested earlier that Jacquet de la Guerre kept the first strain of her A-minor sarabande simple for strategic reasons, for the second strain raises many issues of more self-evident interest to today's analyst (see Example 12.2c). Beginning on the dominant to A with which the first strain concluded, the second quickly reorients us toward G major, with the final A reinterpreted in m. 10 as the second degree poised to descend to the new tonic. This new key serves as a strong articulation of the descent from the E, the fifth scale degree (which was sustained throughout the first section), to the fourth degree. Bars 11–12 confirm both the temporarily reigning D and also its harmonization by G in a leisurely fashion. The D in the background continues to control events for the following four measures, now supported with the new key of D minor. But note the affective change from the blithe treatment of G major to the more plaintive

Example 12.2c Jacquet de la Guerre, Aeolian Sarabande, pt. 2

sojourn in D, to underscore which the downbeats of mm. 14–15 receive acute dissonances.

Most striking, however, is the sucker punch of m. 17. For all its pathos, the D-minor passage seals itself up in m. 16 on an open octave, as if there were nothing left to say. But the downbeat of m. 17 shatters that moment of temporary closure. An unexpected C in the bass under the right hand, which tries to hold onto D by suggesting a return to G, pulls us down through a violent hemiola to A. The right hand scrambles through chromatic inflections to keep up but ultimately surrenders to a relatively weak arrival on A in m. 18; the bass, which had seized the controls in m. 17, performs the resolute stepwise descent and powerful cadential formula that brings us home to A minor.

All of the details I discussed with respect to the first strain also obtain here: each ornament, each change of motion is freighted with implications for the dancer's choreography. But nothing prepares us for that rude awakening in m. 17. A dancer would need to be deaf not to respond powerfully—with physical gesture and facial expression—to that abrupt shift from the closed-up cadence in m. 16 to the explosion that succeeds it without warning. In a sense, it is not only m. 16 that prepares the surprise but the entire sarabande as it has unfolded up until this dramatic moment.

That's why I described the first strain as strategically simple. Jacquet de la Guerre saves her *coup de théâtre* for the last moment, as though the piece has to be dragged kicking and screaming back to its final. Now play the second strain again, as it luxuriates in G major, laments in D minor, and then—unbelievably!—pulls the rug out from under us yet again in m. 17. If this sarabande appeared in a *comédie-ballet*, it might be enacted by a sorceress (say, Lully's Armide) who plays nice until she suddenly unleashes the infernal powers she has kept under wraps. It all breaks loose in m. 17.

But Jacquet de la Guerre doesn't pursue such an end-weighted trajectory in all her binary-form dances. Take, for example, the sarabande from her suite in D minor (see Example 12.3). If we were to encounter this dance in the context of the suite as a whole, we would just have heard the courante conclude on an unrepentant D-minor triad. (In fact, only one unit in this suite—the gigue—ends with the mediant raised to deliver a conventional major-triad conclusion.) Thus, it comes as something of a surprise when the sarabande begins with a D-major sonority. The second beat, typically accented in sarabandes, receives only an embellished tonic in the tenor voice.

Example 12.3 Jacquet de la Guerre, Sarabande, Suite in D Minor

And then she drives the knife in. For that serene opening gets cruelly upended on the third beat, which asserts the minor-key context we knew awaited us. On one level, the B-flat is merely the sixth degree that circumscribes the diapente's upper limit. But its intrusion after the D-major triad sounds excruciating. Moreover, when this pitch recurs on the downbeat of m. 2, it is harmonized as a diminished seventh. The crunch produced by this chord does not find easy resolution: to be sure, the B-flat descends to A, but only after an *échappé* to C-natural over the C-sharp in the bass. More strikingly, the bass's leading tone appears to collapse under the weight of the dissonance and drops abruptly to F.

Although the bass continues on from there to take us in stepwise fashion back to D, the top voice leaps onto C-sharp to arrive on a powerfully asserted (though unstable by virtue of the approach from below) eighth degree in m. 4. Reaching up even more precariously to the mediant, the top line commences a stepwise descent down the octave to the F in m. 8 and its resolution to E for a half cadence. On taking the repeat, we may find the F-sharp in m. 1 even more searing, given that we have just heard F-natural confirmed at the cadence.

A glance at the rhythmic impulses of these first eight bars reveals that Jacquet de la Guerre has decided not to follow the pattern characteristic of the sarabande. If the A-minor sarabande discussed above invites that elegant set of conventional moves, this one aggressively accents downbeats with powerful preparatory anacruses on the third beat. The body's stances and gestures would violate what we expect of a sarabande every bit as much as the harsh harmonic language contests normative practice. Indeed, the two go hand in hand.

The second strain promises at first a moment of relief with a brief arrival on F major, and the long-beleaguered B-flat here operates as a lovely fourth degree. But that promise gets rescinded on the downbeat of m. 11 when the bass's B-flat is greeted with an augmented triad. Nor is this simultaneity the product of an ornament that conceals the untoward dissonance; no, Jacquet de la Guerre notates this chord explicitly on the page.

That diminished fourth between F-sharp and B-flat appears frequently over the course of this suite, making it one of its signature elements. Note that, on a meantone-tempered harpsichord, this interval conjures up the dreaded wolf tone. Voice-leading principles aside, this sonority produces auditory discomfort and even pain. The listener may clap her hands over her ears in an involuntary reflex.

The reader will no doubt still remember that I promised to engage with the olfactory senses. I cannot play or think of this moment without wrinkling up my nose as if in involuntary response to a pungent smell, and the fact that it erupts suddenly after the sweet blandness of m. 10 makes it even more shocking.

To describe the downbeat of m. 11 as pungency is not necessarily to deprecate it: think of the stink of a ripe Époisses, which may seem quite alarming until one realizes (or at least a sophisticated connoisseur of cheese realizes) how delicious it will taste. The performer can temper the odor to some extent: holding onto the G of the embellishment can alleviate the brutality of this moment, but moving as quickly as possible to the F-sharp can enhance its sharpness. Moreover, the sight of the performer screwing up her face in quasi-disgust as she executes this move makes the effect abundantly clear.

This may appear quite fanciful; good German music rarely if ever evokes the sense of smell. But the French do so with some regularity. Recall Gabriel Fauré's "Les roses d'Ispahan," the wavering harmonies of which invite the listener to perceive the perfume of roses and jasmine. Or, to return to the German-speaking world, Mahler's "Ich atmet' einen linden Duft" in the *Rückert Lieder*. Not to mention the whole genre of funk.

The following bar sees the increasingly sore B-flat harmonized more tamely as mediant of G minor and then, through the embellishment, as the upper auxiliary to D minor's fifth degree. If the D-minor chord on beat three suggests that the storm has past, the downbeat of m. 13 explodes in the higher register. A dancer would want to underscore that moment with a dramatic, authoritative gesture. As before, however, the high F serves to instigate an octave descent to the lower F and onward to E, the mode's second degree.

But Jacquet de la Guerre withholds the leading tone that might have harmonized the arrival on E in m. 16. In doing so, she sets up one of her most bizarre strategies, this time played out in the domain of meter as well as harmony. For the first time in this contrarian sarabande, m. 17 seems to deliver an accent on the conventional second beat. The abrupt shift from F to F-sharp in the bass, however, shifts the metric impulse with a hemiola. Above that erratic shift, the top voice breaks apart in a discombobulated manner, creating silences on downbeats and syncopations across bar lines. The diminished fourth in m. 19 recalls the earlier crisis, following which the melody limps home. As if to persuade the incredulous listener of this passage, the composer repeats it to conclude the sarabande.

I have rarely mentioned gender in this essay, and I have no interest in arguing that anything in these dances betrays a feminine sensibility. To be sure, Jacquet de la Guerre mentions her gender as a point of pride in the dedication to her collection when she calls a pastorale she had written for the king "une chose que Personne de mon Sexe n'a encore tentée" (a thing no one of my sex has yet attempted).[17] But far from "betraying" a feminine sensibility, Jacquet de la Guerre's harmonic language and her rhythmic experiments step further outside the norms than do the dance suites of her male contemporaries. No shrinking violet, this female composer pushes the envelope in ways we usually identify as the prerogative of male artists.

Traditional analysts would have little difficulty accounting for these maneuvers; Jacquet de la Guerre makes use of the tonal harmonies Rameau would later teach us how to label. But my finicky attention to detail reveals a crucial quality in the sarabandes: namely, the way this music operates on the basis of moment-by-moment events. An Italian aria of this time would unfold through sweeping gestures, delaying and heightening desire for the next implied point of arrival. To be sure, Jacquet's pieces proceed through standard background progressions as well, and they even construct affect through postponed expectations. These occur, however, at a very low level of activity. Jacquet de la Guerre's music draws the ear into the surface, in accordance with the mode of temporality characteristic of French seventeenth-century culture.

And not only that of the seventeenth century. Recall the introductory section of Berlioz's *Symphonie fantastique* or the balcony scene from his *Roméo et Juliette*, which eschew teleology but keep us on edge by tickling the ear with this nuance or that color: details that in German music would seem like insignificant distractions or would be perceived as sacrificing coherence to "mere" effect. Unless we want to write them off as incompetent (a time-honored reaction, in fact), we have to think more carefully about why French musicians would pursue such effects.

Pungency, kinetic motion, color, simulations of pain and pleasure, touch, taste—and then, analysis. As it developed in the nineteenth century, analysis had as an important ideological goal the demonstration of the solidity of German music in express contradistinction to the perfumed luxury of decadent French repertories. Its methods have proven most fruitful for illuminating the intellectual superiority of Bach, Beethoven, Brahms,

---

[17]. Dedication to her *Pièces de Claveßin* (Paris, 1687).

Schoenberg, and so on. But by their very definition, those same methods aim to expose the ephemerality of what Paul Henry Lang described as "neat little forms, pregnant rhythms, great surface attraction . . . slight and short-breathed . . . elegant"—surely a condemnation by faint praise if ever there was one.

Élisabeth-Claude Jacquet de la Guerre offers the performer and the listener a feast of delights that refuses to remain within a single sensory domain. Her work challenges us to open our observations to experiences not typically included in the enterprise of analysis. Following her hedonistic lead, we may arrive at richer modes of experiencing music of all stripes.

13
Salome in the Court of Queen Christina[1]

Most creative artists lead boring lives; they sit at their desks, and they scribble. For this reason, the screenwriters for biopics usually have to strain to translate the energies of the artworks themselves into compelling narrative plots. Just think of all those movies in which Beethoven or Schubert pines away after an imaginary girlfriend in order to justify the lyric moments in their music.

But Alessandro Stradella might well have been an invention of Alexandre Dumas's fevered imagination. The most brilliant Italian musician of the later seventeenth century, he streaked like a meteor through his brief career, tossing off works of genius, seducing ladies for whom he had been hired for singing instruction, provoking international diplomatic crises when noblewomen refused to hand him over for extradition, and fleeing from *bravi* (hired assassins—predecessors of the Mafia and the Camorra) who managed finally to murder him in 1682 at age 43.[2] A genuine picaresque hero, he even had a sidekick, the composer Carlo Ambrogio Lonati, with whom he carried out his escapades. Known as "il gobbo della regina" (Queen Christina's hunchback), Lonati served as the Leporello to Stradella's Don Giovanni.[3]

Despite Stradella's powerful influence on Handel and many others, he is remembered almost exclusively for his sensationalistic lifestyle, which had already become the stuff of legend by the time of his death. A rash of about half

---

[1] Written for the Voces Nostrates Lecture, UCLA Center for Medieval and Renaissance Studies, January 2010. Delivered as the Robert Kelley Memorial Musicology Lecture at University of Miami (February 2027) and the Stephen Barwick Lecture at Harvard University (February 2017). Also presented at University of Washington, De Paul University, University of Toronto, University of Pittsburgh, Bowling Green University. For more on my career-long engagement with Stradella's music, see chapter 1 in this volume.

[2] The most thorough account of his life is Carolyn Gianturco, *Alessandro Stradella, 1639–1682: His Life and Music* (Oxford, UK: Oxford University Press, 1994). Among many other things, Gianturco establishes his family lineage, which had been drastically distorted in later accounts.

[3] Lonati ceased to be a joke for me when Dr. Cynthia Black presented a lecture-recital based on his music. A worthy companion to Stradella, indeed! See her "Re-Imagining Scordatura in Late Seventeenth-Century Italy: Carlo Ambrogio Lonata's Sonatas of 1701" (Case Western Reserve University, May 2015).

a dozen Stradella operas emerged in the 1840s, and novels based on his life continue to appear with some regularity—bodice-ripping, cloak-and-dagger affairs that pay scant attention to his music. Indeed, most singers know his name only for an innocuous but multiply anthologized tune, "Pietà, Signore," which was actually composed as a hoax in the nineteenth century, probably by the Belgian musicologist and encyclopedist François-Joseph Fétis.[4]

OK, it's time for me to pull the requisite long face of the responsible historian and condemn such nonsense. As a music theorist, I ought to hasten all the more to consider the music without all this hokum: just the notes, ma'am! But I won't—in part because I happen to love stories like this, and in part because Stradella's music proves to be just as outrageous as his audacious lifestyle. The responsible biographies of his life troll dutifully through extant documents (commissions by patrons, financial dockets, police registers, etc.) and then deliver generalized descriptions of his arias, judged as infantile compared to those of his more formally accomplished eighteenth-century successors. It is as if he truly does hold a place in history solely because of his scandal-ridden exploits.

In this chapter I want to make you fall in love, at least a little bit, with Stradella the artist, to seduce you away—if only temporarily—from (no doubt) more edifying composers such as J. S. Bach, to instill in you a taste for the pre-Enlightenment *seicento*. I am aided and abetted in this venture by Stradella's scores, which need only the breath of performance to bring them vividly back to life. And I want to explain why reconstituted sonic experience ought also to qualify as evidence for the historical record.

We teach our students to understand musical grammar according to principles of diatonic tonality: the syntactical norms of the repertories stretching from Arcangelo Corelli through early-period Beethoven.[5] We introduce the patterns to which these composers adhered not as particular to that period or even to Europe but just as the way music is supposed to go, accompanied by universalizing rationales such as the overtone series, physical acoustics, internally consistent logic, or (more recently) trickle-down ideas from

---

[4] Fétis has a lot to answer for, including the invention of the term "tonalité," designed to distinguish European musical practices from those of the French colonies. For a critique, see Jason Yust, "Tonality and Racism," *Journal of Music Theory* 68, no. 1 (2024). *JMT* included a number of responses to Yust's article, including my "'Tonality' and Its Discontents," 149–55.

[5] Beethoven begins to rebel against basic tenets of this model when he substituted modulations to flat-six for the traditional dominant that had always served as the principal counterbalance to the tonic. After that, it was all experimentation.

the neurosciences. It is no wonder that the people we have trained balk at modernist atonality as unnatural, or sneer at earlier or non-Western ways of organizing music as primitive. But although I enjoy Bach and Mozart as much as anyone else, I prefer to understand their compositional habits as manifestations of eighteenth-century cultural priorities,[6] and I have spent most of my career devising approaches to musics of the sixteenth and seventeenth centuries—approaches that allow me to analyze those repertories with the same degree of detail that I bring to Vivaldi or Haydn.[7]

"Oh, no," I hear you saying to yourselves. "What happened to the promise of the lurid and the sensationalistic? Here we are once again in music-theory class!" Well, no theory, no sex. All we have for any of this music are dots on the page, which is why even most musicologists turn exclusively to written documents as their source of historical evidence.[8] But as a performer and coach, I have always considered it my business to make the dots speak. And as titillating as Stradella's scandalous life might be, I actually care far more about the traces he left on paper.

Much of what you hear in his music will sound quite familiar. After all, Arcangelo Corelli played violin in Stradella's ensemble and learned in that context about concerto-grosso orchestration. Handel went so far as to poach some of his predecessor's tunes for his own operas and oratorios: *Israel in Egypt* has several of these. But in at least one important sense, Stradella's music differs quite radically from that of his better-known successors.

If I had to venture one generalization about eighteenth-century musical style, I would point to the premium it puts on predictability. The guidelines of opera seria dictate happy endings, with the monarch always bestowing clemency; the tonal plans through which both instrumental and vocal music unfold pursue a very simple principle derived from the equivalent of the blues pattern; the measure-to-measure procedures rarely depart from well-established formulas. Most important for our purposes, the structural plans of eighteenth-century arias adhere to a single ABA form, which demands that the fully closed first part (A) be repeated after the contrasting section

---

[6] See my "What Was Tonality?" in *Conventional Wisdom: The Content of Musical Form* (Berkeley: University of California Press, 2000), chapter 3. And see again note. 4 concerning the ideological back history of "tonality."

[7] I deal with the sixteenth century in *Modal Subjectivities: Self-Fashioning in the Italian Madrigal* (Berkeley: University of California Press, 2004) and the seventeenth in its sequel, *Desire and Pleasure in Seventeenth-Century Music* (Berkeley: University of California Press, 2012). See also the previous chapters in this collection.

[8] See chapter 4, "Writing about Music."

(B). So precise is this repetition that the music of the third section is not even written out. Rather the composer merely marks "D.C." at the end of the B section, sending performers back to play or sing "da capo"—"from the head" of the score. Sonata procedure as it develops in the later eighteenth century represents a hybrid between the da capo aria and binary dance form.

I have listed the formulaic dimensions of this music not to denigrate the repertories of the Enlightenment but rather to gesture toward their great achievement: the simulation in sound of linear reason, transparency of communication, and the regulation of music by social contract. We enter into a composition of this era secure in the knowledge that we will be able to follow its moves and that it will reinforce the Panglossian premises to which we still cling, even in this postmodernist age. To be sure, every piece has its idiosyncrasies, the individualized turns that differentiate it from all others. Yet they all operate within a hierarchy of conventions that most of us have internalized just as effortlessly as we did our native tongue, which is why it seems "natural" to regard it as the way music—*tout court*—is supposed to go.[9]

Stradella's compositions include many of our familiar markers; his arias have a degree of expansion comparable to those in eighteenth-century operas, and they introduce many of the formulas that will continue to characterize later repertories. Yet he wrote just before the period when all these procedures were expected to confirm foregone conclusions. In short, his music is *not* predictable. Not, however, because he attempted, like the nineteenth-century Romantics, to rebel against established norms, but rather because he was among the foremost practitioners of the seventeenth-century predilection for generating energy arcs that careen ever forward, deferring anticipated points of closure. His predecessors had also trafficked in this kind of breathless activity, but Stradella brought to the table a much-expanded palette of strategies: his pieces are much longer, and they draw upon increasingly radical ways of perpetuating his trajectories. If the eighteenth century favored rational codes of conduct, Stradella and his ilk flaunted the overwhelming power of exceptional individuals.

Eighteenth-century music does not altogether eschew this quality, of course. When performers repeated the opening strain of da capo arias, they were expected to improvise dazzling ornaments, thereby showcasing their technical prowess. But that display is safely buttressed by multiple levels

---

[9] See my *Conventional Wisdom: The Content of Musical Form* (Berkeley: University of California Press, 2000), especially the chapter "What Was Tonality?"

of formal and tonal certainty. As Adorno would later argue concerning jazz, the structure remains rigidly the same, however imaginative the nuances added to the surface. We can discuss at another time whether or not Adorno missed the dialectical dimensions of jazz, or if Farinelli really did qualify as disrupting the certainty of his aristocratic arias by virtue of his embellishments. But my point here is that seventeenth-century sonatas and arias deliberately postpone closure, threatening to override any attempts at bridling.

To the ear accustomed to the assurances of eighteenth-century music, this open-endedness can sound quite disconcerting. Many a musicologist has diagnosed such procedures as displaying a lack of formal sophistication: although some of Stradella's contemporaries would turn exclusively to rounded ABA structure for their arias, he himself persists in ABB' arrangements, in which the third unit risks spiraling out of control. Even if he does usually end up confirming the tonic, he takes his own sweet time doing so and interposes any number of feints and dodges along the way. The next generation would regard such behaviors as unseemly and even label them (in the pejorative sense) as "baroque": witness the multiple levels of constraints eighteenth-century artists imposed in advance upon formal procedure, something akin to encasing radioactive substances in lead containers.

Occasionally, reminiscences of the old style bubbled up in later music. Recall that J. S. Bach was trained as a seventeenth-century musician and only came into contact with tonal processes in his early twenties, when he avidly transcribed Vivaldi's newly published concertos to play on the organ. Yet even after his musical conversion, Bach sometimes hearkened back to the wildness of his youth, performing implosions of well-behaved forms by undisciplined energies. Perhaps the most famous of these occurs in the Fifth Brandenburg Concerto, in which a Stradella-like continuo player gleefully overthrows the carefully choreographed concerto for which it was supposed to provide mere support and then launches into an outrageously extended cadenza. If the apparently uninvited soloist eventually relents and allows the communal ritornello to finish off the movement, the cadenza has raised serious questions concerning authority; the capstone sounds a bit perfunctory after what has preceded it.[10]

---

[10] I discuss this piece at length in "The Blasphemy of Talking Politics during Bach Year," in *Music and Society: The Politics of Composition, Performance and Reception*, ed. Richard Leppert and Susan McClary (Cambridge, UK: Cambridge University Press, 1987), 13–63.

How do such energies operate within the context of seventeenth-century music? Let me start with the issue of operatic plot, since this may be easiest to grasp. I mentioned earlier that the conventions of opera seria—the genre associated with absolutist courts and with the da capo aria—demanded that the drama conclude with the monarch bestowing clemency; the king gets the last word, ensuring happy endings and peace. But a good many seventeenth-century operas feature equivocal finales, often giving unrepentant sorceresses or courtesans the upper hand. This is most obviously true in the topsy-turvy world of commercial Venetian opera, which gloried in rendering stories from classical mythology as sex farces: for instance, Francesco Cavalli's *Giasone*, the most frequently performed opera of the seventeenth century, presents Jason and Medea as the unwitting victims of *commedia dell'arte* tomfoolery. But such inverted power structures sometimes occur even in the aristocratic French *tragédies en musique* performed under the very nose of Louis XIV. The dominant roles of seventeenth-century operas fall to the likes of Monteverdi's Poppea, who assassinates or exiles everyone in her path as she ascends to her coronation, or Marc-Antoine Charpentier's Médée, who triumphantly takes to the sky in her dragon cart to conclude her opera on an ungrounded upbeat, flinging the body parts of Jason's sons as she goes.[11]

Stradella's Salome appears in his oratorio *San Giovanni Battista*, one of a series of fourteen such pieces commissioned in Rome for the Holy Year of 1675. A genre designed to provide audiences with operatic thrills during the Lenten season, the oratorio brought the extravagances of virtuoso singing and dramatic action to stories drawn from the scriptures. Of all biblical narratives, the story of the virago who seduces her stepfather, King Herod, in order to acquire the head of John the Baptist fits most comfortably with those of her sisters Poppea and Medea.

I want to point out that none of these pieces was created by a feminist, even if they star powerful women who survive their respective plots unvanquished and unpunished. Indeed, such plots seem in part to serve as cautionary tales concerning the consequences of having women in positions of influence. But it is possible to read their significance quite differently: in societies in which male subjects found themselves under increasing pressure to take on the burden and constraints of reason, extravagant expressions

---

[11] I deal with these in my "The Dragon Cart: The Femme Fatale in Seventeenth-Century Baroque Opera," in *Desire and Pleasure*.

of feeling, sexuality, and spectacularity were increasingly projected onto women. These ladies may be monsters, but they also serve as the voice of a virtuosic humanity soon to be tamped down and domesticated.

One does not have to look very hard to find a real-life model for uncontrollable women in Stradella's Rome. The inspiration for at least as many fictional and theatrical accounts as our composer, Queen Christina had resided in Rome since her abdication of the Swedish throne at the age of twenty-nine in 1654. During her many years in the Holy City, Christina had experienced adulation, censure, and political intrigue. She accumulated an art collection that rivaled that of the Louvre and founded the Academy of Music; musicians such as Stradella, Corelli, and Alessandro Scarlatti enjoyed her patronage with performances sometimes held in the public theater she founded. When hostile popes were in office, she held performances in her own palace in the Trastevere, where—in defiance of Roman law—she even encouraged women to sing on stage.[12]

As one of the officially sponsored oratorios of 1675, *San Giovanni Battista* featured male singers in all the roles, including that of Salome, in its premiere. But it is difficult not to hear resonances of Christina and Pope Innocent XI in the final standoff between a triumphant Salome and a dispirited Herod that concludes this oratorio: a duet for which multiple manuscript copies survive, thus attesting to its widespread fame. Stradella regarded *San Giovanni Battista* as his best work, and excerpts if not entire performances—with women—may well have taken place in the counterculture spaces afforded by the Queen. Its premiere, however, would have featured a castrato in the role.

I want to turn now to the oratorio itself. The arias sung by John the Baptist himself as he anticipates his martyrdom are magnificent, as are the vainglorious rage arias uttered by an indignant Herod before his abject defeat. But I will concentrate today on Salome herself, or (as she is called in the oratorio) La Figlia: the Daughter.

In keeping with the scriptural narrative, librettist Abate Ansaldo Ansaldi first presents Salome as something of a pawn in a political struggle. The Baptist has publicly condemned Herod for having married his own sister-in-law, thereby compounding the sin of adultery with that of incest. The vengeful wife arranges for her daughter to dance at Herod's birthday celebration—a performance so successful that the king offers his stepdaughter anything she

---

[12] When the pope converted her theater into a granary, Christina merely moved her performances to her own home, where she also experimented with alchemy.

desires, up to half his kingdom. After consulting with her mother, Salome demands the Baptist's head. Herod tries to dissuade her but finally fulfills his side of the bargain. Salome wins.

In Oscar Wilde's infamous version of the story, Salome lusts perversely for John and ends by making love to his severed head. No erotic frisson occurs between Stradella's Salome and Giovanni Battista, but plenty of sexual energy is directed toward Herod, characterized during the oratorio's first half by the Mother, the Daughter, and Herod's chief of staff as having lost his virile appetite. Salome is entrusted explicitly with the task of restoring his potency.

Part II opens with Salome's dance at the birthday party. This particular libretto does not include the conventional narrator who, like the Evangelist in a Passion, fills in the gaps. Instead, Ansaldi writes the entire text as if it were an opera, with nothing more than direct speech delivered by characters. In other words, we experience the seduction and its consequences without commentary or mediation.[13]

Salome's dance number presents her as somewhat kittenish. Her lyrics invoke the nymphs of the Jordan and the stars, challenging them to compare their grace and delight with hers. She states nothing overtly: her images are stock tropes of pastoral poetry, and even her meter follows that of the pastoral siciliano. The burden of the seduction falls to Stradella's music—and, of course, to the performer who must embody it.

Vaghe ninfe del Giordano,	Lovely nymphs of the Jordon,
che movete il ballo al piè.	who move your feet in dance.
Deh, mi dite se gioite	Ah, tell me if you rejoice
dentro l'alma al par di me.	in your soul as much as I.
Anco in ciel le stelle tremule	The shimmering stars in heaven
vezzosetti ogn' hora danzano.	always dance prettily.
Ma per questo non avanzano	But for all that they do not outshine
il mio cor di cui son emule.	my heart, which they emulate.

At first, "Vaghe ninfe" seems to follow conventional figures: its location within dance idioms predisposes it to an easy periodicity (see Example 13.1.).

---

[13] A subsequent Stradella oratorio, *La Susanna*, features a *testo* who proves an unreliable narrator. I composed a deconstructed version of this in my *Susanna Does the Elders*—a play produced in Minneapolis in 1987. See again chapter 1. For more on the significance of mediation in the representation of dangerous women, see my "Excess and Frame: The Musical Representation of Madwomen," in *Feminine Endings: Music, Gender, and Sexuality* (Minneapolis: University of Minnesota Press, 1991).

Example 13.1 Alessandro Stradella, "Vaghe ninfe," mm. 1–22

But within the dance that we, along with Herod, might perceive as innocent, Stradella produces a few special effects: the equivalent of veils opening to reveal tantalizing but forbidden flesh. One of these involves his strategies for repeating his second strain of text. Although the gist of the music recurs, it colonizes a different register—now low, throaty, and suggestive, now suddenly high and exhibitionistic. We cannot anticipate how familiar lines of text will be deployed within the vocal range, each part of which brings its own rhetorical implications.

Another trick you might notice emerges in what pretends at first to be a second verse, though it quickly turns out to have new enticements. On the words "il mio cor," the composer produces a dissonant clash between the bass and the voice, which insinuates an altered pitch. The result sounds something like the self-snuggling gesture made famous by Marilyn Monroe. No wonder Herod collapses in a lustful heap![14]

As you may recall from your years in Bible school, however, Herod balks at his stepdaughter's demand. During their negotiations in the oratorio, Salome holds onto her feigned naiveté as long as possible. Coyly, she pretends to be too bashful to ask for anything, requiring that Herod pull her request from her piece by piece—until she suddenly lays her cards on the table and reminds him of the promise he made in front of witnesses.

In the showstopper of this oratorio, she plays the guilt card. A kitten no more, she alternates extravagantly between vocal registers—between guttural growls and histrionic high notes—revealing her preternaturally adult desires and her indomitable will. Particularly astonishing is her repetition of the last two lines; if she cadences decisively the first time around, she ups the ante exponentially in the second presentation of the word "mirar," which winds its way up by chromatically inflected sequences from her chest voice to a shattering high C. She hurls "quel mostro" with palpable loathing (see Example 13.2).

Deh, che più tardi a consolar la spene	Alas, how much longer will you delay
di questo afflitto core,	to console the hope of this afflicted heart,
che più viver non puo se vive ancora,	who can no longer live if he remains alive,
chi le sue gratie atterra, e discolora.	who tramples and discolors her charms.
Il seren' della fronte oblia l'aurorio e l'ostro,	My brow's serenity loses its ivory and rose,
solo in udir, solo in mirar quel mostro.	in even hearing or seeing that monster.

When I gave this paper as a talk (it was my barnstorming number for a couple of years), I nearly wrecked my voice singing this. But only a performance that displays the recitative's affective polarity—the snarling low notes,

---

[14] See the more extensive treatment of this aria in the final chapter of *Desire and Pleasure*.

the terrifying high ones—can really convey the depth of depravity Stradella has notated. Recall that Stradella influenced both Corelli and Handel, then think of how much cleaning up they had to do to make aspects of his work palatable to the Age of Enlightenment.

But "Deh, che più tardi" is just the warm-up act. What follows this audacious recitative is an extravagant lament. La Figlia begs for mercy—not for John, on whom Herod is all too eager to bestow clemency, but for herself. Only John's death can appease her, can stanch her crocodile tears, can preserve her flawless complexion.

Example 13.2 Alessandro Stradella, *San Giovanni Battista*, "Deh, che più tardi"

Example 13.2 Continued

Questi lagrime e sospiri, che tù miri,   These tears and sighs, which you see,
braman solo, ò mio gran Ré, poca mercè.   desire only, great king, a little mercy.

Aestheticians sometimes ask if music can lie. I've always found this a ridiculous question, especially since it is usually answered in the negative.

We invest so much in this powerful medium that we desperately want it to be true and authentic in all its manifestations. I would offer just this lament as evidence to the contrary: music can lie through its teeth, which is why we need to know how to perform hermeneutic readings. Herod does not, alas, and he pays a heavy penalty for his uncritical responses.

Salome dispenses with the first of her lines in short order: "These tears and sighs that you see. . . ." But she puts her second line—"desire only, my great king, a tiny bit of mercy"—through the wringer of myriad readings. She wheedles, she whines, she demands, she waxes pathetic. My favorite moment occurs when she suddenly moves into a remote key area and pauses there, as if looking around to assess her effect so as to toy all the more productively with Herod's weaknesses. In G. W. Pabst's classic film *Pandora's Box*, Louise Brooks as Lulu stages a mock tantrum to compel Dr. Schön to give in to her demands, and in the middle of her tears she peeks up to see how she's doing. Stradella choreographs precisely this maneuver in his music.

A quick fast-forward to another couple of moments in the oratorio. When Salome finally gets her way, she sings a celebratory dance, "Get up and crown me," an explicit shout-out to Monteverdi's *L'Incoronazione di Poppea*. In contrast to the somewhat cagey dance presented at Herod's birthday, this one is savage: a Dionysian bacchanal over John's dead body, introduced with this recitative:

Cadesti alfine, e nel tuo sangue intrisa	You have fallen at last, and your own tongue,
la propria lingua altrui farà palese	soaked in your blood, will make it plain to all
che donna ancor sa vendicar l'offese.	that women still know how to avenge insults.

In the aria itself, notice in particular the redundant, aggressive ostinato pattern in the solo cello, to which Salome adds her voice in bizarre off-kilter rhythms. This is Kali, the Hindu Goddess of Death, bloody in tooth and claw.[15]

A distant echo of this character appears as Mozart's Queen of the Night, who violates the Enlightenment norms of Sarastro through her anachronistic *seicento* extravagance and her zeal for murderous revenge. And she, like Richard Strauss's Salome, must be purged in the interest of closure. Not so Stradella's heroine. The oratorio concludes with a duet that superimposes Salome's gloating over Herod's remorse. Although the lamenting bass line

---

[15] These excerpts appear in the recording of the entire oratorio by the Academia Montis Regalis, Alessandro de Marchi, conductor. Soprano: Anke Herrmann; Herode: Antonio Abete (Hyperion, 2007).

ought to govern the proceedings, Salome's melody seizes each of Herod's ponderous pitches and uses it as the pretext for her own unmitigated glee. Each examines her or his emotional state and asks "e perchè?" And why?

Salome: Che gioire, che contento provo e sento fra di me! Più felice, più giocondo giorno il mondo non vedè. E perchè dimmi, e perchè?	What bliss, what happiness I feel and sense inside me! A happier, more joyful day the world never saw. And why, tell me, why?
Herod: Che martire, che tormento provo e sento fra di me! Più infelice, men giocondo giorno il mondo non vedè. E perchè dimmi, e perchè?	What suffering, what torment I feel and sense inside me! A more unhappy, sorrowful day the world never saw. And why, tell me, why?

Stradella refuses to resolve the contradiction between his two principal characters and ends instead on a half-cadence—a rhetorical harmonic configuration that demands an answer. The entire oratorio builds, in other words, to this moment, which just leaves us hanging. A recent recording cushions this *coup de théâtre* by adding on an instrumental postlude taken from somewhere else. But Stradella's open end could not have been bested by Bertolt Brecht: the problem is thrown raw into the laps of the listeners.

What is it that gets cleaned up on the way to the eighteenth-century repertories that still stand as our point of reference? For one thing, representations of power. Recall that the appointed monarch in opera seria is always guaranteed his mandate; regardless of the plot, we know in advance that the established hierarchy will prevail—and, moreover, that it will be endorsed as just. This particular convention had to be hardwired in to prevent the catastrophic insurrections staged in seventeenth-century opera. Given its increasing rhetorical force, opera as a genre had to be reined in or else banned. It managed to continue, but only with the proviso of the stacked deck. Shortly after the example of pieces like *San Giovanni Battista*, the rules will dictate that the king always triumphs.

Second, gender comes to be organized according to a strict binary opposition. No one, I think, would claim the seventeenth century as an especially good time for women: this was, after all, the era of the great witch burnings. Nevertheless, this period produced some of our most vivid examples of female agents, whether in real life—as with Elizabeth I and Queen Christina— or in theatrical displays—as with Monteverdi's Poppea, Charpentier's

Médée, or Stradella's Salome. We have to scroll forward to the nineteenth century to find a comparable batch of aggressive women on the stage, and they all pay for their transgressions with violent deaths: a fate that befalls not only Strauss's Salome but also Bizet's Carmen and Berg's Lulu. Yet whatever we make of such characters—whether we regard them as proto-feminist heroines or as monsters created by misogynists—we do need to notice their virtual absence in the eighteenth-century opera, when reason held everything safely in check. (Mozart's Queen of the Night in Magic Flute and Elettra in *Idomeneo*, count as outliers.)

But I am most interested in the music. Eighteenth-century music features predictability on the surface as well as the background. We know in advance where a piece will end, and we receive reassurances throughout that our expectations will be met. Such procedures teach us to play speculative games, to see into the near future; and we are rewarded by finding that most of our projections pan out. This kind of music makes us feel smart, as our reasoning abilities prove accurate over and over again. When something unexpected does occur, we perk up our ears and move our speculations to a higher level. Only very rarely do composers frustrate those higher-level assumptions, and such moments qualify as significant sites for critical discussion. Theorists who develop systematic accounts of musical grammar gravitate to these repertories precisely because their efforts at distilling internally consistent models pay off so well in this repertory.

But not all musics strive for predictability. Stradella wants to surprise, amaze, and even disturb us; we might think of him as the musical equivalent of Caravaggio. The fact that he knows how to manipulate the patterns that will later come to have inevitable results makes his music all the more disconcerting to those of us trained to follow the arias of Handel. His is not an epistemology in which everything always turns out well in the end, and he does not care to honor your carefully honed skills of prediction. The common verdict delivered by musicologists is that he has not yet figured out how to control his structures. But I would explain his predilections differently: by maintaining his right to tailor his structures to the exigencies of each particular dramatic challenge, he manifests a far greater investment in the meanings of formal arrangements than do his successors who buy into the da capo convention in advance.

No one ever claimed that the seventeenth century, with all its reversals of fortunes, religious wars, and power grabs, counted as a comfortable chapter in European history. Alexandre Dumas's swashbuckling novels bring us the excitement and exotic flavor of the period but wrap them up in the formal assurances of later modes of narrative emplotment. Unlike D'Artagnan, however, Stradella does not survive his adventures. Sometimes a voracious princess defeats the monarch, sometimes a piece of music gives you an equivocal conclusion, and sometimes you end up executed by *bravi* right at the peak of your own love story. In the *seicento*, shit happens.

Not that it did not in the Enlightenment: witness the catastrophe of the French Revolution, all the more devastating for occurring in the midst of reason-based cultural texts featuring triumphant kings. If those who cemented the ironclad rules of behavior for opera seria and tonality could pretend thereby to control the real world, they experienced a rude awakening when that world blew up around them. We might say that the tidy, self-referential systems of eighteenth-century music—the same music we often find so conducive to intellectual introspection—qualify as what the Frankfurt School would call false consciousness.

Again, I do not intend to trash such music: some of my own writing celebrates the achievements of Vivaldi, Bach, and Mozart. But we have been hampered in our ability to understand the cultural work accomplished by eighteenth-century composers by our assumption that they simply figured out how music is supposed to go, in accordance with some platonic or universal standard. I believe that we can assess the significance of the music of the Enlightenment only if we take just as seriously the utterances of its predecessors, received not as rough drafts of what would be perfected by future generations but as evidence of other sensibilities responding to other conditions. For all the spectacularity of Stradella's life, his music exhibits even more. And it is for formulations such as "Vaghe ninfe" and "Deh, che più tardi" that we should remember him.[16]

---

[16] For a similar statement, see Philippe Beaussant, *Stradella* (Paris: Gallimard, 1999), 44: "D'ailleurs, lorsque j'acoute sa musique, qui est admirable, pleine de vivacité et d'ardeur, si forte, si allègrement vivante, avec de brusques plongées à vous donner le vertige dans une gravité si inquiète, je me demande si ceux qui ont écrit sur lui l'ont jamais entendue. Je devine, je pressens qu'à l'intersection de ce destin dont on ne raconte que les extravagances joyeuses et de cette musique à la fois débordante de verdeur et d'où s'épanche une si évidente douleur, il y a quelque chose de plus que ce qu'on a dit: exactment à la charnière. Et je voudrais bien savoir quoi." Founder of the Centre de Musique Baroque de Versailles and the Centre des Arts de la Scène des XVIIe et XVIIIe Siècle, Beaussant presents his *Stradella* as a novel.

14

Adorno Plays the *WTC*

On Political Theory and Performance[1]

In 1950, in acknowledgment of the bicentennial of J. S. Bach's death, Theodor Adorno published one of his marvelously cranky rants, "Bach Defended against His Devotees."[2] His immediate target was those "who have made him into a composer for organ festivals in well-preserved Baroque towns" (136). Recall that this diatribe appeared a scant five years after the close of World War II, when Germany was still reeling from the horrific events of the previous decade, and Bach had seemed a relatively uncontroversial figure upon whom to begin the process of rebuilding a sense of national pride. But, as Adorno puts it: "Reaction, deprived of its political heroes, takes complete possession of the composer (135). . . . In being placed into the service of proselytizing zeal, the neo-religious Bach is impoverished, reduced and stripped of the specific musical content which was the basis of his prestige" (136).

Adorno's essay addresses many issues, among them the critique of canonization evident in these quotations. But he dedicates most of this piece to the matter he finds largely ignored by his contemporaries: the "specific musical content" of Bach's music and the problems associated with making that content audible in performance. To the dismay of many readers, Adorno rarely justifies his insights with measure numbers, music examples, or graphs. An account of a whole composition may occupy no more than a single conundrum-laden, impressionistic sentence—the kind of sentence we would flay our students for writing.

---

[1] Keynote for conference, *Performance and Analysis*, Indiana University, February 2009. Published in *Indiana Theory Review* 27, no. 2 (Fall 2009): 97–112.

[2] Theodor W. Adorno, "Bach Defended against his Devotees," in *Prisms*, trans. Samuel Weber and Shierry Weber (Cambridge, MA: MIT Press, 1983), 133–46. See my tribute to the tercentennial of Bach's birth, "The Blasphemy of Talking Politics during Bach Year," *Music and Society: The Politics of Composition, Performance and Reception*, ed. Richard Leppert and Susan McClary (Cambridge, UK: Cambridge University Press, 1987), 13–62.

That withholding of detail has led some to assume that Adorno actually knew very little about music, that his was primarily a political soapbox. Moreover, his cultural-theory devotees often defend his positions without having a clue what any of Adorno's own "specific musical content" might mean. A friend of mine once took a comp-lit seminar focused exclusively on Adorno's book *In Search of Wagner*, and not a single pitch was sounded during the course of the entire semester; sophisticated literary theorists spun elaborate glosses on mysterious expressions like "the circle of fifths," only to become crestfallen when the lone musician in the room explained their literal denotations.

Adorno's refusal to provide documentation might be written off as the arrogance of an ivory-tower mandarin. Yet given the urgency of his agenda and his obvious desire to sound his wake-up call, it seems more likely that he assumed (wrongly, as it turns out) that his readers would know how to supply the missing links, the way one might refer offhandedly to some aspect of Hamlet's character without necessarily citing chapter and verse. Alas, as Adorno would have been the first to lament, and for reasons he expended much effort in explaining, the kind of musically literate reader he had in mind—the kind who could bring to aural memory the preludes and fugues of the Forty-Eight as easily as a contemporary fan can recall Taylor Swift's greatest hits—was fast becoming a vanishing breed.

In this article, I want to revisit the "specific musical content" of Adorno's Bach essay, which I continue to count among the most brilliant disquisitions we have on the possible relationships between analysis and performance. If Adorno does not always spell out explicitly what he means, I will argue that it is well worth our while to meet him halfway: not only for those who want to engage with his polemical arguments but also for those who may benefit from his insights into the music itself.

"Bach Defended against His Devotees" constitutes part of the much larger project Adorno pursued throughout his career: that of reconstructing a history of subjectivity as it has manifested itself in music since the early eighteenth century.[3] He was compelled not by idle intellectual speculation but

---

[3] See the collection of Adorno's music-oriented essays edited by Richard Leppert as *Essays on Music* (Berkeley: University of California Press, 2002). Rose Rosengard Subotnik introduced Adorno to American musicology with her "Adorno's Diagnosis of Beethoven's Late Style: Early Symptom of a Fatal Condition," *Journal of the American Musicological Society* 29 (1976); reprinted in her *Developing Variations: Style and Ideology in Western Music* (Minneapolis: University of Minnesota Press, 1991). I owe my career-long interest in Adorno to Rose and Richard.

rather by his life experience as a German Jew driven into exile by an evil force that presented itself as the apotheosis of the Enlightenment. How, he asked, could those who had produced the greatest monuments of European thought—in philosophy, literature, music—have become the engineers of the death camps? Or as he and coauthor Max Horkheimer state in their preface to *Dialectic of Enlightenment*: "What we had set out to do was nothing less than to explain why humanity, instead of entering a truly human state, is sinking into a new kind of barbarism."[4]

Note that Adorno is not interested in the usual quandary of how Nazis could also have loved the music of Mozart or Schubert: his is a question not of beauty or appreciation but rather of the tensions manifested within the music itself. If Europeans had listened attentively, might they have been able to discern the moment when freedom began to engage with and then surrender to an inhumane form of mechanized reason? As Adorno puts it in his Bach essay:

> Perhaps Bach's innermost truth is that in him the social trend [of rationalization] which has dominated the bourgeois era to this very day is not merely preserved but, by being reflected in images, is reconciled with the voice of humanity which in reality was stifled by that trend at the moment of its inception. (139)

Let me try to translate this into a vocabulary more familiar to us. The musical image of eighteenth-century European rationality is, of course, diatonic tonality. We do not ordinarily consider this way of producing music to have a downside—nor, indeed, to have a social history at all.[5] Even during this period, music theorists (e.g., Rameau) sought to explain tonality as an internally consistent system grounded in the fundamental units confirmed by physical acoustics; its advocates sometimes have implied that it was just waiting there to be discovered like any other natural force by the enlightened denizens of the 1700s. This widespread assumption makes a modal theorist like myself sometimes feel like an advocate for the Flat Earth Society.

---

[4] Max Horkheimer and Theodor W. Adorno, *Dialectic of Enlightenment*, trans. Edmund Jephcott (Stanford, CA: Stanford University Press, 2002), xi. This book was written during the war and first published in Amsterdam in 1947.

[5] See, however, Max Weber, *The Rational and Social Foundations of Music*, ed. Don Martindale, Johannes Riedel, and Gertrude Neuwirth (Carbondale, IL: Southern Illinois University Press, 1958). Music theorists are beginning to turn to questions of ideology. See Jason Yust, "Tonality and Racism," *Journal of Music Theory* 68, no. 1 (2024), along with responses to Yust's article, including my "'Tonality' and Its Discontents," 149–55.

Bach was a modal composer in his early works. To be sure, he knew how to expand on functions in his structural backgrounds, but he differentiated between, say, Dorian and Aeolian and shaped his compositions accordingly. Then, shortly after the publication of *L'Estro armonico* in 1711, he encountered the music of Vivaldi, the precepts of which he internalized by arranging several Italian concertos for organ. From that point forward, he understood his project to be that of converting all the genres he knew into the Venetian dialect.

Many of Bach's works—the Brandenburgs, the da capo arias that appear in cantatas and Passions—operate explicitly according to the Vivaldian format, whereby tutti ritornellos punctuate the background progression while soloists accomplish the task of modulating from pillar to pillar. In contrast to many seventeenth-century procedures, which result in quite different formal plans depending on the particular mode, Vivaldi's model standardizes the background, restricting it to a very powerful sequence of linear steps: the establishment of the tonic, modulation to another key that continues to maintain the fifth degree (either V or III), arrival on another key or two, and then a return to the tonic. With the background already set as a conceptual schema, the composer could concentrate on the middle-level strategies that make the foreordained process seem fresh and exciting, even as it is in effect inevitable—which makes it appear as the material manifestation of reason.[6]

Adorno might have explained Bach's complicity with tonality by examining the works that most obviously represent the composer's modern side. Instead, he chose to focus on the fugues in the *Well-Tempered Clavier*—the pieces critics like Johann Adolph Scheibe disparaged as throwbacks to the past.[7] But according to Adorno, what matters in these feats of imitative counterpoint is the attempt to reconcile the exigencies of a very sophisticated set of inherited procedures with those of eighteenth-century reason as Bach had learned it from Vivaldi.

Few of us know a sufficient number of fugues from the seventeenth century to appreciate the other side of Bach's dialectic. In imitative works by Sweelinck, Froberger, d'Anglebert, or Buxtehude, the principal concern is combinatoriality: the systematic exploration of aspects of a subject that

---

[6] See "What Was Tonality?," chapter 3 of my *Conventional Wisdom: The Content of Musical Form* (Berkeley: University of California Press, 2000).

[7] Johann Adolph Scheibe, a 23-year-old critic for *Der Critische Musicus* in Hamburg, wrote in 1737 that Bach removed "the natural element in his pieces by giving them a turgid and confused style and darkened their beauty by an excess of art." *The Bach Reader*, ed. Hans T. David and Arthur Mendel (New York: Norton, 1972), 238.

might be used for development. This is why composers sometimes called such pieces "ricercars," a cognate of the English word "research." Seventeenth-century fugal works typically exploit such techniques as the augmentation or diminution of the subject's rhythmic units and stretto; many of them build dramatically through increasing animation to meltdowns worthy of 1980s metal bands. By and large, however, they do not follow a linear background progression. Instead, the subject appears in alternation on the final and fifth degree, allowing the listener to concentrate fully on the successive manifestations of the subject. The subject is always front and center; it reveals its inherent richness through a series of virtuosic transformations and superimpositions.

Bach's fugues strive to maintain the importance of the subject, which Adorno equates with the human subject or the self. But Bach also works to modernize the fugue through the objective background formula adopted nearly universally in eighteenth-century European music. Implicit in Adorno's discussion is the understanding that the standardized tonal background brings with it issues of emplotment or narrative, inasmuch as the listener invests emotionally in the trajectory away from and back to certainty traced in the unfolding of each composition.

In short, Adorno asks if Bach managed to preserve the agency of the subject when he required it to go through the paces of the Vivaldian schema, or if submission to Enlightenment rationality made subjects interchangeable and therefore expendable. In Adorno's view, Bach had to accomplish his negotiations between these allegiances in a unique way in each fugue. Otherwise, he only would have been demonstrating in advance the triumph of instrumental reason.

Moreover, Adorno argues that the performer's principal duty is to enact *in sound* the dialectical struggle manifested in each fugue. For him, it is the ability to read the "truth content" of a composition—not the studying of old treatises or playing on period instruments—that makes for historically informed performance. And, given the specter of Auschwitz that hovers over all of Adorno's inquiries, the stakes are very high!

As, indeed, they were for his older contemporary Heinrich Schenker, who similarly sought some kind of truth content in German music beginning with J. S. Bach. We are accustomed to overlooking the metaphysical underpinnings of Schenker's project (relegated to the back of the English translation of *Der freie Satz*), in order to concentrate on his musical insights. And insofar as Schenker located truth in precisely the background Adorno identified with Enlightenment reason, the two men probably would not have agreed about much on the philosophical level. Adorno's principal musical colleague was Alban Berg, whose compositions operated in ways Schenker did not condone. But both Adorno and Schenker regarded music as far more consequential than mere cultural capital, and each grounded his project in performance and in the details of the music itself.

I want to turn now to a few examples to demonstrate what Adorno perceives in each of the fugues he discusses and also to suggest how one might put that understanding into sound. I shall begin with a fugue that still wants to operate like its seventeenth-century predecessors: the E-flat fugue from *WTC II*. Here is some of what Adorno has to say about it:

> The affirmative tone of the E-flat major fugue from the second book of the *Well-Tempered Clavichord* is not the immediate certainty of a sacral community articulated in music and secure in its revealed truth. . . . Rather, in its substance . . . it is reflection on the happiness of musical security, the like of which is possessed only by the emancipated subject, for only it can conceive music as the emphatic promise of objective salvation. This kind of fugue presupposes the dualism. It says how beautiful it would be to bring back its message of happiness from the circumscribed cosmos to mankind. . . . It does not mirror the solitary subject as the guarantee of meaning, but rather aims at its abolition and transcendence in an objective, comprehensive absolute. But this absolute is evoked, asserted, postulated precisely because and only inasmuch as it is not present in physical experience. (138)

Let me try to unpack this. The subject itself is extremely stable: it rises from the tonic to the fifth degree then wends its way eloquently back down. In a sense, it solves within its own span the issues it opens; it is a small, self-contained unit, apparently secure and certain (see Example 14.1a).

Moreover, the first half of the fugue maintains that security by behaving like an archaic motet, with alternating entries on tonic and fifth degree. Even

Example 14.1a J. S. Bach, *WTC* II, E-flat major fugue, subject

after the exposition has clearly ended, the same process continues, now in stretto, simply asserting and reasserting an already established identity. But if this adherence to tonic and fifth degree guarantees one kind of certainty, it does so at the expense of modernity. A seventeenth-century listener might have been content with this process, but a listener from the progress-addicted eighteenth century would begin to detect stagnation and become impatient for something to happen.

Suddenly, in m. 44, the other side of the dialectic kicks in, and Bach begins to modulate. Alas, this restless motion appears to require that we depart from the subject that had cemented the complacency of the first half: The two upper voices alternately try to assert the subject (mm. 47–53), only to be pulled ever downward by the sequencing bass. The threat of stagnation is now replaced by the risk of free fall, as the phrases spiral down mechanically by fifth without an obvious end in sight (see Example 14.1b).

Note that the tenor voice has been silent since m. 43. It enters again in m. 53 in the middle of the downward spiral, as if to put things right (see Example 14.1c). But although it begins with what sounds like the tonal answer to the subject, its harmonic context quickly persuades it to deviate, orienting it instead toward A-flat major; moreover, this entry lies in the middle of the keyboard, shunted between the two hands, and it scarcely makes itself heard against the inexorable bass.

As the bass prepares in m. 58 to confirm A-flat major, however, the soprano enters with a statement of the subject sufficiently powerful to force the bass up to D-natural, which adds its own confirmation of the tonic in stretto. This apparent last-ditch effort saves the day: the subject returns to stop the spiraling and to pull the fugue back to its tonic as well as its principal thematic material, and all ends well. It is even confident enough to throw in

Example 14.1b Bach, *WTC* II, E-flat major fugue, mm. 42–53

at the final cadence the bluesy lowered mediant so favored by seventeenth-century composers (see Example 14.1c).

Adorno argues that this is a specifically new kind of self: not one that bears its own "guarantee of meaning" (like an aristocratic title acquired at birth), but rather one that attains its goal only by braving the possibility of failure and by wrestling with the objective process. When the subject returns, it is in essence transformed because it has learned to constitute itself in a narrative fashion; it even emerges as something of a hero by virtue of stepping in to halt what comes to resemble an automatic modulation machine. Freud, of course, would define this willingness to leave the safe shelter of the maternal home for the tumult of the social world as a necessary stage in the process of self-formation. Bach's E-flat-major fugue anticipates him by over a century and through specifically musical means: the result of his pitting two very different musical imperatives against one another.

But we can only hear this scenario if the keyboardist performs it. The first section should sound stable but increasingly static—an unacceptable quality in the eighteenth century. The performer should resist the impulse to make this section sound more "musical" by introducing apologetic nuances, especially after the cadence that marks the end of the exposition and the new beginning that just reiterates the same tune on the same pitch levels, albeit in stretto. When the sequencing suddenly intrudes, it should sound properly dynamic at first but then mechanical, as each unit just gives way to the next in a musical infinite regress. When the subject finally returns in m. 59, it

Example 14.1c Bach, *WTC* II, E-flat major fugue, mm. 53–end

has to crash in with a dissonance to counter the accumulated momentum of the sequence—a momentum that the entry of the tenor proved powerless to counteract. To quote Newton's First Law of Motion: "Every object in a state of uniform motion tends to remain in that state of motion unless an external force is applied to it"—and the soprano entry here sounds like that external force applying the brakes. Adorno would argue—and I would agree—that this narrative progression is designated by Bach by the details of the score if we know how to discern his "specific musical content."[8]

In the E-flat fugue, Bach split identity off from change to produce his hybrid. But he experimented with a wide variety of other arrangements as well. Of the D-major fugue in *WTC II*, Adorno writes:

> [t]he venerable technique [of imitation] is placed in the service of a driving, thoroughly dynamic, thoroughly "modern" effect. . . . A social deciphering of Bach would presumably have to establish the link between the decomposition of the given thematic material through subjective reflection on the motivic work contained therein, and the change in the work-process that took place during the same epoch through the emergence of manufacturing, which consisted essentially in breaking down the old craft operations into their smaller component acts. If this resulted in the rationalization of material production, then Bach was the first to crystallize the idea of the rationally constituted work, of the aesthetic domination of nature. (139)

The subject of the D-major fugue has two principal components: an opening gambit that calls attention to itself through a repeating pitch, and a four-note tag that sounds like an afterthought (see Example 14.2a). It turns out to be this tag, however, through which Bach manufactures his entire fugue. Never absent, it operates like an especially versatile piece from a set of Tinker Toys: the fugue makes itself up by placing that item end to end or in overlapping patterns.

In the D-major fugue, a detachable resource within the subject itself takes responsibility for engineering the dynamic background: anticipating the

---

[8] Compare this with the first movement of Bach's Brandenburg Concerto No. 5, in which unacceptable tendencies toward both stagnation and runaway motion have to be corrected. See my "The Blasphemy of Talking Politics during Bach Year."

Example 14.2a Bach, *WTC* II, D-major fugue, subject

Example 14.2b Bach, *WTC* II, D-major Fugue, mm. 34–40

mass-production techniques that made the Industrial Revolution possible, it accomplishes all by itself the modulations to the dominant, the submediant, and the mediant, as well as a glorious (if hard-won) return to the tonic (see Example 14.2b). The subject achieves its own *Bildung* with no apparent assistance from the outside. I think of the D-major fugue as the "Little Engine That Could" fugue, with its tireless four-note tag constantly insisting "I think I can!"

It is not difficult to make this process audible, though it requires resisting years of training in "musicality." If we want listeners to hear the extraordinary labor involved in the unlikely self-construction of this fugue, then each statement of the tag has to be made clear. The process of laying this motive end to end and against itself may sound more like a mosaic of discrete tiles than a smooth series of rounded phrases, but I believe the fugue derives its power from precisely this quality. When I play it, I allow my face and body language to emphasize each of its entries (to the horror of my DMA students), and I try to simulate the tremendous effort involved in this process of incremental self-invention.

My next example, the F-sharp-major fugue in *WTC* I, deliberately rejects this kind of stringent homogeneity. Concerning this one, Adorno writes only a single sentence:

> [R]ecall the F-sharp Major Prelude and Fugue of the first book, a fugue once compared . . . to Gottfried Keller's short dance-legend, and which

is not merely the direct representation of subjective grace but moreover mocks all the rules of the very fugue that Bach himself created, through a musical progression in which the motif of the middle part transmits its impulses to the developments as the work unfolds.

Gottfried Keller, a nineteenth-century Swiss author, wrote a story about a little girl named Musa who loves to dance—even in church. King David comes down to tell her that she will be able to dance forever in heaven, if and only if she gives up dancing for the rest of her life on earth. With great difficulty and with the aid of chains, she fulfills her vow, though she sickens and dies from the process. She does indeed get to dance in heaven, though she also discovers there that the ancient Muses sit silent and depressed in the corner; they are soon evicted.

The prelude that precedes the F-sharp-major fugue is a joyful gigue. In comparison, the fugue subject sounds lofty, dignified, noble. From everything we think we know about music from the first half of the eighteenth century, we would expect that particular affect to characterize the entire fugue (see Example 14.3a).

But suddenly, in m. 7, a little hornpipe motive pops up, as if the fugue's authority could not suppress the dancing promised by the prelude (see Example 14.3b).

When I play this fugue, I try to convey a regal, serene posture during the presentation of the subject itself, with the pulse falling at the level of the half note. When the hornpipe enters, however, I reflect its jaunty rhythms in my upper body, which bobs slightly at the eighth-note level, and I allow myself to smile at the joke I am presenting. Most listeners are not accustomed to expecting humor in Bach fugues, and the performer has to dramatize the contrast quite broadly if it is to be grasped as comical by the audience.

Example 14.3a Bach, *WTC* I, F-sharp major fugue, subject

Example 14.3b Bach, *WTC* I, F-sharp major fugue, mm. 6–11

Example 14.3c Bach, *WTC* I, F-sharp major fugue, mm. 31–end

The fugue subject keeps attempting to exert control over its own destiny, but the dance energies persist, effectively hijacking the piece. Notice how in m. 7 the top voice attempts to insert the subject with its last two pitches, only to be undermined; the bass does the same in m. 8 before it succumbs to the dance. A final statement of the subject seems to claim the right at least to closure, but the irrepressible hornpipe comes bubbling up even here. In the last two measures, the noble subject spreads its opening gesture as a benevolent awning, tolerating and even protecting the childlike exuberance of the intrusive motive. In contrast to Keller's story, the two forces in Bach's fugue live together happily ever after (see Example 14.3).

As Adorno points out, this is not how fugues are supposed to operate. Bach violates here the social contract that comes along with genre. It is as if the noble protagonist of a romance suddenly got pushed to the side and rendered virtually irrelevant by a bumptious comic character of the lower classes. We are accustomed to such scenarios in movies, though the comic is usually understood to be the leading figure, with the serious character present only as a straw man. In the basic modus operandi of fugue composition, however, the subject is supposed to be identical with the protagonist, and it is expected to imprint itself all the way through the piece. We might hear this fugue as a social commentary, in which a stodgy aristocracy finds itself undermined by the more vigorous energies of the underclass, which it needs in order to progress.[9] Note that Bach's conclusion is benign: no Bastille, no Terror, no barricades. If only it had been so simple!

A book concerning temporality in eighteenth-century music bears the title *Bach's Cycle and Mozart's Arrow*.[10] Although I admire many of the insights offered by author Karol Berger, I find it difficult to accept Bach's orientation as fundamentally cyclical. To be sure, by the time Mozart came along, teleological structure qualified as simply the way music goes; he never had to question it. Bach, on the other hand, experienced the moment of transition, and he found it necessary to find his own path between radically different ways of being.

And his fugues indicate that he understood very well what was at issue in both. If he most frequently produced music that shot like an arrow, he also retained fluency within an earlier set of options. Indeed, the huge C-sharp-minor triple fugue in *WTC I* operates within Aeolian: it presents entries of the subject on the subdominant within the exposition, cadences most frequently on the subdominant, and ends equivocally poised between its tonic and subdominant—all typical earmarks of Aeolian.[11] He may have taken his cue from Froberger's C-sharp Aeolian ricercar, and Beethoven certainly modeled his Op. 131 (what I will henceforth call the C-sharp Aeolian quartet) after Bach's example.

---

[9] See again my "Blasphemy," in which I argue that the harpsichord leaves its designated role as mere accompanist and usurps control over the piece.

[10] Karol Berger, *Bach's Cycle and Mozart's Arrow: An Essay on the Origins of Musical Modernity* (Berkeley: University of California Press, 2007).

[11] See my *Modal Subjectivities: Self-Fashioning in the Italian Madrigal* (Berkeley: University of California Press, 2004), especially the discussion of Monteverdi's "Ah, dolente partita!" in chapter 1. Bach ends his C-sharp-minor fugue hovering between what we might hear as a picardy version of the tonic or as a dominant preparation for a cadence on F-sharp minor. The presentations of the subject and second countersubject at this moment both point toward necessary resolutions to F-sharp minor—as does Beethoven's Op. 131. Performers should make the implication of pending resolution to F-sharp minor audible in both instances.

For the most part, however, Bach aligned himself with the new temporality of Vivaldian tonality. But he did not just leave his heritage behind. Instead, he undertook a lifelong project of experimentation, fusing the subject-based definition of identity characteristic of earlier imitative genres with the standardized manner of unfolding that was now more or less compulsory. In effect, he was pouring old wine into new wineskins to see what would happen.

Musicians have long recognized *The Well-Tempered Clavier* as a primer for learning fugal composition. Adorno insists that we should also hear it as a document from the crossroads, created by a composer of unsurpassed musical integrity who sought to discover how selfhood might be construed in a world of rationalized process. With the exception of the C-sharp-minor (or Aeolian), which refuses to surrender its modal proclivities, the other fugues I have discussed have anticipated Freud, Ford, and Marx in their strategies; the other forty-four fugues in the *WTC*—to say nothing of the hundreds of fugues Bach wrote for organ, chamber ensembles, and choral groups—pursue other ways of inserting a subject into the objective curriculum of tonality. In Adorno's words:

> [Bach] was not, however, interested in striking a mean between the two elements. His music strove to achieve the indifference of the extremes towards each other more radically than any other until that of the late Beethoven. Bach, as the most advanced master of *basso continuo*, at the same time renounced his obedience, as antiquated polyphonist, to the trend of the times, a trend he himself had shaped, in order to help it reach its innermost truth, the emancipation of the subject to objectivity in a coherent whole of which subjectivity itself was the origin. Down to the subtlest structural details it is always a question of the undiminished coincidence of the harmonic-functional and of the contrapuntal dimension. The distant past is entrusted with the utopia of the musical subject-object; anachronism becomes a harbinger of things to come. (142)

In his discussion of performance per se, Adorno lashes out against original instruments (remember what harpsichords were like in 1950!), against the insistence on inexpressive presentations (remember the old sewing-machine renditions!), and against too-literal applications of historical treatises. For him,

True interpretation is an x-ray of the work; its task is to illuminate in the sensuous phenomenon the totality of all the characteristics and interrelations which have been recognized through intensive study of the score.... [But] the musical score is never identical with the work; devotion to the text means the constant effort to grasp that which it hides. (144)

Effective performance, in other words, requires the combined skills of the analyst, the practicing musician, the historian, and the cultural critic. A tall order! But whoever said that the interpretation of music should be easy?

PART III
SEX AND GENDER REDUX

15

The Classical Closet[1]

I first met Stan Hawkins at a IASPM conference some decades ago. We quickly discovered that we shared a passion for Prince, our local hero in Minneapolis where I then lived. In 2007, Stan arranged for me to come to the University of Oslo for residencies over the course of five years. During those visits, I came to know him much better and also became acquainted with his wonderful students. At once urbane and earthy, funny and deeply serious, Stan became one of my closest colleagues and friends, and I have witnessed with joy his increasing prominence in musicological conversations concerning gender and sexuality in popular music.

Most of the essays in Stan's Festschrift rightly focused on popular-music topics, the area within which Stan has made his greatest contributions. In other circumstances, I might also have chosen a similar focus: the songs that circulate through our digital platforms influence the shaping of gender and sexuality far more than any other medium—certainly more than the exalted canon we perpetuate in conservatories and academic music programs. I insist on including popular music in my history surveys, even though I have had to fight constantly in order to do so.

But for Stan's Festschrift, I want to address a spectrum of sexual identities only barely hidden within classical music. As I rummage through what I'm calling the Classical Closet, I will deal largely with the music itself and the ways in which listeners tolerant of difference might hear it. I emphasize "hear," because I mean to privilege moments of reception rather than focusing exclusively on the site of the composer. For composers do not own the meanings that attach to their pieces, and audience members tend to cherish pieces that resonate with their own experiences, regardless of original intentions. We find in our favorite tunes expressions of interiority, deeply personal feelings that rarely make it to the level of verbal utterance. That

---

[1] Keynote for international conference, *Gender and Music: Practices, Performances, Politics*, Örebro University, Sweden, March 2016. Published in *Popular Music and Identity: Festschrift for Stan Hawkins*, ed. Kai Arne Hansen, Eirik Askerøi, and Freya Jarman (Oxfordshire, UK: Taylor & Francis, 2021), 50–59.

Making Sense of Music. Susan McClary, Oxford University Press. © Oxford University Press 2025.
DOI: 10.1093/9780197779798.003.0016

is the principal reason we turn to music, why half the population wanders around sporting earbuds.

I am drawing my examples from a backlog of class discussions. In the bad old days, music-history teachers were expected to present a heteronormative version of classical music. Musicologists do not differ from other kinds of instructors in this regard: as Louis Althusser pointed out, education counts as an Ideological State Apparatus, one of the strategies by means of which a society transmits its dominant structures from generation to generation.[2] Since the survival of the species depends upon at least *some* intimate contact between members of the opposite sex, educators—formal and informal, academic and domestic—have always focused a good deal of their energy on shaping gender roles and sexual behaviors in ways that will maximize reproduction. But that imperative too often becomes a set of draconian precepts that weigh heavily on women and on anyone who would deviate from what American evangelicals call the principle of One Man and One Woman.

In the early years of my teaching career, I dutifully presented the canon the way God had meant for it to be. Only gradually did I come to recognize my efforts as policing, as honor-bound tenets of pedagogy that dismissed comments that might have opened up unwanted topics. Because in order for the Ideological State Apparatus of the music-history survey to operate smoothly, I had to behave as a passive conduit between received wisdom and the students to whom I was supposed to impart sanctioned knowledge. Occasionally, however, a student would raise a question and then refuse to back down in the face of my programmed response. Such experiences drew my attention to the uncomfortable role I was playing and forced me to decide whether to continue to operate as a cog in the great wheel of musicological verities or, instead, to pay attention to the ways some students resisted absorbing those presumably objective truths. Needless to say, I find the needs of my students more compelling than the formal abstractions and institutionally codified factoids I had been trained to deliver.

When I think back to such episodes that have occurred throughout a teaching career that now spans half a century, I can only conclude that classical music is deeply, deeply queer. It didn't so much take radicals like me to bring these strains to the surface. Rather, musicology has been doing its best to obfuscate such issues from the get-go. And that's why bright students

---

[2] Louis Althusser, "Ideology and Ideological State Apparatuses," in *Lenin and Philosophy and Other Essays*, trans. Ben Brewster (London: New Left Books, 1971).

ask those embarrassing questions with such frequency. The issues are completely obvious to anyone who hasn't been brainwashed.

Let's start with European music history's greatest affront to normative gender roles: the castrati of the Italian baroque. Although the earliest operas featured men singing in the tenor or baritone ranges, in keeping with the natural post-pubescent male voice, the premiere of Monteverdi's *Orfeo* in 1607 cast castrati to sing the parts of all the female characters, including Euridice.[3] In 1631, Stefano Landi's *Sant'Alessio* starred no fewer than ten castrati playing both male and female roles.[4] When opera exploded onto the public stage in Venice in the late 1630s, women performed most of the female roles, but the romantic heroes all sang in the treble range—and so it continued until the French Revolution deposed the aristocracy along with all its decadent pleasures.[5] The newly emerging middle classes sought to realign genders with reproductive efficacy, which involved the systematic imposition of those binary oppositions we know all too well.

Think about it: for nearly two hundred years, Italian opera—the reigning genre at the time—relied upon transgendering technologies. Producing the men who could provide the sound demanded by audiences required radical surgery performed on boys before their voices changed. The church simultaneously outlawed these operations and became their principal beneficiaries, as popes and other high officials competed for the right to display the greatest virtuosi. Despite the rigorous scholarship devoted to studying this phenomenon, the novel *Cry to Heaven*, by Anne Rice of Lestat-the-Vampire fame, remains one of the most effective accounts of how these individuals lived and worked.[6]

---

[3] See my "Gender Ambiguities and Erotic Excess in Seventeenth-Century Venetian Opera," *Desire and Pleasure in Seventeenth-Century Music* (Berkeley: University of California Press, 2012), chapter 4.

[4] See William Christie's remarkable production of *Sant'Alessio*, available on DVD. Christie, of course, makes use of countertenors.

[5] For a novel that explores the fate of castrati who became freakish outcasts after they suddenly fell out of favor, see Dominique Fernandez, *Poporino, or The Secrets of Naples*, trans. Eileen Finletter (New York: Morrow, 1976).

[6] Anne Rice, *Cry to Heaven* (New York: Knopf, 1982). But see also Martha Feldman, *The Castrato: Reflections on Natures and Kinds* (Berkeley: University of California Press, 2016); Roger Freitas, "The Eroticism of Emasculation: Confronting the Baroque Body of the Castrato," *Journal of Musicology* 20, no. 2 (Spring 2003): 196–249.

Of course, many prominent rock and pop stars also sing in the soprano and alto ranges. For more on this phenomenon and comparisons with the castrati, see chapter 16, "Soprano Masculinities," and Freya Jarman, *Angels, Demons, Lovers, and Lunatics: The Queer Meanings of Singing High Notes* (New York: Oxford University Press, forthcoming).

Our greatest testimony to the cultural authority wielded by male sopranos and altos survives in the thousands of musical scores written to showcase their dazzling abilities. When the castrati's world collapsed at the end of the eighteenth century, those scores also were consigned to oblivion. Not coincidentally did early musicologists found their canon on the works of the prodigiously heterosexual J. S. Bach, father of at least twenty kids and of the great German tradition. Scholars celebrated Bach's great contemporary George Frideric Handel for his edifying English oratorios, even as they tried desperately to forget the scandal of his Italian operas, all of them starring castrati. They also sidelined his Italian cantatas, many of them set to explicitly homoerotic libretti written expressly for him by Cardinal Benedetto Pamphili, a prominent member of an ecclesiastical gay subculture in Rome.[7] And they concocted far-fetched stories that attempted to prove Handel's heterosexuality.[8]

But in the 1960s, along with other widespread cultural revolutions, a few intrepid souls began to look again at Handel's operas, regarded as unperformable since the 1700s, not the least because they required someone to sing the parts designed to showcase those vanished rock stars of the baroque stage. The great conqueror Julius Caesar an alto? Are you kidding? Yet the music itself proved sufficiently compelling that opera houses began to mount productions.

The first revivals simply transposed the offending parts down an octave so that "real men" could sing them without disrupting the prevailing gender economy. Baritones Walter Berry, Norman Treigle, and Dietrich Fischer-Dieskau all played Caesar, setting straight the original confusion. But because Handel had composed his love duets with the assumption that the lovers would have identical sounds as they intertwined, this strategy left Caesar and Cleopatra essentially in different beds. Heteronormativity was gained at the expense of the erotic frisson Handel had written into his scores.

The next solution cast women in the castrato roles, with Dame Janet Baker and others singing in the right tessitura (if not necessarily with the right sound).[9] Yet this strategy introduced queer resonances of its own, for now we

---

[7] See Ellen T. Harris, *Handel as Orpheus: Voice and Desire in the Chamber Operas* (Cambridge, MA: Harvard University Press, 2004).

[8] Gary Thomas, '"Was George Frideric Handel Gay?': On Closet Questions and Cultural Politic," in *Queering the Pitch: The New Gay and Lesbian Musicology*, ed. Philip Brett, Elizabeth Wood, and Gary C. Thomas, 2nd ed. (New York: Routledge, 2006), chapter 8.

[9] Nevertheless, one of my favorite performances stars an exceedingly butch and sexually charismatic Dame Sarah Connolly as Caesar at Glyndebourne.

had women making love to each other on the stage. Of course, we had learned to accept this convention because of cherished pants roles such as Mozart's Cherubino or Strauss's Octavian. But, as we have since learned from private diaries and letters, that convention itself had long served as a crucial site for women who derived immense erotic pleasure from watching same-sex activities on the stage. In the years when Gluck's Orfeo was commonly sung by a woman, lesbians streamed to opera houses to catch a glimpse at behaviors still denied to them in real life.[10]

To the chagrin of those women who greatly enjoyed this strategy, countertenors have increasingly assumed the roles designed for castrati.[11] At first, only a few men chose to specialize in the falsetto parts of their voices. But as the market for countertenors has expanded, vocal techniques have also developed such that the leading singers sound quite ravishing—indeed, so ravishing that several new operas (George Benjamin's *Written on Skin*, Salvatore Sciarrino's *Luci mie traditrici*, Kaija Saariaho's *Only the Sound Remains*) call for countertenors to sing the leading roles.[12] Yet today's countertenors almost always play their parts with three-day stubble to remind us that they are NOT castrati.

Treble singing, however, counted as only one of the scandalous elements in the parts written for baroque castrati. Even within the societies for which these entertainments flourished, many of the roles were designed to violate norms of male behavior. Take, for example, the title character in Francesco Cavalli's *Il Giasone*, the most successful opera of the seventeenth century. Cavalli and his librettist, Giacinto Andrea Cicognini, took the myth of Jason and Medea and made it into a sex farce befitting Venice, the Las Vegas of its time. Before Jason shows up on the stage, his fellow Argonauts have been complaining of his effeminacy—of the fact that he wants to do nothing but loll around in bed all day with his mysterious lover. Comic characters have already cracked castrato jokes, not aimed directly at Jason but reminding us at every turn about the miracle that makes his voice possible.

---

[10] See the many essays in *En Travesti: Women, Gender Subversion, Opera*, ed. Corrine E. Blackmer and Patricia Juliana Smith (New York: Columbia University Press, 1995), 135.

[11] Joke Dame, "Unveiled Voices: Sexual Difference and the Castrato," in *Queering the Pitch*, chapter 7.

[12] Benjamin Britten called for a countertenor to sing Oberon in his *Midsummer Night's Dream* (1960), and Philip Glass wrote his music for Akhnaten for countertenor (1983). But both chose that voice type expressly because it would sound queer: Britten for the king of the fairies, Glass for a pharaoh who seemed to have had an androgynous appearance. Only within the last twenty years have composers begun to use this voice for roles not marked as queer. See "Soprano Masculinities," chapter 16.

When Jason finally does appear, it is to sing not a heroic aria but rather an autoerotic lullaby about the pleasures of lovemaking. "Delizie, contenti" resembles Prince's song "Do Me, Baby" not only in its use of high voice but also because the lyrics of both songs present the male lover as submissive, begging his partner to take the lead. Moreover, both feature harmonic progressions that tilt through the subdominant toward the supine. This is *not* what manhood was supposed to be, not now nor in the mid-seventeenth century. No wonder generations of musicologists have tried to shield us from such perverse gender constructions.

Fortunately, modern stage directors have become much less squeamish about the queerness of Venetian operas. Watch, for example, countertenor Christophe Dumaux performing "Delizie, contenti"; as he sings, Dumaux wallows in masturbatory languor, intensified by the appearance from beneath the sheets of extra arms and hands.[13] Not even his three-day stubble can put this travesty straight!

As I mentioned earlier, Handel often composed Italian cantatas on homoerotic texts about Greek mythological figures such as Narcissus and Ganymede. Narcissus, as you recall, was Apollo's lover until Apollo killed him in an accident; Apollo's tears caused his beloved's body to change into the flower that bears his name. Ganymede was a beautiful boy, forcibly abducted by Jupiter, who had assumed the guise of an eagle. A few decades later, Franz Schubert too composed songs about Ganymede's rapturous ascent into heaven in the talons of his sugar daddy, and Narcissus also figures among his personae.[14]

But not all Schubert's queer-tinged songs turn out to be pleasurable. "Der Erlkönig," his Opus 1, written when he was 17, brings together pedophilia and supernatural horror in ways that should still shock us today. Over the years, several of my gay students have interpreted the song as a scenario of father/son incest, with the "good father" trying to dispel the child's fears and the "bad" one—the Elf King—relentlessly enticing, then threatening, and finally murdering him. In this reading, the famous galloping rhythms in the piano become the impulses of sexual aggression, of anal rape. Composer

---

[13] https://www.youtube.com/watch?v=FWWsHP7OooM
[14] See Kristina Muxfeldt, "Schubert, Platen, and the Myth of Narcissus," *Journal of the American Musicological Society* 49, no. 3 (Autumn 1996): 480–527, and her *Vanishing Sensibilities: Schubert, Beethoven, Schumann* (New York: Oxford University Press, 2012); see also Lawrence Kramer, *Franz Schubert: Sexuality, Subjectivity, Song* (Cambridge, UK: Cambridge University Press, 2003).

Georg Friedrich Haas has published an analysis that presents the same reading in extremely graphic detail.[15]

I wouldn't argue, of course, that this is the only interpretation; a few years ago, most of us would have dismissed such a reading out of hand. But as I have discovered in class discussions, Schubert's setting of Goethe's gothic ballad clearly has the potential to awaken memories of childhood abuse. Indeed, many have quoted part of Schubert's quasi-autobiographical story, "My Dream," to argue for the composer's own family trauma:

> My father took me once again into his favorite garden. He asked me if I liked it. But the garden was wholly repellent to me and I dared not say so. Then, flushing, he asked me a second time: did the garden please me? Trembling, I denied it. Then my father struck me and I fled.

In a horrifying performance of "Der Erlkönig," Ian Bostridge stresses the sinister way Schubert sets even the opening lines, with a cry of horror on the words "father and his son" and a creepy, insinuating presentation of "he holds him securely, he keeps him warm."[16]

In the wake of disclosures concerning the abuse of thousands of children at the hands of the clergy, as well as the cover-ups that ignored the pleading voices of victims, we need to take such readings far more seriously. Music can take us to ecstatic highs, but it can also trigger deep-seated fears and anxieties. We go to music for the whole range of experiences, which seem to the listener more immediate—that is, without mediation—than any of the other arts. As a teacher, I have to be prepared for all responses and to deal with them sympathetically.[17]

But back to the pleasure zone for a while. I lectured recently on Debussy's *Prelude to the Afternoon of a Faun*, the composer's response to the infamous poem by his friend Stéphane Mallarmé. Analysts often point to the opening C-sharp in the solo flute and its refusal to conform to any of the harmonic

---

[15] See George Friedrich Haas, "On Schubert's 'Erlkönig,'" *VAN Magazine* (Feb. 4, 2016). See also the graphic descriptions of those alternating roles abusers take in Hanya Yanagihara's harrowing novel *A Little Life* (New York: Anchor, 2015).

[16] https://www.youtube.com/watch?v=mmx4MN3xZpM.

[17] I delivered a version of this paper as a keynote, titled "Not in Kansas Anymore: Bringing Sexualities into Music Studies," at the LGBTQ Studies and Music Education Symposium, Champaign, IL, May 2016. Even the discipline responsible for training young students now takes seriously the need to prepare teachers to deal with a full range of sexualities. My colleague Matthew Garrett has played a central role in bringing these issues to bear. See Garrett and Joshua Palkki, *Honoring Trans and Gender-Expansive Students in Music Education* (New York: Oxford University Press, 2021).

contexts within which Debussy places it. The passionate middle of the piece moves into D-flat, the enharmonic respelling of that initial sore pitch, and though the music swells and throbs toward closure, the anticipated cadence returns us to the original environment in which the stubborn C-sharp stands outside, resisting assimilation. It still lingers on in the ear after the final cadence, a kind of added sixth atop the E-major surroundings.

After class I received an email from one of my students, who offered a compelling queer reading of these details. If that C-sharp sounds like a point of pleasure (as the sixth degree has done since the Renaissance), then its refusal to conform to traditional harmonic syntax makes it a sexual outlaw of sorts. Only in the middle section—a fantasy? a safe space, hidden away from the world?—does it give full voice to its own desires in its own realm. And if the Faun has to return eventually back into reality, he has experienced bliss at least temporarily on his own terms, and his C-sharp holds out the hope of revisiting that island of unbridled pleasure sometime in the future.

All this resonates with Mallarmé's poem, which starts with the line "I must perpetuate these nymphs," flickers in and out of wet dreams, and attempts at the end to go back to sleep in order to reach that moment of *jouissance* once again. Nijinsky's outrageous choreography, which concludes with the Faun masturbating into a scarf, only translates Mallarmé's and Debussy's energies onto the dancing body.[18]

It should not be difficult to arrive at a queer reading of *Salome*: an opera based on a prohibited play by a notorious homosexual who would serve time at hard labor for his crimes against nature. We might understand Oscar Wilde's *Salomé* as a manifestation of loves that dare not speak their names—of obsessive, overwhelming passions addressed to illicit objects of desire. From the viewpoint of Saint Oscar, Salomé appears as a martyr on the altar of forbidden sexual practices.

Historian Sander Gilman has documented how Strauss latched onto this play in large part because of the Wilde scandal, and the composer assumed quite rightly that his impeccable heterosexual credentials would protect him from the fate that befell its playwright.[19] But Strauss may have been the least appropriate composer for this task of setting Wilde's delicate, pointillistic text, which he steamrollers with Wagnerian angst. In his opera, Strauss's title character takes her place beside the other *femmes fatales* of late Romantic

---

[18] https://www.youtube.com/watch?v=EvnRC7tSX50

[19] Sander L. Gilman, "Strauss, the Pervert, and Avant-Garde Opera of the Fin de Siècle," *New German Critique* 43 (1988): 35–68.

opera, the queer elements of Wilde's play put straight in a parable of lurid female lust. So overwhelming is Strauss's music that restaging proves difficult, and many directors strive for pornographic and misogynist presentations.

But a Salzburg production by Götz Friedrich starring Teresa Stratas in the title role manages to present the final speech as a moment of divine transfiguration. In the video recording of this production, the entire sequence appears in a single camera shot, and as Stratas reaches the climax, she moves into a pose characteristic of Baroque paintings of saints in ecstasy. This, I believe, is how Wilde envisioned it. Queer, disturbing, transgressive, without question—yet also somehow sacred.[20]

My last example concerns a particularly successful attempt at queering the classics: Matthew Bourne's production of Tchaikovsky's *Swan Lake*. Like classical music, classical ballet conceals its ideological agendas deep within the closet. We encourage little girls to imagine themselves floating weightlessly in pink tutus, thereby helping to instill lifelong eating disorders.

What we forget is that dancing *en pointe* began in the nineteenth century as a way of representing non-dead women, zombie spirits who prey on living men. The first ballerina to deploy this special-effects technique, Maria Taglioni, did so in 1832 (after much very painful experimentation) for her father Filippo's choreography of the ghost tale *La Sylphide*; *Giselle* and *Swan Lake* followed this tradition closely, after which it just became the way female dancers were supposed to move. And the tutu itself. Ever wonder why this convention came into being in the olden days when a glimpse of stocking was looked on as something shocking? Well, nineteenth-century ballet houses operated as thinly veiled brothels. At the ends of performances, wealthy men came backstage to collect partners for the evening, and they paid extra to sit in the front rows. The tutu offered a good deal more than a glimpse of stocking.

Nonetheless, as a cultural medium of the nineteenth century, classical ballet did present a rigorously heteronormative set of images, with fragile, swooning women borne aloft by strong, dependable men. Dance historian Susan Leigh Foster has argued that male dancers wielded the ballerina's stiffened body as a kind of phallic extension, thereby displaying a highly sexualized masculine prowess.[21] A more stringently gendered division of

---

[20] https://www.youtube.com/watch?v=Op1VoQXXARs, at the 7-minute mark.
[21] See her "The Ballerina's Phallic Pointe," a lecture-performance at danceworkbook.pcah.us/susan-foster/the-ballerinas-phallic-pointe.html.

labor is hard to imagine (even if the ballerinos in tights with bulging packages more than flirt with homoerotic display).[22]

Of course, that very stringency invites parody, and the Ballets Trockadero de Monte Carlo has long presented hilarious versions of *Swan Lake* with male dancers in drag. Such spoofs poke fun at the artificiality of ballet, and seeing large, hairy men twirling in pirouettes while attired in tutus does take something of the solemnity out of the art form. Yet parodies and send-ups notwithstanding, *Swan Lake* continues to cast a strange spell over many viewers, as the film *Black Swan* demonstrated once again. How many little girls overlooked the grossly mutilated feet shown repeatedly in the movie and merely raced home to put on their tutus?

Matthew Bourne reached for something beyond parody in his reworking of this ballet. To be sure, parody certainly enters into his production, especially in the scenes in which the chorus dances to moves borrowed from contemporary popular genres. But more than that, he sought to deconstruct the gender economy of ballet, rereading it through the lens of same-sex love. In his version, the young prince resists the blandishments of court (as does Siegfried in the original, for that matter, where the queen mother is trying to pressure him into marriage). But Bourne's prince finds his transcendent ideal in the charismatic Adam Cooper, the leader of a flock of male swans. In the scenes focused on the troupe, Bourne has to butch up the gestures and steps previously identified with fluttering birds, and these dances prove revelatory, inviting us to hear Tchaikovsky's music, its gestures and accents, in altogether new ways—in ways no longer tied to the flightiness we might anticipate.

Most astonishing, however, are the pas de deux, the equivalent of love duets in opera. These required the choreographer to dispatch with the gendered binaries handed down by tradition. What would it look like to have two symmetrical partners, each equally active and passive, mutually nurturing? To find out, watch Bourne's staging of the famous pas de deux in Act II between the prince and the swan.[23] Although this duet speaks directly to the same-sex narrative Bourne traces throughout his version, it also offers a mode of emotional interaction that does not demand a division of labor guaranteed in advance by gender. Many a straight woman has gazed longingly at Bourne's

---

[22] Arved Ashby has reminded me of this dimension of classic ballet. See his chapter on Tchaikovsky, "Love's Balletic Inverse," in his *My 1980s Gayboy Playlist* (punctum, 2005). Ashby's extraordinary book also includes chapters on Bruckner, Prince, Berg, and Nirvana.
[23] https://www.youtube.com/watch?v=q4LDNlc_AQI, at 55:35.

images, wishing that such reciprocal patterns occurred more frequently on stage—and also in their own personal relationships. Bourne directs a glaring light back on the ideological assumptions underpinning the conventions of classical ballet and its music.

Might other works similarly find liberation in restagings? Once given permission to think along these lines, we can easily find places where narratives suggesting same-sex love suddenly get shoved back to heteronormative structures for closure. Recall Bellini's *Norma*, in which two women sing ravishing duets with one another, despite the fact that they love the same Roman lout. At the end of the opera, the lout shows up, thereby putting a heterosexual face on Norma's passions. Adalgisa gets disappeared, and Norma walks nobly into the flames with the lout. How much more satisfying—in terms of the narrative tensions within the opera itself—if the two women were to join hands in martyrdom, or if they simply walked off the stage and into a fulfilling life together, leaving the lout to return to Rome or go to a casino or whatever.

I leave other possibilities to your imaginations. But I hope to have demonstrated how very shallow the veneer of mainstream behaviors really is in classical music. Such issues arise in my classroom not because I drag them in but because they have always been there: in Plato's desire to exclude the musical practices of the Lydians from the Republic because of their effeminacy, or in the struggles of Hildegard von Bingen to have her voice and those of her nuns heard in a culture that demanded the silence of women.

Nineteenth-century German idealist aesthetics, with their emphasis on absolute music, managed to make us forget how pervasive these themes have been throughout music history—and also how this aesthetic foundation justifies itself by universalizing its particular privileges of gender, sexuality, ethnicity, race, and class. I still like a lot of classical music. I just prefer it with a twist.

16

Soprano Masculinities[1,2]

Castrati. Even after decades of teaching about seventeenth-century music, I still find this the most difficult topic to broach with students. I have learned how to avoid or present with exquisite nuance many other potentially uncomfortable issues that arise over the course of music history. But one cannot circumvent the castrati when trucking through the survey of European art music. Whatever I might want to say on the appointed day concerning Cavalli or Handel or the emergence of public opera houses gets shoved to the side as my students pose their inevitable questions concerning anatomy and the surgical procedures of bygone eras. I dutifully answer them, attempting to minimize sensationalism and struggling to get back to the music as quickly as possible. Expressions of prurience, disgust, and horror flash across their faces. I try to speak over the sounds of tittering and gagging. The fact that the messenger who brings these ill tidings is a well-known feminist probably does not help.[3]

---

[1] Keynote for the conference *Popular Music and Gender in a Transcultural Context*, University of Oslo, March 2011. Published in *Masculinity in Opera*, ed. Philip Purvis (London: Routledge, 2013), 51–79. I have added a new section concerning recent operas composed specifically for countertenors at the end of the chapter.

[2] This chapter is memory of Christopher Small (1927–2011). As I prepared to send this chapter to Philip Purvis, I learned that Christopher Small—whom I counted as a dear friend—had just died at age 84. A project such as this one would never have occurred to me without Chris's brilliant books: *Music—Society—Education* (Hanover, NH: Wesleyan University Press, 1996); *Musicking: The Meanings of Performing and Listening* (Hanover, NH: Wesleyan University Press, 1998); and *Music of the Common Tongue: Survival and Celebration in African American Music* (Hanover, NH: Wesleyan University Press, 1999). Chris and his spouse, the late Neville Braithwaite, taught me to understand the profound impact of African American culture on all of us and to appreciate the centrality of musicking to human life. I dedicate this in loving memory of Chris and Neville.

And as I was preparing the final version of the essay, I acquired Anthony Heilbut's newly released book, *The Fan Who Knew Too Much: Aretha Franklin, the Rise of the Soap Opera, Children of the Gospel Church, and Other Meditations* (New York: Knopf, 2012), which contains a chapter titled "The Male Soprano." Like my essay, this chapter compares the high-range singing of gospel performers with that of rock stars and castrati. Heilbut's earlier work influenced my own account of Claude Jeter of the Swan Silvertones; see my *Conventional Wisdom: The Content of Musical Form* (Berkeley: University of California Press, 2000), chapter 1. I am delighted to see him drawing many of the conclusions that appear in this chapter.

[3] I deal with this problem in chapter 15 from a somewhat different angle.

In truth, I do not know of a way of defending the physical mutilation visited upon hundreds of young males during this period, and I quite share my students' squeamishness on that score. But they also resist the notion that audiences might have wanted to hear men sing in the high tessituras typically associated with women, and they often hear even performances by countertenors as irredeemably repugnant. Because they perceive the sonority itself as signifying damaged manhood, they find it nearly impossible to understand the aesthetic values of the two hundred years of European music designed for castrati.

Part (but only part) of the problem involves biology. Children and adult females can sing in the treble range because their vocal cords are relatively short. With the onset of puberty, both males and females experience hormonal changes that produce a wide variety of secondary sex characteristics. For men, this includes the lengthening of vocal cords and the resultant lowering of the voice. Societies that value a strict binary distinction between men and women sometimes exploit the signs of physical maturation by exaggerating male facial hair, female curves, or the manly timbre of the baritone voice. When, as often happens, such signs of difference are raised to the level of ideology, they can come to seem natural and universal, as unwavering dictates of physiology itself. A quick glance at world cultures and the history of Western fashion, however, will reveal how very diligently human beings work to manipulate and interpret even the most fundamental of body parts and functions.

The meanings of voice change are far from natural or universal, even at the level of individual experience. Boys first encounter their voices and shape their sense of sonic identity as children, and one of the most traumatic events in puberty involves the unbidden alienation from that sound that had served as their conduit for subjective expression. With puberty, a boy has to accommodate a switch from one concept of his own essential sound to another, very different one. With respect to voice, in other words, the possibility of a stable "natural" condition is already deeply compromised. This may be why so much cultural effort has to be expended on making the transfigured sonority seem vastly superior to its childhood predecessor—at least in societies in which this particular sign of difference is viewed as advantageous.

Many societies, however, have valued and continue to value the sound of men singing in a high tessitura. In the most extreme instances—including, alas, the Italian *seicento*—they have learned how to circumvent sexual maturation altogether through surgical procedures practiced since antiquity not only on livestock but also on humans.[4] Yet less dire solutions also motivate adult males to produce sounds in the soprano range, and these manifest themselves in a wide variety of circumstances.

In the 1980s I began paying attention to popular music for the first time in my life, and the new medium of music video—with stars such as Prince and Michael Jackson who specialized in displaying transgressive sexual personae—offered me invaluable assistance as I tried to explain some of the pleasures of early modern opera. I still must deal with the physiological and cultural dimensions of the castrati in my classes, of course. But I am better able now to help my students grasp and even appreciate seventeenth-century vocal music.

I want to begin my essay by discussing some of the reasons recent popular musicians have chosen to sing in their highest range and also explain how the falsettist sonority registers for its various fan bases. Following this excursion, I will return to the baroque opera that served as my own starting point, and finally to a new cluster of operas composed explicitly for the countertenor virtuosos who have emerged in the early twenty-first century. Together, these very different artists—castrati, falsettists, countertenors, female singers *en travesti*—provide us with what I call soprano masculinities.

Since the advent of sound recording, the genres and conventions developed by African Americans have shaped musical practices in all corners of the globe. Put succinctly, the twentieth century witnessed a profound African-Americanization of Western culture. Virtually all the musics that have emerged as our common soundtrack over the course of the last hundred years—blues, jazz, rock, hip-hop—have their roots in this community.[5]

The single most important incubator for musicians and their proliferating idioms is the African American church, which frequently features male gospel singers who produce high falsetto moans and melismas. Although they scale the heights of their ranges, their high-pitched vocals rarely have anything to do with gender-bending. They serve rather to simulate—through a practice

---

[4] A forerunner of my uncomfortable lectures on the castrati occurred every year in my fundamentalist Bible-study classes when we arrived at the story of the Ethiopian eunuch in Acts, chapter 8. "What is a eunuch?" we would chirp. Our teacher, who wanted to focus instead on his extraordinary conversion, would always sidestep the question. Her failure to answer us candidly resulted one year in our calling a visiting preacher named Enoch "Brother Eunuch" by mistake. Who knew?

[5] For a brilliant account of this tradition, see Small, *Music of the Common Tongue*. See also my review of Richard Taruskin's *Oxford History of Western Music* (Oxford, UK: Oxford University Press, 2005) in *Music and Letters* 87, no. 3 (2006): 408–13, and chapter 1 of my *Conventional Wisdom: The Content of Musical Form* (Berkeley: University of California Press, 2000).

relating back to those of ancestors from West Africa—the ecstatic condition of "getting over," and their extravagant sounds are understood within their communities as performances of charismatic virtuosity (with the stress here on "vir") and spiritual leadership.

Take, for instance, the recording in 1952 by the Swan Silvertones of "Jesus Keep Me near the Cross."[6] Falsettist Claude Jeter begins his upward trajectory after the hymn itself has been presented in a relatively straightforward way. As the others in the group set out an ostinato on the words "just beyond the river," Jeter enacts his intense yearning to push through to another state of consciousness. Over and over, he strives to attain rapture through his efforts. The makeshift congregation assembled in the studio for this recording adds audible approbation, cheering him on at each successive stage. Far from transgressive, in other words, his soprano sonorities offer for the faithful a model of what it would feel like to transcend earthly burdens. Moreover, as he strains to go higher and higher, he pulls his listeners along with him. At last he reaches F'—an eleventh above middle C—an event roundly celebrated by those who have identified with his arduous journey and its cathartic triumph.

Many singers other than Jeter also work within this tradition. Listen, for instance, to Aaron Neville crooning Schubert's "Ave Maria" or to Kirk Franklin exploring sacred erotic tropes worthy of Heinrich Schütz in his "Something about the Name Jesus." Occasionally a white critic will ask such artists why they sing in women's ranges. But within the aesthetic context of the gospel church, the notion that gender might be at issue in performances of soprano masculinity seems ludicrous.

The practices of African American gospel have long since spilled over into the secular realm. In genre after genre—including blues, jazz, R&B, doo-wop, girl groups, Motown, soul, disco, and even hip-hop—leading musicians more often than not have honed their skills in church and simply deployed them again in their new contexts. I recently heard an R&B group in Cleveland that calls itself Swanktify, thereby acknowledging precisely this hybridized legacy. The divine Aretha Franklin inherited her rhetorical power from her father, the legendary preacher C. L. Franklin, whose astonishing

---

[6] Re-released on *The Swan Silvertones* (Specialty Records, 1993). For a more extensive discussion, see chapter 1 of my *Conventional Wisdom*. See also Anthony Heilbut, *The Gospel Sound: Good News and Bad Times*, 3rd ed. (New York: Limelight, 1989), and *The Fan Who Knew Too Much*.

sermons are available online. Whether singing anthems such as "Respect" or hymns like "Amazing Grace," Aretha invests everything she touches with the spiritual zeal she developed in the worship service.[7]

This blurring between sacred and secular spheres has resulted in the presence in popular music of thousands of falsettists who continue to operate within the gender-neutral aesthetic assumptions of gospel. Before moving to Motown as songwriters and recording artists, the late Nick Ashford and his partner Valerie Simpson (Ashford & Simpson) developed their craft in a Harlem church. Ashford often matched his wife's voice note for note, and they took turns raising the ante with high-pitched melismas.

A spectacular instance of secularized gospel is Earth, Wind & Fire's perennial hit "Reasons" featuring the extraordinary Philip Bailey, who can soar far above what most castrati were expected to perform.[8] In interviews, Bailey has stated that he doesn't understand why dewy-eyed couples want to have "Reasons" performed at their weddings, for the lyrics of "Reason" actually express a cynical attitude concerning one-night stands ("After the love game has been played / All our illusions were just a parade / And all the reasons start to fade / After all our reasons why / All the reasons were a lie").[9] But in my experience playing this track for very different audiences, the words of this song almost never register to listeners, virtually all of whom respond instead to the powerful pseudo-spiritual trajectories of the music and the tender quality of the vocals.

Bailey begins with his silky voice already in a middle-soprano range. He seduces through his effortless, incomparably elegant delivery. As the song progresses, he presses increasingly into the stratosphere in ways that resemble Claude Jeter's attempts to "get over" and with much the same emotional effect—except that he goes much higher, finally reaching C'' two octaves above middle C. My students hear this gospel-inflected fervor as "passion," a term that counts as the highest praise for them, and they inevitably get teary as soon as I push "Play." Such is their rapture that I can never bring myself to read the lyrics to them. But just imagine Tom Waits singing those same words.

"Reasons" manifests a stark discrepancy between lyrics and musical semiotics—precisely the kind of discrepancy that makes many scholars wary

---

[7] Aretha Franklin, "Amazing Grace," on *Amazing Grace* (Atlantic, 1972).

[8] Originally released on Earth, Wind & Fire, *That's the Way of the World* (Columbia, 1975).

[9] See the discussion in Robert Walser, "Groove as Niche: Earth Wind & Fire," in *This Is Pop: In Search of the Elusive at Experience Music Project*, ed. Eric Weisbard (Cambridge, MA: Harvard University Press, 2004), 266–67. As the notes throughout this essay demonstrate, I owe much of what I know and understand concerning popular music to my husband, Robert Walser.

of hermeneutical analysis. But only if we imagine that signification inheres strictly in the verbal medium, only if we try to reduce the import of a song to its lyrics, can we declare a song such as "Reasons" resistant to or inappropriate for musical interpretation. Indeed, the fact that millions of fans swoon to this song without having the vaguest idea of its heartless words makes the project of musical hermeneutics all the more pressing. And the tendency of listeners to hear Bailey through the filter of gospel conventions, as well as the unequivocally macho funk of Earth, Wind & Fire's instrumentalists, usually discourages them from worrying about gender or sexual identity at all as he sings.

But some artists have taken their gospel-inspired sounds and styling in directions that call explicit attention to such concerns. The late disco artist Sylvester, for instance, brought many of the verbal and musical tropes he absorbed in church into the hedonistic environment of post-Stonewall gay nightlife as he belted out disco anthems such as "Power of Love" in his exquisite soprano-range voice.[10] The extravagantly cross-dressed former member of a group named the Cockettes, Sylvester left no doubt that he intended his falsetto—with which he displayed vocal pyrotechnics similar to those of Jeter and Bailey—as transgressive of traditional gender codes. He operated as a part of a new culture that aggressively and exuberantly asserted its rights to disrupt the ways the dominant realm dictated how masculinity was to be performed. This was what we used to call Gender Fuck in all its glory.

Stripped of its drag paraphernalia, "Power of Love" might have fit quite comfortably within certain gospel contexts, even with the pounding dance beat backing up the vocals. Such rhythmic practices regularly incite congregants in evangelical churches to "get happy." But Sylvester deliberately took his ecstatic, ambiguous sonority and put it in the service of the rites of a new cultural agenda, exploiting for all he was worth the fact that he was trying to sound (and look) something like a woman. He qualifies, along with Donna Summer and Gloria Gaynor, as one of the leading Divas of Disco.

Of course, he was not the first pop star to flirt with using these aural signs to confuse gender norms. In a more innocent time, Little Richard could sport high vocals and spectacular grooming without creating sexual panic; most rock 'n' roll fans in the 1950s remained oblivious to the connotations of Richard Penniman's stage persona when he performed songs like the frenetic

---

[10] Sylvester (James), "Power of Love," *Call Me* (Megatone, 1983).

"Tutti Frutti." He could call himself the Queen of Rock without raising suspicions. Even less plausibly, the Village People sang explicitly gay-coded songs such as "YMCA," and Freddie Mercury called his band Queen while sporting Castro-clone fashions yet still somehow passed under the radar. Willful ignorance concerning same-sex subcultures allowed many artists to play both sides of the fence, hiding in plain view from those who would prefer not to know, even while shouting their sexual preferences from the rooftops for the benefit of those celebrating their newfound freedoms.

Even within disco culture, certain prominent heterosexual musicians and fans sought to pull the soprano sound back over into a realm in which gender was not at issue. The Bee Gees (i.e., the Brothers Gibb) and the film featuring their music, *Saturday Night Fever*, attempted to reclaim the falsettist and even disco itself for heterosexuality. Their sound might be compared productively to that of earlier Boy Groups: recall, for instance, the hair-raising soprano whoops of Frankie Valli and the Four Seasons in songs such as "Sherry," "Big Girls Don't Cry," or (with no apparent irony intended) "Walk Like a Man."[11] But no one could mistake Sylvester's purpose and message. However much he may have channeled gospel rhetoric in his songs, he meant to be understood as joyously, flamboyantly Queer.

The presence of a figure like Sylvester muddied the waters a bit for subsequent artists. Once high-pitched singing was purposely associated with gender-bending, the task of deciding whether or not that style of delivery counted as queer became far more difficult. Prince exploited these ambiguities strategically throughout his career. Although he was primarily or even exclusively heterosexual in his personal life, he often presented himself as queer in the hairstyles, clothing, and stage mannerisms borrowed variously from icons such as Little Richard, Sylvester, James Brown, Sly Stone, and Rick James.

But he went further in his assertion of androgyny: for a while, he famously dropped his name in exchange for a symbol comprising the traditional signs for male and female. For such transgressive acts, he received praise

---

[11] I often use "Sherry" in my courses in historical performance practice, especially when discussing Giulio Caccini's instructions for how to produce the *esclamazione*. If we did not have this recording as documentation, we would never imagine Valli's forced, arpeggiated falsetto as the authentic mode of rendering this song. What if Caccini were trying to describe something that alien to our sensibilities?
   Valli has enjoyed something of a renaissance with the award-winning Broadway show *Jersey Boys* (2004), which features many of the hits he recorded in the 1960s.

in the 1980s and 1990s from poststructuralist theorists who perceived him as fighting against traditional binary arrangements of gender and sexuality, though he also suffered considerable abuse from homophobes.[12]

Prince has a relatively low voice, naturally situated in the baritone range, and his songs are sometimes performed in that register. But he also figures among the most dazzling falsettists of our time, and many of his most important hits feature his very high sound. In contrast to Philip Bailey, Prince frequently manipulates his voice in ways that beg to call normative sexuality into question. Recall, for instance, the weird, squeaky sonority that prevails throughout most of "Kiss." Drawing attention precisely to vocal register and gender in this song, he has the female dancer mouth his baritone rendition of the word "kiss": he looks at her aghast.

I want to focus here on Prince's "Do Me, Baby," in part because I will return to elements of it when I discuss the seventeenth-century castrato.[13] Singing with a somewhat tremulous quality that sometimes recalls the catlike sound of Claude Jeter, Prince pleads with his lover to pleasure him. He positions himself as the passive partner in this encounter, attempting to maintain a steady state of arousal as long as possible. Occasionally he seems on the verge of losing his control, and he then slips momentarily down into his lower voice for a defenseless moan. Toward the end of the second verse, however, he allows himself to explode in ecstasy. The gospel goal of "getting over" here is clearly sexual climax, as he ascends gradually to a rapturous, full-voiced pitch within the coloratura.

It is not merely the fact of the high tessitura that makes "Do Me, Baby" sexually ambiguous but also the abjection projected in the song's lyrics and its cyclical harmonic progression. As we shall see, these qualities sometimes appear as well in the music written for some of the characters sung by castrati. When I play "Do Me, Baby," I find that most of my students find this particular persona extremely sexy, and they go wild along with him in his climactic cadenza. What I strive to do is help them to relate that performance of masculinity to those of the baroque.[14]

---

[12] See Robert Walser, "Prince as Queer Poststructuralist," *Popular Music and Society* 18, no. 2 (Summer 1994): 79–89; my *Conventional Wisdom*, chapter 5; *Prince: The Making of a Pop Music Phenomenon*, ed. Stan Hawkins and Sarah Niblock (Aldershot, UK: Ashgate, 2011). See also Hawkins, *The British Pop Dandy: Masculinity, Popular Music and Culture* (Aldershot, UK: Ashgate, 2009).

[13] Prince, "Do Me, Baby," *Controversy* (Warner Bros., 1981).

[14] See also the discussion of "Do Me, Baby" and baroque opera in chapter 15.

As the mainstream public became more aware (if not always more accepting) of gay culture, it sometimes linked suspicions of sexual deviance with such voices. The late Michael Jackson was idolized for his gorgeous sonority, already offered with flawless perfection in his hits with the Jackson Five, yet also subjected to gossip concerning not only his sexual orientation but even his physiology. Was he really a falsettist? Or did his voice betray the possibility that he never passed through puberty, never developed secondary sex characteristics? For it wasn't only Jackson who faced the trauma of a changed voice but also millions of fans for whom his sound in "I'll Be There," recorded when he was only eleven years old, could not be improved upon.

Never has a pop star's autopsy attracted such attention as Jackson's—and not only because of the question of drugs. Although the coroner reported explicitly that Jackson's genitals were normal and intact (what other autopsy in recent memory has been called upon to address this?), his celebrated voice continues to provoke questions. Musicologists Stan Hawkins, Susan Fast, and Jacqueline Warwick have attempted to put such rumors to rest.[15] But the fact that male singers have *sometimes* been physically altered to preserve their angelic vocals—together with Jackson's well-known desire to cling like Peter Pan to childhood and his penchant for undergoing extreme plastic surgery—make it unlikely that the scandal attached to his voice will ever truly disappear.

Another strand of soprano masculinities exists prominently in popular music: the lead singers in hard-rock and heavy-metal bands. Although this strand seems far removed from the gospel legacy we have been tracing, it also has roots in African American practices. Recall the deep influence of bluesman Robert Johnson's falsetto on British rockers such as Eric Clapton and Robert Plant; Plant's strained mode of delivery also owes much to that of Janis Joplin, who in turn learned her styling from blues and gospel artists such as Big Mama Thornton.

But hard rock has long since separated itself from its roots, even if audible residues remain. For the lead singers in these bands, the most obvious influence on vocal production is the sound of the heavily amplified and distorted electric guitar. Of course, rhetorical excess also plays an important role. Recall the ways Aerosmith's Steven Tyler whets his fans' appetites for his high-pitched keening in, for instance, "Dream On."[16] Only three and a quarter minutes into

[15] See Stan Hawkins and Susan Fast, ed., *Michael Jackson: Musical Subjectivities*, special issue of *Popular Music and Society* 35, no. 2 (2012).
[16] Aerosmith, "Dream On," *Aerosmith* (Columbia, 1973).

the song does he finally cut loose and present his refrain up an octave from its earlier iterations. Tyler occasionally flirts with drag in his videos and stage performances, most famously in his "Dude Looks like a Lady," and even his "normal" attire—flowing scarves, feathers, heavy eye makeup—plays with gender in ways that characterized late-'80s metal bands such as Poison and Dokken. But the lead singers in none of these bands choose the falsetto range because they want to sound like women. Within their community of fans, their sonorities register as hypermasculine assaults on cultural norms.[17] And they strive to match the effect of the screaming guitar in their vocals.

Or take Judas Priest's Rob Halford. Although Halford's bondage gear may read as unambiguous evidence of his affiliation with a particular gay subculture, many fans understand the leather and chains merely as assertions of masculine force, and his piercing vocals in songs like "Between Hammer & Anvil" do so as well.[18] As he blasts out his refrain toward the end of the song, he rises to the challenge of matching the timbre and sonic power of the electric guitar.

What does any of this have to do with opera? In the pages that follow I will not add anything new to what we know about seventeenth- and eighteenth-century castrati—a field of research that has recently taken on new life, especially with the superb work of Roger Freitas and Martha Feldman.[19] As I argued in chapter 15, my concern here is rather more pedagogical, stemming as it does from my decades of attempting to introduce the topic to students and to coach singers learning to perform these repertories.

When countertenors first began performing the roles designed for castrati in the early years of the historical-performance movement, many of them employed a mode of sound production that recalled the sonorities characteristic of Monty Python drag skits. Called upon to mimic sopranos, countertenors adopted the conventions men often use when trying to sound like women. No wonder students recoiled in disgust or else giggled helplessly. I confess

---

[17] See Robert Walser, *Running with the Devil: Power, Gender and Madness in Heavy Metal Music* (Middletown, CT: Wesleyan University Press, 1993), especially chapter 4, "Forging Masculinity."
[18] Judas Priest, "Between the Hammer and the Anvil," *Painkiller* (Columbia, 1990).
[19] See Roger Freitas, *Portrait of a Castrato: Politics, Patronage, and Music in the Life of Atto Melani* (Cambridge, UK: Cambridge University Press, 2009); and Martha Feldman, *The Castrato: Reflections on Natures and Kinds* (Berkeley: University of California Press, 2015). Feldman also examines the spectacularity of castrati in her *Opera and Sovereignty: Transforming Myths in Eighteenth-Century Italy* (Chicago: University of Chicago Press, 2009). See also chapters 3 and 4 of my *Desire and Pleasure in Seventeenth-Century Music* (Berkeley: University of California Press, 2012).

that I too greatly preferred hearing women singing such roles during those years.

A deliberate use of such vocal qualities for the sake of parodic female impersonation occurs in René Jacobs's brilliant production of Francesco Cavalli's *Calisto*, in which Giove (a baritone) disguises himself as the goddess Diana in order to seduce the innocent nymph Calisto. Although Jennifer Williams Brown has argued persuasively that the original Venetian production assigned the scenes featuring Giove-as-Diana to the same woman who was cast as Diana, Jacobs has his baritone Marcello Lippi camp up these scenes with a hooty falsetto.[20] The result is utterly hilarious, though it also underscores the potential ridiculousness of having men sing in their feigned voices.

But the roles designed for castrati were not intended to be heard as ridiculous. Indeed, these singers within their plots were cast as heroes and lovers, powerful in battle and irresistible in romantic engagements with women. They should *not* bring to mind John Cleese—or, for that matter, Jacobs's Marcello Lippi masquerading as Diana.

When I work with countertenors, I have them listen to the pop singers discussed above. Falsettists do not have to sound like capons in order to reach those high notes; we have thousands of instances of gospel, soul, and heavy-metal singers who project unequivocal power while singing as high as any baroque castrato. No one gags when listening to Philip Bailey or Prince or Rob Halford, nor do they imagine that physical defects cause them to sound that way.

Some of this project has been rendered considerably less urgent by the emergence of a generation of countertenors—Andreas Scholl, Michael Chance, Derek Lee Ragin—who demonstrated that they can sing in their upper registers without imitating the utterances of drag queens. Just as players have learned to negotiate the challenges posed by natural trumpet, which seemed virtually impossible in the early years of the authentic-instruments movement, so singers have developed the capacity to perform the repertories composed for castrati in ways that do not sound effeminate or bizarre. They project clarion tones that make palpable once again why seventeenth-century audiences demanded something resembling this sonority.

---

[20] See the invaluable preface by Jennifer Williams Brown to her edition of *La Calisto*, in which she details what we know of the original production. Francesco Cavalli, *La Calisto*, ed. Jennifer Williams Brown (Madison, WI: AR Editions, 2007), xv. Jacobs's recording, which is also available on commercial DVD, was released by Harmonia Mundi in 1993. Note that Jacobs is a formidable countertenor himself.

Let's review some of the basics. First, with a few exceptions such as Rome, where ecclesiastical authority forbade women from singing in public, castrati did not typically perform the roles of female characters.[21] The phenomenon thereby differs considerably from that of the boy actor on the Elizabethan stage—a topic studied in exhaustive detail by Shakespeare scholars in the heyday of Queer Theory.[22] In other words, castrati did not proliferate owing to a collision between biology and the law. We must search more deeply for an explanation.

Second, for all the gender-bending featured in seventeenth-century opera, the castrati played the roles of heroes. In the strange, topsy-turvy world of Venetian opera, *only* castrati qualified as appropriate romantic idols. Tenors and baritones, whose voices testified to their physical maturity, could only play the parts of fathers, kings, or philosophers. With elevated social responsibility came severe behavioral restrictions: men in opera acquired the phallus only if they agreed to retire the penis.

But this odd arrangement is not so foreign to our own day. As Marjorie Garber has argued, pop stars in film (James Dean, the young Leonardo DiCaprio, Johnny Depp) and music (Michael Jackson, Justin Bieber, boy groups from doo-wop to 'N Sync) often feature the image of the ephebic youth: still beardless yet old enough for sexual activity.[23] The libretto of Cavalli and G. A. Cicognini's *Giasone* (Venice, 1649) goes out of its way to describe its lead character in precisely this way just before his first entrance: though he does not yet have to shave, he has proven exceptionally fertile, given that he has already fathered two pairs of twins. As they say in pop culture, chicks dig it—and have done so for a very long time, perhaps even as far back as the troubadours, many of whom began their careers in their teens.

---

[21] See William Christie's remarkable production of Stefano Landi's Roman opera *Sant'Alessio* (Rome, 1631; Warner Classics, 1996), which features no fewer than eight countertenors, several of them in female roles. Monteverdi's *Orfeo* (Mantua, 1607), featured a castrato singing the part of Euridice. For more on Roman casting, see the discussion of Stradella in chapter 13. Venetian opera, however, featured the female *prima donna* as prominently as its castrato *primo uomo*.

[22] See, for instance, Stephen Orgel, "Nobody's Perfect: Or Why Did the English Stage Take Boys for Women?" *South Atlantic Quarterly* 88, no. 1 (1989): 7–29; Bruce Smith, *Homosexual Desire in Shakespeare's England: A Cultural Politics* (Chicago: University of Chicago Press, 1991); Susan Zimmerman, ed., *Erotic Politics: Desire on the Renaissance Stage* (New York: Routledge, 1992); Peter Stallybrass, "Transvestism and the 'Body Beneath': Speculating on the Boy Actor," in Zimmerman, ed., *Erotic Politics*, 64–83; Valerie Traub, *Desire and Anxiety: Circulations of Sexuality in Shakespearean Drama* (New York: Routledge, 1992); Jonathan Goldberg, *Sodometries: Renaissance Texts, Modern Sexualities* (Stanford, CA: Stanford University Press, 1992); Goldberg, ed., *Queering the Renaissance* (Durham, NC: Duke University Press, 1994).

[23] Marjorie Garber, *Vested Interests: Cross-Dressing and Cultural Anxiety* (New York: Routledge, 1992).

Cavalli not only casts Giasone (Jason of the Golden Fleece) as a castrato, but he also gives him little music that sounds heroic. His paramour, Medea, represents the voice of desire in this opera, while Giasone happily adopts a passive pose. In his famous entrance aria, "Delizie, contenti," the love-depleted Jason sings of how he has had enough of desire, and he creates a languid energy vacuum with the rocking quality of the lullaby, inviting his female partner to assume the active role.[24]

As it turns out, the image of the sleepy, sexually passive protagonist stretches back into the Renaissance. In his "What Knights Really Want," Stephen Orgel demonstrates how this trope manifests itself in epics such as Spenser's *The Faerie Queene*.[25] Baroque opera also indulges frequently in the plot device of the male sleeping beauty: Alidoro in Cesti's *Orontea* conveniently slumbers while the eponymous queen expresses her desires in a monologue, and Renaud in Lully's *Armide*—albeit a tenor—spends much of the opera lying helplessly in a trance while the sorceress who has produced this enchantment acts upon him according to her whim.

As mentioned earlier, this ruse of somnolent seduction still operates in our own popular culture. Prince's "Do Me, Baby" features the same lullaby-tinged stasis as Cavalli's "Delizie, contenti" and in the service of the same sexual fantasy. The decadent pleasures of Venetian opera, which seemed so incomprehensibly perverse only a few years ago, have returned with a vengeance—if one may associate "vengeance" with such sweet passivity.

But it is perhaps in the love duets of Venetian opera that the raison d'être for the castrati becomes most evident. In the late sixteenth century, the *concerto delle donne* of Ferrara made ensembles of soprano *virtuose* a kind of fetish.[26] Seventeenth-century musicians strove to preserve the sounds and imagery that the legendary Ladies of Ferrara had made available, suddenly banishing the sonorities of unaltered males to the margins and simulating in their part writing the erotic intertwining of bodies traced by identical voices. The violin, and especially the trio sonata that featured two treble instruments, came to the fore in part because of this cultural craze.

In the love duet between closely matched voices, the depiction of lovemaking reaches its zenith. Think, for instance of "Pur ti miro, pur ti godo,"

---

[24] René Jacobs's production of *Giasone* (Harmonia Mundi, 1988) stars Michael Chance as Giasone. I have never had any difficulty getting students to accept Chance—who sounds something like Philip Bailey—as alluring.
[25] Stephen Orgel, "What Knights Really Want," in *Thinking Allegory Otherwise*, ed. Brenda Machosky (Stanford, CA: Stanford University Press, 2010), 188–207.
[26] See chapter 3 of my *Desire and Pleasure in Seventeenth-Century Music*.

the duet that concludes Monteverdi's *L'Incoronazione di Poppea*. Nerone and Poppea have traced a path of destruction throughout the opera: they have killed off the philosopher Seneca, sent Ottavia (Nero's wife) into exile, and corrupted the moral fiber of everyone around them. Poppea's naked ambition has not been hidden from view, and the Emperor Nero's abominations are too well known to require rehearsing. Yet here at the end they sing one of the most ravishing compositions ever penned.[27]

The outer sections of the duet unfold over a descending-tetrachord ostinato, a device that sustains a single region indefinitely through a repeating bass figure. It was commonly used to simulate trancelike affective states, whether lament or—as in this case—sustained erotic rapture. While the bass guarantees insulated security (often simulating entrapment in laments), the voices interact in the manner of the *concerto delle donne*: they intertwine, take turns being on top, rub up against each other in aching dissonances, resolve sweetly together. Its dissonances lose their poignancy when Nerone sings his line down an octave rather than producing the minor seconds that finally force Poppea to bend to his will.

The middle section of the duet turns more active, as the lovers tease each other with a variety of possible key trajectories. Whereas the first section maintained a kind of timeless bliss, here the singers cavort, nipping at each other in the musical equivalent of the love bites featured in so many lyrics of this time, or in what Stephen Greenblatt calls "friction to heat" in the rapid repartee in Shakespeare's romantic comedies.[28] But after this episode of mutual arousal, Nerone and Poppea settle back down into their ostinato and its promise of endless pleasure. The ideal mode of lovemaking as represented in music followed the ideals set out by the Three Ladies of Ferrara, even when the participants included men, even when the price of reaching that ideal required *extremely* extreme makeovers.

But that was then, and this is now. What are our options for modern productions when faced with the question of casting the soprano hero? Many recordings of baroque operas cast a tenor or even a baritone in the roles of Monteverdi's Nerone or Handel's Caesar, and much of the erotic quality

---

[27] The text of this duet had appeared in 1641 in *Il Pastor regio* by composer Benedetto Ferrari, and its music bears a striking resemblance to the many other ostinato-based pieces by Ferrari. Like most multi-section pieces of this time, *L'Incoronazione di Poppea* changed for the purposes of different productions. Whoever wrote it, this duet stands out as one of the most beautiful and—given the circumstances of the plot—most lethal in the repertory.

[28] Stephen Greenblatt, *Renaissance Self-Fashioning: From More to Shakespeare* (Chicago: University of Chicago Press, 1988).

comes through even with the octave displacement. Indeed, a resolutely heterosexist listener may prefer to hear the woman sound like a woman, the man like a man. But such performances pry the lovers apart and put them in separate beds; instead of caressing and licking each other, they swat at each other as if with towels at a distance, and they can never dissolve into the single undifferentiated unit that stood as the telos of duets such as "Pur ti miro."

Female mezzo-sopranos have long stood in for castrati, most famously in Gluck's *Orfeo* and then, with the baroque-opera revival, in Handel's opera seria. Dame Janet Baker made a career of singing these male roles, and later Dame Sarah Connolly emerged as a remarkably effective Julius Caesar. A number of female musicologists have written of their pleasure in witnessing on the operatic stage what they can read as romantic relationships between women, and they would prefer that countertenors stay away from this one terrain women had managed to inhabit—if by default—for a couple of centuries.[29] And surely gender-bending always was one of the delights of hearing castrati in heroic roles.[30] Moreover, many female singers sound more powerful in the designated ranges than the often fragile sonority of feigned voices, especially in cavernous performing spaces like the Metropolitan Opera in New York.

On the other hand, the sonority produced by a woman singing low in her range does not have the same effect as that of a man singing high in his, even when the pitches remain the same. The heroic quality of assailing the improbable heights, which is present in Claude Jeter, Prince, and Steven Tyler, is fundamental to the aesthetic. A woman situated within the comfort zone of her range projects something quite different.

In the 1950s and 1960s, as the historical-performance movement began to experiment with countertenors for Handel revivals, some composers seized upon this new voice type for their own purposes. Thus, such roles are related—at least tangentially—to the issue of the baroque castrato. But the logic behind operas of this sort needs special treatment.

The premiere of Benjamin Britten's *A Midsummer Night's Dream* in 1960 featured the pioneering British countertenor Alfred Deller as Oberon. In casting Oberon, King of the Fairies, as a countertenor, Britten sought to

---

[29] See the essays in *En Travesti: Women, Gender Subversion, Opera*, ed. Corrine E. Blackmer and Patricia Juliana Smith (New York: Columbia University Press, 1995).
[30] See Wendy Heller, "Daphne's Dilemma: Desire as Metamorphosis in Early Modern Opera," in *Structures of Feeling in Seventeenth-Century Expressive Culture*, ed. Susan McClary (Toronto: University of Toronto Press, 2012).

create a male character whose voice, in the words of Philip Brett, "is far from the ardent tenor of the romantic era and as close as one can get nowadays to the *primo uomo* of eighteenth-century *opera seria*, the castrato. Along with the historical reference, however, goes the association of unmanliness, and thus of gender liminality, that haunts the modern image of the homosexual. Squeaking in a falsetto voice, the emasculated, misogynistic boy-desiring Oberon is almost literally a figure of the closet."[31] Britten may have intended to code Oberon as queer—as he did Peter Quint in *The Turn of the Screw* and oddly constructed figures in his other operas.[32]

In other words, just as Handel revivals were attempting to encourage listeners to accept the countertenor voice as the pinnacle of the gender hierarchy, Britten's dramatic deployment of that vocal type relied on the negative implications that had plagued the male soprano since the end of the eighteenth century.[33] The more heroic timbre of today's virtuosic countertenors can therefore change the dynamics of the opera, pulling it away from the sound ideal (along with its connotations) that Britten seems to have had in mind. Recall that Britten, Poulenc, and others also intended the Pleyel harpsichord rather than the historically modeled instruments now *de rigueur*. Thus, the authenticity bind with which we struggle operates quite differently in this situation. Should we consider resurrecting the Pleyels languishing in the basements of our performing institutions? Should we train countertenors who can approximate Deller's timbre?

Philip Glass's *Akhnaten* focuses on a visionary Egyptian pharaoh who appears to have had androgynous physical characteristics; some authorities have suggested he was a hermaphrodite, though others interpret these attributes as symbolizing a sacred fusion between male and female.[34] For the premiere in 1984, Glass cast countertenor Paul Esswood in the title role, in

[31] Philip Brett, "Britten's *Dream*," in his *Music and Sexuality in Britten*, ed. George E. Haggerty (Berkeley: University of California Press, 2006), 118.

[32] Brett's courageous discussions of coded homosexuality in Britten inspired the development of Queer criticism in musicology. Throughout his career, he dealt with great sensitivity with this closeted composer who marked so many of his morally equivocal characters as homosexual. See again Brett, *Music and Sexuality in Britten*. See also Peter Franklin, *Britten Experienced: Modernism, Musicology and Sentiment* (Abingdon, UK: Routledge, 2024). Franklin's book responds to an extraordinarily condescending book by Christopher Chowrimootoo, *Middlebrow Modernism: Britten's Operas and the Great Divide* (Berkeley: University of California Press, 2018).

[33] Wayne Koestenbaum has shown that nineteenth-century voice manuals link the falsettist with degeneracy and unnaturalness. In his words, "the discourse of degenerate voice (one of several models of the unnaturally produced self) enfolds and foretells the modern discourse of the homosexual." Koestenbaum, "The Queen's Throat: (Homo)sexuality and the Art of Singing," in *Inside/Out: Lesbian Theories, Gay Theories*, ed. Diana Fuss (New York: Routledge, 1991), 217–23.

[34] For more on the genesis and sexual politics of this opera, see John Richardson, *Singing Archaeology: Philip Glass's* Akhnaten (Hanover, NH: Wesleyan University Press, 1999).

part because of the emergence of such singers to perform roles originally intended for castrati. Unlike Britten, Glass does not mean for this voice type to point to sexual deviance. His Akhnaten treasures his wife, the great beauty Nefertiti, and one of the most gorgeous tableaux in the opera allows us to listen in on the exquisite harmony of the royal couple—in sound (if not in content) reminiscent of the duet between Nero and Poppea.

The casting of a countertenor in the role allows Akhnaten to sing his hymns in an ethereal voice that transcends ordinary reality. As Glass writes, "The effect of hearing a high, beautiful voice coming from the lips of a full-grown man can at first be very startling. In one stroke, Akhnaten would be separated from everyone around him."[35]

Yet this choice also underscores the physical abnormalities attributed to the pharaoh. For David Freeman's North American and English production, Robert Israel designed a bodysuit to make countertenor Christopher Robson look like the deformed version of Akhnaten. As Glass writes concerning the reception of this decision: "A number of people in our audiences were quite upset by Christopher's appearance on stage.... Near the end of the New York City Opera run, we received a letter denouncing us for (1) having found some poor hermaphrodite; (2) forcing him to display his deformities in public; and (3) making him sing my music!"[36]

In this production in particular, the countertenor's sonority raised the specter of abnormality and monstrosity. It thereby resonates with the surgical scandal associated with the castrati and with the questions that circulated concerning Michael Jackson's body. Once again, it suggests damaged manhood—rather than the virile brilliance of Philip Bailey or Rob Halford or even Farinelli, the most celebrated of the eighteenth-century castrati.

A new generation of countertenors since 2000 has inspired a new cluster of attitudes toward the male soprano. Not only do they star in the baroque dramas designed for the castrati, but the roles written specifically for them by leading composers no longer suggest deviance or monstrosity. This is in part because of the appearance of so many brilliant performers.

But more important is the fact that audiences have grown used to queer and nonbinary gender identities. Same-sex marriage became legal throughout the United States in 2015, and transitioning (despite political moves to block

---

[35] Philip Glass, *Music by Philip Glass*, ed. Robert T. Jones (New York: Harper & Row, 1987), 156.
[36] Ibid., 164–65. The original Stuttgart production presented Esswood with his normal body.

it) now occurs quite often.[37] In the movies, we have seen the rise of Timothée Chalamet from ephebic roles (e.g., *Call Me by Your Name*) to epic hero (in *Dune*). TV has given us *RuPaul's Drag Race*, *Pose*, and *Transparent*. The unapologetic queer self-presentations of Sylvester, Prince, and others helped to topple the compulsory heteronormativity that had ruled the stage and screen since the early 1800s.

Indeed, the twenty-first century has witnessed nothing less than the triumph of the *primo uomo*. Peter Sellars has an extensive history of engaging countertenors for his productions, beginning with his stagings of baroque operas (Handel's *Giulio Cesare*, 1990, and *Theodora*, 1996; Purcell's *The Indian Queen*, 2015), and continuing to the extraordinary trio of narrators in John Adams's *El Niño* (2008). In May 2024,[38] he showcased countertenor Reginald Mobley in an event that juxtaposed traditional spirituals with arias from Bach cantatas, thereby bringing together two historically separate performance traditions that drew on the same voice type.

I have written elsewhere about Kaija Saariaho's casting of Philippe Jaroussky in her collaboration with Peter Sellars in *Only the Sound Remains* (2015).[39] In her settings of two ancient Noh dramas translated by Ezra Pound, Jaroussky channels the uncanny voice of spirits in uneasy contact with human characters performed by Davóne Tines. Saariaho's quasi-spectral orchestration supplements the sounds of these specters.

Jaroussky also shows up as the allegorical figure of Music in Matthew Aucoin's *Eurydice* (2021), seducing Orpheus away from his bride. (Jaroussky wins competitions as a break dancer, and he busts some moves in the opera's wedding scene.) George Benjamin's *Written on Skin* (2012) features an androgynous youth, sung by Bejun Mehta, whose unearthly beauty unsettles everyone around him. Countertenor Iestyn Davies performs the role of Francisco de Ávila in Thomas Adès's *The Exterminating Angel* (2016), while Brett Dean in his *Hamlet* (2017) casts his comic Rosenkrantz and Guildenstern as countertenors.

By the time the Metropolitan Opera staged Glass's *Akhnaten* in 2019, no one any longer questioned what it meant for a man to sing in the high register. Superstar Anthony Roth Costanzo's gorgeous vocal production in

---

[37] Six of my students have transitioned during their graduate work, the first in 1979. Among them, Jack Halberstam and Stephan Pennington have become major figures in transgender studies.

[38] Sellars, Park Avenue Armory, May 21, 2024. The concert addressed the crisis of climate change in conjunction with the Armory's COAL + ICE exhibition.

[39] McClary, *The Passions of Peter Sellars: Staging the Music* (Ann Arbor: University of Michigan Press, 2019), chapter 5.

solos and in duets with J'Nai Bridges embodied in sound the baroque ideal of male soprano as hero. More recently, the Met's production of Gluck's *Orfeo* presented him as a kind of guitar god. If we needed reminding that countertenors have naturally low voices, Roth Costanzo has presented solo versions of Mozart's *Le Nozze di Figaro* in which he sings all the roles.

When I first wrote this piece, I worried that stringing together baroque castrati, gospel singers, and queer pop stars might seem contentious. The last decade, however, has seen unanticipated changes in music composition, in performance practices, and in the real world—a world in which formerly subcultural self-presentations have become mainstream. Who could have imagined that opera would move to the avant-garde of gender construction?

Of course, the representation of gender is always fraught. In the wake of the Dobbs decision, many of these bold expressions may well get peeled back. Several states have already prohibited drag performance, and the right to same-sex marriage—recognized only a decade ago—is clearly endangered. For now, however, we are experiencing a renaissance in nonbinary operatic expression.

Feminists have long focused on the cultural forces that operate to produce "femininity," and men are no less products of social mediation. Shifting attitudes toward something as fundamental as the male voice demonstrate this process at work. As Robert Walser puts it, in one of the few statements I fervently wish I had penned myself (and so will simply appropriate):

> Masculinity is forged whenever it is hammered out anew through the negotiations of men and women with the contradictory positions available to them in such contexts. It is also forged because masculinity is passed like a bad check, as a promise that is never kept. Masculinity will always be forged because it is a social construction, not a set of abstract qualities but something defined through the actions and power relations of men and women—because, with or without makeup, there are no "real men."[40]

But even if there are no "real men," we have a surfeit of superb male vocalists. And some of them sing soprano.

---

[40] Walser, *Running with the Devil*, 136.

17
Sister Campers[1]

There exists no dignified name for us. Fag hags? Fruit flies? Labels that disparage both us and the gay men we love. Nor are we widely recognized as a category. Absent even from the LGBT lineup (unless the indeterminate "Q" is attached), we qualify as shadowy figures at best, trooping along with our friends, fully acknowledged within the community itself but otherwise mostly invisible.[2]

Yet many prominent female stars of twentieth-century music—Judy Garland, Bette Midler, Cathy Berberian, Diamanda Galas, Madonna—have sprung from our ranks. Heterosexual women all, they signal their affiliations with gay men through their over-the-top performances of femininity, sentiment, and parody, and they owe much of their success to the enthusiastic responses and support of gay men. Especially crucial during times when this community still dared not publicly speak the name of its love, when it lost so many to AIDS, such women continue even now to galvanize gay male fans by means of their camp sensibilities.

If not comparable to the fabulous women listed above, I have always engaged in camp—in my own humble way—even within my musicological work. Indeed, in the mid-1970s when I could not find an academic job, I considered taking my show to bathhouses, aspiring to do with classical music what Bette Midler was achieving so brilliantly with pop. The misunderstandings that have greeted my publications often result from the inability of certain readers to comprehend the codes of camp and who consequently interpret my insider jokes as evidence of hostility. And my greatest accolades have come from gay males who recognize those same

---

[1] Dedicated to the dozens of gay men who have sustained me and brought me joy over the course of my life. You know who you are. (I hasten to add that I also have close male friends who are not gay.)
   I first wrote this piece for a book on camp edited by Philip Purvis; see *Music & Camp*, ed. Christopher Moore and Philip Purvis (Middletown, CT: Wesleyan University Press, 2018). But I got cold feet when we got to the copyediting phase. This is its maiden voyage—unless I get cold feet again.

[2] For an overview of such relationships in popular culture from the male side, see Mark Harris, "Missing the Gay Best Friend," *New York Times* (March 11, 2024). Harris is responding in part to the FX miniseries *Feud: Capote vs. the Swans* (2024).

turns of phrase and regard them as hilarious, as special signs intelligible to them alone.

How to explain this phenomenon? I cannot remember a time when I did not gravitate toward individuals I would later identify as gay. At age seven, when I was in second grade, my best friend was a flamboyant kid (I still remember his name) who was just a lot more fun than anyone else. Neither he nor I had the slightest idea of homosexuality—or, indeed, any kind of sexuality whatsoever. Something else drew us together, and so it has been with countless other friends to this very day. I can stand up in front of a large audience to give a talk and in a single scan of the room pick out my likely compatriots. It goes both ways: those men usually come forward in the Q&A, their queries posed with an unmistakably camp inflection, thereby signaling to me that they know that I know that they know, and so on. My husband, Rob Walser, has observed this routine time and time again, and it still mystifies him. Somehow or other, a kind of current (sometimes called gaydar) locates us immediately to one another. When we speak afterwards, it is as if we have always known each other. Right off the bat, we hoot and holler, camp and carry on.

I have no idea how widespread this phenomenon is, but I assume that women like me have always existed. The fact that men with same-sex inclinations used to have to live mostly in the closet makes it difficult to ascertain the status of their female friends. In the decades since musicology began to pay attention to homosexuality, those who want to argue against that orientation for Handel or Schubert trot forth as evidence possible girlfriends or wives.

But to anyone familiar with gay subcultures, those women prove nothing whatsoever. If one were to rely on elements from Peter Ostwald's biography of Robert Schumann, one could make a case for considering Clara a serial fag hag, coupled first with Robert and then with his protégé, Brahms.[3] To be sure, she had seven children with Robert, and I do not doubt that she loved both him and Johannes sincerely and deeply. We may never know, but we should keep in mind that having close female companions or even wives and children does not necessarily support claims of heterosexuality—or at least not *exclusive* heterosexuality. Simply adding this category (whatever we

---

[3] Peter Ostwald, *Schumann: The Inner Voices of a Musical Genius* (Boston: Northeastern University Press, 1985).

choose to call it) to the list of potential relationship-types changes the terrain substantially.

When Bradley Cooper's biopic *Maestro* opened in late 2023, many critics understood Leonard Bernstein's relationship with Felicia Montealegre to indicate a bisexual orientation; I read him as a gay man who wanted to have a family (as well as the public appearance of normalcy) and so married a female soulmate. As a denizen of the theater world, Felicia would have been very familiar with such identities and roles; even the parties shown in the movie feature high camp as a cultural currency. And their banter during their courtship, including her explicit acknowledgment of Bernstein's orientation, resonates with the kinds of conversations I have had with gay friends I came close to marrying.

Somebody, Somewhere, a recent series on HBO/Max, presents this kind of relationship more openly than anything I have seen in the commercial media. Its principal characters—Sam (a straight woman) and Joel (a gay man)—become inseparable when they meet up again years after their high-school graduation; they sustain each other during moments of emotional distress, and they lift their spirits through nonstop camping. No other relationship in the series or, indeed, in much of television, comes close to displaying this kind of intimacy and profound caring. Although both love sex and chat about it all the time, the show gives no hint that they might eventually make love with each other. It's just not that kind of partnership. And yet if the series were set in the 1950s and Joel needed credibility for, say, an appointment as conductor of a major symphony orchestra, they might well have gotten married. If one or both of them wanted children, they would even have performed the necessary act. But that would not define the core of their relationship.

In a world in which gay men faced pressure to conform, and even prosecution if their sexuality became known, countless marriages of this sort have occurred. When I was in graduate school, scarcely closeted senior faculty informed their gay advisees—my beloved friends—that they would not recommend them for jobs if they did not (and they used this phrase) "bite the bullet," as they had; they did not want to perpetrate what they labeled as (and they used this phrase) "Harvard bachelors."[4] At best, the resulting marriages occurred between individuals who were aware—as

---

[4] Imagine their consternation when the gay magazine *After Dark* published an interview with Assistant Professor David Del Tredici (complete with naked pictures, available online on Google). In the interview, David claimed that the Harvard faculty would offer him tenure and that he would turn them down. They did indeed offer, and he did indeed turn them down. He soon scandalized the serialist mafia with his Alice pieces. Decades later, in 2009, the LGBTQ Study Group at the AMS

Montealegre was—of what was going on. But I witnessed a number of catastrophic pairings, with uninformed wives who became chronic alcoholics when they learned too late what everyone else had always known about their spouses. All of which is to say that musicologists have some serious disambiguating to do!

Fag hags are rarely lesbians, in part because lesbians usually don't traffic in the particular sensibility that draws us fag hags to gay men. I have many lesbian friends, and I treasure them. But although we might josh around from time to time, we do not camp (except, maybe, in tents). When I began coming out as a feminist scholar, my obvious affiliations with gay men sometimes caused other women in the field to view me with suspicion. It is no coincidence that Philip Brett, Gary Thomas, and Mitchell Morris served as my principal means of moral support during those years. I framed my questions and methods in ways that closely resembled theirs, as they, too, labored to bend musicology to accommodate other kinds of identities. The writing of the late queen of queer theory, Eve Kosofsky Sedgwick, influenced me far more than that of the more usual feminist sources. I would give anything to have quipped:

> Has there ever been a gay Socrates? Has there ever been a gay Shakespeare? Has there ever been a gay Proust? Does the Pope wear a dress? If these questions startle, it is not least as tautologies. A short answer, though a very incomplete one, might be that not only have there been a gay Socrates, Shakespeare, and Proust, but that their names are Socrates, Shakespeare, and Proust.[5]

To try to theorize camp is to encounter another of those "I know it when I see it" problems. Susan Sontag's famous essay on camp always seemed to me to abscond with the term, thereby marginalizing the very world from which it springs.[6] She makes camp virtually the same as irony. But you can ironize

---

arranged a special event in which David and I engaged in conversation. It was if we had seen each other the day before, as we fell into old rhythms, alternately giggling wildly at his outrageously dirty lyrics and weeping with unrestrained sentiment. David passed in 2023. To me, he will always be that beautiful, flamboyant leather queen in assless chaps.

[5] Eve Kosovky Sedgwick, *Epistemology of the Closet* (Berkeley: University of California Press, 1990), 52.
[6] Susan Sontag, "Notes on Camp," in *A Susan Sontag Reader* (New York: Farrar Straus & Giroux, 1982), 105–19.

your every utterance (think of Mahler) and never come close to registering as camp.

The great icon of this sensibility is, of course, Judy Garland. When police arrived at an obscure bar called Stonewall to break up a party of homosexuals mourning her death in 1969, the patrons fought back, thereby kicking off the Gay Liberation Movement. Garland had long attracted a following of gay men. Over the years, her nightclub acts, in which she became audibly and visibly corroded by drugs, alcohol, and relationship fiascos, offered an image of sacrificial femininity with which so many fans identified.

How far back does that bond with Garland go? A few years ago I watched *The Wizard of Oz* with my friend Paul Attinello, and we were stunned when we saw all those long-familiar figures through our adult eyes. There is Dorothy, happily skipping along with her trio of gay male friends: the Scarecrow, the Tin Man, the Cowardly Lion. No sexual danger here! Paul and I scrolled back to earlier layers of memory to try to recover how in the world we understood those characters when we were kids. Then we looked at each other and realized that we had been reconstructing precisely that variety of bond throughout our lives. Well, hello there, Dorothy! Hello, Tin Man!

Garland carried her devotees with her until her death and long after. In *Wizard* and also in her concerts, she brought into public view structures of subjective experience her fans necessarily had to hide away. Of course, her performances also had to appeal to mainstream audiences who related to her on entirely different levels. A charismatic actress and singer, she touched millions of straight fans as well. Hell, my mom loved Judy Garland. But she wouldn't have gone to the barricades on learning of her demise.

Part of the appeal comes from her willingness to belt out numbers, which is why she often appeared with the likes of Ethel Merman and Barbra Streisand.[7] These women had ruled on the Broadway stage as divas, with voices that frequently shed the ladylike and lunged for the dramatic, whatever the consequences. Garland had a whole raft of mannerisms and tics that suggested some kind of suppressed energy, emotions released finally in those glorious (if often ragged) climaxes. It's as if she fears that underneath that fabulous exterior lurks merely . . . Frances Ethel Gumm. Fragments of her own tormented history—always a key part of her mythology—float to the surface, to be overcome, at least temporarily, by those hard-won high notes.

---

[7] See for instance www.youtube.com/watch?v=W7AViKc52P0.

Watch some of the many drag queens impersonating Garland to see what they value in her image: the insecurities manifested by the nervous self-touching of hair and face, the arms that sometimes shoot out in premature anticipation of eventual release, the full-body joy at the moments of transcendence. And the tragic countenance of the torch singer, yearning bravely if hopelessly for a love that cannot be.

Of course, having a gay male fan base does not automatically qualify an artist as a fag hag. One imagines that many a diva, whether on the Broadway stage or at the Met, has received this particular kind of adulation with ambivalence.[8] Especially at times when all these signals had to remain covert and unacknowledged, we mostly lack verbal evidence. But occasionally Garland seems to have spoken more directly to her special fans. In a television interview in 1967, she was asked point-blank about her homosexual fans, who had been targeted in a recent article in *Newsweek*. At first she tried to deflect, feigning not to know what that reporter was talking about. But as Irv Kupcinet, the interviewer, persisted, she angrily erupted: "For so many years I've been misquoted, rather brutally treated by the press, but I'll be damned if I'd like to see my audience mistreated."[9]

YouTube also offers a performance of "Over the Rainbow" from *The Judy Garland Show* in 1955 in which she comes out dressed like a tramp with scruffy beard and mustache.[10] This might seem simply cute—a reference, perhaps, to Chaplin's iconic figure or Red Skelton's Freddie the Freeloader. But then she sits down at the edge of the stage and delivers her signature tune. Her voice trembles and breaks, she visibly weeps as she sings of a freer life beyond the rainbow—itself now the universal emblem of LGBTQ rights as this song is its anthem. Her transgendered self-presentation invites individuals who struggle with gender identity to hear those words as relating particularly to them.

In the decades following Stonewall, both artists and their fans have enjoyed the luxury of more open modes of communication. Madonna, for instance, first became a star not on MTV but rather in gay bars, where her soundtracks offered irrepressible grooves for hedonistic dance. She has continually made her fierce bond with these men known, especially in her aggressive support of AIDS research and advocacy for those infected with

---

[8] On the phenomenon of the opera queen, see Wayne Koestenbaum's fabulous *The Queen's Throat: Opera, Homosexuality, and the Mystery of Desire* (Da Capo, 1993).
[9] www.youtube.com/watch?v=C35sw0JfLxM
[10] See www.youtube.com/watch?v=ss49euDqwHA

HIV. In her mega-shows, she features both gay men and women—not just as shadowy figures backing her up but choreographed in ways that simulate same-sex activity. Watch, for instance the video of her performance in Rio de Janeiro, the last concert of her 2023–24 Celebration Tour, before an audience of a million and a half, a large percentage of them gay men. Particularly moving is her performance of "Live to Tell," during which photos of artists and friends lost to AIDS pop up one by one, finally to fill the entire wall behind her.[11]

Madonna's performances testify publicly to her connections with or deep interest in particular gay communities. Her book *SEX*, for instance, brought to broader public attention the Bondage and Discipline games then emerging among some lesbian subcultures. The song "Vogue" and its accompanying video developed from her acquaintance with a stylized genre of dance practiced by Latino and African American men in Harlem ballrooms. But although her borrowings helped to mainstream such possibilities, they also sometimes sidelined the very artists from whom she learned. One of the stars of the voguing scene, Willi Ninja, enjoyed a short burst of personal fame owing to the video before he was eclipsed by the next fad. Many people who saw Ninja after her video even assumed that he was imitating Madonna. Reverence can quickly turn to appropriation. The second season of the TV series *Pose* focuses on this particular appropriation and its devastating effects on the queens whose livelihoods and sense of purpose depended on their performances.

But Madonna's relationship to gay culture runs much more deeply than the occasional rip-off. She also shares the idols of her fans. In "Vogue," Madonna rightly heads her list of fabulous celebrities with Judy Garland. But even before that, her videos had displayed her impersonating—as a kind of same-sex drag—Marlene Dietrich, Marilyn Monroe, and many others from this pantheon. Indeed, if her reworking of tunes with new scenarios in her shows demonstrates anything, it is that gender itself is necessarily a form of drag. Identity can never be stable, is always a sort of performance, a kind of camp. It may prove difficult for a drag queen to mimic "Madonna," given her own chameleon-like endeavor. She inevitably beats would-be impersonators to the punch.

And that goes as well for women striving to follow in Madonna's footsteps. Lady Gaga has attempted to assume Madonna's mantle: she pursues the

---

[11] See the performance at https://www.youtube.com/watch?v=67_YxU0BXj8.

camp qualities of her predecessor's performances and even produced her own overtly gay anthem, "Born This Way." But Lady Madonna still wears her mantle and seems reluctant to hand it over. In her 2015 album, *Rebel Heart*, she speaks back with "Bitch, I'm Madonna"—a queeny, slap-down line if ever there was one. In fact, the album revels in the word "bitch," as she comes roaring back, demanding the center stage she never relinquished.

Nothing can compete with this brand of catfighting in the world of camp. Think, if you will, of the famous bouts between Bette Davis and Joan Crawford. But Madonna is no Margo Channing, ready to move on for Eve Harrington, even if her version of the latter does have to wear a meat dress to compete. In the terrain of transgression, Madonna has always Been There and Done That.

The single most important reason for Madonna's staying power continues to be her songs—those dozens of dance-club hits that have appeared at regular intervals over the course of the last forty years. As mentioned above, these brought Madonna her first acclaim, and they show no sign of slacking off. She may have had many wannabes over the years, but they pale in their musical impact next to her. Even the very term "wannabe" was coined to refer to her imitators. By far the most successful woman in the history of music (well, prior to Taylor Swift), Madonna has owed much to her loyal gay male fans.

I have spent most of this essay with popular culture, since sister campers are more self-evident and more frequently recognized in that terrain. But occasionally a fag hag pops up in classical music. Married for fourteen years to Luciano Berio, Cathy Berberian rose to the challenges of even the most abstruse experimental scores.[12] But Berberian seems to have done more than just execute the complex instructions set forth for her in scores written "for her" by avant-garde composers. Indeed, she appears to have had a good deal to do with the creation of many of those "scores," even if the composers frequently neglected to acknowledge her side of their collaborations.

I first encountered Cathy Berberian's work in my undergraduate music-history survey in Carbondale, Illinois, in 1966. My teacher, the late Wesley Morgan, had managed to acquire the famous 1962 LP that contained Luciano Berio's *Circles*, Sylvano Bussotti's *Frammento*, and John Cage's *Aria with Fontana Mix*.[13] Although I'm sure Professor Morgan encouraged us to

---

[12] For recent research concerning her career, see *Cathy Berberian: Pioneer of Contemporary Vocality*, ed. Pamela Karantonis, Francesca Placanica, Anne Sivuoja-Kauppala, and Pieter Verstraete (Farnham, UK: Ashgate, 2014).
[13] Time Records, 1962.

focus on the experimental notational devices displayed in the composers' scores, my attention fixed itself permanently onto the sounds produced by what the album cover identifies merely as "the voice of Cathy Berberian."

The question of authorship invariably arises when we consider the relationship between the composers listed as owners of intellectual property such as *Circles*, *Frammento*, or *Aria* and the "voice of Cathy Berberian." Although others can and do perform these scores, Berberian's renditions qualify as virtually definitive, for they feature not only her "voice" (as extraordinary as that instrument may be) but also her imagination, wit, musicality, fierce intelligence, and ability to camp in any style of music available. Compare these with the all-too-common scratch-and-sniff presentations of open scores, in which performers do everything in their power to prevent rhetorical interaction with their listeners. I do not believe that Berberian was capable of bridling her communicative talents; everything she performed came alive with her humanity.

When chance composers such as Cage engaged with her, they risked losing the abstract, cerebral dimension of their experiments. In short, taking a chance with Cathy meant surrendering control. The artistic sensibility we hear in these pieces—the hilarity, the vulgarity, the hair-raising virtuosity, the ravishing sonic beauty—belongs to her alone.

But Cage himself indulged in camp with considerable frequency, even if our academic emphasis on his philosophy usually tries to steer us away from hearing those traces. I once witnessed a surprise performance of *4'33"* at the subway entrance in Harvard Square during rush hour. A truck pulled up and deposited a grand piano at the kiosk; Cage materialized, performed his famous work with great solemnity, then popped up cackling with glee like a two-year-old who has just blown out the candles on a birthday cake before he disappeared into the puzzled throng. He brought the same mischievous edge to *MusicCircus* and other performance pieces. Thinking along these lines allows for a very different reading of his work.

I've always liked to imagine Cage with Berberian in the studio producing *Aria*, whooping it up while recording their campy love song to one another. And lo: a photo of precisely such a moment has appeared on the internet among images of Berberian. If Berio stifled her naughty side, Cage happily brought it forth in all its queer glory.

When I first heard this track, serialists still held an iron grip in composition departments in North American universities; in order to garner any respect, one had to toe the twelve-tone line, devoting one's talents to what Philip

Glass later recalled as "that creepy music." But *Aria*, which Berberian opened unceremoniously with "HAMPART-ZOUM," was (as they say on Monty Python) something completely different. As the colored blobs in Cage's score flashed by, Berberian delivered a hard country twang for "COULD ENTER YOUR HEART/NON TANTO/HOW SO?/GIOVANE."[14] Musicologists didn't talk in those days about the sexual orientation of composers such as Cage or Boulez, and the marriage of Berio and Berberian had yet to shatter. Certainly my undergraduate teacher was not going to raise such issues. But I already detected in Berberian's performance the height of camp—not "camp" in the wishy-washy sense theorized by Susan Sontag but the in-your-face fag-haggotry flaunted in 1970s bathhouses by Bette Midler.

Berberian's associations and performances after the split-up from Berio underscores this predilection. She met her closest gay male friend, Sylvano Bussotti, when she was still living with Berio in Milan in 1959. Bussotti was completing his *Pièces de chair II* on homoerotic texts. According to David Osmond-Smith, "When she showed him what Cage had produced for her the previous winter, Bussotti decided to insert a *Voix de femme*—a reminder that men are not the only admirers of pretty boys—among the male gasps and sighs.... Berio, working upstairs at the piano, heard laughter and came down to investigate."[15] How well I know that spousal response to the peculiarly intimate cackling that gushes forth at such encounters.

Paul Attinello explains the aftermath: "Bussotti had become a close friend of Berberian, and at first Berio evidently found this amusing. However, fairly soon, Bussotti became Berberian's closest confidant, introducing her to camp aesthetics and the pleasures of outrageous spectacle; she was an extraordinarily good student, modifying her stage persona from dark-haired wife to flamboyantly platinum-haired *grande dame* by the mid-1960s."[16] David Osmond-Smith comments elsewhere that Berio "was never to forgive Bussotti for leading her down [the path to camp] with such zest."[17]

With zest, indeed. In 1979, Berberian broadcast on Dutch Radio what she called *Cathy's KRO Solo Talk Show*, transcripts of which appear in the recent book devoted to her. Much of what she says relates to her favorite performances by opera singers. But occasionally she goes on a campy

---

[14] Cage, *Aria* with *Fontana Mix*, Berberian recording, https://www.youtube.com/watch?v=a15xkowPEPg

[15] *Berberian*, 24.

[16] David Osmond-Smith and Paul Attinello, "Gay Darmstadt: Flamboyance and Rigour at the Summer Courses for New Music," *Contemporary Music Review* 26, no. 1 (February 2007): 113

[17] Quoted in *Berberian*, 14.

rampage. She begins one, for example, with: "Did you know that some singers sustain ... that the high notes are controlled by the asshole? Did you know that? It's true! My hand on the Bible." (37) See the interview for the continuation.

At another moment she explains her philosophy of performance: "You *always* have to manipulate an audience. That's what an audience is for. It should be like putty in your hands. You should be able to play on an audience like you play on an instrument and they *like* being played with, if you know how to play. You have to tickle them, you have to squeeze them, you have to scratch them a little and sometimes you have to give 'em a punch in the jaw. But you also have to make them enjoy, huh?" (44)

I have drawn extensively from *Cathy Berberian: Pioneer of Vocality*. Yet I find the book curiously reticent about really plunging into the fag-hag dimension of her work, especially in Anne Sivuoja-Kauppala's chapter, "Cathy Berberian's Notes on Camp." Relying heavily on Sontag, Sivuoja-Kauppala strives to use Berberian as support for the position that camp need not belong to the gay male community, and she offers the label "feminist camp" for this purpose.

Now, as a self-identified feminist *and* a fag hag, I regard "feminist camp" as something of an oxymoron. To be sure, a feminist may also engage in camp—but not, I think, as a manifestation of her feminism. As Osmond-Smith and Attinello make clear, Berberian revealed that side of her personality—a side previously unknown to her husband—when she began to hang out with Cage and Bussotti, who were (let's face it) a lot more fun than Luciano. After the marriage broke up, she followed her gay friends with abandon.

Berberian began to compose her own pieces, including *Stripsody*, from 1966. Clearly inspired by the work she had done with pieces like Cage's *Aria*, *Stripsody* features the sounds of cartoons—and thus the title, which appears far more risqué before one hears the piece. The notated pages of this piece bear a strong resemblance to those of Cage and Bussotti, except that they're unambiguously hilarious.

Videos of Berberian performing *Stripsody* may be viewed on YouTube. They show a middle-aged Armenian-American lady in what appears to be a living room, with a hairdo worthy of a John Waters character, gleefully producing the sound effects of long-forgotten Saturday morning cartoons. John Zorn's *Road Runner* (1986), in which an accordionist plays a montage of cartoon sounds, comes a bit too close to *Stripsody* for comfort; he cites only Carl Stalling of Warner Bros. fame among his influences. Even after her death in 1983, Berberian continued to fuel the imaginations of composers who left her name off the docket.

Berberian pointed the way toward what came to be called postmodernism—an often campy rejection of the dour seriousness of serialism. I hear her sensibility in the jumble of symphonic excerpts and Swingle Singers riffs layered over Mahler in Berio's *Sinfonia*. And I greatly prefer introducing my students to Cage through her performance of *Aria* than through his Zen ponderings or prepared-piano pieces. Berberian's performance of *Aria* and her *Stripsody* announce the end of Modernist posturing.

Music history owes a great deal to Berberian. Most obviously, her example inspired an explosion of performance artists and singers who specialize in extended vocal techniques. She made full use of rude sounds never before regarded as having a place within music, now fundamental to the work of Meredith Monk, Diamanda Galas, Laurie Anderson, and countless others—all women, by the way, and only now receiving some degree of recognition.[18]

Berberian's mercurial fluctuations between the sublime and the ridiculous influenced my own prose style as I struggled to break away from the stiff academic conventions prescribed for me by teachers and editors. I can trace the fact that I camp it up in my writing (apparent throughout this collection) to Berberian's transgression of Modernist propriety, and I tried to pay homage in my Foreword to *Berberian*, "Cathy Berberian—Modernism's Bette Midler."[19]

I have, of course, merely scratched the surface of what should become a target for much more research. At the very least, I hope to have helped dispel some of the demeaning or pitying accounts of fag hags that appear from time to time.[20] I also want to insist that this category be taken into account when we consider the women who had close relations with gay or possibly gay men. But can anyone watching Margaret Cho or Madonna or Cathy Berberian really doubt the agency of these divas who can out-camp their brothers any day? I mean, *really*!

---

[18] Alex Ross, "Guided by Voices," *New Yorker* (January 5, 2015).
[19] *Berberian*, xxv-vi.
[20] See, for instance, the piece by Rohin Guha, "The Myth of the Fag Hag and the Dirty Secrets of the Gay Male Subculture," *Jezebel* (January 25, 2014). But see also the interview with Monica Davidson on her documentary *Handbag* in *Gay Star News* (March 21, 2013).

18

Kaija Saariaho, Mater[1]

Before her untimely death in June 2023, many of us regarded Kaija Saariaho as the greatest living composer—not the greatest *woman* composer (though she certainly was this), but the greatest, period. Over the course of the last fifty years, Kaija created masterpiece after masterpiece, winning most of the international awards available to musicians and securing a permanent place in the programming of symphony orchestras, chamber groups, and opera houses. And she did so without surrendering a bit of her artistic integrity to a populist strain of postmodernism. Even as her stringent musical language challenges listeners still anchored in traditional idioms, she has proved able to engage and electrify many of them.

In contrast to many of her Modernist colleagues who often write in order to explore abstract schemata, Kaija composed to communicate. With the opening sonority of each of her works, she establishes a vibration that resonates deep inside the listener's body, along with a spectrum of overtones that grow out of that originary sonority but that also foreshadow the complex contradictions that will compel us to identify with and follow the web she weaves. I am quite sure that I do not breathe between the beginnings and conclusions of her compositions, and I continue to live inside those sonorities long after I have left the performance space.

Although audiences may respond first to the astonishing sensual beauty of her music, they soon sense the psychological and ethical urgency of her work. In this essay, I want to focus on Kaija's vocal repertory and, in particular, on her unprecedented focus on motherhood. Mothers rarely appear as major characters in the history of opera or, for that matter, in mainstream cinema.[2] Given that all humans come into being only by means of this process, pregnancy, labor, and childbirth qualify as literally universal

---

[1] Invited keynote for the seventieth birthday of Kaija Saariaho in October, 2022. I could not travel to Helsinki, for health reasons, but a shorter version of this essay was published in a special issue of *Finnish Music Quarterly* and presented to Kaija on her birthday. Available at www.fmq.fi.

[2] For a discussion of this problem in film, see Naomi Scheman, "Missing Mothers/Desiring Daughters: Framing the Sight of Women," *Critical Inquiry* 15/1 (1988): 62–89.

experiences. Yet these experiences are mostly regarded as unworthy of artistic attention, especially compared with the romanticized sex act that leads up to impregnation: the center of virtually all our conventional plots. As the United States grapples to respond to the recent ban on abortion—*even* in cases of rape or incest, *even* to save the life of the mother—we have discovered the ignorance and callousness of many of our lawmakers. Some of them have even brought murder charges against women who miscarry, estimated to occur in as many as one in four pregnancies. Pregnancy has become a life-or-death proposition.

Like many other female artists, Kaija long resisted identifying as a "woman composer." But her perspective changed radically when she became pregnant and gave birth to her first child, Aleksi Barrière, in 1989. Rather than regretting this transformation in her life, she saw it as an opportunity. In her words: "As a mother, I have access to many things that men could never experience. Before having children, I really was up in the air most of the time. The earthly aspect became more present with children. Has my music changed with motherhood? Of course."[3]

In choosing to identify herself in her music as a woman and a mother, Kaija risked a great deal. She reports that "I really felt some people's suspicions when I had my first child, suspicions like: this is the end of her serious music, she'll become too sentimental."[4] And some of her subsequent works received contemptuous reviews from critics who specifically ridiculed her decision to foreground such issues. When I give talks about these pieces, I still have to field vehement objections from female composers and musicologists who insist that women should stick to the gender-free abstractions developed by their male colleagues; they actually express fear in the face of Kaija's breaking of long-established taboos. It is not only abortion, in other words, that provokes controversy but also the alternative—namely, childbearing.

Some of those who object make use of the dreaded term "essentialism." In the wake of Judith Butler's groundbreaking work, many music scholars have warded off discussions of gender as theoretically suspect, as a reduction of complex phenomena to a simple male/female dichotomy. Feminist music criticism began to emerge in precisely the same year that Butler published

---

[3] Kaija Saariaho, "My Library, from Words to Music" (1987), trans. Jeffrey Zuckerman, *Music and Literature* 5 (2014): 22.
[4] Many women opt to leave their vocation, given the extraordinary tensions involved. See also Ligaya Mishan, "When Women Artists Choose Mothering over Making Work," *New York Times Style Magazine* (Dec. 1, 2023).

Gender Trouble, and such charges stopped that enterprise cold in its tracks. We went from pre-feminist to post-feminist musicology overnight, saving the discipline the pain of having to delve into the often-tortured history of such issues as gendered terminology and misogynist representations in music. Many female composers, already beleaguered by their marginalization, have avoided at all cost drawing attention to their sex.

Let's return to the word "sentimental," which Kaija used to describe how women composers are expected to sound. European music theory has long made use of gendered binary oppositions: A masculine theme stakes out the turf for standard symphonies, while a sweet lyric theme allows for some relief before being assimilated to the key of the first theme in the recapitulation, exactly the way a wife is expected to take on the name of her husband. Masculine cadences are the ones that absorb all the energy leading up to that point, while feminine ones deflect demurely. Men act as the agents in operas, while female characters mostly get acted upon—or else (like Carmen) pay dearly for usurping agency. And given such associations, what artist of any integrity would want to identify with those weaker positions?

Yet female novelists, poets, and visual artists often understand their experiences as women as central to their artistic agendas. Nobel laureate Toni Morrison wrote from her experiences as a Black woman; Frida Kahlo drew on her life as a disabled Mexican woman for her representations. Would we wish it otherwise? Would we admire Morrison more if she had written novels about disaffected college professors, or Kahlo if she had dribbled paint randomly on her canvases?[5]

When she was young, Kaija immersed herself in literature by women. She writes:

> In the beginning of my compositional studies, I tried in vain to find a model in the world of music; female composers were few and far between. No doubt this is why I was interested in the lives of female writers, and took pleasure in reading their diaries, letters, and biographies, in addition to their works. Besides Virginia Woolf, the two figures who meant the most to me were Sylvia Plath and Anaïs Nin [because] of their urge to combine—at

---

[5] In fact, Morrison did confront criticism on this score. In a review of her novel *Sula*, a critic wrote that she was "far too talented to remain only a marvelous recorder of the Black side of provincial American life," that she had to transcend the "limiting classification 'Black woman writer'" and "address a riskier contemporary reality." Sara Blackburn, *New York Times* (December 30, 1973). I suspect that Kahlo faced similar charges.

least that's what it seemed to me—a "woman's life," meaning their roles as mother, and their artistic careers.... I was searching for a way of life, I was reading these diaries as survival manuals.[6]

If the equivalent of Woolf or Plath did not exist in music then, they do now, thanks in large part to Kaija's own brave imagination. And so, when I discuss Kaija as "woman composer," it is because she has given voice to so many dilemmas particular to women. I might add that she asked me to write program essays for her productions, because she knew I wouldn't shy away from such issues.

Her 2021 opera, *Innocence*, features three principal women: Tereza, whose child was murdered in a school shooting; Patricia, the mother of the shooter; and Stela, an unsuspecting bride whose potential for reproduction hangs in the balance. Ten years after the violent incident, both mothers still suffer the repercussions of that act—guilt and immeasurable loss—as they find themselves face to face at a wedding celebration. Stela will learn over the course of the opera how her choice of husband risks perpetrating a toxic gene pool. Of course, many other survivors in the opera also give voice to trauma, including the multilingual students who testify to their inability to lead normal lives, as well as their teacher and a priest, who castigate themselves for failing to protect their charges. I happened to be on a panel discussion with Kaija in November 2015 when she learned of the terrorist attack on the Bataclan Concert Hall in Paris, and she feared that her son might have been a victim; I sat with her as she suffered for several hours waiting to hear of Aleksi's fate.

The subject matter of *Innocence* (2021) seems ripped from the front page of yesterday's headlines with ever more frequent school shootings. But Kaija had been grappling with the joys and dangers of motherhood since she first decided to compose texted music. Her 1996 song cycle, *Château de l'âme*, for instance, includes, along with love songs, a ritual chant from ancient Egypt focused on the healing of children. Yet it is in her two operas *Adriana Mater* (2006) and *Émilie* (2010) that she confronted these issues most powerfully.

Kaija, her eloquent librettist Amin Maalouf, and the ubiquitous Peter Sellars developed the plot of *Adriana Mater* when she mentioned that she could feel two hearts beating inside her body during her pregnancy. The protagonist, Adriana, has been raped during wartime (bringing to mind the women of Ukraine and Israel/Gaza who are now suffering such assaults on

---

[6] Saariaho, "My Library," 13–14.

a daily basis). In the crucial middle act of the opera, Adriana's sister tries to persuade her to terminate the pregnancy that resulted from that rape. (May I remind you that some states have banned abortion even in cases of rape.) But Adriana, echoing Kaija's imagery, replies that she feels that second heartbeat; even while fearing that the child might inherit the violent tendencies of his father (also Stela's dilemma in *Innocence*), she chooses to carry it to term. In this crucial scene, which takes place in the precise middle of the opera, we hear Adriana's avowals of maternal tenderness, continually shadowed by feelings of dread and terror. Kaija adds voices to her underscore, reminding us of that embryonic human presence inside her, which manifests itself in tension with her verbal sentiments.[7]

Oui, je suis sûre, Refka, je suis sûre....	Yes, I am sure, Refka, I am sure....
Non, Refka, je ne suis sûre de rien.	No, Refka, I am not sure of anything.
Je sens seulement, je sens un coeur,	I only feel, I feel a heart,
Un deuxième coeur qui bat tout près du mien.	A second heart that beats close to mine.
Qui est cet étranger qui m'habite?	Who is this stranger that inhabits me?
Un frère? Un autre moi-même? Un ennemi?	A brother? Another myself? An enemy?
Dans ses veines coulent deux sangs, deux sangs mêlés,	In its veins two bloods flow, two bloods mixed,
Le sang de la victime, et le sang du bourreau.	The blood of the victim, and the blood of the executioner.
Comment répandre l'un sans répandre l'autre?	How to spill one without spilling the other?
Un jour, mon enfant naîtra, je le tiendrai dans mes bras,	One day, my baby will be born, I will hold him in my arms,
Je le prendrai contre mon sein pour le nourrir.	I will take him to my breast to nourish him.
Pourtant, ce jour-là,	Yet that day,
Oui, même ce jour-là,	Yes, that very day,
J'en serai encore à me demander,	I will still be asking myself,
Comme je me demande à cet instant,	As I ask myself at this moment,
Comme je me demande à chaque instant du jour et de la nuit:	As I ask myself at each moment day and night:
Qui est cet être que je porte?	What is this being that I carry?
Qui est cet être que je nourris?	What is this being that I nourish?
Pour me rassurer, je me dis parfois	To reassure myself, I tell myself sometimes
Que toutes les femmes, depuis Eve,	That all women, since Eve,
Auraient pu se poser ces questions,	Must have asked themselves these questions,
Ces mêmes questions:	These same questions:
Qui est cet être que je porte?	What is this being that I carry?
Qui est cet être que je nourris?	What is this being that I nourish?
Mon enfant sera-t-il Caïn, ou bien Abel?	Will my baby be Cain? Or perhaps Abel?

---

[7] https://www.operaonvideo.com/adriana-mater-saariaho-paris-2006/. See segment at 48:10–53:50.

But this decision does not qualify as an unambiguous triumph for the anti-abortion crowd. The remainder of the opera traces the ways in which both Adriana and her son, Yonas, must handle the consequences in their lives that bear the mark of Cain. The shame of his conception leads Adriana and her sister to lie to Yonas about his origins. When he learns the truth outside the home, he seeks to murder his father as revenge. He stops at the last minute before shooting, allowing Adriana to claim that he is after all her child rather than his father's.

Yet despite this rather bittersweet reconciliation at the end, the opera traces the terrible consequences of this pregnancy on the lives of everyone involved; it follows that initial fetal heartbeat through its years-long aftermath. Kaija and Maalouf do not offer easy solutions or celebrate childbirth as an unalloyed good. Adriana never regrets her choice, but she has nonetheless lived in anguished uncertainty ever since. In the opera's last moments, Yonas kneels before his father, now blind and homeless, while reaching out to his mother. He is the bridge they created, however unwittingly. Listen to how Kaija holds you in suspense at the end, flickering between potential resolution and that condition of not knowing that has gripped Adriana since the day she first learned of her pregnancy.[8]

Cet homme méritait de mourir,	This man deserved to die,
Mais toi, mon fils,	But you, my son,
Tu ne méritais pas de tuer.	You don't deserve to kill.
Depuis que tu es né, et avant même la naissance,	Since you were born, and even before your birth,
Je me demande si tu serais un jour capable de tuer.	I have wondered if you one day would be capable of killing.
Même quand tu étais au berceau, je ne pouvais m'empêcher	Even when you were in the cradle, I could not prevent myself
De surveiller tes cris, le fond de ton regard, et tes gestes.	From surveilling your cries, the depth of your glance, and your gestures.
Il fallait que je sache	I needed to know
Si le sang qui coulait dans tes veines,	If the blood that flowed in your veins,
Était celui du tueur,	Was that of a murderer,
Ou bien le mien.	Or rather mine.
Quand, autour de moi, on s'inquiétait, on se méfiait,	When those around me worried, when they had doubts,
Moi, je m'efforçais de croire	I forced myself to believe
Que le sang était neuter et muet,	That blood was neutral and mute,
Que le sang ne décidait de rien,	That blood didn't decide anything,
Qu'il suffirait que je t'aime, que je te parle,	That it sufficed that I love you, speak to you,

---

[8] See segment 1:59:40–2:18:50.

Que je t'élève avec droiture,	That I raise you properly,
Pour que tu sois aimant, et réfléchi, et droit.	For you to be loving, sensitive, and moral.
Mais il y avait constamment en moi,	But there was constantly in me,
Constamment, la torture du doute,	Constantly the torture of doubt,
Constamment, cette question obsédante, têtue:	Constantly this stubborn, obstinate question:
Si un jour, te tenant, une arme dans la main,	If one day, you had a weapon in your hand,
Devant un homme que tu haïrais,	man you hated.
Devant un homme qui mériterait le pire châtiment...	Facing a man who deserved the worst punishment,
Ce jour-là, le frapperais-tu?	On that day, would you strike him?
Ou bien ferais-tu, au dernier moment, Un pas en arrière?	Or perhaps at the last moment, you would take a step back?
Si tu étais vraiment le fils de cet homme, Tu l'aurais tué!	If you were really the son of that man, You would have killed him!
Aujourd'hui, j'ai enfin la réponse:	Today, I finally have my answer:
Le sang du meutrier s'est apaisé en côtoyant le mien.	The murderer's blood was allayed in flowing with mine.
Aujourd'hui, ma vie, que je croyais perdue, Est enfin retrouvée.	Today, my life, which I believed lost, Is finally found.
Nous ne sommes pas vengés, Yonas, Mais nous sommes sauvés.	We are not avenged, Yonas, But we are saved.
Viens, approche-toi, entoure-moi de tes bras!	Come, embrace me in your arms!
J'ai besoin de reposer ma tête en instant Sur une épaule d'homme.	I need to rest my head for a moment On the shoulder of a man.

The stakes are even higher in Kaija's monodrama of 2010, *Émilie* (libretto, Amin Maalouf). Émilie, Marquise du Châtelet, died in childbirth in 1749 at age 42, just as she was completing her translation of Isaac Newton's *Principia*—long the standard version of this crucial study in France. An accomplished physicist, astronomer, mathematician, musician, and writer, she was an intimate friend of Voltaire and a strong influence on the Encyclopedists. Scientists who recently have assessed her pioneering work find that she anticipated aspects of Einstein's Relativity and the game theory that makes possible much of our digitized culture.

As Émilie approaches the due date for both her translation and her child, she has a strong presentiment that she will not survive labor. The monodrama traces her warring emotions during her final days: her memories, scientific speculations, fears, hopes, and desires. But this towering intellectual knows—just as surely as any criminal on Death Row—that her days are numbered, that she is now in countdown. (Many states also greatly restrict abortions that would save the life of the mother.)

The penultimate section of the opera, "Principia," opens with the low, ominous rumble characteristic of Saariaho as she sets out the fundamental over which her melodic lines and harmonies will unfold. We hear Émilie express her fear—not fear of death or of abandonment by her feckless lover, Saint Lambert, but fear that she that she might die before finishing her translation. Like any of us trying to remain calm in the face of a publishing deadline, she recites her daily schedule in scarcely controlled monotone as a marimba ticks off clock time in the background. But we hear her anxieties churning away in the background in the form of urgent, syncopated figures. Her only peace of mind comes when she immerses herself in her work, escaping her condition to contemplate the cosmos, gravitation, and tides. See the sections in italics in the following excerpt, which suddenly lift the listener out of the nervous patter of Émilie's terror and allow us to hover in those luminous, undulating, timeless sonorities only Saariaho can produce.

After vacillating between the real world of danger and the life of the mind, Émilie pushes toward the goal and imagines holding her completed book in her arms. She sings out her title in triumph even as the orchestral conclusion simulates the onslaught of violent contractions. Those high notes so often associated with sexual excess or suicidal impulses in traditional opera here signal intellectual achievement colliding with biological imperatives as she anticipates a double birth—or, more probably, a double death.[9]

Ce n'est pas tant la mort que je redout,	It isn't so much death that I dread,
Ce qui m'angoise, ce n'est pas non plus votre tiédeur	Nor is it your indifference that gives me anguish,
Saint-Lambert, mon ami, mon amant,	Saint-Lambert, my friend, my lover,
Bien que j'en souffre.	though I do suffer from it.
Mon angoisse, ma frayeur,	My anguish, my terror
Et je'n rirais presque,	(and I almost laugh at it),
C'est de mourir sans achever	is to die without having finished
Ma traduction de Newton.	my translation of Newton.

Philosophiae Naturalis Principia Mathematica.

Je ne songe plus à rien d'autre!	I dream of nothing else!
Je me lève à neuf heures, quelquefois à huit,	I get up at 9, sometimes at 8,
À trois heures, je m'interrops pour un café;	at 3, I stop for coffee;
Je reprends le travail à quatre heures.	I start working again at 4.
"La Lune gravite vers la Terre,	*"The moon gravitates toward the Earth,*
et par la force de la gravité elle est	*and by force of gravity it is*

---

[9] Saariaho, *Émilie*, "Principia": https://www.youtube.com/watch?v=0qo1zbsk8Z8.

continuellement retirée du mouvement rectiligne et retenue dans son orbite."	*continually pulled from rectilinear movement and retained in its orbit."*
Je m'arrête à dix heures, je dîne,	I stop at 10, I dine,
Voltaire assiste à mon souper,	Voltaire joins me for supper,
Nous causons jusqu'à minuit.	We chat until midnight.
Ensuite je me remets à l'ouvrage	Then I return to my work
Jusqu'à cinq heures du matin.	until 5 in the morning.
"La force qui reticent la Lune dans son orbite est en raison réciproque du carré de la distance des lieux de la Lune au centre de la Terre."	*"The force that keeps the Moon in its orbit is reasoned as the inverse of the square of the distance of the Moon to the center of the Earth."*
C'est à cela que je m'acharne,	It is that which drives me
Et que j'épuise mes dernières forces.	And for which I spend my last energy.

Fluxum et refluxum Maris ab actionibus
Solis ac Lunae oriri debere

"Il y a deux espèces de marées, solaires et lunaire, qui peuvent se former indépendamment..."	*"There are two types of tides, solar and lunar, that can form independently..."*
J'ai quasiment fini.	I have almost finished.
Je dois encore revoir mes épreuves,	I must still review my drafts,
Ajouter quelques commentaires,	add some commentaries,
Mais l'essentiel est fait;	but the essence is done;
Si mes funestes pressentiments	if my dire forebodings
s'avèrent mensonger	prove false,
bientôt je porterai mon livre dans mes bras.	soon I will carry my book in my arms.

Principes mathématiques de la philosophie naturelle

Compare this character with the myriad simpering victims and femmes fatales of opera history. As Nicholas Stevens has argued, these stereotypes have returned with Mark Anthony Turnage's Anna Nicole Smith and Thomas Adès's aging Duchess in *Powder Her Face* holding center stage among newer works.[10] *Émilie* both celebrates the accomplishments of a major thinker of the Enlightenment and records the price she paid for an ill-considered affair—a fatal pregnancy that cost her her life.

Saariaho's score smolders with the spectralist images of ecstatic longing that her music so often conveys, but it also features violent interruptions

---

[10] Nicholas Stevens, "Lulu's Daughters: Portraying the Anti-Heroine in Contemporary Opera, 1993-2013" (PhD dissertation, Case Western Reserve University, 2017).

as well as brief reminiscences of the harpsichord the marquise played as a young prodigy. Émilie de Châtelet is now taking her place, alongside Einstein and Oppenheimer, among those scientists whose breakthroughs have served as grist for the operatic stage. But in contrast with the composers who have portrayed those great men, Saariaho insists on the body in addition to the mind.

In so doing, she has courted certain dismissive reactions. One critic wrote concerning *Émilie*: "How and why a female composer would want to produce yet another hormonally ravaged female character is beyond me."[11] He also referred snidely to Maalouf's "pregnant" libretto. I ransack my memory for other operatic women in the travails of childbirth and come up only with Sieglinde and Mélisande. By contrast with the duels, seductions, and drinking choruses scattered throughout the entire repertory, the genuinely universal phenomena of pregnancy, labor, and delivery remain nearly absent. As for all those staged representations of women pursuing ambitions in mathematics, physics, and astronomy—hmmm, forgive me if I can't think of one right now

"Sentimental" is scarcely the adjective that comes to mind to describe the horrifying subject matter and often brutal sonorities Kaija produces in *Adriana Mater* or *Émilie*. Our laws concerning pregnancy are so harsh in part because we fail to acknowledge the very personhood of women. In the history of opera, women may express emotions, but they still mostly conform to patriarchal concepts of what women should be like; the gender-specific existential struggles they often endure rarely find a place on the stage.

Of course, Kaija also composed for male characters, most memorably in her portrait of troubadour Jaufré Rudel in *L'Amour de loin* (2000) and the ghostly encounters in *Only the Sound Remains*.[12] But regardless of her subject matter, her musical language dives deep inside her subjects, inviting listeners to share the contradictory strands of lived experience. Music has an unmatched capacity to instill empathy, to immerse us as if without mediation in the feelings of someone entirely different. The other arts share some of that ability, but music's rhythmic embodiment, its infinite shades of sounds, its dynamic trajectories bypass the eye and the page to register directly on the listener's interiority.

---

[11] Igor Toroni-Lalic, "Kaija Saariaho's Émilie, Opéra de Lyon," *the desk.com* (March 9, 2010).
[12] For more on these works, see my chapter on Saariaho in *The Passions of Peter Sellars*. Concerning the use of the countertenor voice in *Only the Sound Remains*, see "Soprano Masculinities," chapter 16 of this volume.

No one does this more effectively than Kaija Saariaho, whose decision to allow her experiences of motherhood to permeate much of her work will inspire audiences and composers for generations to come. Hers is precisely the voice we need to hear in our troubled time when the decisions faced by Adriana and Émilie risk criminal charges. Yet even when Kaija engages with social issues, it is always her music—her ability to draw the listener into her deep resonances and dense contrapuntal webs, the unparalleled range of colors and fragrances she creates, the sheer sonorous beauty of her works—that finally matters. We will miss her.

19

Mahler Making Love

Mengelberg's Adagietto[1]

Some thirty years ago, Gilbert Kaplan published a startling article in the *New York Times* concerning the interpretation of the Adagietto movement of Gustav Mahler's Symphony No. 5 by conductor Willem Mengelberg.[2] According to Mengelberg, Alma and Gustav Mahler had told him that the composer designed the movement as a declaration of his love for her. In Mengelberg's words, which appear on the first page of his own performing score (see Example 19.1 for facsimile):[3]

Diese Adagietto war Gustav Mahlers Liebeserklärung an Alma! Statt einer Briefes sandte er ihr dies im Manuscript, weiter kein Wort dazu. Sie hat es verstanden und schrieb ihm: Er solle kommen! (<u>beide haben</u> mir dies erzählt!!!)[4]

Mengelberg's score also included lyrics that fit the melody in the first violin's opening gambit, converting it into a love song:[5]

---

[1] Commissioned by Jeremy Barham for a collection focused on Mahler, gender, and sexuality. Published in *19th-Century Music* 47, no. 3 (2024): 219–38.
[2] Gilbert Kaplan, "A Dirge? No. It's a Love Song," *New York Times* (July 19, 1992).
[3] Mengelberg made use of colored pencils when making his annotations. See www.oup.com/us/makingsenseofmusic for the facsimile in color.
[4] Willem Mengelberg, personal score of the Adagietto from Mahler's Symphony No. 5. "This Adagietto by Gustav Mahler is a declaration of love to Alma! Instead of a letter, he sent her this in manuscript with no words attached. She understood and wrote to him: He should come! <u>Both of them</u> told me this!!!" Mengelberg underlines "beide haben" three times and highlights many other parts of this text as well for emphasis. Collection Haags Gemeente Museum, The Hague/Mengelberg Stiftung. My thanks to the Museum for use of the facsimile and to Dane-Michael Harrison for helping me to acquire it.
[5] It is not entirely clear who wrote these lyrics. Some (Henry Louis de La Grange and Gilbert Kaplan) have attributed them to Mengelberg himself, though Peter Franklin has expressed doubts that Mengelberg would have defaced Mahler's score with his own attempts at poetry. Franklin also points to the similarities between this verse and some of Mahler's own lyrics and notes that Mengelberg writes "1.Vln" before the poem. Personal correspondence (13 July 2022). Many thanks to Professor Franklin for his insights here and elsewhere in this chapter.

Example 19.1 Willem Mengelberg facsimile, p. 1

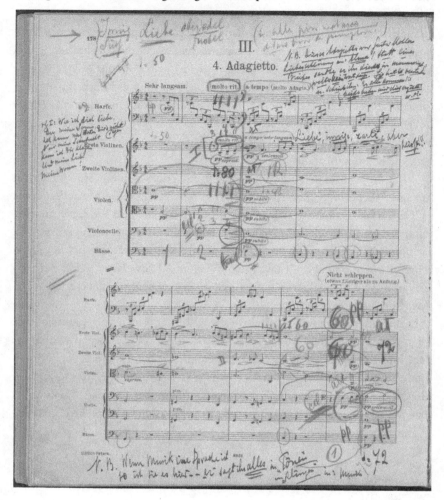

Wie ich dich liebe,
Du meine Sonne,
Ich kann mit Worten Dir's nicht sagen
Nur meine Sehnsucht
Kann ich Dir klagen
Und meine Liebe
Meine Wonne!

How I love you,
You, my sun,
I cannot tell you in words
Only my longing
Can I bewail to you
And my love
And my bliss!

And, of course, Mengelberg left us a recording from 1926 of this movement—his understanding of the score rendered in sound.[6]

Such detailed information concerning an historical performance of a composition would ordinarily thrill musicians. Yet few conductors have followed Mengelberg's suggestions, preferring instead to present the Adagietto as a kind of elegy, appropriate for the memorial service Leonard Bernstein offered for Robert Kennedy (1968) or for the soundtrack of Luchino Visconti's *Death in Venice* (1971).[7] Many listeners know the movement from the latter source, and they expect to experience that same dark, mournful episode when they hear the whole symphony.

When I play Mengelberg's recording in my courses, many students erupt in rage. His performance strikes them as something close to sacrilege; it's as if the apostles portrayed in Leonardo's *Last Supper* had suddenly jumped up and danced the cancan. No matter how much I point to the marginalia scribbled in Mengelberg's score, they simply will not accept such a radical refiguration of one of their favorite movements. They claim to find particularly offensive Mengelberg's tempo and his use of special effects such as extravagant portamenti and rubato.

In this essay, I will review what we know about performance practices that seem to have informed Mengelberg's recordings and the ways in which his decisions might be defended. But I suspect the problem is much deeper than one of mere performance practice, which is where most critics stop their discussions. Rushing in once again where angels fear to tread, I will argue that Mengelberg reads Mahler's score as presenting an explicit sexual encounter. Stay tuned.[8]

---

[6] Willem Mengelberg, Mahler, Symphony No. 5, Adagietto, https://www.youtube.com/watch?v=dWxCKJBr0QM.
  A remastered performance may be heard at https://www.youtube.com/watch?v=2HQpJdORX6w. Mahler's autograph score appears on YouTube with a very different performance: https://www.youtube.com/watch?v=JV6r4KTSQ6c

[7] Leonard Bernstein, funeral for Robert F. Kennedy, June 8, 1968. An excerpt of this performance is available at https://www.youtube.com/watch?v=aVax4yKCBUI. Luchino Visconti, *Death in Venice* (1971). Franco Mannino conducts the Orchestra dell'Accademia Nazionale di Santa Cecilia in this film adaptation of Thomas Mann's death-obsessed novella. Visconti designated Aschenbach, the protagonist, as a composer rather than a writer, and the ubiquity of the Adagietto on the soundtrack has led many viewers to link Aschenbach with Mahler himself. Mannino's performance may be heard at: https://www.youtube.com/watch?v=UoGqwhUXI8c.

[8] Recall that another beloved piece of presumably "absolute music," Alban Berg's *Lyric Suite*, has similarly been unmasked as an intimate love message with the discovery of Berg's annotated score to his then-mistress, Hanna Fuchs-Robettin (Franz Werfel's sister!), in which he reveals his codes. George Perle, "The Secret Program of the Lyric Suite," *International Alban Berg Society Newsletter*, note 5 (June 1977): 4–12.

Mengelberg and Performance Practice

Mengelberg's annotations and Alma's testimony qualify as external evidence—information not available from the composer's autograph or the printed score. Like all external evidence, these depend on the reliability of sources—often in short supply when it comes to Alma, to whom I will return later. But with respect to tempo, we have reports that Mahler himself seems to have performed the movement in about the same time as Mengelberg's seven minutes;[9] a brief review of recordings by Bruno Walter, another close associate of Mahler, reveals that he clocked in at about eight minutes.[10] By contrast, many later recordings last much longer, with one by Bernard Haitink taking nearly fourteen minutes; Hermann Scherchen's 1964 performance logs in at over fifteen and a half minutes.

What about internal evidence—details available in the printed scores we all can see? My students eagerly point to the tempo designation, *Sehr langsam* (very slow). But Mahler, alas, does not indicate the level of meter that should move slowly. Videos of Bernstein reveal him conducting with each eighth note receiving a heavy pulse.[11] In his Norton Lectures, he discusses at length the tonal ambiguity of the movement's opening sonority, which comprises only the pitches A and C in the harp and strings.[12] If we do not already know this movement and fill in the missing tonic by force of habit, we will learn only on the downbeat of m. 3 that the movement is in F major (see

---

[9] According to Robert Philip, "The Adagietto from Mahler's Fifth Symphony is a movement that was taken much faster on 78 rpm recordings than in most later performances. De la Grange lists the timings for several recordings, from Mengelberg in 1926 through to modern times. The performances recorded on 78s by Mengelberg (1926) and Walter (1938) are under eight minutes, neatly fitting two 78 rpm sides. All the recordings from later years are substantially longer, ranging from Solti at 9 mins 40 secs to Haitink at 13 mins 55 secs. But suspicions that Walter and Mengelberg might have speeded up their performances have to be put against timings of Mahler's concert performances: 7 1/2 in Hamburg in 1905 (in Walter's copy of the score) and 7 minutes at St. Petersburg in 1907. Both Mengelberg and Walter were closely associated with Mahler and heard Mahler conduct this work. This does not prove that Mengelberg and Walter took the music at the pace they wanted to in the recording studio, but it makes it far more likely than if Mahler had habitually taken the movement much more slowly in concert." In Philip's *Performing Music in the Age of Recording* (New Haven, CT: Yale University Press, 2004), 38.

For more on the tempo of this movement and Mahler's sense of composerly authority, see Gilbert E. Kaplan, "Mahler and Tradition: Is There or Isn't There? Gilbert E. Kaplan and Peter Franklin in Search of One," *Musical Times* 133, no. 1797 (November 1992): 559–63.

[10] Several of Bruno Walter's performances of the Adagietto appear on YouTube. As it turns out, Mannino's timing in *Death in Venice* is surprisingly close to Walter's.

[11] Leonard Bernstein, Adagietto: https://www.youtube.com/watch?v=Bj6KLv7kv2Q

[12] Bernstein, "The Delights and Dangers of Ambiguity," *The Unanswered Question: Six Talks at Harvard*. Norton Lectures (Harvard, 1973). Mahler excerpt, https://www.youtube.com/watch?v=A7O5zcQPRQQ

Example 19.1). But those opening pitches could as easily be harmonized as belonging to A minor (the key of Movement 2), and Bernstein's performance entreats listeners to suspend the equivocality of that sonority for as long as possible. This performance decision has the effect of setting the rate of motion at that very low level of meter; he asks the listener to attend to each successive pitch in the harp as an event in and of itself. Many other conductors have followed his example.

The movement's harmonic rhythm, however, operates on the level of the half note, as do the arpeggios in the harp. When I am coaching performers, I frequently argue that harmonic rhythm and pulse go together, though dipping below the rate of the chord changes may sometimes occur for particular affective purposes. But when that happens, the music loses its relationship to physical motion and produces a kind of suspended animation. This is what so many Mahler fans want to experience with the Adagietto—that sense of hovering somewhere beyond time and space, something akin to the end of *Das Lied von der Erde*. Obviously, this solution "works": if it did not, it would not have become the principal way we now hear this movement.

But if we take seriously the lyrics scribbled in the margin of Mengelberg's score and if pulses occur on the half note, matching the harmonic rhythm, then we find that the opening segment of the movement is transformed from a dirge into a completely viable and astonishingly beautiful *Lied*. In Mengelberg's performance, the arpeggiation in the first two bars presents a relatively uninflected backdrop, establishing the pulse but reserving expressivity for the entrance of the song in m. 2. (After singing along with the Mengelberg recording, try vocalizing along with Bernstein's or Haitink's performances. Those simple melodic gestures no longer have the coherence expected of song but convert to something else—wonderfully effective, of course, but not song.) My string students at the Cleveland Institute of Music report that Mengelberg's tempo would alleviate the strain they experience when performing this movement. Moreover, he also makes readily audible the cross-rhythms produced by the harp, drawing the accompaniment much closer to the two-against-three patterns so loved by Schumann and Brahms in their Lieder and piano compositions as a way of conveying inner tremulousness. In other words, the Adagietto becomes an entirely different piece, with different cultural associations and affective charges, in the Concertgebouw recording.

One more bit of internal evidence before we move on. The Adagietto appears as the fourth of five movements in a highly complex cycle. Mahler demands a separation—a long pause—between the first two movements and the following three; on one side of the pause, we have Mahler's characteristic funeral marches (C-sharp minor) and cataclysmic storms (A minor). After the pause, Movement 3 (designated as Part II) transports us into a radically contrasting world with waltzes in D major. A third part comprises the Adagietto, followed by the pastoral rondo of Movement 5, also in D major, with strategically placed flashbacks to the Adagietto. The F-major Adagietto itself sits nested between the two exuberant D-major movements.

If rendered as an elegy, the Adagietto seems to return us to the funereal affects that dominate the first part of the symphony. To be sure, such a narrative trajectory is not atypical of Mahler's cyclic imagination: he often dangles hope in front of us before quashing that utopian vision with devastating violence. In most standard performances of the Fifth, the joy and vigor of Movement 3 are disrupted by the mournful introspection of Movement 4 before Movement 5 attempts to restore exuberance. But if the Adagietto so easily undercuts the D-major world of Movement 3, the celebratory promises extended by Movement 5 now ring hollow, as false consciousness. Adorno includes this finale among his examples of failed jubilation, inspiring his famous line that "Mahler was a poor yea-sayer."[13]

Mengelberg's performance inflects the cycle's sequence of events differently. Rather than retreating to the darker impulses of the opening movements, his Adagietto builds upon the optimistic swerve initiated by Movement 3 and completed by Movement 5. That long pause Mahler indicates thereby creates a firewall between the first part of the symphony and the succeeding three movements, a juxtaposition between "before" and "after." And we already know that Mahler met, fell in love with, and married Alma Schindler during the time he was composing this symphony. Recall that Alma understood the Adagietto as his marriage proposal, which she accepted ("Er solle kommen!" as she reported to Mengelberg). With this in mind, we might well hear the movements that precede the long pause as representing Gloomy Gus before Alma transformed him into lover, husband, and father. Mahler even braids reminiscences of the Adagietto into the celebratory finale. (These reminiscences can sound brutally sardonic if the Adagietto has appeared as a site of melancholy retreat.) In other words, much more weighs on the performance decisions made for the Adagietto than our

---

[13] Theodor W. Adorno, *Mahler: A Musical Physiognomy*, trans. Edmund Jephcott (Chicago: University of Chicago Press, 1992), 137.

understanding of that movement alone. The cycle as a whole varies in its global meanings depending on the tempo taken for this movement.[14]

Tempo is not the only element that causes Mengelberg's Adagietto to stand apart from other performances. He also makes extreme use of portamenti, which add considerably to the sensuality of his recording. Of course, these portamenti also appear in almost everything Mengelberg conducted: they count as a trademark idiosyncrasy.[15] Bruno Walter's recordings do not share this predilection: as the late Richard Taruskin quipped, "compared with Mengelberg, Walter is practically Roger Norrington."[16] We know from historic recordings that divas and violin virtuosos of the time similarly made regular use of such gestures. Mengelberg kept this practice alive for the full orchestral ensemble of the Concertgebouw, which he trained to maintain what seems to have been an earlier style. When he conducted other orchestras, he found that most of them no longer had the skills necessary to execute simultaneous slides. But the Concertgebouw learned over the course of his tenure and in unusually long rehearsals to follow his dictates.[17]

To what extent does the Adagietto simply conform to Mengelberg's usual approaches? Is this nothing more than standard-issue Mengelberg? To a listener coming to Mengelberg's recordings for the first time, the fluctuations in tempo and the portamenti may sound indiscriminate; they seem

---

[14] See William Kinderman, "Aesthetics of Integration in Mahler's Fifth Symphony," in his *The Creative Process in Music from Mozart to Kurtág* (Urbana: University of Illinois Press, 2012), for a superb discussion of the relationships between the Adagietto and the other movements, especially the finale. My take is somewhat different from his.

Peter Franklin also discusses the place of the Adagietto in the context of the whole symphony. "Given the character of Mahler's relationship with Alma, one can but note that, in the regenerative cycle symbolised by the Fifth Symphony as a whole she thus appears to have merited no more than a fragrant adagietto, whose function is to lead into Mahler's first truly celebrative rondo-finale, where that now so famous theme is irreverently recast as a jaunty dance. Was Alma, on one level, no more than the charming key to her master's pleasure? When Mahler implicitly mocks the material of a real Adagio, as in the Ninth Symphony, the effect is one of agonising self-torture. Might we not indeed interpret the Adagietto of the Fifth as staged or 'set up' in a rather deliberate way? Is there not something a touch 'culinary' in its indulgence, however fond, in a kind of sentimentality at which the Rondo-Finale will merrily raise an eyebrow?" (Adorno had described the movement as 'culinary sentimentality.") Kaplan, "Mahler and Tradition," 562.

[15] Listen, however, to Mengelberg's 1930 recording of Ravel's *Bolero*, which sets up and maintains an astonishingly insistent groove to the very end: https://www.youtube.com/watch?v=0YRTtjGcXC0

[16] Richard Taruskin, "Making a Stand against Sterility," *New York Times* (2 February 1997). Richard died on July 1, 2022, when I was completing this essay. A musicologist and public intellectual of unparalleled breadth, he and his zingers will be sorely missed.

[17] Robert Philip writes that ". . . the unusual approach to portamento . . . was a stylistic feature which he developed with [the Concertgebouw] over a long period of rehearsal, and that it was not a style which could be transferred to other orchestras when Mengelberg visited them." Philip, *Early Recordings and Musical Style: Changing Tastes in Instrumental Performance, 1900–1950* (Cambridge, UK: Cambridge University Press, 1992), 197.

ubiquitous. Fortunately, YouTube has made many of his performances—of Bach, Beethoven, Brahms, Tchaikovsky—available online, making comparisons relatively easy. Studying these makes it clear that although he includes these devices in his basic toolkit, he wields them in a variety of ways for different expressive purposes.[18]

In Mengelberg's reading of Mahler's Fourth, for instance, the exaggerated portamenti occur only in the third movement. The opening movement, however, features quite extraordinary attenuations of time, beginning in m. 3 with the three pickup notes marked "etwas zurück haltend."[19] With each iteration of this figure, the ritardando becomes greater, until the line threatens to break. But this rendition does not constitute mere indulgence. Listening closely to Mengelberg's recording, we can hear him isolating the pitch F-sharp as always extremely vulnerable: it functions both as the fifth scale degree in B minor (the implicit key of the sleighbells) and as leading tone to G major, the ostensible key of the symphony. In Mahler's movement, the progression from B minor to G major always hinges on that pivotal F-sharp. It is as if Mahler were pushing by dint of sheer willpower that illogical move from the savagery of the sleighbells to an always-tentative pastoral loveliness. If, as many commentators have suggested, this symphony deals with memories of childhood, then that F-sharp is a sonic equivalent of Proust's madeleine, the threshold that bridges the gap between the harsh present of adulthood and an idyllic past, the surface of Alice's looking glass. Few other recordings make that point, which has profound consequences for the entire symphony.[20] In other words, Mengelberg's performance decisions are not arbitrary idiosyncrasies.

The third movement of the Fourth, marked "Ruhevoll, poco adagio," presents a calming lullaby after the scordatura-laden eeriness of the preceding movement. And it is here that Mengelberg deploys his portamenti, which simulate soothing caresses.[21] Both "poco adagio" and "adagietto" signal some

---

[18] For examinations of Mengelberg's performances of these other repertories, see Samir Ghiocel Golescu, "The Recorded Heritage of Willem Mengelberg and Its Aesthetic Relevance" (PhD dissertation, University of Illinois, 2014). He notes: "There is no other conductor born as early as Mengelberg or earlier to have conducted as much 20th-century music as Mengelberg did" (p. 2, n. 2).
[19] Mengelberg, Mahler, Symphony No. 4: https://www.youtube.com/watch?v=J18wFaVjbPw&t=1634s
[20] The first recording of this symphony or any other Mahler symphony, in 1930 by the New Symphony Orchestra of Tokyo, conducted by Hidemaro Konoye, presents this moment in a way that closely resembles Mengelberg's interpretation, suggesting that such readings were relatively common practice in the earlier twentieth century. https://www.youtube.com/watch?v=e1Tu0TQZ-sk. My thanks to Jonathan Guez for bringing this recording to my attention,
[21] Mengelberg, Mahler Symphony No. 4, Movement 3, at 25:40.

sort of modification of the more usual "adagio." Mengelberg takes this movement and the Adagietto at about the same tempo, and so long as the Adagietto stays within its initial songlike section (through m. 11), the two movements resemble each other in their simulation of tenderness.

In fact, Mengelberg most often resorts to portamenti when he wants to convey tenderness. As one scrolls through other recordings, one can begin to anticipate the movements that he will approach in this fashion: the second movement of Beethoven's 5th and the third movement of his 9th, for instance.[22] Most shocking, perhaps, to ears accustomed to the more pristine executions that followed the historical-performance revolution is his rendition of the Air from Bach's Third Orchestral Suite.[23] Utterly gorgeous and exceptionally tender, this recording raises the uncomfortable questions: Whose historical performance practice are we seeking to recover? Why do we believe that our "crisp" renditions are more authentic than Mengelberg's?[24] Might we consider a revival of the early-twentieth-century version of baroque sensibility? At least we have recorded evidence for this style of interpretation, as opposed to the guessing games we necessarily bring to our claims to have reconstructed eighteenth-century tastes. But Mengelberg's claim to historical authenticity is, of course, much stronger when it comes to Mahler.

Mengelberg's Adagietto

As already mentioned, Mahler opens his movement with the pitches A and C—pitches that do not immediately declare a specific key (see Example 19.1). During this passage of ambiguous hovering, Mengelberg chooses to emphasize only the pitch C in the harp. Because this pitch is displaced from the metric pulse, he creates a cross-rhythm in anticipation of the movement's downbeat, producing something like an eager intake of breath in anticipation of the melody's entrance. And in m. 2, the first violin gradually moves up by step from the suspended C to F, thereby establishing the key and meter

---

[22] Mengelberg, Beethoven Symphony No. 5, Movement 2: https://youtu.be/LkqKnyRdZy8?t=400; Beethoven Symphony No. 9, Movement 3: https://youtu.be/9TYc8uNbRU4?t=1649.

[23] Mengelberg, J. S. Bach, Air, Orchestral Suite No. 3, https://www.youtube.com/watch?v=vvTxkdHdKlw

[24] On the fetishizing of "crispness" in reviews of baroque music, see Addi Liu, "How Did Early Music Get So 'Crispy'?," *EMAg, The Magazine of Early Music America* 28, no. 2 (May 2022): 40–47. Whatever adjective we might want to assign them, most of Mengelberg's recordings stand as the polar opposite of "crispy."

to commence its *Liebeslied*. Mahler clearly regarded this juncture as significant yet deeply fragile, for he marks the entrance with a variety of indications (*espress., molto rit.*, a crescendo from *pp* to a sudden return to *pp* at the downbeat, and a tenuto marking each pitch of the anacrusis—now in eighth notes, making each step emphatic up against the triplets in the harp). The arrival itself is rendered both inevitable and vulnerable by the appoggiatura that delays F in the melody. The fact that the strings must suddenly return to the pianissimo of the previous measure delivers a sense of urgency halted by shy reticence (Mahler marks the melody's continuation *seelenvoll*).

Less noticeable, perhaps, is the cello's descent from its sustained A down to G, whence it drops not to the expected F but to C, positioning it temporarily as an inner voice (Mengelberg circles this drop in his score for emphasis). The line's arrival on the withheld tonic, F, is supplied here by the harp and bass. But what might seem like a mere detail of part-writing at the beginning will take on ever greater significance as the Adagietto proceeds, for the configuration A–G–F in the cello will become the cadential formula of choice in this movement.

Recall that the expansion of a sixth to an octave was the cadential formula of choice in polyphony before 1600.[25] The fifth scale degree that we mostly pay attention to at cadences (owing in part to the shorthand of figured bass) is simply the strongest harmonization of the tenor voice's second scale degree before it descends to the final. I will argue in my analysis that Mahler works over the course of this movement to restore that earlier practice in which the relationships between tenor and *canto* determine the syntax, with the harmonic bass operating only occasionally as a significant feature. In other words, the contrapuntal intertwining of the lovers determines the unfolding of the Adagietto at the most fundamental level. It qualifies not only as motivic and as a crucial element in the movement's narrative unfolding but also as a step in Mahler's ongoing critique of standard tonal practice.

Although Mahler's love song unfolds with unusual simplicity, he makes its mostly triadic contour more poignant by means of nonharmonic tones that linger tenderly before moving onward. Mengelberg's first portamento occurs in m. 3 when the melody overshoots its move to the mediant with a

---

[25] For extended discussions of how these configurations work grammatically in sixteenth-century polyphony, see my *Modal Subjectivities: Self-Fashioning in the Italian Madrigal* (Berkeley: University of California Press, 2004). For an account of how and why the change of focus occurs, see my *Desire and Pleasure in Seventeenth-Century Music* (Berkeley: University of California Press, 2012).

brief B-flat appoggiatura.[26] In mm. 6–8 he also highlights B-flat with slides. But although all of these dramatize that particular pitch, they receive quite different inflections. Robert Philip has noted that

> [i]n Europe one orchestra, the Concertgebouw under Mengelberg, continued to play with very prominent portamenti right through the 1930s, in defiance of the general trend elsewhere. It is clear from recordings that his was not just a broad habit, but that, certainly in some instances, Mengelberg required specific fingerings at particular places. Some of the slides in his recordings are too eccentric to have been the result of more general instructions.[27]

And it is in these various shades of portamento that Mengelberg displays his artistic control and also animates with extraordinarily explicit detail his concept of the love scene Mahler has notated.

We do not have technical terms for such nuances, but we can describe how they operate with respect to the melodic line. The slide in m. 3 emphasizes the significance of the arrival on A; the one leading into the downbeat of m. 5 contributes a touch of urgency; the one in m. 6—which follows a brief B-natural—returns with great sincerity and a touch of pleading to the B-flat, its importance enhanced by its ornamental D; the one in m. 7 marks F-sharp (a qualifying embellishment of G), before another slide takes us back to B-flat in m. 8. If one were singing this, one's face would take on a different expression for each of these. Mengelberg would have specified the speed and intensity for each individual portamento, thereby producing a virtually speechlike articulation of Mahler's melody. We know that he micromanaged the Concertgebouw, and the results are on full display in this opening passage. Note that he also chooses to land cleanly on many pitches; he even moves to the half cadence in m. 9 with detached pitches (also indicated in his score), thereby breaking up the slur Mahler indicates. In other words, his portamenti are strategic and calculated.

---

[26] Peter Franklin has pointed out that Mahler's original draft had the melody continuing by step only to the mediant. The B-flat of the final version intensifies the arrival on A, and Mengelberg's portamento intensifies it even more. In Kaplan, "Mahler and Tradition," 562. Facsimiles of both versions appear on p. 563. Note that in the recapitulation of the movement, in m. 76, the score retains the stepwise motion of Mahler's draft.

[27] Robert Philip, *Performing Music in the Age of Recording* (New Haven, CT: Yale University Press, 2004), 100.

The opening melody halts in m. 9 on a precadential G (scale-degree 2), extending an invitation for an answer. And overlapping the conclusion of the first violin's song, the cello enters in response with exactly the same melody, though each of the melodic pitches in the violin's opening statement is now doubled in length. Not only is the cello's sound heavier than that of the violin, but Mahler's augmentation of note values makes this response more ponderous, even if he cautions the conductor not to drag and to perform this passage a bit more flowingly ("etwas flüssiger als zu Anfang" than at the beginning, albeit "seelenvoll"). It surely does not require extensive familiarity with topic theory to identify this as a love duet.

Yet after a mere four bars, the cello moves from the security of diatonic F major through a series of chromatic inflections toward a cadence in m. 19 on a sorrowful A minor—the road not taken by the violin after the ambiguous A/C introduction. This arrival on A receives the confirmation of a perfect authentic cadence (PAC)—the only one in the movement. The answering partner has swerved away from the violin's promise of bliss toward a morbid domain (see Example 19.2). Yet even here, Mahler's orchestration plays tricks on the ear, for the cello suspends its statement in m. 17 on C in a 6/4 position, leaving it to the second violin to complete its line to A. If the cello has brought us to this contrasting realm, it loses courage to follow through (though it does return in m. 20 to ratify mournfully this eventuality). The ways Mahler pulls his voices into substitutions and overlappings creates a sense that they finish each other's sentences, as if murmuring intimately to one another.[28]

In m. 23, however, the violin returns, coaxing the bass line to move very slowly with it in tenths from A through G to F. As already mentioned, this proves to be the cadential formula of choice in this movement. But at this particular moment, with its rhetorical suspension of A and C, the whole relationship seems to hang in the balance.[29] Although the cello continues to

---

[28] My thanks to Jonathan Guez for this insight and image.

[29] Adorno subscribes to the "mournful" and "melancholy" interpretations of this movement, but he rightly points to the extraordinary effect of the pause and reset in m. 23. He writes of this moment (which he labels an *Abgesang*): "[Mahler] can therefore invent melodies that clearly have the character of sequels, essences of the closing themes of sonata form; of such kind, for example, is the *Abgesang* figure in the Adagietto of the Fifth Symphony. Its character derives, no doubt, from its drawn-out beginning, a hesitation that checks the flow of time and disposes the music to retrospection. Essential to such closing models is the descending second, an interval for which Mahler had a general predilection. It imitates the falling voice, melancholy like the speaker whose endings fall. Without the intrusion of meanings, a linguistic gesture is transferred to music. Of course, something as commonplace as the descending second only functions as a gesture when accentuated; the Adagietto has been rich in descending seconds previously, but only through their lengthening in the *Abgesang* do they become something special. In general, Mahler's music inclines to the descending.

Example 19.2 Mengelberg facsimile, p. 2 (mm. 12–33)

Devotedly it accedes to the gravitational slope of musical language. Yet as Mahler expressly assimilates this gradient, it becomes colored with expressive values that it otherwise lacked in a tonal context. This contrasts Mahler with Bruckner. The differences of inflection stand for diverging intentions, Bruckner's affirmation and Mahler's discovery of solace in unrelieved mourning. However, the Mahlerian characters seldom inform the individual figures as purely as in this *Abgesang*. Usually they are also determined by their relation to what has preceded them." (Adorno, 48) On p. 136, however, Adorno writes: "The Adagietto of the Fifth, despite its important conception as an individual piece within the whole, borders on genre prettiness through its ingratiating sound."

interject its questioning chromaticism into its harmonization, it joins the other forces in m. 30 for a joyous pre-cadential harmony that leads to a confirmation of F major. Here again, however, the first violin concludes with its open invitation on G, and a displacement in the resolution in cello and bass allows for the extension of a weakly grounded F major for another four bars before a delayed resolution in m. 37. The necessary components of the PAC occur, but Mahler adjusts them in minute ways that make the conclusion seem provisional. He will return to this passage at the end of the movement, though with significant modification.

Thus far, we have heard uncertainty followed by a tender expression of love in the violin, a pessimistic response in the cello, before the violin radiates its warmth and security to lure the cello and its questioning to full-throated concurrence. If the movement concerns the budding courtship of the Mahlers, this first section reveals tender confidence in contrast to the depressive persona of this symphony's first two movements. In Mengelberg's recording, it is the violin that presents the caressing portamenti, with the cello only following suit once, in m. 12, where it is still echoing the violin. Otherwise, the cello insists on a declarative mode of articulation, further shaping the still-different affects of the two lovers. After a bit of resistance, the two entities agree to unite in F major (the second violin enters to endorse the agreement between the principals). And that's as far as the verbal description on the first page of Mengelberg's score goes.

The movement, however, does not stop there with a scenario that would feel quite at home in the Biedermeier modesty of Schumann's *Frauenliebe und Leben*. If Mengelberg's violations of standard practice involved nothing more than tempo and portamenti, I would not be writing this essay, largely because Robert Philip, Peter Franklin, and others have already covered those issues quite well. But Mengelberg seems to take the verbal cues recorded on the first page of his score as license to move beyond a vague sense of "love" to produce in sound an explicit sexual encounter in the middle section of the movement. This is the portion of the recording most likely to raise the hackles of my students and friends. Indeed, few pieces of classical music—perhaps not even Wagner's *Tristan und Isolde*—present such audacious sexual imagery. Teleological trajectories and deferred arrivals are one thing; ardent fondling and the cries of intense pleasure Mengelberg simulates are another. He delivers something much more explicit than "love," the vaguely erotic label sometimes affixed to the Adagietto in the wake of Gilbert Kaplan's revelations.

At the top of his score, Mengelberg has written "Innig/süss/Liebe, aber edel" (Ardent/sweet/love, but noble), all of which clearly apply to the Adagietto's first section. Does the adjective "noble" indicate chastity? It certainly might for anyone who finds actual sex dirty and ignoble. But I do not see a contradiction. Some of our culture's most powerful expressions of religious devotion—the Song of Songs, Sufi poetry, Saint Teresa of Ávila's accounts of Divine Union (complete with moans), the Holy Sonnets of John Donne—draw heavily, sometimes shockingly, on sexual metaphors.[30] For sacred and profane versions of love share a search for transcendence, of escape from the rational world into something that challenges worldly existence, even if it does so by means of the body. And, of course, music's incorporeality has long served as a readily available site for such experiences. This is why we can regard *Tristan* (an opera with special meaning for the Mahlers) as profoundly sexual and yet profoundly spiritual.

According to their diaries and letters, Mahler had resisted Alma's overtures in the belief that he was too old for her.[31] With the Adagietto, he proclaims his willingness to enter into a full-fledged relationship with her: noble love, to be sure, but also a commitment to the physical engagement such a relationship would entail. I am not trying to convert this extraordinary movement into an obscene scenario, but Mahler is not telling Alma he just wants to hold her hand.

In her important book, *Sex Sounds*, Daniele Shlomit Sofer traces the ways music often simulates sexual activities and also the ways musicologists and theorists try desperately to ignore or resist such matters.[32] Focusing on electronic music of the last seventy years, Sofer demonstrates how often electronic musicians, from Pierre Schaeffer in his *musique concrète* to the latest

---

[30] See the chapters on Divine Love in my *Desire and Pleasure in Seventeenth-Century Music*.

[31] Alma recorded in her diary on 1 January 1902 about Mahler's difficulties in consummating their relationship: "What I have to write today is terribly sad. I called on Gustav—in the afternoon we were alone in his room. He gave me his body—& I let him touch me with his hand. Stiff and upright stood his vigour. He carried me to the sofa, laid me gently down and swung himself over me. Then—just as I felt him penetrate, he lost all strength. He laid his head on my breast, shattered—and almost wept for shame. Distraught as I was, I comforted him.

"We drove home, dismayed and dejected. He grew a little more cheerful. Then I broke down, had to weep, weep on his breast. What if he were to lose—that! My poor, poor husband!

"I can scarcely say how aggravating it all was. First his intimate caresses—and then no satisfaction. Words cannot express what today I have undeservedly suffered. And then to observe his torment—his unbelievable torment! My beloved!" *Gustav Mahler: Letters to His Wife*, ed. Henry-Louis de la Grange and Günter Weiss, rev. and trans. Antony Beaumont (London: Faber & Faber, 2004), 95.

[32] Daniele Shlomit Sofer, *Sex Sounds*: *Vectors of Difference in Electronic Music* (Cambridge, MA: MIT Press, 2022).

hip-hop producers, feature the sounds of female pleasure in their works. As her title *Sex Sounds* signals, she argues that the erotic figures into music not only through metaphors of desire but also as sonic representation. Many of Sofer's observations resonate strongly with the Adagietto as Mengelberg performed it. Bear with me while I trace some of the ways the conductor choreographs the details of Mahler's score. If you're prudish, you might want to stop reading now.

In standard-issue pornography, male pleasure is made visible through penile erection and ejaculation; evidence of female pleasure, however, is conveyed largely by way of the auditory—through gasps and moans taken to testify to sexual climax (recall Meg Ryan's simulated orgasm in a crowded diner in *When Harry Met Sally* or Donna Summer's "Love to Love You, Baby"[33]). But this trope has also appeared in European art music at least as far back as Cipriano de Rore's madrigal "Da le belle contrade d'oriente."[34] To stay closer to Mahler's moment, we might also consider the cistern scene in Strauss's *Salome*, for which the composer asks a solo double bass to produce a sound simulating "the repressed moans and groans of a woman" ("so dass ein Ton erzeugt wird, der dem unterdrückten Stöhnen und Ächzen eines Weibes ähnelt"). Thus, although I would like to maintain gender neutrality in my reading of the Adagietto (and although I know full well that men often moan during intercourse), I find it very difficult not to hear this passage as a simulation of female arousal and orgasm. Is this Mengelberg's invention? Or might we credit Mahler himself with this swerve into the explicitly sexual?

The middle section of the Adagietto moves into a far more impassioned terrain featuring erratic melodic behavior and bewildering shifts in implied key centers (see Example 19.3). The serene certainty of the opening section—the extension and acceptance of the marriage proposal—retreats into the past as our lovers move on to consummation. Once again, the first violin takes the lead, now in a low, sultry register over a troubled C minor. The appoggiaturas that have marked this movement become more prevalent, accentuating ubiquitous wide leaps in the violin line. But after a passage of harmonic instability and anguished searching, marked "etwas drängend"

---

[33] Sofer discusses at length the collaboration between Summers and Giorgio Moroder in the composition and production of this cut. The two have very different accounts of the song's genesis. Sofer, *Sex Sounds*, 105–23.
[34] See my discussion of "Da le contrade d'oriente" in my *Modal Subjectivities*. Cipriano presents the scenario of a woman thrashing about and moaning in the throes of passion, framed by the ostensibly rational account of her male partner. I discuss this madrigal also in chapter 3, "Evidence of Things Not Seen."

318   MAKING SENSE OF MUSIC

Example 19.3 Mengelberg facsimile, p. 3 (mm. 34–55)

(somewhat urgent), Mahler suddenly airlifts us in m. 46 to G-flat major—a moment of unanticipated *jouissance* that halts the action and takes us to an intensely bodily out-of-body terrain, a sudden jolt into another world described so often by Saint Teresa as "union." The harp, which has served as a trusty timekeeper throughout the movement, withdraws discreetly.

As the first violin continues, it returns to its initial motive of three ascending pitches leading to an appoggiatura, but now repeated in rapid succession and with greater and greater insistence. The meter, which had provided some degree of grounding thus far, seems to lose its mooring. Mahler himself notates ornamental grace notes before many of the melodic leaps, which occur with ever-greater frequency. Between mm. 54 and 70, fifteen of these figures occur, and Mengelberg leans into those grace notes (virtually ignored by many conductors) to produce especially pronounced portamenti.

In m. 58, the violin appears to get stuck on E-flat, over D-flat (V/G-flat) in the bass (see Example 19.4). As if in response to the violin's dammed-up frustration, the bass moves slowly down to arrive at B-natural—V/E—thereby converting that stuck E-flat to D-sharp. During this passage, the violin thrashes about wildly, delivering blissful moans (first once, now twice per measure), and apparently compelling the bass to accommodate through a series of bewildering key changes. Listen to Mengelberg's nearly dizzying slides during this passage. But as the violin presses for release, the bass descends methodically by semitones, undergirding a series of unexpected modulations with a steely linear rationality; it continues its initial chromatic descent from D-flat (formerly C-sharp) through to B, to A (functioning as a temporary V/D), and then on through G-sharp to G-natural, which will yield—though not in the cello—to F. Underscoring the significance of these pitches, Mengelberg circles them multiple times in red and blue pencil and with an array of arrows in the margin, all pointing toward this moment in the score.

F major qualifies, of course, as the Adagietto's home key, making m. 72 a kind of recapitulation. But what an odd arrival this is! To be sure, it counts as the end point of the desire trajectories Mahler has been whipping up, made more urgent rhetorically by the many expressive designations (*zurückhaltend, morendo, molto rit.*) leading up to this moment. Yet the downbeat scarcely even counts as a cadence. Indeed, the appearance of F here sounds much more like the flat-sixth degree in relation to the pedal on A (F arrives through what seems like a tetrachord descent from A toward E) than like a return to tonic: it evokes a world of fantasy rather than a concession to reality. Our ears will need a while to adjust to this sleight of hand, not least because Mahler blurs the difference by withholding the appearance of F in the bass until m. 74. To be sure, the harp, which had absented itself throughout the lubricious middle section, punctuates the return in m. 72 with an F-major arpeggiation, but with its Fs tucked into a preparatory V6/4 before returning to the ambiguous extension of A and C that Bernstein discussed in his lecture.

320 MAKING SENSE OF MUSIC

Example 19.4 Mengelberg facsimile, p. 4 (mm. 56–79)

Nearly completely isolated, the violin reaches in m. 72 its long-awaited conclusion. It arrives, however, on D rather than the tonic, as if holding on to that last moment of pleasure before collapsing to C in postcoital exhaustion two and a half octaves below (marked *glissando*). For the violin, the rest of the world disappears momentarily; even the bass line, which has proceeded as if intending to present its A–G–F formula, absents itself at the last moment, allowing the violin (albeit doubled by the viola) to perform this moment of blissful fulfillment alone.

The urgency of the Adagietto has now diminished. As if too depleted to continue, the first violin even surrenders its song to the second violin, which presents the opening strain with the slower note values of the cello's first response earlier in the movement. When the cello enters in m. 82, it does not offer the reciprocal echo of the first section (the second violins have already produced this), nor does it move into an agonized, questioning key as it did before. Instead, it seems merely to render an endorsement, an amen. However secure that confirmation might seem, Mahler delays resolution by having all instruments hover on a sustained, timeless C (mm. 85–87), held twice as long as in the corresponding passage in the opening section (see Example 19.5).

The first violin picks up the thread of its initial argument in m. 87, as the cello follows (as so often before) in tenths with the violins, A–G–F. As in the opening section, the instruments build to a pre-cadential 6/4 chord, as if in preparation for a final arrival. But this time, Mahler has the cello eschew the extended dominant function he gave it in mm. 30–33, choosing rather to have both violin and bass move into a pentatonic region; they drop their conventional contrapuntal roles as they both move deliberately, emphatically, through pentatonic intervals toward repose. Once again as in m. 3, the bass drops in m. 97 from G down to C. But then it continues its pentatonic descent, proceeding in parallel tenths with the violin down from G to F for the movement's conclusion. Ever the gentleman, the cello reaches its tonic, then waits a full bar for the violin to descend to the mediant. The perfect authentic cadence—the linchpin of tonal practice—has no business in this movement.

Many analysts have noted the strong resemblance of these concluding bars to those of Mahler's setting of Rückert's "Ich bin der Welt abhanden gekommen," an extended experiment with pentatonic time-suspension on which Mahler was working at the same time as this symphony. But Mahler opens the song by unveiling his pentatonic framework interval by interval, and it operates largely within that exotic terrain.[35] By contrast, the Adagietto comes to this collection only at its conclusion, as the apotheosis of the cadential formula first hinted at with the drop in the cello in m. 3, but presented ever more confidently as the movement progresses. The Adagietto seems, in other words, to have worked its way painstakingly toward this discovery rather than taking the pentatonic realm as given from the outset, as if the

---

[35] Recall that Friedrich Rückert was a celebrated expert in Oriental languages and translator of many Middle Eastern texts. His poetry served as a kind of gateway for Mahler into that world, with its very different religions and notions of temporality. This song and *Das Lied von der Erde* stand as his most explicit responses to the East that Rückert had opened for him.

Example 19.5 Mengelberg facsimile, p. 5 (mm. 80–conclusion)

particular version of lovemaking developed throughout the movement has had the effect of pushing the composer step by step toward a new grammatical framework.

Music and Sexuality, Redux

As I have argued elsewhere, the PAC is a mechanism for producing desire in music. Even in medieval music, the leading tone serves to enhance the expectation of resolution onto a particular pitch. What we call "tonality," as it emerged over the course of the seventeenth century, involved the harnessing of that configuration—previously restricted to cadences—so as to prolong its urgency for longer and longer durations. By means of this new arrangement, composers could defer resolution while maintaining goal-oriented drive. In the 1600s, the relationship between such strategies and breathless sexual longing remained part of the expressive apparatus.[36]

But as this convention settled into "the way music is supposed to go," it became less clearly related to desire per se (though moments like the bridge between the third and fourth movements of Beethoven's Symphony No. 5 still make the connection audible; try stopping your recording just before Beethoven finally drops the beat at the beginning of the finale). Over the course of the nineteenth century, as composers manipulated tonal mechanisms to defer the release of tensions for ever-longer spans, the paltry PAC came to seem incommensurate with the floods of pent-up desire leading to the final cadence; Wagner had to find other solutions for the ends of the *Ring* and *Tristan*. To compensate, nineteenth-century symphonies often featured emphatic, militant conclusions to signify the triumph of the indomitable subject, and Mahler, as one of Beethoven's acolytes, delivered such endings on a regular basis. But few regard such processes as having anything to do with desire, even though we rely on that phallic display—the musical equivalent of the "money shot" in old-fashioned pornography—as a guarantee of tonal closure and also of masculinity.

Many of the people for whom I play Mengelberg's Adagietto decry the conductor as "effeminizing" Mahler. No one doubts the virility of Mahler's music, even as we want him and his colleagues to pass as somehow "sexless" in their music. Recall that Mengelberg indicates an entirely heteronormative scenario—nobody is insinuating here that Mahler was gay. And yet the idea that he as a straight man might have experienced sensual pleasure during lovemaking seems to diminish his masculinity, to provoke a kind of sexual panic, making such inquiry almost as scandalous as Schubert's

---

[36] For a formal account of this transformation and its initial attachment to breathless longing, see my *Desire and Pleasure*. See also "What Was Tonality?" in my *Conventional Wisdom: The Content of Musical Form* (Berkeley: University of California Press, 2000), chapter 3.

Jeremy Denk extends my images concerning harmonic tension and sexuality in his *Every Good Boy Does Fine: A Love Story, in Music Lessons* (New York: Random House, 2022), particularly in chapter 4. He writes later in his book: "Like idiots, we all made fun of *Feminine Endings* when it came out in 1991, for being so wild in its imagery, and yet now I can see how vital it was," 336.

peacocks.[37] I find myself in the bizarre position of trying to out Mahler as a sexual being!

The problem involves what counts as proper expression of masculinity. Of course, male composers have been producing musical simulations of sexual pleasure at least as far back as the Renaissance madrigal; they know, in other words, what it feels like. Indeed, throughout the Baroque, the erotic ideal of mutual arousal of equal subjects prevails, in opera-seria duets between a male castrato and female soprano and also in the trio-sonata texture of much instrumental music. But starting in the eighteenth-century Enlightenment, composers increasingly projected such qualities as swooning and vulnerability onto imagined female subjects. For desire implies agency and control, while pleasure requires vulnerability, a trait culturally ascribed to women and other presumably passive partners.

In part because of this cultural taboo, love duets in Romantic opera more often than not trace a pattern of seduction and conquest; the boy continues to be in charge. Listing the very few exceptions—Berlioz's night scene between Aeneas and Dido, Wagner's "O sink hernieder" in the second act of *Tristan und Isolde*, Verdi's "Un bacio" duet in *Otello*—reveals how very rarely composers dare to represent reciprocal exchanges between even heterosexual partners. In all of these, the male figure lets go (at least temporarily) of his primacy; he surrenders himself to his partner—a mature woman who does not have to be coaxed into submission. They become interchangeable, merging into a single identity. One of the revelations of Matthew Bourne's brilliant *Swan Lake* is his reimagining the famous pas de deux as a duet between two equal subjects. His choreography lays bare the extraordinary sexism hardwired into the basic technical grammar of standard ballet, in which the virtuosic ballerina seems to rely entirely on the support and agency of her partner. One does not have to be a gay viewer to covet the kind of relationship Bourne enacts in this production.[38]

I would like to add the Adagietto to this very short list, for Mahler's compositional strategies strongly resemble the scenarios I have just mentioned.

---

[37] I allude here to the scandal concerning Schubert's sexuality. See Maynard Solomon, "Franz Schubert and the Peacocks of Benvenuto Cellini," *19th-Century Music* 12, no. 3 (Spring 1989): 193–206. See also my "Constructions of Subjectivity in Schubert's Music," in *Queering the Pitch: The New Gay and Lesbian Musicology*, ed. Philip Brett, Elizabeth Wood, and Gary C. Thomas, 2nd ed. (New York: Routledge, 2006), 155–203.

[38] Matthew Bourne, *Swan Lake* (2012 production), https://www.youtube.com/watch?v=tm6MGWeE-as&t=631. For more on the gender politics of classical ballet choreography, see Susan Leigh Foster, "The Ballerina's Phallic Pointe," in her *Corporalities* (Routledge, 1995).

All traces of assertion have been left outside the bedroom door in the Adagietto. The sole PAC in m. 19 appears as an attempt to resist the pleasure proffered by the violin's opening *Liebeslied*. After this exception, most of the Adagietto's phrases and sections close with stepwise motion in tenths between melody and bass. I admit that one might regard the opening violin as Gustav proposing, with Alma hesitating before accepting. But for a variety of reasons—the traditional gendering of treble and bass voices, the extravagant moaning in the violin, the choreography of the climax in m. 72—it makes more sense to hear the violin as Alma, the pessimistic cello as Gustav before he surrenders to tenderness. In presenting such a scenario to his prospective wife, he is assuring her that he finds mutuality and her *jouissance* as the highest form of erotic exchange. The Talmud teaches that an effective male partner must value his lover's pleasure above his own, and Mengelberg's performance suggests that Mahler knew his way around a woman's body.[39] Well might Alma have exclaimed: "Er solle kommen!"

I find resistance to contemplating Mahler making love—even conjugal love—puzzling, especially since musicologists often scurry to propose possible female partners for composers who remained single. Think of all the bogus girlfriends posited for Handel, Schubert, or Brahms.[40] Beethoven's single letter to a still-unidentified woman, the "immortal beloved," still gets more attention than the details of most of his works, in part because it stands as a rare trace of his presumed heterosexuality. That homophobia fuels such scholarly activity seems obvious.

Yet, at the same time, we have a very long tradition of mocking or deprecating the wives of composers. How could any particular woman deserve to have made love to J. S. Bach or Mozart? In other words, straight bona fides scarcely count as positive in composer biographies. And no woman has had quite so much scorn heaped on her as Alma Schindler, so often characterized as a she-devil who counted Gustav Klimt and Alexander von Zemlinsky among her lovers, who bewitched Mahler and wrecked his final years, driving him to seek counsel from Sigmund Freud. Just recall the anguished notes in the margins of Mahler's Symphony No. 10, as well as the

---

[39] And we know he did. See Morten Solvik and Stephen E. Hefling, "Natalie Bauer-Lechner on Mahler and Women: A Newly Discovered Document," *Musical Quarterly* 97, no 1 (Spring 2014), 12–20. Bauer-Lechner kept a chronicle of Mahler's affairs, including the one involving her, before he encountered Alma.

[40] For an enlightening and often hilarious account of the bogus girlfriend issue, see Gary C. Thomas, "'Was George Frideric Handel Gay?' On Closet Questions and Cultural Politics," in *Queering the Pitch*, 155–203. See also chapter 17.

much-reported scene in which she shows up at their home with Walter Gropius in tow. She may still be best known in North America for Tom Lehrer's cruel satirical song based on her obituary.[41] (Lehrer echoes popular sentiments when he sings, "Their marriage, however, was murder. He'd scream to the heavens above, 'I'm writing *Das Lied von der Erde*, and she only wants to make love!'") Moreover, after Mahler's death, Alma continued to draw on the prestige of her status as his widow, even after her marriages to Gropius and Franz Werfel, passing on sometimes-dubious information and shaping her late husband's legacy. Hugh Wood summarized "the Alma Problem" in these words: "Often she is the only witness, and the biographer has to depend on her while doubting with every sentence her capacity for telling the truth. Everything that passed through her hands must be regarded as tainted."[42] Mengelberg's annotated score and reports of the Adagietto's origins fall easily in line with Alma's self-serving mythologizing.

So when we resist Mengelberg's performance of the Adagietto, do we do so because we reject Alma's influence out of hand? And might we do so because we cannot bring ourselves to imagine that kind of ardent lovemaking between our beloved composer and . . . *that woman*? Or, indeed, with ANY woman? Better, no doubt, to slow it down, eliminate the portamenti, and render it as an elegy.

At the bottom of Mengelberg's score (see again Example 19.1), we see the following: "N.B. Wenn Musik eine Sprache ist so ist sie es hier, er sagt ihr ALLES in Tönen, in Klingen, in Musik" (Nota bene: If music is a language then it is so here; he tells her EVERYTHING in tones, in sounds, in music. Mengelberg underlines the word "ALLES" three times.) I freely admit that none of my prose can or should substitute for the power of Mengelberg's performance. So why should I bother to write about it?

I do so in part for the sake of performance theory. However much Mahler marked up his scores with expressive directives, we know that the "tones, sounds, music" Mengelberg and Alma took as self-evident rely on interpretation. Mengelberg heard Mahler himself conduct this work, but we have no

---

[41] Tom Lehrer, "Alma" (1965): https://www.youtube.com/watch?v=QL6KgbrGSKQ. Ken Russell presents a more sympathetic portrait of Alma in his film *Mahler* (1974), which shows Gustav's own affairs as well as his contempt for his wife's compositions. https://www.youtube.com/watch?v=PGq7TFoxB4E

[42] Hugh Wood, "The Alma Problem," *Guardian* (December 2, 2010). But see also Seth Monahan, "'I Have Tried to Capture You . . .': Rethinking the 'Alma' Theme from Mahler's Sixth Symphony," *Journal of the American Musicological Society* 64, no. 1 (Spring 2011): 119–78.

way of knowing whether the composer indulged in the portamenti that make this performance so charged erotically. Drawing on Alma's verbal testimony, Mengelberg works to convert Mahler's notation into the sonic gestures he understands to correspond with that testimony.

The vast difference between Mengelberg's performance and those of most other conductors stands as proof that notation cannot guarantee the transmission of any particular cluster of sensibilities or meanings. The Adagietto has been convincingly rendered variously as an explicit simulation of sexual passion, as an escape from the exigencies of time and space, as a funereal reminiscence. None of these is transparently the way the movement is supposed to go. Even if we embrace the concept of classical music's ineffability, someone still has to take those scores and render them in sound. Even if we desire drastic performances, we have to get there by means of (dreaded term!) *the music itself*. And that requires analysis, gnostic or otherwise.[43]

I confess that I am ambivalent about the prospect of future conductors following Mengelberg's lead to produce or even amplify the moans in the middle of the Adagietto. If Mengelberg offers us a reading of the movement informed by Alma's (and perhaps Gustav's) testimony, copycats could easily push those gestures into the realm of salacious caricature. In other words, although I find this recording deeply compelling and illuminating, I also recognize how easily representations of women's sexuality can slide over into pornography. I would not want to see the Adagietto reduced to a dirty joke. As Richard Taruskin reminded us repeatedly, performing and writing about music always raise difficult ethical issues.[44]

But I also pursue music analysis and contemplate extreme readings such as Mengelberg's in the interest of cultural history. Michel Foucault argued persuasively that bodies, affects, desires, pleasures, and sexualities all have histories that leave traces in cultural artifacts. I have long contended that music offers perhaps the most detailed evidence for such apparently ephemeral experiences, usually understood as universal or deemed unworthy of serious scholarly attention. In the words of the divine Louise Brooks, our quintessential Lulu in G. W. Pabst's *Pandora's Box* (1929):

---

[43] I allude here to Caroline Abbate, "Music—Drastic or Gnostic," *Critical Inquiry* 30 (2004): 505–36. I am one of her gnostics.

[44] See his *The Danger of Music and Other Anti-Utopian Essays* (Berkeley: University of California Press, 2008) and *Cursed Questions: On Music and Its Social Practices* (Berkeley: University of California Press, 2020).

In writing the history of a life I believe absolutely that the reader cannot understand the character and deeds of a subject unless he is given a basic understanding of that person's sexual loves and hates and conflicts.[45]

In this essay, I have risked (once again) effing the ineffable in order to bring such traces into the realm of analysis and history. Mengelberg's annotations and his performance present the historian with a precious opportunity for linking musical procedures with the hedonistic fin-de-siècle Viennese culture whence it sprang, with Mahler's complex subjectivity, with an all-too-rare representation of conjugal lovemaking. I'd rather not hear it as a dirge.

---

[45] Louise Brooks, "Why I Will Never Write My Memoirs," *Focus on Film* (March 1978). Reprinted in *Lulu in Hollywood* (Minneapolis: University of Minnesota Press, 2000). My thanks to Keith Fitch for this quotation. I also want to thank Peter Franklin, Lawrence Kramer, Danielle Shlomit Sofer, Marcelo Rebuffi, Samuel Bivens, and Jonathan Guez for their invaluable responses to this essay.

Index

For the benefit of digital users, indexed terms that span two pages (e.g., 52–53) may, on occasion, appear on only one of those pages.

Adorno, Theodor W., 8, 22, 30, 91, 109, 219–20, 232–46, 307, 313–15
Arcadelt, Jacques, 156–58, 170–71, 172
  "Margot labourez les vignes," 156–58
Aretino, Pietro, 159, 163–64, 165, 166, 167, 173
Artusi, Giovanni Maria, 20, 60–61, 166–67
Attali, Jacques, 38, 50, 61–62, 81, 180
Attinello, Paul, 283, 288, 289

Bach, Carl Philip Emanuel, 8, 100–1, 113, 140
Bach, Johann Sebastian, 13, 22, 91, 99, 139, 140, 150, 171, 187–88, 220, 232–46
  Brandenburg Concerto, No. 5, 220, 239–40
  Cantata 140, *Wachet auf*, 100–1
  French Suite No. 5 in G, "Loure," 8–10
  Partita II for Accompanied Violin, Chaconne, 99–100
  Well-Tempered Clavier, 232–46
Bacilly, Bénigne de, 200–1
Bailey, Philip, 264–65, 276
Beethoven, Ludwig van, 12, 66, 70, 91, 111–12, 325
  String Quartet Op. 132, in A Minor, Op. 132, 126
  String Quartet Op. 131, in C-Sharp Minor, 244
  Symphony No. 5, 53–62, 323
  Symphony No. 9, 40–41, 89–90, 101–2, 106–7, 111–12, 173–74
Bellini, Vincenzo
  Norma, 259
Benjamin, George, 105, 117–18, 119, 253
  Written on Skin, 117–18, 253, 277
Berberian, Cathy, 279, 286–90
  Stripsody, 289–90
Berio, Luciano, 116, 286–88
  Sinfonia, 116, 290
Berlioz, Hector, 51, 113, 206, 214, 324
  Symphonie fantastique, 51, 214
  Les Troyens, 324
Bernstein, Leonard, 281–82, 304, 305–6, 319
  West Side Story, 116

Bizet, Georges
  Carmen, 41–42, 114–15, 128–29, 143, 229–30
Body, 2, 16–17, 30, 93–103, 144, 166, 261
  and brain, 7, 64
  embodiment, 13, 57, 85, 93–103, 196–215, 241, 242, 284
  erotic, 9, 20, 97, 102–3, 166–78, 302–28
  and gender, 2, 31–32, 73–81, 166–78, 260–78, 291–301, 302–28
  metaphor, 7–9, 14, 57, 74–75, 94
  as taboo, 16–17, 93–94, 101, 166, 316
  transcendence of, 14–15, 93–103, 316, 317–18
Boulez, Pierre, 105–6, 110, 119, 287–88
Bourne, Matthew
  Swan Lake, 257–59, 324
Brahms, Johannes, 280–81, 306, 325
Brett, Philip, 37, 274–75, 282
Britten, Benjamin, 112
  Midsummer Night's Dream, 118, 253, 274–76
  Turn of the Screw, 274–76
Brooks, Louise, 228, 327–28
Brown, Rae Linda, 143n.18, 149
Bussotti, Sylvano, 286–87, 288, 289

Cage, John, 50–51, 287–88, 289, 290
Calvin, John, 86–87, 98, 154, 157–58
Castrati, 251–54, 260–62, 267, 269–76
Cavalli, Francesco, 50, 253
  Calisto, 270
  Giasone, 23, 221, 253–54, 271–72
Cavell, Stanley, 46–47, 83
Chambonnières, Jacques Champion de, 13, 205–6
Charpentier, Marc-Antoine
  Médée, 221, 229–30
Cherokee ancestry, 18, 27–28, 121–22, 133–34
Christina, Queen of Sweden, 216, 222, 229–30
Corelli, Arcangelo, 33–34, 42–43, 137, 218
Council of Trent, 96–97, 154, 164
Countertenors, 118, 254, 262, 269–70, 274–78

Couperin, François, 200, 205–6
Couperin, Louis, 95
   Prélude in G Minor, 187–95
Crook, David, 163, 164
Cropper, Steve, 198–200

Dawson, William, 143, 150
Debussy, Claude, 128–29
   Afternoon of a Faun, 255–56
Del Tredici, David, 281–82n.4
Derrida, Jacques, 34, 90
Du Bois, W.E.B., 144, 149, 150
Dvořák, Antonin, 132n.18, 133–34, 142–44, 149

Earth, Wind & Fire, 208
   "Reasons," 264–65
Eastman, Julius, 142, 143–44
Ewell, Philip, 19, 135–36, 137, 141

Farinelli, 219–20, 276
Feminism, 2, 15–16, 30, 31–32, 35, 37, 87, 123–24, 292–93
Floyd, George, 18, 135–36, 148–49, 150
Forster, E.M.
   Howard's End, 15–16, 53–62
Foucault, Michel, 30, 170, 327
Franklin, Peter, 112, 274–75, 302, 307–8, 311–12, 315
Frescobaldi, Girolomo, 50–51, 187–88
Freud, Sigmund, 239, 245, 325–26
Froberger, Johann Jakob, 12–13, 187–88, 189–94, 235–36, 244

Garland, Judy, 279, 283–84, 285
Gershwin, George, 115, 142–43
Gesualdo, Carlo, 50–51, 118
Gjerdingen, Robert O., 32–33, 181n.7
Glass, Philip, 31, 104, 116, 191, 287–88
   Akhnaten, 118, 253, 275–76, 277–78
   The Photographer, 31
Gluck, Christoph Willibald
   Orfeo, 252–53, 274, 277–78
Grieg, Edvard, 17–18, 120–34
   "Røtnams-Knut," *Slåtter*, Op. 72, 125–33

Halford, Rob, 269, 270, 276
Halvorsen, Johan, 125–26, 127–28
Handel, George Frideric, 216–17, 218, 230, 252, 254, 280, 325
   Giulio Cesare, 252, 273–74, 277
Hasty, Christopher, 179, 187
Hawkins, Stan, 65, 249, 268

Hildegard von Bingen, 139, 259
Hoffmann, E.T.A., 57, 61–62, 101
Hurston, Zora Neale, 144, 149

Identity politics, 120–34
Ingarden, Roman, 93–94
IRCAM, 23, 106, 107, 116–17, 206
Ives, Charles, 3, 133–34

Jackson, Michael, 23, 262, 268, 271, 276
Jacobs, René, 97, 270, 272
Jacquet de la Guerre, Élisabeth-Claude, 139, 188, 196–215
   keyboard suite in A minor, 202–10, 212
   keyboard suite in D minor, 210
Jenkins, Christopher, 19, 138, 141
Jeter, Claude, 263, 264, 265, 267, 274
John of Salisbury, 154–55
Josquin des Pres, 156, 171

Kaplan, Gilbert, 302
Kerman, Joseph, 11, 16, 46–47
Kim, Earl, 5
Kramer, Lawrence, 38–39, 109

Landi, Stefano
   Sant'Alessio, 251, 271n.21
Lasso, Orlando di, 153–65
   "Matona, mia cara," 20
   Missa je ne menge point de porc, 158–65
Leppert, Richard, 30, 35–36, 109
Lewin, David, 51–52, 110–11
Louis XIV, 99–100, 106–7, 187, 221
Lully, Jean-Baptiste, 197
   Armide, 210, 272
Luther, Martin, 154, 156

Maalouf, Amin, 294–300
Madonna, 77–81, 279, 284–86
   "What It Feels Like for a Girl," 77–81
Maguire, Matthew, 31–32
Mahler, Alma Schindler, 302, 305, 307–8, 316, 324–27
Mahler, Gustav, 41, 128–29, 142, 145–48, 282–83, 290, 302–28
   Das Lied von der Erde, 306
   "Ich atmet einen linden Duft," 213
   "Ich bin der Welt abhanden gekommen," 321–22
   Symphony No. 4, 309–10
   Symphony No. 5, Adagietto, 302–28
McGilchrist, Iain, 7–11, 14, 16, 83–84
Mengelberg, Willem, 302–28

Messiaen, Olivier, 50–51, 105, 114, 116, 117, 119, 206
Metaphor, 7–8, 9–10, 14, 57, 63–64, 74–75, 94, 316
Metric level and performance, 13, 96–97, 241, 305–6
Midler, Bette, 279–80, 287–88, 290
Milton, John, 89–90
Modal theory and analysis, 6–7, 9, 12, 19, 29–30, 35, 73–77, 126–27, 130–31, 180–87, 191, 201–2, 311
  and tonality, 29, 42–43, 91, 130–31, 136, 140, 201–2, 234
Monteverdi, Claudio, 6, 20–21, 29–30, 50, 97, 137–38, 166–78, 181–87, 188–89
  "Ah, dolente partita," 138–39
  "Ahi, com'a un vago sol," 181–87
  "Cruda Amarilli," 9, 20, 34–35, 186–87
  Incoronazione di Poppea, 221, 228, 229–30, 272–74
  "O Jesu, mea vita," 171
  Orfeo, 4, 28, 97, 182, 251
  "Sì, ch'io vorrei morire," 166–78
  Vespro della Beata Virgine, "Duo seraphim," 97, 99, 102, 187
Morrison, Toni, 132, 149–50, 293
Mouton, Jean
  "Nesciens mater virgo virum," 95–97
Mozart, Wolfgang Amadeus, 38, 158, 234, 244, 325–26
  Don Giovanni, 5, 56, 59
  Magic Flute, 228–30
  Nozze di Figaro, 252–53, 278
music pedagogy, 4, 5, 6, 8, 9–10, 12, 135–50, 217–18, 250
music theory, 45–62, 135–50

Newcomb, Anthony, 5, 28
Newton, Isaac, 10, 179–80, 188–89, 239–40, 297–99

Osmond-Smith, David, 288, 289

Palestrina, Giovanni Pierluigi da, 97, 166–67
Paul, Saint, 2, 63
Penniman, "Little" Richard, 265–66
Plato, 86–87, 106–7, 137, 259
Price, Florence, 142–50
  String Quartet No. 2 in A Minor, 144–50
Prince, 149, 249, 262, 266–67, 270, 274, 276–77
  "Do Me Baby," 254, 267, 272

Rabelais, François, 153, 158, 159, 165, 173

Rachmaninoff, Serge, 3, 112, 130
Rameau, Jean-Philippe, 8, 49, 127, 140, 197, 206, 214, 234
Reich, Steve, 114, 116
Rimsky-Korsakov, Nicolai
  Scheherazade, 172–73
Romanesca, 181–82, 201–2
  difference from Gjerdingen's "romanesca," 181–82, 201
Romano, Giulio, 166, 173
Rore, Cipriano de, 51, 73, 78, 80–81, 137–38
  "Da le belle contrade d'oriente," 16, 73–77, 317
Russell, George, 130–31, 136

Saariaho, Kaija, 17, 105, 113–14, 116–17, 119, 291–301
  Adriana Mater, 116–17, 294–97, 300, 301
  L'amour de loin, 116–18, 300
  Château de l'âme, 294
  Émilie, 116–17, 297–300, 301
  Innocence, 116–17, 294–95
  Only the Sound Remains, 253, 277, 300
Sandow, Greg, 40, 53, 109
Schenker, Heinrich, 8, 58, 139, 140, 141, 201–2, 236–37
Schoenberg, Arnold, 16, 50–51, 106, 110–11, 115–16, 119, 136–37
  Harmonielehre, 136–37
  Moses und Aron, 113–14
Schubert, Franz, 37, 51–52, 60–61, 65–72, 80, 145–48, 216, 234, 254–55, 280, 323–24, 325
  "Der Erlkönig," 254–55
  String Quartet No. 15, Op. 161, 65–72, 80–81
Schumann, Clara Wieck, 138, 280–81
Schumann, Robert, 4, 150, 280–81, 306, 315
Schütz, Heinrich, 179, 187, 263
Sciarrino, Salvatore, 105, 118, 119
  Luci mie traditrici, 118
Sedgwick, Eve Kosofsky, 282
Sellars, Peter, 32, 43, 117, 277, 294–95, 300
Sermisy, Claudin de, 19–20, 158–60, 164–65
  "Je ne menge point de porc," 158–60, 164–65
Shadle, Douglas, 142–43
Small, Christopher, 14–15, 43–44, 94, 115, 148–49, 260
Sontag, Susan, 282–83, 287–88, 289
Stradella, Alessandro, 5–6, 15, 21–22, 27, 28, 42, 44, 216–31
  San Giovanni Battista, 21–22, 28, 33, 221–31
  La Susanna, 15, 31–32, 33
  Susanna Does the Elders (McClary), 32

Strauss, Richard, 51–52, 256–57, 317
    Salome, 20, 21–22, 112, 228–30, 256–57, 317
Stravinsky, Igor, 112, 113–14, 124, 128–29
Streisand, Barbra, 39, 283
Subjectivity, 12, 13–14, 38–39, 61–62, 63–81, 174, 191, 233–34, 245, 328
Subotnik, Rose Rosengard, 30, 35–36, 233
Sylvester, 265, 266, 276–77

Taruskin, Richard, 14–15, 22, 87, 107, 115–16, 124, 131–32, 308, 327
Tchaikovsky, Pyotr Ilyich, 3, 37, 173–74, 257–59
    Swan Lake, 257–59, 324
Temporality, 7, 13, 14, 20–21, 22, 31, 40, 63–64, 88–92, 93–103, 128–29, 173–74, 179–95, 196–97, 214, 244–45, 321–22
Teresa of Ávila, Saint, 97, 171, 316, 317–18
Tonality, 12, 19, 32–33, 36, 47, 49, 130–31, 173–74
    history of, 12, 20–21, 29–30, 32–33, 34, 36, 42–43, 49, 50, 60, 137–38, 179, 191, 231, 234, 245, 322–23

Tyler, Steven, 268–69, 274

Valli, Frankie, 266
Vivaldi, Antonio, 20–21, 22, 71–72, 220, 235, 236, 245

Wagner, Richard, 20, 86, 90, 233, 256–57, 315, 323, 324
    Tristan und Isolde, 20, 90, 155, 315, 323, 324
Walser, Robert, 10, 39, 43–44, 65, 266–67, 268–69, 278
Walter, Bruno, 305, 308
Wexler, Jerry, 198–200
White, Hayden, 38–39, 61–62
Wieseltier, Leon, 206
Wilde, Oscar, 256–57
    Salome, 223, 256–57
Williams, Raymond, 65, 185–86

Yust, Jason, 135, 216–17, 234

Zarlino, Gioseffo, 6–7, 29